HABITATIONS
OF THE
VEIL

SUNY series, Philosophy and Race

Robert Bernasconi and T. Denean Sharpley-Whiting, editors

HABITATIONS
OF THE
VEIL

Metaphor and the Poetics of Black Being
in African American Literature

REBECKA RUTLEDGE FISHER

Published by State University of New York Press, Albany

For information, contact State University of New York Press, Albany, NY
www.sunypress.edu

Production by Eileen Nizer
Marketing by Michael Campochiaro

Library of Congress Cataloging-in-Publication Data

Fisher, Rebecka Rutledge.
  Habitations of the veil : metaphor and the poetics of black being in African American literature / Rebecka Rutledge Fisher.
      pages cm. — (SUNY series, Philosophy and race)
  Includes bibliographical references and index.
  ISBN 978-1-4384-4931-9 (hc alk. paper) 978-1-4384-4932-6 (pb alk. paper)
  1. American literature—African American authors—History and criticism.
2. Metaphor in literature. I. Title.

  PS153.N5F536 2013
  810.9'896073—dc23   2013002463

10 9 8 7 6 5 4 3 2 1

I dedicate this book with much love to my husband, Edwin B. Fisher,
and my mother, Billie Rutledge Killens.

Contents

Acknowledgments

I want first to thank my family for their continuous love and support. My husband, Edwin B. Fisher, has supported me unfailingly throughout the long durée of this project. I lovingly dedicate this book to him and to my mother, Billie Rutledge Killens, who has always been my biggest fan and most stalwart believer. Mommy, I love you and could not have done this without you. My father, Vince Rutledge, Sr., has long been a man of no-nonsense faith. I thank him for his calming presence and unstinting strength. My late grandmother, Mrs. Alice W. Smith, bequeathed me her love of books and words. She is still with me every day. My godparents, Deloris and William Bell, provided me the warmth and comfort of a home away from home during my graduate school days, and saw me through the first iteration of this project. Bill, the book is done! Friends and colleagues have provided support, wisdom, and cheer all along the way: James Coleman, María deGuzman, Gerald Early, Trudier Harris, Errol Henderson, Mae Henderson, Donald H. Matthews, Itabari Njeri, John McGowan, Linda Wagner-Martin, and Rafia Zafar. For reading parts of this project at various stages, and/or listening to presentations drawn from it and providing me invaluable feedback, I thank the following colleagues, who are also dear friends: Minrose Gwin, Ruth Salvaggio, Nahum Chandler, Hortense Spillers, Nicole Waligora-Davis, Hilary Holladay, and John Charles. The editors of SUNY's Philosophy and Race series, Robert Bernasconi and T. Denean Sharpley-Whiting, championed my project and believed in it from the start. Andrew Kenyon of SUNY Press provided a sage ear and lasting enthusiasm. An early draft of this book was completed with the support of the Spray-Randleigh Fellowship at the University of North Carolina at Chapel Hill, and a summer residential fellowship at the Virginia Foundation for the Humanities.

$\sim$

An earlier version of chapter 4 appeared in *ESQ: A Journal of the American Renaissance* 54.1–4 (2008): 55–74. A shorter version of chapter 7 appeared in *Obsidian: Literature in the African Diaspora* 11.2 (Fall/Winter 2010): 14–42.

Herein lie buried many things which, if read with patience, will reveal the strange meaning of being black

—W. E. B. Du Bois, *The Souls of Black Folk*

Introduction

The Poetics of Being Black

The Souls of Black Folk (1903), from which the epigraph to this introduction is drawn, is but one instance of Du Bois's particular brand of historical narration and metaphorical innovation, wherein he proclaims unhesitatingly, in a voice that should evoke an unsettling ring of truth as we survey our own contemporary political landscape, that "the problem of the twentieth-century is the problem of the color-line,—the relation of the darker to the lighter races of men in Asia and Africa, in America and the islands of the sea" (*Souls* 372). From the perspective of the present study, it is not simply Du Bois's prescient political outlook that draws us near to him, and him close to us. Rather, Du Bois's book, radical for its time and labeled "dangerous" by a number of Southern reviewers because, one Southern writer claimed, it would incite black men to "rape" white women, continues to be so very important to the present generation of readers because from our moment in history, we can see that Du Bois not only revolutionized the way racialized being (or, as Du Bois termed it, "being black") was, and continues to be, discussed in this country; he also brought to bear upon his analysis of race exceptional, and perhaps unsurpassed, philosophical metaphors of "being black," or, what I will refer to as "black being," that were alternately (and at times simultaneously) spiritual, secular, historical, economic, feminist, and, importantly, humanistic in nature.

Indeed, the open-endedness of Du Bois's ontological and epistemological metaphors—their fluid capacity to transgress categories of discursive signification (such as the category of race) and thus their ability to challenge social and theoretical commonplaces and generate alternative social and political meanings— marks them as an exemplary mode of conceptual expression, and allows me to place Du Bois at the core of my analysis of the philosophical possibilities of metaphor and its relation to concepts of black being in the African American literary tradition. The metaphorical processes at work in Du Bois's seminal text continue to elucidate the philosophical trajectory of his discourse on black being, and thus they provide a firm foundation for the critical and ontological inquiry I undertake in this book.

1

In this study, I draw upon Du Bois's conceptual uses of metaphor in *Souls* as a frame through which to examine how African American writers throughout the history of the tradition have long put into practice what the philosopher Paul Ricoeur would later describe as language's—and specifically metaphor's—knowledge of its relation to being. For example, when Ricoeur's frequent interlocutor on the question of being, the phenomenologist Martin Heidegger, writes that "language is the house of Being," we are clearly reminded of Du Bois's desire that readers of *Souls* should, as he writes, patiently "study my words with me" as they enter into the language of his text, which describes, in "vague uncertain outline the spiritual world in which ten thousand thousand Americans live and strive" (359). If language is the house of being, then being is likewise housed in the world of text and exemplified in narrative. For Du Bois, the worlds "within and without the Veil" collide in text and produce the existential and plural world of African American souls, which he portrays for the reader in fourteen essays that he calls "thoughts."

It seems natural that Du Bois's "thought" should assume a central role when one determines to examine the relation of metaphor and being in the African American literary tradition. *Souls* contains at least three of the major philosophical metaphors that, throughout the twentieth and twenty-first centuries, have persisted in African American philosophical, social, and political thought to the extent that they have taken on psychosocial descriptive qualities as they express black being: the veil, the color-line, and double consciousness. In its ultimate significance as a multidisciplinary work of considerable magnitude, *Souls* is itself regularly evoked as a trope of sorts, one that often serves as the incipit of African American literary studies as well as black political theory, as the continuing inauguration of urban and rural sociological study in America, and as a modern philosophy of being that insists upon the values of ethical social action. From the vantage point of *The Souls of Black Folk*, this study assumes a diachronic perspective. From Souls, I look back to the incipient moments of the literature in the eighteenth century, and forward to the beginnings of the postmodern era, drawing upon Du Bois's tropological thought as a critical lens through which to survey the intersections of philosophical metaphor and articulations of being that appear in a select number of canonical texts. As I do so, I describe a poetics that I see emerging from these intersections. I have called this poetics a "poetics of black being."

The metaphors that found this poetics of black being have consistently appeared in African American texts across a long span of time, nascent not simply in the inaugural moments of the literature itself, but also in the historical moments that occasion the modern era: the revolutions (French, American, and Haitian) that collectively signal the inception of modernity at the end of the eighteenth century. The opposite limit of the period I examine is marked by the conclusion of World War II, the rise of the modern Civil Rights movement, and the early glimmers of African decolonization, which together augur the onset of the postmodern era in the mid-twentieth century and the provisional end (in some schools of thought) of the modern era, though the use of such metaphors of black being persist in various guises—they inhabit a variety of veils—up to the present time.

While scholars have long extolled the virtues of metaphorical expression in African American texts, heretofore there has been no overarching study that seeks to trace the continuum of epistemological and ontological thought alive in these metaphors. I survey the poetics of such metaphors in a number of familiar works that appear throughout the modern period: Olaudah Equiano's *The Interesting Narrative of the Life of Olaudah Equiano, or Gustavus Vassa, the African. Written by Himself* (1789); Frances Ellen Watkins Harper's *Sketches of Southern Life* (1872); W. E. B. Du Bois's "The Conservation of Races" (1897), and *The Souls of Black Folk* (1903); Richard Wright's *The Man Who Lived Underground* (1944); and Ralph Ellison's *Invisible Man* (1952). Though I can lay no claim to a comprehensive study that presents an exhaustive overview of all the texts that constitute the African American literary tradition, I have undertaken a series of close readings of texts that offer exemplary conceptual metaphors of being. The readings I provide here may be only incisions in an immense corpus of works, yet they advance a hermeneutic suggested by the metaphorics of major African American texts. My hope, then, is that my analysis suggests a theory of metaphor alive in these works, a theory that will be of use in interpreting other texts concerned with the poetics of black being.

Part I of the study, comprising the Introduction and chapters 1 and 2, provides the theoretical framework for this study and discusses the theories of metaphor and being that inform my project. The Introduction offers an overview of the study. It succinctly summarizes each chapter, includes a discussion of the concept of being and my use of the concept in this work, and centers W. E. B. Du Bois's philosophical metaphorics as the critical framework for the book. The chapters of Part I deepen our understanding of the ways in which philosophical metaphors have taken shape in African American literary thought by providing a genealogy of this tradition's epistemological and ontological conceptualizations, from the early written and oral literature, to the modern discursive stylings of

Du Bois and Zora Neale Hurston (specifically viewing "Characteristics of Negro Expression" as a contribution to the philosophy of ordinary language), to the convoluted textures of the black postmodern novel, as practiced, for instance, by Ralph Ellison. Chronicling the evolution of thought on black philosophical metaphor as it critiques the exclusion of this discourse from any number of treatises on the subject, these chapters provide a genealogy of black conceptual metaphors in oral and written forms, underscores calls for ethical and moral activism that are usually found at the heart of these constructions, and encourages us to look more closely at the relation between race, metaphor, and being.

Part II, comprising chapters 3 through 8, presents close analytic readings of philosophical metaphors of being that appear throughout the tradition, both before and after Du Bois's signal use of ontological and epistemological metaphor at the turn of the twentieth century. The chapter studies of Part II serve to exemplify and elucidate the theory that undergirds my overall argument, as it is presented in Part I. In chapter 3, "A Poetics of Becoming," the first chapter of literary analysis, I begin with Equiano, since he stands at the wellspring of the African American literary tradition. In his *Narrative*, Equiano adumbrates a finely wrought expression of his own sense of being in such a way that makes clear its relation to the formation of modern nation-states as well as the discourses of the Christian Church that were so important to him. Equiano's eighteenth-century autobiography exemplifies his era's tensions between notions of being based in the sacred (the dominance of the church as the major organizing force of Western society) and those anchored in the secular (the rise of the nation-state as the church fell into decline). It is thus crucial to understanding conceptual metaphors of black being in the incipient moments of modernity.

In chapter 4, I discuss how Frances Ellen Watkins Harper extends Equiano's eighteenth-century metaphorics of the sacred and the secular into the Reconstruction era of the late nineteenth century, testing its limits by adding to it the concerns of the feminine. In addition to voicing the conditions of black female existence, Harper's onto-theological metaphorics prize a certain mysticism of being that is subtended—as is Equiano's—by radical notions of freedom and liberty, and in this way she continues an African American literary tradition grounded in metaphorics of national belonging and spiritual existence that is so remarkable in the work of Equiano, Phillis Wheatley, Maria Stewart, David Walker, and Frederick Douglass, among others. This is so even as her use of religious metaphor evolves toward the quasi-secular expression of black being that would emerge in the new century with Du Bois's metaphors of the veil, the color-line, and double consciousness.

Du Bois, Wright, and Ellison, three major thinkers of the first half of the twentieth century, serve as the foci of chapters 5, 6, 7, and 8. Each capitalizes upon the spiritual metaphors of the black vernacular and critical traditions founded in the eighteenth and nineteenth centuries even as they unveil modern metaphors of black being that tend toward the secular. Du Bois, as I have said, plays a central role in how the function of ontological and epistemological metaphor in African American thought would be used from his time onward. Certainly if one draws upon the definition of the "color-line" given by Du Bois in *The Souls of Black Folk*, one sees that it functions as a concept-metaphor of both social realities and historical/political/economic problematics. However, Du Bois's definition of this conceptual trope also makes clear that the concept of the color-line comes into existence practically as a result of the rise of modern nation-states that took shape during the revolutionary time of Equiano. It tells us that double consciousness and what Du Bois calls "the shadow of the veil" result, in good measure, from the widely varied forces that converge around the formation of the modern nation-state, a point I expound in chapter 2. Seeing Du Bois's concept-metaphors in this light holds significant implications for our reading of related ontological metaphors of belonging, duality, and veiling/revealing that we see at work in the writings of Equiano and Harper, among other early figures who emerged during the era of nation formation.

The prescience of Du Bois's concept-metaphors in *Souls* is made possible, I suggest in chapter 5, by his metaphorization of the very notion of race itself in his 1897 essay, "The Conservation of Races." Du Bois explicitly deconstructs the idea of race by, essentially, metaphorizing it, and in so doing he exposes its anti-humanist import, the aspects of raciology that undercut the ideals of the Enlightenment (including the twin ideals of liberalism and democracy), as well as the critical ontology conveyed by the word "race" itself. When Du Bois calls "race" "the vastest and most ingenious invention for human progress,"[1] he reaches back to the time of Equiano and Harper, whose metaphorics and social activism contribute to a deconstructionist theory of race that had been at work in African American thought as early as the eighteenth and nineteenth centuries. By looking back to and drawing upon this literary and activist history, Du Bois uses "Conservation" to lay the groundwork for his concept-metaphors of the veil, the color-line, and double consciousness in *Souls*, which serve as the analytic foci of chapter 6.

Though they both silently and openly reject it as a model, the conceptual metaphorics of *Souls* lights the path followed by Wright and Ellison. Each writer proffers signal modernist metaphorical constructions that are as much concerned with the poetics of being as those of Du Bois. Such constructions reflect the challenges that, for Wright and Ellison, Sigmund

Freud's psychoanalytic theories of consciousness posed to conventional Western philosophies of being. Through my analyses of selected works by these writers, I identify and critique the shortcomings of psychoanalytic theories of consciousness when applied to concepts and expressions of black being.

Each of the writers I treat—from Equiano to Ellison—was deeply concerned with creating what Richard Wright would call, in the conclusion to his 1945 autobiography, *Black Boy*, a vital "sense"—that is, a meaning, an understanding—of the "inexpressibly human" nature of black being. By way of their ontological metaphors, they demonstrated, as did Wright himself, their commitment to building "a bridge of words between [themselves] and that world outside, that world which was so distant and elusive that it seemed unreal" (*Black Boy* 384). At the level of their most conceptual metaphorical operations, these authors propose alternative, even revolutionary ways of knowing and being in the world, an epistemology of modern black being that is, as Toni Morrison states regarding African-descended subjectivity, "prized but not privileged" ("Home" 12).

This study differs from those important and necessary projects that undertake an exploration and explication of what has been called a politics or even a poetics of "black identity." For what I am after in this book is an inquiry into a philosophical concept—being—as it is manifested in the literary expression of a people deemed—through self-determinative modes as well as modes externally and overly determinative—"black." Indeed, identity forms its own concept as an object of philosophical inquiry. While I historicize and analyze the ways in which what I call metaphors of black being accord with modern discourses on freedom and subjectivity, I do not analyze a politics of racial identity that would accompany social struggles for black liberation or resistance. Even as it contextualizes and conceptualizes a "poetics of black being" within such crucial historical contexts as abolitionism, black nationalism, and the modern Civil Rights movement, my study distinguishes between ideologies of black "identity" that may be aligned with what has come to be called "identity politics," and concepts of "being" that engage the longstanding philosophical debate over the nature of human subjectivity and consciousness. While "identity" may be defined, for the purposes of my study, in terms of one's relation to society, government, and geopolitical spaces,[2] I use the term "being" as it relates to concepts of self-consciousness, that is, who one is in relation to oneself within the contexts of these social structures. Thus how one expresses oneself metaphorically in light of evolving intellect, imagination, feeling or emotion, and in relation to one's own body and the community of beings one inhabits, is of paramount importance in this study. Even as I suggest the importance of the semantic distinction between identity and being, the concepts can never be cleanly separated, for their margins continually push one against the other, and regularly overlap, at times making them indistinguishable. Nevertheless, in addressing more pertinently the second of these concepts, being, this study anatomizes the ways in which African American writers, across nearly 200 years of writing, have devised philosophical metaphors to give expression to their sense of black being, their conception of an ontology. It situates them firmly within a critical (and, importantly, revisionist) African American humanistic tradition that pushes at the confines of white Western concepts of *humanitas*. Through the relation of metaphor and being, these writers not only reflect critically upon the world about them, but also insist upon decisive and ethical humanistic action in response to that world.

A Question of Black Being

At this point, it would be good to take a moment to expand further upon and contextualize the concept of "being" and its relationship to metaphor before going on to a more pointed discussion of metaphor theory and expressions of black being in the next two chapters. Martin Heidegger, whose philosophical writings Richard Wright began studying in earnest in the 1940s[3] (and this in spite of Heidegger's racism, a social ill that likewise afflicted his philosophical predecessors Immanuel Kant and Georg W. F. Hegel), was the twentieth century's foremost Western philosopher of the concept. In *Being and Time* (1929), Heidegger presents "Being-in-the-world" as a quasi-spiritual concept that is central to understanding human existence (83), for it signifies not only being in relation to other worldly entities (entities that may be living or inanimate, but that are not human), but, more pointedly, it indicates the quality of concern that is constitutive of human being, which he calls "Dasein."

Dasein is a term that may be translated, in the vernacular, as "existence," but it is usually and best left untranslated. Heidegger sees Dasein, which is a combination of two German words, "Da," meaning "there," and "sein," meaning "being," not as equivalent to a holistic self, but as a subject constituted temporally and existing in space without being limited to any specific time or place. For Heidegger, Dasein is characterized not only by its historicity, but also by its care and concern, which are crucial ways of Being-in-the-world:

Dasein's facticity is such that its Being-in-the-world has always dispersed [zerstreut] itself or even split itself up into definite ways of Being-in. The multiplicity of these is indicated by the following examples: having to do with something, producing something, attending to something and looking after it, making use of something, giving something up and letting it go, undertaking, accomplishing, evincing, interrogating, considering, discussing, determining. . . . All these ways of Being-in have concern as their kind of Being. . . . Leaving undone, neglecting, renouncing, taking a rest—these too are ways of concern; but these are all deficient modes, in which the possibilities of concern are kept to a "bare minimum." (83, italics in original)

In short, a crucial characteristic of Dasein is its "care," or "concern," which Heidegger uses as an "ontological term for existentiale" (sic 83). Care, he writes, "is always concern and solicitude if only privately" (238–39). Each of the writers I discuss in this study, from the eighteenth century through the twentieth, employs ontological metaphors to project a sense of being that is not simply concerned with what Heidegger calls "private" care, but care, and more importantly caring action, in the public sphere. Specifically, each calls for concerted humanistic action in response to the horrific situations of chattel slavery in the eighteenth and early nineteenth centuries, and in battle against Jim Crow discrimination, racial and economic injustice, and segregation in the late nineteenth and twentieth centuries. While the central aspect of Dasein as Heidegger conceives it certainly lies in its modes of caring action or doing, each author examined in this study places vital importance upon humanistic action that will ameliorate or eradicate social ills that emerge from racist thought and practices, an emphasis that is lacking in most European and American treatises on being. (Jean-Paul Sartre is, of course, a notable exception in this regard, though his own work on the topic has not escaped the criticism of Frantz Fanon, for instance.[4]) While I underscore throughout this study that a sense of noetic movement (from one pole of thought to another) provides for metaphor and its "possibilities," a Heideggerian notion that correlates well with Ralph Ellison's more pointed concept of and insistence upon human possibilities (I consider this point in chapter 8 of this work), I also emphasize that such movement is specifically conceived in response to the harsh realities of Western racial injustice. In all of this, one notes the ways in which Wright's and Ellison's metaphors silently comment upon and quite obviously evolve from Du Bois's metaphors of the veil, the color-line, and double consciousness. Yet Du Bois's own metaphors of being do not emerge *sui generis*, as I argue above. Indeed, Du Bois profits from even as he modernizes and partially secularizes the anagogic metaphorics of Equiano and Harper, who then serve as his literary forebears.

Thus I encourage a consideration of the writings of these authors (and of others who contribute metaphors of being to the tradition of African American literature and who thus help establish this poetics of black being) as conceptual, complex, and nuanced statements of philosophical thought demanding the very sort of close reading and critical analysis that we have become accustomed to giving works such as Dante's *Inferno*, Montaigne's *Essais*, Franklin's *Autobiography*, and Sartre's *Nausée* (to mention four examples that represent the genres under examination in this study). Care is, for instance, a central theme critically and polemically at play in Wright's *The Man Who Lived Underground*, a theme that is not always credited in the literature on this work, but to which I turn my attention in chapter 7. Ellison casts care as "love," and features within his expansive metaphorics an insistence upon a moral democratic practice. Chapter 8, entitled "A Love Called Democracy," expounds this point.

Throughout this study, I will use terms such as "being," "consciousness," "subjectivity," and "existence" rather than the less familiar "Dasein," though I hope my meaning will nonetheless be clear. I will also refrain from capitalizing the term "Being" in my own usage, though, when needed, I will reproduce it as it is used by Heidegger and others. I will use instead the lowercase "being" to indicate at once an embrace of ideas of existence, consciousness, care, humanistic action and concern, and a refusal of metaphysical concepts of absolute presence or determinate selfhood. In *Being and Time*, Heidegger used Dasein as a rejection of Aristotelian categories of being (including the notion of "essence," which Heidegger sought to counter), and universalist "Being" or absolutist notions of "Being" that came about in the work of both Kant and Hegel. Like Nietzsche, Heidegger sought to refute these absolutist notions. He would do so later in his oeuvre by placing Being "under erasure"—the *sous rature* adapted, somewhat differently, by Jacques Derrida in *Of Grammatology* (1967)—showing both the unreliability of the term and its indispensability.

Even so, Heidegger's later thinking on *humanitas* does not "think" the essence of human being in ways adequately radical to deconstructing the privileging of what might be called white Western being. This I point out in chapter 4 of this study when I read his concept of a primordial *homo humanus* critically against the philosophy of black being exemplified in the poetry of F. E. W. Harper, and again in chapter 7, when I read Heidegger critically in light of the thought of Richard Wright. Later in his oeuvre, in 1947, Heidegger intended to recuperate a sense of universal humanism once its earlier, degenerated form had been put to rest. Thus he proposed a renascent humanism that cherished not an absolute sense of being (as was prized in the Hegelian dialectic), but a pluralistic humanist perspective.

This proposition was articulated in Heidegger's well-known "Letter on Humanism." Written in response to a query from the French philosopher Jean Beaufret,[5] who had posed to Heidegger a number of questions regarding his approach to phenomenology, among them, significantly, the question of how to restore meaning to the term "humanism," Heidegger argues:

> Your question not only presupposes a desire to retain the word "humanism" but also contains an admission that this word has lost its meaning. It has lost it through the insight that the essence of humanism is metaphysical, which now means that metaphysics not only does not pose the question concerning the truth of Being but also obstructs the question, insofar as metaphysics persists in the oblivion of Being. But the same thinking that has led us to this insight into the questionable essence of humanism has likewise compelled us to think the essence of man more primordially. With regard to this more essential *humanitas* of *homo humanus* there arises the possibility of restoring to the word "humanism" a historical sense that is older than its oldest meaning chronologically reckoned.[6]

Although Heidegger claims the project of conceptualizing a "primordial" man, a conceptualization that will, he argues, restore to humanism its sense and purpose even as it works to avoid the pitfalls of a false metaphysics, he continues to embrace a conceptualization that focuses, almost exclusively, on white Western human being. As Heidegger puts it to his Japanese interlocutor, the practically anonymous Professor Tezuka of "A Dialogue on Language": "I was trying to think the nature of phenomenology in a more originary manner, so as to fit it in this way back into the place that is properly its own within Western philosophy" (*On the Way to Language* 9. My emphasis.). Given his purposeful situation of his project at what he considers the origins of the genealogy of Western philosophy alone (to the exclusion of the philosophical traditions of non-Western societies such as Japan), his vision of *homo humanus* is, quite obviously, not anterior to or conceived radically against concepts of race and racialized being that crystallized in the West during the modern era. Indeed, as Heidegger indicates, his own conceptualization of being—which still holds its place as the preeminent conceptualization of being in twentieth century Continental philosophy—remains largely ascribed to the confines of Western European historicity without challenging the philosophy and limits of such historicity. Rather, Western historicity is, for him, the "standard conception": ". . . [S]pace and time do not only serve as parameters [of the "neighborhood" of Being, that is, its simultaneous "nearness" and "remoteness"]; in this role, their nature would soon be exhausted—a role whose seminal forms are discernible early in Western thinking, and which then, in the course of the modern age, became established by this way of thinking as the *standard conception*" (*On the Way to Language* 102. My emphasis). Heidegger's "neighborhood" of Being, the originary one from which all others are cast as simply derivative, appears to remain segregated, a gated community in which black being is neither welcome nor recognized.

~

Metaphor, which Heidegger ultimately rejected as locked within an outmoded version of metaphysics and which Jacques Derrida critiqued for its linkages to what he called a "white [Western] mythology,"[7] may nonetheless push past the gates that separate beings into racialized communities. This is, at least, the way in which I see conceptual metaphors at work in African American thought. At times, such thought takes shape in what has been called, in light of Ludwig Wittgenstein's work on language games, a philosophy of ordinary language. (I address such through a discussion of Zora Neale Hurston's work on vernacular metaphor in "Characteristics of Negro Expression" in chapter 1.) At other times, these conceptual metaphors engage much more directly ideas of conscious being under debate in Enlightenment-era continental philosophy, as reflected in the work of Equiano (whom I read against other contemporary philosophical writers on church, state, and race, such as Alexander Pope and Immanuel Kant). At still other times, the metaphors under examination debate the challenge Freudian psychoanalysis raised to continental philosophy's concepts of being, mind, consciousness, and language, a point I make in chapters 7 and 8. At all times, however, these metaphors have been inherently ontological and onto-theological, and often orientational. For their functioning, they depend, either implicitly or explicitly, upon the verb "to be," and thus they reflect upon human existence and experience, and regularly serve as linguistic and literary modes of personification. They also speak to one's place in the world (even as one seeks to negotiate the gap between temporality and the atemporal), or a sense of displacement from it, since they not only voice proscribed being in the face of racial oppression, but also deviate from accepted conventions of language and thus challenge traditional categories of meaning, a movement that I examine consistently throughout the chapters of this book.

Because they both profit from a long but under-examined tradition of philosophical metaphorics in African American literature and have left an indelible mark on the conceptual processes of metaphor that come in their wake, W. E. B. Du Bois's metaphorics serve as a powerful and productive critical framework through which to examine and analyze the tradition of philosophical metaphor in African American writing. In *Habitations of the Veil*, I draw upon the theory implicit in Du Bois's work to analyze African American metaphors of being as they are embedded within the social and intellectual upheavals from which they emerge and which they critique and clarify. I aim to establish these conceptual metaphors as tropes that function at the level of discourse and that articulate black being after a manner that is crucial. While attaining their status as what Aristotle calls the mark of genius, black philosophical metaphorical constructions, as we learn from our understanding of Du Boisian metaphorics, regularly do the work of epistemology and speculative thought that is so unyieldingly demanded by the social context in which the writer writes. The metaphors I examine in this study point out the problem of language encountered by many African American thinkers, since the existing lexicons of their societies are often simply inadequate to the issues and questions they encounter in being—in conscious lived experience. In response, many of these writers regularly make of ordinary language a conceptual discourse intent upon critiquing conventions of meaning as they establish new meanings and exhort humanistic activism, and this is regularly done through metaphorization. They put into play a critical discourse capable of conveying their lived experiences: metaphoric discourses of black being emerge from their writings in a humanistic gesture toward a social praxis aimed at ensuring a viable future for black people. This study introduces a new hermeneutic of these cultural, linguistic, and textual structures of metaphor.

I

Inhabiting the Veil

On Black Being

1

Being and Metaphor

There is more to be said about the concept of being, and particularly about the relationship between concepts of black being and metaphor, but first a fair amount of context is necessary to ensure our understanding of the discourses surrounding these concepts. This context will permit us to see more clearly how African American philosophical metaphors appeared in the literature well before Du Bois's seminal work in *The Souls of Black Folk*, even as they have persisted throughout the modern and postmodern periods in the aftermath of Du Bois's pivotal contributions.

African American philosophical metaphors have long demonstrated a penchant for voicing being or consciousness, and yet they have consistently participated in a genealogy of African American and, more broadly, Western philosophical thought whose historiography largely excludes them. Beginning with the classical period and granting significant attention to the modern contributions made by Zora Neale Hurston, chapter 1 discusses a number of theories specific to philosophical uses of metaphor in both African American and white Western aesthetic discourses before addressing its regular appearance in African American literary and cultural expression. Chapter 2 examines in detail the evolution of thought on the role of philosophical metaphor in African American literary theory, criticism, and philosophy, in particular.

Most of us understand metaphor generally as an ornament of language. African Americanists have long noted metaphor's capacity to enact what Henry Louis Gates, Jr. has called parodic signification.[1] In the African American tradition, these might be such metaphors as "you sho' is propaganda," and "sobbing hearted," both of which Zora Neale Hurston gives as examples of metaphor in her 1934 essay, "Characteristics of Negro Expression." However, while metaphor certainly operates as this sort of linguistic and textual embellishment—what some philosophers of language call "mere" or "fancy" metaphor, but what I will refer to more pertinently in this instance as vernacular metaphor—it also functions in modes that may be characterized as philosophical. On the one hand, vernacular metaphors constitute what Samuel Taylor Coleridge saw as the "primary imagination," which "perceives and operates within the ordinary world" through language (Hawkes 47). Philosophical metaphors, on the other hand, "[re-work] this world, and [impress their] own shape upon it" (47) in such a way that they reveal their epistemological potential and ontological qualities. These might be such metaphors as "I'll make me a world," which James Weldon Johnson uses in his 1927 poem, "The Creation." Johnson's metaphor carries at least two senses: in the first sense, the poet indicates an intention of creating a world around him or her; in the second sense, the poet collapses the distinction between self and world by articulating his/her intention to remake him/herself as a world, as a sphere of habitation for the spirit, soul, and mind. Such an image of world-creation connotes systemic knowledge. Philosophical metaphors are said to accomplish this world-making process through such modes as resemblance, deviance, and analogy. The especial focus of this study is upon those modes that are described as epistemological and ontological, those that, like Johnson's metaphor, are specifically concerned with the nature and meaning of being.

Western philosophical inquiry into the intersecting nature of metaphor and being dates back to the time of Plato and Aristotle, and actually appears in the works of both philosophers.[2] Metaphor has today remained at the center of a number of contemporary debates on being alive in much continental philosophy for two related reasons. First, as the aesthetician Clive Cazeaux puts it, "the fact that key epistemological concepts have metaphors at their root, for example, 'mirroring,' 'correspondence,' [and] 'sense datum,' is taken as evidence of the contingent, communal, subjective basis of knowledge" [sic]; and second, "because metaphor (as a form of dislocated or dislocating predication) works by testing the appropriate with the inappropriate, it is seen as a means of challenging the boundaries whereby one subject defines itself in relation to another."[3] That Aristotle, even more so than Plato, stands at the center of this epistemological but transgressive contemporary perspective on metaphor is central to this debate, as witnessed in the work of the Italian philosopher Guiseppe Stellardi. Aristotle's perspective on metaphor provides the foundation for both a semantic theory of metaphor and for what Stellardi calls "a possible conjunction between poetics and ontology, which if carried forth to its logical consequences, would place metaphor right at the heart of the processes of knowledge acquisition."[4]

This conjunction between poetics, ontology, and epistemology explains why Aristotle's definition of metaphor is largely considered to found the cornerstone of contemporary metaphor theory. While his *Rhetoric* contains a detailed treatment of tropes, Aristotle's major treatise on metaphor appears in the *Poetics*, a classical work on the origins of tragic drama and epic poetry, and one of the earliest works of western literary theory. There he defines metaphor as "the application [to something] of a name belonging to something else" (108). In Aristotle's analysis, metaphor is defined in four modes, each of which entails a "movement" or shifting of meaning. The definition is extended and fairly laborious, but it must be grasped if we are to understand the fundamental workings of metaphor.

The first mode of metaphor takes place in the movement "from the genus to the species," or from a general concept (a genre or universal type) to its outward form or specific manifestation. The metaphorical example Aristotle gives is, "Here stands my ship." In this instance, the verb "stands" functions as the genus, which takes the place of the species, "lying at anchor." The metaphor then consists in drawing the image of a ship "lying at anchor" to the mind of the reader via the use of the genus "standing." The second mode comes about when metaphor moves in the opposite direction, that is, when the species takes on the function of the genus. An example of this mode is found in a quote Aristotle draws from the work of the poet Homer: " 'truly has Odysseus done ten thousand deeds of worth': for [the species] 'ten thousand' is [part of the genus] 'many,' and Homer uses it here instead of 'a lot.'" An instance of the third mode, in which metaphor moves from one species to another, is found in such a phrase as "[killing a man by] 'draining out his life with bronze,'" that is, with a weapon made of bronze. This example provides a metaphor whose core is, essentially, a metonym. (A metonym is a word that is used as a substitute for something with which it is closely associated. In this case, the word "bronze" comes to stand in for a dagger or sword.) And lastly, metaphor may operate "according to analogy," where "*b* is to *a* as *d* is to *c*; for [the poet then] will say *d* instead of *b*, or *b* instead of *d*" (Aristotle 108). In the analogical mode of metaphor, the poet is free to make outright substitutions of words that evoke similar imagery or that carry similar meanings, and that therefore test the limits of meaning conveyed in each word. As an example, Aristotle writes, "the wine-bowl stands to Dionysus as the shield does to Ares: so [the poet] will call a wine-bowl 'shield of Dionysus' and a shield 'wine-bowl of Ares'" (109).

Aristotle considers metaphor the most important of the five principal tropes, the others being simile, metonymy, personification, and synecdoche.

Indeed, in the *Rhetoric*, he concludes that "simile is also a metaphor; the difference is but slight,"[5] and that metaphors can likewise take the shape of metonymy and synecdoche. Aristotle allows that writers may employ catachresis (which is more than simple malapropism) in the making of metaphors by inventing relationships between images, objects, and actions. To do this, the writer must take advantage of definitions accepted in the language-culture, such as "to scatter seed is to sow" (109) if he or she wishes to invent a metaphor such as "[scattering] radiance from the sun," which "has no name," or whose semantic and logical relationship was heretofore nonexistent (109). The writer may then turn about to say, "sowing god-wrought radiance," a metaphor whose inventive conceit is ensured only by the participation of the reader or auditor. The success of innovative metaphors depends fully upon the reader/auditor's being able to understand the relationship implied in the metaphor itself. In other words, the metaphor must make sense in the culture and society in which it is expressed, even if the relation it claims is distant. It is nonetheless important to note that each of the modes of metaphor described by Aristotle implies a logical relation that ties the terms of the metaphor together, and thus we see that metaphors can indeed serve ornamental purposes, but they can as well serve as propositional structures of meaning.

From Aristotle's definition, we see that metaphors can be words or phrases; they can be simple or complex. In the *Poetics*, they are described as a type of dynamic naming that can also be, especially in the fourth mode, analogy, vehicles for making new meaning and for reasoning. Importantly, Aristotle identifies them as the cornerstone of specific sorts of aesthetic language use in various genres of writing, particularly epic poetry and drama. Central to our understanding of metaphor and its use in African American literature is that Aristotle points toward mimesis, or representation, as foundational to metaphor, for in transferring the name of one thing to something else, there must be present some sort of recognition of the word that makes the transference work. In other words, metaphors make sense because they lead the reader or auditor to recognize the similarities between two seemingly disparate concepts or actions, as in "sowing god-wrought radiance." Hence (and this point Aristotle does not make directly) metaphor itself may be understood as inherently paradoxical, even as it extends toward a provisional unity of thought. Metaphor presents a continuity within an apparent discontinuity.

This dialectic of metaphor, wherein metaphor effects the displacement of one sense or meaning by substituting another, by claiming the nearness (contiguity) of another conceptual image whatever its semiotic distance, obtains not only between the similar and the dissimilar (between sameness and difference), but also between the written and the spoken. The oral/aural seems to be as significant as writing to the role of metaphor in literature, especially since metaphor serves, in speech as well as in writing, to make the spectator of the play or reader of a poem "see" things that would not otherwise be perceived. Aristotle writes that the "liveliness" of metaphor is achieved by "using the proportional [analogical] type of metaphor and by being graphic (i.e., making your hearers *see* things)." And by "'making them see things' I mean using expressions that represent things as in a state of activity" (*Rhetoric* 190. Italics in original).

Effective and ingenious metaphors, Aristotle argues, exploit this dialectical relation between the aural and the visual, the oral and the literate, for their function. What is more, Aristotle, in underscoring the importance of action ("things as in a state of activity") as well as perception ("making your hearers see things"), makes clear the centrality of agency and embodiedness to the conception and success of metaphors. For only bodies, whether they be human, animal, or celestial (as in plants, stars, and galaxies, which we significantly and metaphorically refer to as heavenly bodies), can undertake activity, and only human beings are thought capable of using advanced reasoning, engaging in action as they perceive differences and conceive linguistic innovations. Thus, from the inception of the history of the theory of metaphor, there courses the importance of representation, displacement, and epistemological deviance. Aristotle underscores the centrality of sound, sight, speech, and writing to successful and powerful metaphors. And, perhaps most critical to the purposes of this study, Aristotle makes clear the relation of phenomenological presence and metaphor, casting into clear relief the bond between ontology (as a central element of metaphysics) and the ordinary and poetic uses of metaphorical language.

The paradoxical nature of metaphor—its process of articulating discontinuity within continuity, its recognition of similarities in dissimilar entities, its collocation of the written and the oral/aural, and its simultaneity of transcendence and immanence—makes it uncommonly well-suited to the double-voiced character of modern African American cultural forms such as Spirituals, the blues, and gospel music. Metaphor simply abounds in the African American vernacular tradition. This is nowhere better exemplified than in the Sorrow Songs, which Du Bois treats at length in *Souls* as early African American poetry set to music, not unlike the early poetry of Europe sung in feudal and pre-modern monarchical lands by troubadours.

Many of the Spirituals date back to at least the eighteenth century, at the inception of the modern period. Canonical Spirituals such as "Swing Low, Sweet Chariot," do not simply allude to the promise of home represented by the lines referring to an afterlife in heaven ("Steal away, steal away, steal away to Jesus / Steal away, steal away home"), but also evolve over time to suggest the metaphorical train of the underground railroad, which would carry the slave northward to earthly freedom. The Spiritual "Go Down, Moses," puts forward analogical metaphors that consist in drawing an implicit comparison between the situation of the Jews in captivity and that of African slaves in bondage, a lyrical gesture that has been made explicit in such eighteenth-century writings as the narratives of Quobna Ottobah Cugoano[6] and Olaudah Equiano. Many scholars agree that "Go Down, Moses" is a transgressive song of open protest, a defiant melody that might only have been sung in the absence of white slaveholders and overseers.[7]

Late nineteenth- and twentieth-century blues songs, which evolved from Spirituals and work songs, are widely characterized as double-voiced expressions of concerns and care.[8] Their lyrics operate via metaphor, allusion, and innuendo. The double-voiced character of the blues is described by Albert Murray as being at once sacred and profane, a duality that supports what I see as the evolution of the use of metaphor in modern African American literature. Witness the "How Long Blues," first recorded in 1928: "The brook runs into the river, the river runs into the sea / If I don't run into my baby, a train is going to run into me / How long, how long, how long?" The repeated interrogatory phrase "how long?" is drawn from the Spiritual and gospel traditions, which regularly produced songs that queried God on the duration of human suffering. (How long must earthly suffering endure before the slave reached her heavenly rest? How long would men's sins prevail before the vengeful coming of the Lord?) Various elements of metaphor contribute to the figurative nature of language in the "How Long Blues": the repetition of words and themes; the play of orientational tropes (as discussed by Lakoff and Johnson, 15) that capitalize on sundry uses of the prepositional phrase "run into"; and the echoing of the first line by the second. Billie Holiday's "Fine and Mellow" (1939), one of her more memorable blues performances (many commentators agree that while Holiday at times recorded blues standards, she was more of a jazz vocalist than a blues singer[9]), employs metaphor more forthrightly: "Love is just like a faucet / It turns off and on / Love is just like a faucet / It turns off and on / Sometimes when you think it's on, baby / It has turned off and gone." We understand the simile, the explicit comparison—Aristotle's "full blown" metaphor—between love and a faucet, as a humorous trope employing ontological and somewhat personified descriptions of "love" and "faucet" because popular Western culture understands "love" as a capricious human sentiment that we may hope to contain (through the controlling mechanism of the faucet), but can never quite manage to fix.

The literature of African America is no less ripe with metaphor than its oral tradition. Metaphor is seen in its earliest examples, beginning with the often discussed "trope of the talking book" in the eighteenth-century narratives of John Marrant (*A Narrative of the Lord's Wonderful Dealings with John Marrant, a Black (Now Going to Preach the Gospel in Nova Scotia) Born in New-York, in North-America*, 1785) and Olaudah Equiano (*The Interesting Narrative of the Life of Olaudah Equiano, or Gustavus Vassa, the African. Written by Himself*, 1789), among others.[10] Sojourner Truth's metaphors of "substance" and "shadow," and her ontological declaration of herself as a "sign unto this nation,"[11] along with Frances Ellen Watkins Harper's layered framework of metaphor, memory, testimony, and being in *Sketches of Southern Life*, punctuate the mid-nineteenth century in preparation, as I show in chapter 4, for Du Bois's metaphorics of black ontology in *Souls*. Likewise, Paul Laurence Dunbar's 1895 poem "We Wear the Mask" anticipates the "two-ness" of African American existence expressed most poignantly and poetically by Du Bois nearly a decade later. Dunbar most famously writes: "We wear the mask that grins and lies/It hides our cheeks and shades our eyes/This debt we pay to human guile/With torn and bleeding hearts we smile/And mouth with myriad subtleties." The mask of which Dunbar sings foreshadows Du Bois's figures of the "veil" and the "color-line," as well as the latter's germinal trope of "double consciousness."

Standing at the crossroads of a metaphorical and ontological tradition of modern black expression, Du Bois develops these tropes at length and with eloquence not only in *The Souls of Black Folk*, but across his oeuvre, as I discuss in chapters 5 and 6. In the African American literary tradition, Du Bois's tropes are rivaled in importance only by Ralph Ellison's metaphor of "invisibility" as elaborated in *Invisible Man*. Du Bois's metaphorics provide a bridge between Dunbar's "mask that grins and lies" and the invisible man's determination to "yes 'em to death" with false acquiescence. Just as Ellison's narrative inherits much from Du Boisian metaphorics, it also underscores the crucial sense of double consciousness that provides the motivity to *Souls* as well as to James Weldon Johnson's *The Autobiography of an Ex-Colored Man* (1912/1927), which is taken by many critics to be a model for Ellison's novel.[12] Johnson, in one of his narrator's more explicit moments, writes that the "delicate" and "subtle" concerns that weighed upon the thought of the "coloured man" gave

> every coloured man, in proportion to his intellectuality, a sort of dual personality; there is one phase of him which is disclosed only in the freemasonry of his own race. I have often watched with interest and sometimes with amazement even ignorant coloured men under cover of broad grins and minstrel antics maintain this dualism in the presence of white men. (*Autobiography* 21–22)

Ellison, whose protagonist likewise suffers from a multiple sense of being akin to double consciousness, begins *Invisible Man* with a chiasmus (from the Greek for "a placing crosswise"), a metaphorical construction resembling an "X," not unlike the image of the crossroads that figures so prominently in the blues music Ellison loved: the novel's prologue is actually the introduction to the memoir of the narrator, who tells us near the conclusion of the novel that the "end was in the beginning" (*Invisible Man* 431). We the readers know that even as the end is in the beginning, the beginning is also in the end; the past is prologue to the present time of the novel.

Ellison's structures of time and space in *Invisible Man* were, as is well known, strongly influenced by Richard Wright's 1944 novella, *The Man Who Lived Underground*. Wright highly valued and regularly profited from textual metaphors that revealed both a critical ontology and a critical epistemology, such as those pioneered by Du Bois. He calls our attention to metaphorical matters of the text when he opines, in the 1937 essay, "Blueprint for Negro Writing" (which, in chapter 7, I read in context with earlier aesthetic statements on the role and function of tropes in literature written by F. E. W. Harper and Du Bois), that the "image and emotion" of literature "possess a logic of their own." He insists that affect and imagery— including, specifically, figures of language such as conceptual metaphors that approach the level of catachresis—are capable of granting form, meaning, and access to a new and better world. Like *Souls* before it, *The Man Who Lived Underground* paradoxically points the way to life in such a world through the complexity of its philosophical metaphors. I see Wright's fundamental metaphor of psychic and bodily descent as emblematic of the ways in which archetypal ontological tropes of death and life, guilt and freedom, time and space, memory and oblivion, and dreaming and waking facilitate the African American text's demand for a new and better world.

A Philosophy of Ordinary Black Being: Hurston's "Characteristics of Negro Expression"

Wright would, of course, implicitly (though not explicitly) distance himself from Du Bois and other earlier black writers in "Blueprint for Negro Writing." Nonetheless, "Blueprint," an indispensable piece on African American language, culture, and political aesthetics regarding the function and mission of the artist, was published three years after what was probably the single most important essay on African American language to appear before World War II, Zora Neale Hurston's "Characteristics of Negro Expression" (1934). In many ways, Wright and Ellison alike would profit from the insights on vernacular expressions of black being that Hurston documents in "Characteristics" and puts into play in her fiction, though Wright in particular would distance himself from Hurston's art.[13] Hurston's discussion of metaphor as foundational to African American vernacular expressions such as the blues and folklore, and as relational to its social context resonates in crucial ways with Aristotle's classical discussion of metaphor in the *Poetics*. Thus it actually advances the question of ontological metaphor towards what mid-twentieth-century philosophers would come to call the philosophy of ordinary language.

A product of what is now known as the "linguistic turn" in philosophy during the 1950s and 1960s, the philosophy of ordinary language emerged in contrast to analytic philosophy. While the latter treats with some suspicion what it sees as language's tendency toward opacity, ordinary language philosophy claims that meaning resides precisely in the use of words, that words mean what they are used to mean in certain contexts. Though Hurston is generally not read within the context of this discourse, she is, in fact, the first African American literary and cultural critic to have published a piece specific to language, sociolinguistics, and cultural expression among African Americans before 1950,[14] and thus her short piece on language is the most pointed and, perhaps, most important work of sociolinguistics and the philosophy of ordinary African American language produced prior to the Black Aesthetic movement. It therefore bears an extended discussion, after which I will elaborate the ways in which Hurston, Wright, and Ellison engage Du Bois's theory of metaphor in its insistence upon a philosophical grounding in the exigencies of everyday black being.

The original venue for Hurston's essay, published the same year as her first novel, the semi-autobiographical *Jonah's Gourd Vine*, was *Negro: An Anthology* (1934). Edited by the British shipping heiress Nancy Cunard, a poet, writer, and biographer whose passion for African and African American culture and history was well known in transatlantic circles, *Negro* was not only large and broad in scope (it contained at least 231 entries and was divided into seven sections, including "America," "Negro Stars," "Music," "Poetry," "West Indies and South America," and "Africa"), it also boasted of such African American contributors as W. E. B. Du Bois, Langston Hughes, Sterling Brown, and Arna Bontemps. White authors who contributed to the collection included William Carlos Williams, Theodore Dreiser, and Cunard herself. The then fledgling writer Samuel Beckett, whose most famous work is the play *En attendant Godot* (*Waiting for Godot*, 1952), undertook a number of translations for inclusion in the work. Among these is the piece "Murderous Humanitarianism," submitted by The Surrealist Group in Paris and signed by André Breton, Paul Élouard, and René Char, among others.

Negro constituted something of an act of daring. While *The New Negro* (1925) was presented by its editor, Alain Locke (who also contributed to Cunard's anthology), as the voice of the Harlem Renaissance, the throaty song of the New Negro poet and intellectual in the United States, *Negro* laid claim to the world as its stage. In her anthology, Cunard implicitly framed the cultural artifacts of African-descended peoples as "diasporic." The term exists nowhere in her Foreword to the work, yet it is silently spoken from each page comprising the text. She also framed the book as one that responded to the needs of the Negro through the activism of the Communist Party, and this she did explicitly.

Hurston seems to have been oblivious to Cunard's purpose. In her autobiography *Dust Tracks on a Road* (1942), she makes no note of her involvement in producing *Negro*. In fact, she does not mention it at all. The very structure of Hurston's essay on "Negro expression" appears to serve a specific purpose quite apart from that of Cunard. Hurston's goal seems not to have been the disruption of any sort of authority—imperialist, capitalistic (these were Cunard's stated aims for *Negro*), or otherwise. She strikes one as being much more intent upon expressing what she describes, in a letter to Carl Van Vechten, as the beauty of "Negrodom" and the complexity of its expression, which she chronicled not through the singular practice of writing, but multiply through story, song, and dance.

"Characteristics" unfolds in twelve parts: "Drama"; "Will to Adorn" (which treats metaphor and simile, the "double-descriptive," "verbal nouns," and "nouns from verbs"); "Angularity"; "Asymmetry"; "Dancing"; "Negro Folklore"; "Culture Heroes"; "Examples of Folklore and the Modern Culture Hero"; "Originality"; "Imitation"; "Absence of the Concept of Privacy"; "The

Jook"; and "Dialect." I will limit my discussion to the two sections of the essay that are most pertinent to the focus of this study: "Drama" and "Will to Adorn."

It should not be lost on us that Hurston, like Aristotle, approaches her theory of figurative language through a discussion of human action, human drama. In the *Poetics*, Aristotle defines metaphor as reliant upon mimesis—representation—for its formation. He addresses metaphor not simply through a discussion of the parts of speech, but also through the major genres of his day: epic poetry and tragic drama. Primary or "primitive" epic poetry such as that composed by Homer—whose work Aristotle prized above almost any other poet—was largely oral. Indeed, it was mimetic—it was *performed* and, because of its metaphorical innovations, it bore, as Alexander Pope saw it, the mark of inventive genius.[15] In speaking of metaphor, which is her major concern in the first two sections of the essay, Hurston likewise insists upon the importance of the relation between metaphor and mimesis, and she does so in terms of the dramatic mimicry that she sees at the center of black cultural life.

The "Negro's universal mimicry" is "evidence of something that permeates his entire self. And that thing is drama," Hurston writes (1019). In a way that reflects the anthropological work she had been carrying out since 1926,[16] Hurston's discussion of the drama that characterizes everyday Negro expression analyzes it in something of a naturalistic way, that is, with regard to environmental and social relations, and, perhaps most importantly, in relation to vernacular culture. (As an anthropologist, Hurston makes clear throughout the essay that her focus is the black "folk" or what she calls the "average Negro" [1022] and not middle-class African Americans, whose culture is, in her eyes, derivative of that of whites.) The peculiar language that Hurston sees the Negro employing in his/her self-expression is highly imagistic and replete with terms capable of enacting the drama of black existence. "His interpretation of the English language is in terms of pictures" (1019), Hurston insists.

Hurston's choice of "interpretation" as a key term in this phrase appears quite deliberate. She might instead have chosen the word "translation," which would indicate a movement or transference of meaning across the boundaries of two or more different linguistic and social contexts. While "translation" indicates an articulation of meaning across language's own limits, "interpretation" would instead indicate the act of taking meaning to a point of exchange and there rendering it otherwise in a gesture of displacement. Where translation appears to be directly linked to language as it is written, interpretation refers to language as it is spoken. Thus by choosing "interpretation" as a critical term of analysis, Hurston remains true to her goal of discussing the performative (mimetic) aspects of Negro vernacular expression (performance in language being one of the central tenets of the philosophy of ordinary language). "Interpretation" permits Hurston to shed light on what she sees as the dramatic and mimetic nature of African American speech as it displaces white American norms, and there, for her, lay the very essence of African American culture.

Hurston goes on to argue that everyday African Americans routinely use metaphorical analogy in their version of American English: this newly interpreted language is expansively employed to "describe [one act] in terms of another," and this sort of systemic analogy is the basis for "the rich metaphor and simile" that characterize folk expression (1019). These metaphors are, to Hurston's mind, "primitive," since it is "easier to illustrate" meaning by way of pictures "than to explain because action came before speech" (1019). In fact, she concludes, the Negro "thinks in hieroglyphics." And this compared to the thought process of "the white man," who "thinks in a written language" (1020).

The analogy Hurston provides ("Let us make a parallel," she writes) in support of her controversial contention that the Negro's "language and thought are 'primitive'" is striking. It underscores the significance of her decision to employ the term "interpretation" rather than "translation." Interpretation highlights an act of not only excavation, of tunneling through layers of signification in order to attain to a deeper, hidden meaning; it also emphasizes the act of exchange Hurston sees at work in black vernacular expression. We should recall that the "parallel" that Hurson draws itself functions as an analogy, a tropological form that Aristotle deems to be one of the four fundamental types of metaphor.[17] Beginning with yet another metaphorical construction, a simile, described by Aristotle as a "full-blown" metaphor,[18] Hurston writes: "Language is like money. In primitive communities, actual goods, however bulky, are bartered for what one wants. This finally evolves into coin, the coin being not real wealth but a symbol of wealth. Still later even coin is abandoned for legal tender, and still later for checks in certain usages" (1019–1020).

Hurston likens the barter system, an early system of trade characterized by economists as cumbersome and inconvenient, to the Negro's ostensibly "primitive" use of language. Bartering evolved into a more sophisticated monetary system in which coin came to be exchanged for goods. We might add that the use of money in lieu of barter allows for a more extensive network of exchange in a marketplace. Barter severely limits the number of players in a market, because it largely eliminates intermediaries or "middle men": it demands that those who wish to make the exchange make it more or less directly with one another. Bartering seems to be, like the so-called "primitive" Negro expression Hurston describes, a system in which the only ones who can participate are those who "belong" to the language community in question, those who are situated in the cultural tradition of the local place. Quite possibly, it is the anthropologist in her that leads Hurston to see the Negro's expression in such naturalistic terms. Ferdinand de Saussure, the father of modern linguistics whose work I discuss further below, built his analysis of human language in good measure upon similar concepts of value and exchange, though Saussure was more likely to value the "check words" that Hurston attributes to whites.

It must be pointed out that, from the perspective of Claude Lévi-Strauss, to reference the thought of yet another modern sociolinguist and anthropologist, such expression does not indicate the "ineptitude" of so-called "primitive people" for abstract thought, as Hurston argues in her essay. Hurston insists that a more evolved, conceptual language expressed in "check words" remains the province of whites. Lévi-Strauss, who regarded highly the work of Hurston's mentor, Franz Boas, takes the counterview:

> It has long been the fashion to invoke languages which lack the terms for expressing such a *concept* as "tree" or "animal," even though they contain all the words necessary for a detailed inventory of species and varieties. But, to begin with, while these cases are cited as evidence of the supposed ineptitude of "primitive people" for abstract thought, other cases are at the same time ignored which make it plain that the richness of abstract words is not a monopoly of civilized languages. In Chinook, a language widely spoken in the north-west of North America, to take one example, many properties and qualities are referred to by means of abstract words: "This method," Boas says, "is applied to a greater extent than in any other language I know." The proposition "the bad man killed the poor child" is rendered in Chinook: "The man's badness killed the child's poverty"; and for "The woman used too small a basket" they say: "She put the potentilla-roots into the smallness of a clam basket."
>
> In every language, moreover, discourse and syntax supply indispensable means of supplementing deficiencies of vocabulary. And the tendentious character of the argument referred to in the

last paragraph becomes very apparent when one observes that the opposite state of affairs, that is, where very general terms outweigh specific names, has also been exploited to prove the intellectual poverty of Savages. . . . The proliferation of *concepts*, as in the case of technical language, goes with more constant attention to properties of the world, with an interest that is more alert to possible distinctions which can be introduced between them. This thirst for objective *knowledge* is one of the most neglected aspects of the *thought* of people we call "primitive." Even if it is rarely directed towards facts of the same level as those with which modern science is concerned, it implies comparable *intellectual application* and methods of observation. In both cases the universe is an *object of thought* at least as much as it is a means of satisfying needs. (Lévi-Strauss, *The Savage Mind*, 1–2. Emphasis added.)

Lévi-Strauss's conclusions, of course, appeared in 1962, well after the publication of Hurston's "Characteristics" and after Hurston's death in 1960. Nonetheless, Lévi-Strauss not only quotes Hurston's mentor, Franz Boas, in his critical comments countering the supposed lack of abstract thought among so-called "primitives" (above, I have highlighted Lévi-Strauss's references to the "concepts," "knowledge," "thought," and "intellectual application" of such to peoples); he also echoes Ferdinand de Saussure's pioneering findings.[19]

In his authoritative 1914 work (published posthumously by his students as the *Course in General Linguistics*), Saussure opined that "[s]cholars were . . . wrong in assuming that the absence of a word proves that the primitive society knew nothing of the thing that the word names" (*Course* 225). In "Characteristics," Hurston seems unwilling substantiate her notions of what she calls black "primitive" expression, which in some ways went against the prevailing linguistics of her day. Yet we can be certain of the force of her opinion, delivered through the tropological form of analogy: if Negro expression is primitive expression likened to a primitive system of trade known as bartering, and if bartering is itself a limited form of economic interaction, it becomes clear that, in Hurston's logic, the "primitive" forms of metaphor used by the class to which Hurston refers are largely viewed by members of that group itself as closed social media of exchange that unfold within what James Weldon Johnson referred to as the "freemasonry of the [Negro's] own race" (*Autobiography* 22). These forms thus require their own interpretation from someone inside the group, a task that Hurston readily takes up.

The implication one draws from Hurston's analogy is that systems of language likewise evolve as systems of exchange wherein language not only carries concepts that are embellished by human linguistic inventiveness and enhanced by the drama of human experience, but also, on quite another register, carry an exchange value relative to a sense of community, social class, and even racial and ethnic identity. While Hurston's stance on the "primitive" nature of African American expression ignored significant aspects of Saussure's and Boas's theories of primitive language, her adaptation of a value-based perspective of language was not out of line with the currents of linguistic theory in the 1920s and 30s. Indeed, it had been sanctioned in Saussure's *Course*.

Saussure had largely been concerned with value in relation to synchronic linguistics, but made it clear that value was of "prime importance" to the general study of linguistics. For him, language is a system of "pure values" whose "characteristic role" is "to serve as a link between thought and sound" (*Course* 111–12). In defining more pointedly the role of value in language, Saussure returned to his conclusion regarding the arbitrary nature of the sign:

> Linguistics then works in the borderland where the elements of sound and thought combine; *their combination produces a form, not a substance.* These views give a better understanding of what was said before about the arbitrariness of signs. Not only are the two domains that are linked by the linguistic fact shapeless and confused, but the choice of a given slice of sound to name a given idea is completely arbitrary. If this were not true, the notion of value would be compromised, for it would include an externally imposed element. But actually values remain entirely relative, and that is why the bond between the sound and the idea is radically arbitrary. The arbitrary nature of the sign explains why in turn the social fact alone can create a linguistic system. The community is necessary if values that owe their existence solely to usage and general acceptance are to be set up; by himself the individual is incapable of fixing a single value. (Italics in original, 113)

Having addressed the question of linguistic value, and being duly careful to avoid the sense of essentialism carried by the notion of language producing a "*substance*" rather than a "*form*," Saussure would eventually come to issues of race and ethnicity in relation to language. He felt certain that "a common language [would not imply] consanguinity, that a family of languages [does not necessarily match] an anthropological family" (222), but he did believe that ethnic identity was reinforced by common language usage: "The social bond tends to create linguistic community and probably imposes certain traits on the common idiom; conversely, linguistic community is to some extent responsible for ethnic unity. In general, ethnic unity always suffices to explain linguistic community" (223).

In spite of Saussure's insistence on the centrality of the linguistic community when it comes to evolving a system of language, in late twentieth-century theory, Henry Louis Gates, Jr. emphasized—after a fashion that seeks to critique what he characterizes as a pertinent oversight—Saussure's assurance that the "signifier . . . is fixed, not free, with respect to the linguistic community that uses it. The masses have no voice in the matter."[20] (Curiously enough, however, in his theorization of African American vernacular expression, Gates does not locate African American vernacular speech along the diachronic/syntagmatic x-axis of Saussure's model—the axis of dynamism and change—but along the synchronic/paradigmatic y-axis, the static axis of language to which Saussure grants the preponderance of his attention as he formulates his theory of structuralist linguistics. I shall return to this point shortly.) Yet Saussure's conclusion should ultimately be read in its fuller context. Saussure's comment that the signifier is "fixed, not free" should be interpreted only in the greater context of his ideas regarding the simultaneous, but seemingly incongruous "immutability and mutability of the sign" (74). As Wade Baskin, editor of the English translation of the *Course* puts it, "It would be wrong to reproach F. de Saussure for being illogical or paradoxical in attributing two contradictory qualities to language. By opposing two striking terms, he wanted only to emphasize the fact that language changes in spite of the inability of [individual] speakers to change it" (*Course* 74ff). Although Saussure was quite clear in arguing that no single member of a linguistic community could alter the course of language, he did agree that through an innovation (made by one or more speakers of whatever race or ethnicity) subsequently adopted by the group, a community of speakers could indeed alter language. The ability of language to evolve through linguistic communities is especially important in understanding diachronic language, which is mapped along the x-axis. Saussure writes:

> [E]verything in diachronic language is diachronic only by virtue
> of speaking. It is in speaking that the germ of all change is found.
> Each change is launched by a certain number of individuals

before it is accepted for general use. . . . the new form, repeated many times and accepted by the community, [becomes] a fact of language. But not all innovations of speaking have the same success, and so long as they remain individual, they may be ignored, for we are studying language; they do not enter into our field of observation until the community of speakers has adopted them. (*Course* 98)

It is useful to return to Hurston with Saussure's words in mind. As we have seen, Hurston grants close attention to the African American community of speakers, but does not ignore whites. When writing of white communities of speakers, or of persons belonging to various European ethnic groups (which Hurston does not specify), she deems their language to be more highly evolved: "Now the people with highly developed languages have words for detached ideas. That is legal tender" (1020). By contrast, she argues, the "primitive man," and by implication Hurston here refers to the Negro, "exchanges descriptive words." Even if a so-called "primitive" being such as the Negro is possessed of "detached words in his vocabulary—not evolved in him but transplanted on his tongue by contact," Hurston maintains, he must first refashion this vocabulary and "add action" so as to "make it do [sic]" (1020). This is the reason for such "characteristic" Negro expressions as "sitting-chair" and "chop-ax," Hurston tells us. She juxtaposes these sorts of Negro expression, which she terms "double-descriptives" and which she also describes as metaphorical action-words, against what she deems abstractions or concepts used primarily by whites. The Negro "has in his mind the picture of the object in use. Action. Everything illustrated. So we can say that the white man thinks in a written language and the Negro thinks in hieroglyphics" (1020).

There is something unsettling about the ease with which Hurston assigns "true" Negro expression the label of "primitive" and associates advanced thought and expression with whites alone.[21] And it is striking that she is less than progressive in her views regarding the possibilities inherent in black speech and knowledge. Yet in arguing assiduously that Negro words are action words and are of a piece with the oral culture of which they form the largest and most significant element, Hurston's analysis accomplishes an extraordinary measure from the perspective of contemporary theory. While poststructuralism has tended to characterize metaphor rather simplistically as a form of verbal and literary ornamentation that is inexorably tied to the transcendent and the abstract (and placed firmly on Saussure's vertical synchronic/paradigmatic y-axis), Hurston insists upon its predicative qualities, in which metaphor performs acts of verbalization that exemplify the immanent and the embodied, the everyday. Put otherwise, Hurston argues, *avant la lettre*—that is, before the "linguistic turn" in philosophy, and before the revolution in metaphor theory that was ushered in by Paul Ricoeur's work on the topic in 1975, and before Gates's work in *The Signifying Monkey* (1988)—that metaphor does exactly what poststructuralists claim it cannot do.[22] She demonstrates that it is living rather than static, and this living quality of metaphor permits us to draw further conclusions: that metaphor moves capriciously between the paradigmatic and syntagmatic lines of Saussure's axis of language; that it is epistemological, such that it is capable of voicing the structures of meaning at work in a community; and that it is ontological—it is immanent and embodied at the same time that it gives expression to the fluid and living ideals of a group of people.

For Hurston, Negro expression, especially its metaphorical forms, is redolent of the everyday lives of ordinary African Americans. Again, it is important to note that Hurston's analysis is a class-based one. This she herself argues when she differentiates between the "average Negro" and the "sophisticated" Negro, who has no real culture, in her estimation. In "average Negro" life, "[a] bit of Negro drama familiar to us all is the frequent meeting of two opponents who threaten to do atrocious murder one upon the other," she narrates (1020). Significantly, this line stands alone as a paragraph in the essay; it marks a transition in the text, and serves to introduce the paragraphs that conclude the essay's first section, "Drama." In the wake of this declaration, Hurston renders language ironically and strategically mute. While for Hurston, the body takes the place of metaphorical language as a focal point, language still speaks from the silence of the mimetic: "Who has not observed a robust young Negro chap posing upon a street corner, possessed of nothing but his clothing, his strength, and his youth?" Hurston asks. Important to her is the innate drama that characterizes two young people who take on the mantle of performance, and that which they perform is the everyday use of black language. Such performance, such drama, Hurston argues, is inherent to the cultural traditions of black folk, just as Aristotle insisted—through his attention to epic, tragedy, and his fleeting reference to comedy—that drama is germane to the cultural traditions of the Greeks. As Hurston places her two actors in motion, their embodied genders speak their words for them. The body, and the social presence it affords them, seem to be all the two young players need. Through the body, the girl's shoulders and hips put forth all the action. The "chap's" eyes and posture "speak" with authority, she tells us, and "no one ever mistakes the meaning" (39). With this line, Hurston links her philosophy of ordinary language with phenomenology and the black body with metaphorical expression, disallowing the possibility that any meaning could slip away in the process.

Hurston alerts us to something important here, but never quite arrives at crystallizing its significance; she seems more interested in the supposed "primitive" characteristics of the people she describes. Yet we can still get closer to the philosophical import of such performativity as Hurston illustrates. Reflecting upon the phenomenological possibilities inherent in ordinary language philosophy, such as that which Hurston employs, Paul Ricoeur writes that as an intellectual and philosophical project, phenomenology tries

> to extract from lived experience the essential meanings and structures of purpose, project, motive, wanting, trying and so on. I note in passing that phenomenology [. . .] had already attacked problems which are now in the forefront of the school of linguistic analysis with the philosophy of action. But if it was phenomenology, it was existential phenomenology in the sense that these essential structures imply the recognition of the central problem of embodiment, of *le corps propre*. Anyhow, whatever might be the relation between phenomenology and existentialism [. . .] this kind of philosophizing did not yet raise any particular problem of language, for a direct language was thought to be available. This direct language was ordinary language in which we find words like purpose, motive, and so on. This is why I now believe that there is an intersection of the philosophy of ordinary language and phenomenology at this first level. (*The Rule of Metaphor* 316)

I take Ricoeur's assessment of the relation between phenomenology and the philosophy of ordinary language to be particularly instructive to any reading of Hurston's "Characteristics of Negro Expression," which not only analyzes the levels of metaphoricity at work in black performativity and black vernacular discourse, but also posits a theory of embodied agency—action—alive in folk expression, even if she does not assess this language for its possible contributions to black knowledge and radical action, as does Richard Wright. One might say that Wright presents an example of the existential phenomenology of black knowing and black agency, indirectly extending Hurston's focus on drama in everyday black life by introducing his reader to Bigger Thomas and Fred Daniels, two everyday "black boys" (like Wright himself) whose daily trials and heavy existential burdens were meant to force upon readers the realities of black life by dramatizing black experience.

Ralph Ellison chose a different pathway in his fiction. Hurston's emphasis on black vernacular expression and the black body is cast into relief yet again when we consider that Ellison, who metaphorically rendered the black body "invisible" in his novel (implying that the ontological condition of invisibility was a universal human condition that applied to all African American men if not, in fact, all African Americans), challenged Hurston's and Wright's links between black corporeality and black epistemology and ontology. Even if in a differential fashion—one focused on literature as well as orality and mimesis, and concerned with black folk traditions as well as the crises of the emerging black middle class—Ellison is one of a small number of mid-twentieth-century African American writers who take up the task of characterizing black expression that Hurston began, in light of Du Bois's own articulations in *Souls*, near the close of the Harlem Renaissance. In doing so, Ellison returns us to the phenomenology of metaphor so wonderfully on display in Du Bois's work. It is a phenomenology that is rooted in black folk culture: Ellison trusts that black folk culture has a radical message to bring to the world. He anchors his phenomenology of black being in vernacular expression, and through his criticism of this expression, especially in the forms of the blues and jazz, elevates these vernacular forms to the realm of "high" art without wishing to "dry up the deep, rowdy stream of jazz until it becomes a very thin trickle of respectable sound indeed."[23]

Likening the underlying message of his novel to the quest for existential identity each American must undertake, Ellison proffers the propositional metaphor of home as democracy and, by extension then, democracy as love (see "Brave Words for a Startling Occasion," 1953). Democracy is the ideal that each American, of whatever color, must grasp, for it is only by realizing the ideal of democracy (a radical democracy, Ellison argues implicitly) that Americans can overcome the oblivion of invisible black being and corporeality, and live up to the moral call issued by the man for whom Ellison was named. Ralph Waldo Emerson, to whom Ellison often referred, in a moment of ruminating and theorizing the state of American politics, called for politics as an expression of love. Ellison goes so far as to echo Emerson in the novel, prompting his protagonist to ponder this very point. In the final chapter of this study, I argue that Ellison's concern in deploying the metaphor of love as democracy is to give voice to a sense of homelessness or a crisis of belonging that culminates in a state of social invisibility and that is, itself, indicative of a crisis in American democracy. The black state of invisibility is a crisis that, Ellison seems to say in a moment of great phenomenological and existential import, can be overcome only by love of an active, moral, and maternal sort.

As did Ellison, Hurston actually hearkens back to Du Bois and his work on African American culture in *The Souls of Black Folk* and elsewhere. If for Du Bois it is in the vernacular, spiritual expressions of African Americans that one may find the "souls" or being of black folk, it is so for Hurston as well, even if she disagrees with Du Bois's characterization of the Spirituals as "Sorrow Songs."[24] Wright likewise considered African American folklore, Spirituals, and the blues to be a font of "racial wisdom" ("Blueprint for Negro Writing" 1405), and he agreed with Du Bois, Hurston, and Ellison that Negro culture stemmed from the black church and African American folklore. However, Wright argued that black folk expression, especially in the Spirituals, was not only a simple stage along the way to transcending an overly simplistic black ontology, but that black folk expression in the Spirituals and other vernacular forms could, at the same time, be tapped as a source for the transcendence of the worldly limits of racism and oppression, a way of attaining, however tenuously, a state of psychic freedom and the realities of bodily freedom.

≈

In light of path-breaking works such as those I examine in this study, works that show conceptual metaphors to be central not only to African American expression, but indeed African American culture more broadly defined, many African Americanists—theorists and philosophers alike—agree on the importance of metaphor as central to voicings of black consciousness and being. I shall come to the philosophers in chapter 2, but will attend here to some of the pertinent analyses that have been proffered by a number of literary theorists and critics.

Karla F. C. Holloway, for instance, is quite specific about the noetic location in which she situates her inquiry in *Moorings and Metaphors* (1992), which, not withstanding its pointed focus on gendered language, resonates with my own study in its aims: "Its center is where behavior, art, philosophy, and language unite as a cultural expression within an African-American literary tradition. . . . My primary argument is that black women's literature reflects its community—the cultural ways of knowing as well as ways of framing that knowledge in language" (1). Holloway, influenced significantly by Hurston's approach to the study of African American culture, espouses a perspective that is easily linked to Hurston's philosophy of ordinary language, given her focus on the orality in African diasporic women's literature. She focuses on a specific feminine metaphor—the goddess ancestor—in black women's texts, and argues for the distinctiveness of black women's writing vis-à-vis that of black men (25, 92). Specifically, she argues that a "woman-centered principle" grounds "black women's literature," and that this principle "emphasizes the cultural representation of language. What connects language and creativity is that for women, biologically confronted with the possibility of creation, motherhood embraced or denied is unique to her sense of self" (26). In her attention to the particularities of black women's writing (from West Africa as well as the United States), Holloway wants to avoid what she sees as the strictures of a "scriptocentric historicism" of women's literature. Instead, she describes a "mooring" that ensures a critical relationship between "the spoken texts of myth and the (re)membered consciousness within the literate word" (25). Seeing orality as the core or soul of literacy, Holloway argues that it is from this soul that black women writers' consciousness comes forth. And, importantly for her, the metaphors that "identify black traditions of literary theory are those that reach outside of Western history for their source" (24).

While I would agree with Holloway that African diasporic literary traditions often reach beyond the boundaries of (white) Western thought in order to found its poetics, I am not certain of what it means to insist that the tropes that identify the "black traditions of literary theory" come from beyond the boundaries of "Western history" and, presumably, its aesthetics. New World African writers look back to the Continent, the "motherland," but also look within the new culture they were forced to create for the sources of their aesthetics and their systems of meaning; they are thus both "in the West," and not of it, to adapt a Biblical phrase. The words of Christ in John 17:9–16, which resonate significantly in much African American vernacular discourse, speak of Christ's people as being in the world but not of it. This is, in fact, a wonderful poetic anticipation of Heidegger's secularized use of the phrase "being-in-the-world," in which being is defined in simultaneous relation to temporality and spatiality. Eighteenth- and nineteenth-century African Americans regularly used Christ's phraseology as the basis of their expressions of consciousness, ethics, and morality; quite often, it emerged from within the West as a stringent spatio-temporal critique of Western processes of racism and oppression. In an ironic foreshadowing, Christ, just before being betrayed by Judas and denied by the Apostle Peter, prayed to God for his followers even as he spoke of their existential temporalities as related to space: that life on earth was limited, but life beyond the world was eternal. It is in this eternal and at times liminal temporality that the saved would actualize their being, and we see such a creed reflected in many of the philosophical metaphors I examine in this study.

Houston A. Baker, Jr.'s attention to Western theoretical perspectives, including those of Heidegger, does not at all sit well with Holloway (Holloway 103–104). Baker's aim in *Blues, Ideology, and Afro-American Literature: A Vernacular Theory* (1984) is to go beyond if not, in fact, reverse his earlier work in *The Journey Back* (1980). There, he writes, he "envisioned the 'speaking subject' creating language (a code) to be deciphered by the present-day commentator" (1). In *Blues*, by contrast, Baker no longer sees a speaking black subject, but a black subject spoken and displaced by language itself: the "code" speaks the subject, who suddenly finds him- or herself "decentered" in Baker's thought. He explains: "I was convinced that I had found such specificity in a peculiar subjectivity, but the objectivity of economics and the sound lessons of poststructuralism arose to reorient my thinking" (1). His reorientation leads him to formulate a blues theory, which he terms a "matrix" that stands as a "cultural invention": "a 'negative symbol' that generates (or obliges one to invent) its own referents" (9). Like Holloway, however, I, too, remain unconvinced of the value of proposing that the African American subject be necessarily decentered in a wholesale application of Western theoretical constructs to the question of black being. For reasons I propose below, I believe that poststructuralist theory should be further challenged to accommodate African American ontological and epistemological perspectives, which strain at and test its limits.

Henry Louis Gates, Jr.'s 1988 book, *The Signifying Monkey: A Theory of African-American Literary Criticism*, has been of remarkable importance to scholarship on figurative language and intertextuality in African American literature, as Holloway's work makes clear. For this reason, I engage him extensively here. His theory of "Signification" undertook a valuable intervention in the theorization of African American rhetorical language. As he analyzes the orders of meaning that evolved under the auspices of the European concept of signification, Gates is concerned in his study to "define a carefully structured system of rhetoric, traditional Afro-American figures of signification, and then to show how a curious figure becomes the trope of literary revision itself" (44).

In order to demonstrate his point, Gates reminds us that the standard Western use of the term signification "denotes the meaning that a term conveys, or is intended to convey" (46). The advent of Saussurean linguistics in the early twentieth century changed all that because it shifted the denotation of signification onto the linguistic and literary grounds of criticism: "Since Saussure, at least, the three terms *signification, signifier, signified* have been fundamental to our thinking about general linguistics and, of late, about criticism specifically. These neologisms in the academic-critical community are homonyms of terms in the black vernacular tradition perhaps two centuries old" (46). Gates dates the African American usage of the word signification, which "[supplanted] the received term's associated concept," at about 1787, 200 years before the time of his own writing. If this is so, then the slaves' emptying of the prior term and supplementation of new meaning is coterminous with the early days of the American nation, as the country was coming to form itself as a nation-state and as concepts of American citizenship, individualism, and national belonging were taking shape. It is not lost on Gates that, as he notes in *Figures in Black* (copyrighted in 1987, but not published until 1989), ideas of race that were anchored in an emerging pseudoscience were also crystallizing during this Enlightenment era. Gates sees the slaves' "witty" disruption of middle- and upper-class white signification as a "guerrilla action" that denotes a "Signifyin(g) black difference" (*Signifying Monkey* 46–47), countering the dehumanizing signification that was ascribed to black difference in white Western philosophy and social discourse. And while he is quite aware of the traps that lay awaiting those who naïvely postulate a concept of origins—such as that which might be associated with tracing this sort of language use back to "[some] Black genius or community of witty and sensitive speakers" (46)—he insists upon the intentionality that founds his project. That is, he believes that "some genius[es]" innovated the "homonymic pun" of "signifyin(g)" to differentiate the black enslaved interlocutor from the free white interlocutor, who was much more familiar with the conventional English usage of the term. And though he easily terms such usage "punning," he clearly argues for this innovation as a "complex act of language" (47). The enslaved's "signifyin(g)" difference, articulated from the Revolutionary era through the time of the Civil War and beyond through the semiotics of the slaves' descendants, disrupted Western conventions of language, forging an epistemological deviance whose import is difficult to miss.

As Gates puts it, there are "scores" of "revised words" "which snobbishly tend to be written about as 'dialect' words or 'slang'" (47):

> But to revise the term signification is to select a term that represents the nature of the process of meaning-creation and its representation. Few other selections could have been so dramatic, or so meaningful. We are witnessing here a profound disruption at the level of the signifier, precisely because of the relationship

of identity that obtains between the two apparently equivalent terms. This disturbance, of course, has been effected at the level of the conceptual, or the signified. How accidental, unconscious, or unintentional (or any other code-word substitution for the absence of reason) could such a brilliant challenge at the semantic level be? To revise the received sign (quotient) literally accounted for in the relation represented by signified/signifier at its most apparently denotative level is to critique the nature of (white) meaning itself, to challenge through a literal critique of the sign the meaning of meaning. What did/do black people signify in a society in which they were intentionally introduced as the subjugated, as the enslaved cipher? Nothing on the x axis of white signification, and everything on the y axis of blackness. (47)

With a provocative statement that black people, who are represented as the "subjugated, as the enslaved cipher" (47), themselves perform the act of signification inversely, Gates makes a signal and suggestive argument. These subjugated speakers, by simply placing nothing on "the x axis of white signification, and everything on the y axis of blackness," did not simply "colonize the white sign," but proffered a "meta-discourse" (47). They "defined their ontological status as one of profound difference vis-à-vis the rest of society" (47). Taking the opportunity to refute certain aspects of Saussure's structuralism, which we have already encountered, Gates vigorously demonstrates that this enslaved community of speakers not only emptied of its meaning a term in wide use among free middle- and upper-class whites; they deliberately chose the term that served as the cornerstone of European and Euro-American theories of meaning. As Gates puts it, "Contrary to an assertion that Saussure makes in his *Course*, the 'masses' did indeed 'have [a] voice in the matter' and replaced the sign 'chosen by language'" (47).

Let me tarry a moment here over Gates's signal adaptation (48–49) of Saussure's axis of language, which is itself quite well known to literary theorists. Gates's "horizontal" x-axis, which he names as the axis of Standard English and white signification, is actually in Saussure's model the axis of diachrony: it indicates the contiguity (nearness) of signs, linked together in a chain of speech, and evolving over time. It is the syntagmatic axis whose combinations comprise consecutive units of language, "supported by linearity" (Saussure 123). Gates's y-axis, onto which he maps the signifyin(g) difference of black language, runs vertically in Saussure's model. It is the paradigmatic/synchronic axis that Saussure calls the "axis of successions . . . on which only one thing can be considered at a time" (Saussure 80). This axis indicates the state of language at any given moment. In the *Course,* Saussure's focus is on paradigmatic/synchronic linguistics (y-axis), rather than syntagmatic/diachronic linguistics (x-axis); he was mainly concerned to examine and theorize relatively isolated language states, even as he acknowledged and repeatedly underscored the fact that language was in constant modes of diachronic change and evolution.

Mapping Gates's y-axis of the black vernacular onto Saussure's y-axis of paradigm/synchrony would cast Gates's theory of the fluid "signifyin(g)" difference of black expression into something of a contradiction, given that, according to Saussure, the y-axis of paradigm/synchrony allows the linguist to freeze language in time, and there study it. Gates, conversely and by virtue of his claims regarding the inventiveness and fluidity of black speech (which, in turn, provides the foundation of black literature), ignores the contradiction. He insists upon the play—rather than the stasis—of the y-axis of language, and values much of this play for its relation to rhetoric and tropes. For Gates, the play of black speech gives rise to a black ontology: its inscription in the speakerly text of African American literature allows the black subject to write her- or himself into being. To this important point I will return shortly.

But here, first, a clearer understanding of other, now conventional ways in which Saussure's axes have been adapted is crucial to grasping the import of metaphor as it relates to such queries and conundrums, especially since Gates's work has been so influential. Neither of these axes was discussed in relation to metaphor and metonymy until the linguist Roman Jakobson did so in his signal essay, "Two Aspects of Language and Two Types of Aphasic Disturbances" (1956). In his studies of aphasia, Jakobson came to identify what he characterized as two oppositional aspects of language: similarity and contiguity. Jakobson would follow Saussure in arguing that these two aspects coincide so frequently in spoken language that they could be seen as occurring simultaneously. Even so, the character of the two uses of language allowed Jakobson to identify two distinct principles of speech, which he chose to name under the rhetorical figures of metaphor and metonymy. Jakobson thus opposed two terms that had never before been set in opposition. And he did so with, it seems, less than precision. As the editors of the *Norton Anthology of Theory and Criticism* explain,

> Jakobson's distinction between metaphor and metonymy in "Two Aspects of Language and Two Types of Aphasic Disturbances"

(1956) became for him—and for many others following him—a key to language itself. Derived from studies of aphasia (inability to speak), Jakobson detected two primordial principles of language use: similarity and contiguity (i.e., resemblance and nearness). . . . Jakobson chooses to call these metaphor and metonymy, using the names of two rhetorical tropes that had not previously been set in opposition. . . . Jacques Lacan, building on Sigmund Freud's opposition between "condensation" and "displacement" in the rhetoric of dreams, sees in the relation between metaphor and metonymy the general psychoanalytic laws governing symptoms and desire.[25]

Jakobson's opposition was taken to affirm and even replicate Freud's earlier distinction between condensation and displacement in dream-work. In turn, Freud's "condensation" came to be aligned with Jakobson's idea of metaphor; his "displacement" was taken to be emblematic of metonymy. Jakobson's influential argument goes as follows:

Every form of aphasic disturbance consists in some impairment, more or less severe, of the faculty either for selection and substitution or for combination and contexture. The former affliction involves a deteriorization of metalinguistic operations, while the latter damages the capacity for maintaining the hierarchy of linguistic units. The relation of similarity is suppressed in the former, the relation of contiguity in the latter type of aphasia. Metaphor is alien to the similarity disorder and metonymy to the contiguity disorder. ("Two Aspects of Language" 1265–66)

Though Jakobson did allow for the peculiarities of verbal style in what he referred to as "normal verbal behavior," and argued that the processes of both metonymy and metaphor are continually operative in such behavior, he also embraced, in resonance with Jacques Lacan's work on Freud in the 1950s, Freud's structuralist characterization of the unconscious work of language. Jakobson writes:

A competition between both devices, metonymic and metaphoric, is manifest in any symbolic process, be it intrapersonal or social.

Thus in an inquiry into the structure of dreams, the decisive
question is whether the symbols and the temporal sequences
used are based on contiguity (Freud's metonymic "displacement"
and synecdochic "condensation") or on similarity (Freud's
"identification and symbolism"). (1268)

No less an authoritative interpreter of Freudian thought than Lacan
reinforced the dichotomy that Jakobson introduced. While Lacan saw
metaphor as emblematic of "symptom," metonymy itself became a signifier
of desire. Indeed, Lacan's views on metaphor, which I discuss in the Ellison
chapter, were read by the theorist Jean Laplanche as analogous to Freud's
theory of and formula for repression (where metaphor functions as the
return of the repressed and undertakes a transcendent movement of rising
not unlike that of the metaphysical). And although Lacan rebutted what he
saw as a misreading of his theory,[26] the metaphysical die was nonetheless cast,
it seems, for metaphor. Even Paul Ricoeur permitted himself a provisional
statement that metaphor's character is inherently metaphysical (*The Rule of
Metaphor* 288).

However, metaphor's action cannot be read as purely "metaphysical," for
if, as Jakobson would have it, metaphorical action is limited to identification
and symbolism while metonymy is attributed the power of displacement,
how can metaphor also be defined in terms of Freudian condensation? Of
"the work of condensation," Freud writes:

The first thing that becomes clear to anyone who compares
the dream-content with the dream-thoughts is that a work of
condensation on a large scale has been carried out. Dreams are
brief, meagre and laconic in comparison with the range and wealth
of dream-thoughts. If a dream is written out it may perhaps fill
half a page. The analysis setting out the dream thoughts underlying
it may occupy six, eight or a dozen times as much space. This
relation varies with different dreams; but so far as my experience
goes its direction never varies. As a rule one underestimates the
amount of compression that has taken place, since one is inclined
to regard the dream-thoughts that have been brought to light as
the complete material, whereas if the work of interpretation is
carried further it may reveal still more thoughts concealed behind
the dream. I have already had occasion to point out that it is in
fact never possible to be sure that a dream has been completely
interpreted. Even if the solution seems satisfactory and without

gaps, the possibility always remains that the dream may have yet another meaning. Strictly speaking, then, it is impossible to determine the amount of condensation. (*The Interpretation of Dreams* 924–25)

By Freud's definition, the dream-thoughts, which are "a work of condensation," are "brief," and "meagre," yet escape full interpretation. If this is so, then the sense of metaphor itself (as a process of condensation of any number of fragmented dream elements and thus as a *combinational* force) defies satisfactory comprehension, for in its action, some of the nuances of meaning not only always slip away, but often deviate from the "literal" meanings of words and referents.

In other words, while metaphor does serve to substitute one word-image-sound for another, and thus its action may be seen as symbolic, its action is also one of displacement. As the term "metaphor" itself implies ("metaphor" in the Greek means "to transfer"), metaphors regularly transgress categories of meaning by supplanting one word, phrase, or even a discourse with another.

None of this is to treat fully Roman Jakobson's seemingly arbitrary dichotomy of metaphor and metonymy, which has been taken up admirably in the work of Ricoeur, who points out that metonymy often functions as a type of metaphor, and thus a strict dichotomy of the two is impossible.[27] Further, it casts into question Jakobson's structuralist conclusion that the "principle of similarity [metaphor] underlies poetry," while prose, "on the contrary, is forwarded essentially by contiguity. Thus, for poetry, metaphor— and for prose, metonymy—is the line of least resistance and consequently the study of poetical tropes is directed chiefly toward metaphor" (1269). Jakobson's dichotomy of metaphor and metonymy leaves more questions unanswered than resolved. It, in fact, leaves open the possibility of collapsing his axes, the y-axis of metaphor and the x-axis of metonymy, one on top of the other, so that the linguistic action of either cannot be neatly determined through a structuralist analysis.[28]

Even so, Jakobson's dichotomy has had great influence over the thinking of such poststructuralist and postmodernist theorists as Ihab Hassan. Hassan's "schematic" figure (Fig. 1) distinguishing modernism from postmodernism (given in his seminal 1987 essay, "Toward a Concept of Postmodernism"[29]) is emblematic of the ways in which, following Jakobson's example, metaphor and metonymy have been theorized and juxtaposed in poststructuralist and postmodernist theory more generally. (I reproduce Hassan's model in Figure 1):

↕	↔
Modernism	Postmodernism
Romanticism/Symbolism	Pataphysics/Dadaism
Form (Conjunctive, closed)	Antiform (Disjunctive, open)
Purpose	Play
Design	Chance
Hierarchy	Anarchy
Mastery/Logos	Exhaustion/Silence
Art Object/Finished Work	Process/Performance/Happening
Distance	Participation
Creation/Totalization	Decreation/Deconstruction
Synthesis	Antithesis
Presence	Absence
Centering	Dispersal
Genre/Boundary	Text/Intertext
Semantics	Rhetoric
Paradigm	Syntagm
Hypotaxis	Parataxis
Metaphor	Metonymy
Selection	Combination
Root/Depth	Rhizome/Surface
Interpretation/Reading	Against Interpretation/Misreading
Signified	Signifier
Lisible (Readerly)	*Scriptible* (Writerly)
Narrative/*Grande Histoire*	Anti-narrative/*Petite Histoire*
Master Code	Idiolect
Symptom	Desire
Type	Mutant
Genital/Phallic	Polymorphous/Androgynous
Paranoia	Schizophrenia
Origin/Cause	Difference-Différance/Trace
God the Father	The Holy Ghost
Metaphysics	Irony
Determinacy	Indeterminacy
Transcendence	Immanence

Figure 1.

In this model, which is directly influenced by Hassan's readings of both Jakobson and Saussure, the left column represents the vertical y-axis, and the right column stands for the horizontal x-axis. Hassan's schema dichotomizes not only paradigm and syntagm—the paradigmatic nature of the y-axis and the syntagmatic nature of the x-axis—as Saussure and Jakobson did; it also sketches binary events, movements, and modes of expression such as presence/absence, synthesis/antithesis, root-depth/rhizome-surface, signified/signifier, *lisible* (readerly)/*scriptible* (writerly), mastercode/idiolect, transcendence/immanence, and, importantly, metaphor/metonymy. Hassan, admitting a lack of stability in each axes' purported characteristics, describes his schema in this way:

> The preceding table draws on ideas in many fields . . . aligned with diverse movements, groups, and views. Yet the dichotomies this table represents remain insecure, equivocal. For differences shift, defer, even collapse; concepts in any one vertical column are not all equivalent, and inversions and exceptions, in both modernism and postmodernism, abound. Still I would submit that rubrics in the right column point to the postmodern tendency, the tendency of indeterminacy, and so may bring us closer to its historical and theoretical definition. (280–81)

In devising this table, Hassan adapts with only minimal critique Jakobson's opposition of metaphor and metonymy, and though he admits that the characteristics that found his model are themselves "insecure, equivocal," he nonetheless feels certain that the right column represents the openness of postmodern and poststructural indeterminacy, while the left column represents the rigidity, stasis, and metaphysics of modern structuralist thought. Even so, Hassan's admission of the equivocal nature of his categories (the possibility that the two axes might collapse one atop the other) lends additional force to my observation that a strict opposition of these two axes is difficult if not impossible to sustain.

Even with his own incisive and well-informed critical stance, Gates's study does not discuss or interrogate Jakobson's opposition at all, nor does Hassan's schema, published the year before Gates's *Signifying Monkey*, factor into his analysis. Gates looks instead to what is actually Lacan's adoption of Jakobson's theory, though Gates frames Lacan's theory as coming to him directly from Saussure (49). Gates's analysis focuses mainly on homonyms and a genealogy of African American texts that "Signify" upon one another, even as they "Signify" upon European standards of denotative language that would be represented on the very vertical axis that Gates uses to indicate the contestatory difference of black language (50). For Gates, these texts therefore constitute at once metanarrative as well as metadiscourse, thus they instantiate a discourse on narrative and knowledge. And, in doing so, I would add, they also instantiate a discourse on being.

It is this latter point that I intend to pursue further through the chapter studies of the present book. Gates's theory has been of considerable influence, and is quite fine and path-breaking. However, his interpretation of rhetorical language in African American literature and his mapping of black vernacular expression onto the vertical y-axis—the rooted axis of structural determinacy—not only confounds the distinction between linguistic diachrony and synchrony as demonstrated by Saussure, Jakobson, Lacan, and Hassan (who, quite purposely, maps rhetoric onto the x-axis rather than on the y-axis, as Gates does). It also risks ontologizing black textuality in such a way that African American writers (and, by extension, those communities of black life that the writers sought to represent in all their complexity) are relegated to the position of non-being without the text—to adapt with a sense of irony Derrida's well-known phrase that there is nothing outside of the text, *they are nothing without the text.*[30]

Gates argues that African Americans insisted upon literacy and, more specifically, textuality as the central means of showing themselves to be worthy of the moniker of the "human" because this was the proof that white Western epistemology demanded of them. By arguing that African Americans strove to *prove* their very humanity by demonstrating that they could not only write, but could author a *literary* text,—and that, through such authorship, they "write themselves into existence"—Gates appears, in the first instance, (un)wittingly[31] to enclose African American poetics within a literary typology (the paradigmatic dictates of the y-axis) that is subservient to the white Western discourse on aesthetics and national belonging that he so strongly interrogates. In a well-known passage from *Figures in Black*, Gates writes:

> I would hope that it is obvious that the creation of formal literature could be no mean matter in the life of the slave, since the sheer literacy of writing was the very commodity that separated animal from human being, slave from citizen, object from subject. Reading, and especially writing, in the life of the slave represented a process larger than even "mean" physical manumission, since mastery of the arts and letters was Enlightenment Europe's sign of that solid line of division between human being and thing. (24–25)

Gates continues this line of argumentation throughout the pages of *The Signifying Monkey*, for it was an argument that he had made earlier in his introduction to *The Slave's Narrative* (1985), co-edited with Charles T. Davis. For example, in *The Signifying Monkey*, Gates contends that Janie Crawford of Hurston's *Their Eyes Were Watching God* (1937) "writes herself into being by naming, by speaking herself free" (207); Celie of Alice Walker's *The Color Purple* (1982) does likewise, he claims. As Gates puts it, "Celie writes herself into being as a text, a text we are privileged to read over her shoulder. . . . Celie is a text in the same way in which Langston Hughes wrote (in *The Big Sea*) that Hurston was a book—'a perfect book of entertainment in herself.' We read Celie reading her world and writing it into being, in one subtle discursive act" (245).

Gates's meaning in these instances is compelling: through an act of literary self-creation, African American writers, from the eighteenth century through the twentieth, have used textuality as a means of creating *being*. They had, to adapt Audre Lorde's much used phrase to my purposes here, taken the master's tools (Prospero's symbolic books and language) not to dismantle his house, but to build a perceptible temple of the black self, a habitation of the black spirit that was recognizable and knowable, even in an age when the black body (and, by extension, the black mind) was generally deemed inscrutable.[32] Being, in this instance, appears to refer not only to an imagined existential spatiality, wherein the effect of a self-conscious black presence is brought about through a concerted use of figurative rhetorical language in a literary text; it also relates to the prevailing notions of race that occupied the social thought of the writer's time. That is, it intimates that writers of African descent not only acknowledged the questions and doubts whites had raised about their very existence as human beings, but they bought into and validated them by responding to them. If, as Gates writes in *The Slave's Narrative*, the slave narrative not only serves as the foundation of African American literature (and this point is certainly debatable, given the centrality of oral poetry—the Spirituals—to the early African American literary tradition), but also "represents the attempt of blacks to *write themselves into being*" (xxiii), it must, at the same time, attest to the anxiety of the black author—a certain existential angst—in the face of white doubt and denigration. Such writing is not so much art as it is argument.

On the other hand, as the novelist and philosopher Charles Johnson points out in *Being and Race* (1988), all literature is argumentation: "each literary form, style, or genre is a different, distinct mode of reasoning, of shaping what is to body it forth intelligibly" (6). Those readers familiar with Aristotle's definition of metaphor in the *Poetics* and the *Rhetoric* will recall immediately the ways in which Johnson's precept regarding the "body[ing] forth" of reasoning resonates with Aristotle's principle of metaphor: that metaphor serves as the vehicle for the bodying forth of reality, what phenomenologists and existentialists refer to as lived experience.

In this way, metaphor, full of its inherent mimetic qualities and essential to Gates's theorizing, is shown to be an aspect of logic, and this is particularly so, but not exclusively so, in its analogical or propositional form: *a* is to *b* as *c* is to *d*. This denotation of metaphor is demonstrated by reviewing metaphor's relationship to rhetoric and discourse alike. As Paul Ricoeur points out in *The Rule of Metaphor*, metaphor is both an aspect of rhetoric and of speculative enunciation, since each of these modes of expression—in order to be successful—must draw from a society's storehouse of common knowledge and culture for validation. Thus while Ricoeur agrees with Aristotle that metaphor is an aspect of rhetoric (which Aristotle defined as "the faculty of observing in any given case the available means of persuasion"[33]), he also sees rhetoric's development as necessarily emerging out of vernacular ("popular" and "common" are the adjectives Ricoeur uses) culture, wit, and wisdom. It is worth citing Ricoeur at length on these points. On rhetoric and philosophy, he writes:

> With Aristotle we see rhetoric in its better days; it constitutes a distinct sphere of philosophy, in that the order of the "persuasive" as such remains the object of a specific *technê*. Yet it is solidly bound to logic through the correlation between the concept of persuasion and that of the probable. In this way a philosophical rhetoric—that is, a rhetoric grounded in and watched over by philosophy itself—is constituted. . . . Aristotle was careful to define what he calls *technê* in a classical text of his *Ethics*. There are as many *technai* as there are creative activities. A *technê* is something more refined than a routine or an empirical practice and in spite of its focus on production, it contains a speculative element, namely a theoretical enquiry into the means applied to production. It is a method; and this feature brings it closer to theoretical knowledge than to routine. (28)

And on rhetoric and the vernacular, he continues:

> Rhetoric does not develop in some empty space of pure thought, but in the give and take of common opinion. So metaphors and

proverbs also draw from the storehouse of popular wisdom—at least, those of them that are "established." This qualification is important, because it is this topology of discourse that gives the rhetorical treatment of *lexis* and metaphor a background and an aftertaste different from those of the *Poetics*. (30)

Ricoeur's reading of Aristotle qualifies rhetoric not as ornate oration or political persuasion, but as a "distinct" *techné*, a method of inquiry that is capable of producing discourse. The linkage, then, between a rhetorical theory of metaphor (with its attendant and distinct *techné*) and dialectic (as a central process of philosophical reason) assures us that rhetoric is kept "under the sway of logic and, through logic, of philosophy as a whole" (*Rule of Metaphor* 28). For Ricoeur, rhetoric is "a phenomenon of the intersubjective and dialogical dimension of the public use of speech" (29). As such, rhetoric is effective only in its measure with accepted ideas among the populace, for this is how it gains its persuasive quality. Nonetheless, the so-called "death" of rhetoric, which Ricoeur locates in the "excess of formalism in the nineteenth century" (30)[34], was knelled by its collusion with the popular. To locate metaphor exclusively under the auspices of rhetoric, whose negative fate was sealed by its relation to the public sphere and its performative nature (supposedly indicating its distance from philosophical, speculative thought), underscores a signal problematic for revisionist theories of metaphor, such as those advanced by Gates, Holloway, and even the present author.

So, keeping this problematic in mind, let us return briefly to the claim Charles Johnson makes for seeing literature as argumentation, considering more fully now the relationship between plot and its main devices (the most ingenious of which, Aristotle points out, is metaphor) and the mode of argumentation that Johnson maintains all plot must take up:

[W]hatever else it may be dramatically, each plot—how events happen and why—is also an *argument*. . . . If plot is anything, it is a vehicle of reason . . . If some writers find plot to be a difficult problem to solve, I would wager it is because they also find it difficult to engage in the ballet of argumentation, and also because they are not familiar with the many forms that reason or reasoning can assume. It is this basic, genuinely exploratory element in creative writing that leads some phenomenologists such as Maurice Merleau-Ponty to conclude that philosophy and fiction—both disciplines of language—are about, at bottom, the same business. Merleau-Ponty, of course, goes farther than that, making it clear in *Sense and Non-Sense* [1948; Eng tr. 1964] that our lives are inherently metaphysical insofar as each moment of perception, each blink of the eye, involves the activity of interpretation; perception is an *act*, and this observation puts the lie to that ancient stupidity that says the processes of philosophy and fiction are two different enterprises—they are sister disciplines, I would say, and unless a critic realizes this, his position is simply untenable. (32; italics in original)

To be tenable, then, according to Johnson, any reading of African American texts must at once engage art and argument, poetics and critical discourse. After a fashion, the critic must agree with Ralph Ellison, who once proclaimed, in "The Art of Fiction," a 1955 interview he granted to the *Paris Review*, that he "[recognized] no dichotomy between art and protest,"[35] here referring to a reasoned aesthetic argument against a status quo such as Jim Crow discrimination.

In Gates's study, it would seem that Zora Neale Hurston and Alice Walker alike engage not only in the poetics (and aesthetics) of black being, but they also partake of and contribute to an ever evolving and engaged philosophy of black being that is highly critical of the failings of its white Western counterpart. Even so, Gates implies that Hurston and Walker both undertake what he sees as the literary process of "writing oneself into being" differently than does, for example, Ishmael Reed. While Hurston has given us a "paradigmatic signifyin(g) text because it figures signifyin(g) as both theme and as rhetorical strategy," Reed, on the other hand, has rendered a signifyin(g) text "for still another reason" (217). Gates explains:

> Reed's concerns, as exemplified in his narrative forms, seem to be twofold: (1) the relation his own art bears to his black literary precursors, including Hurston, Wright, Ellison, and Baldwin; and (2) the process of willing into being a rhetorical structure, a literary language replete with its own figures and tropes, but one that allows the black writer to posit a structure of feeling that simultaneously critiques both the metaphysical presuppositions inherent in Western ideas and forms of writing and the metaphorical system in which the blackness of the writer and his experience have been valorized as a 'natural' absence. (218)

It seems that while Hurston and Walker have given us novels that exemplify how the heroine of the "speakerly" text writes herself into what

Gates sees as determinate being, Reed has gifted us with exemplary texts that will into being a rhetorical structure of feeling. Because his own writing, and particularly *Mumbo Jumbo* (1972), is primarily concerned with the novel as a form, Reed's is a gesture apart, according to Gates. One dares say that, in Gates's view, while Hurston and Walker provide us with texts that define the subject by writing that subject "into existence," Reed writes in contrast to the texts that make up the African American canon, which, Gates argues, insists upon determinacy and conventions of closure largely through its major tropes. Taking up an oppositional artistic stance, and insisting upon an "aesthetic play," Gates argues that Ishmael Reed has produced work that "figures and glorifies indeterminacy" (227). Gates tells us that Reed accomplishes this task through "Signifyin(g), by repeating received tropes and narrative strategies with a difference. In Reed's differences lie an extended commentary on the history of the black novel" (217). Gates's critique of Reed's third novel is lauded by Johnson as "provocative" and "thorough" (*Being and Race* 66). Gates tells his reader that *The Signifying Monkey* itself "at the very least began with (and at most was shaped by) [his] explication of Reed's difficult novel" (218), which seems to exemplify the characteristics of Hassan's x-axis of postmodernism and poststructuralism. While it appears, in Gates's argument, that writers such as Hurston and Walker write themselves forcibly onto Gates's y-axis of determinate black being, succumbing to the West's demand for proofs of black humanity, he sees Reed's refusal of such demands as a valuable stroke of indeterminacy.

It has become a scholarly commonplace to reference Gates's work obliquely by contending that thus and so author "wrote him or herself into being." The phrase has won such wide usage that it is now itself a perhaps unconscious trope, a performance of critical discourse now largely taken for truth. I cannot dismiss this conclusion out of hand, for I find that it bears some trace of legitimacy: many writers of various backgrounds have spoken of the ways in which the practice of reading and writing aided them in understanding exactly what it was they thought, how they processed their experiences, and, indeed, who they were in the moment of writing and beyond. However, the perspective I advance in this study is one that is borne out by my readings of central philosophical metaphors in African American texts that serve as a representative sampling of works across the tradition: a certain grasp of one's sense of being—however permeable and evolving—is required before one even enters into the act of writing for public (or even an intended private) readership. From the reader's perspective, the completed act of writing (that is, the published text) discovers consciousness even as the writer him- or herself has revealed it. Metaphorical concepts of black being are never fully determinate because the conceptual action of metaphor is not absolute. It constitutes, rather, an open tautology, in the sense that Édouard Glissant gives that term in *Poetics of Relation* (1988). In the following chapter, we shall see whether and how such a perspective has been espoused by African Americanist philosophers who look to black texts—and the question of black being therein—as the scaffolding of their speculative enterprise.

2

African American Philosophy and the Poetics of Black Being

African American literature has long articulated a philosophy of existence and experience, a fact witnessed by the frequency with which African American philosophers have turned to literary texts not in an aesthetic interrogation of the nature of the literary object, but in order to craft a philosophy that debates the knowledge delivered through prose (and, though less often, through poetry and drama) as it works to clarify what we believe we know for certain about life, the world, social values, and racialized being. Though he is not what one might call a "practicing" philosopher, Charles Johnson, whom we have already encountered, turns with assurance to fiction in his 1988 book *Being and Race*. Other philosophers practicing in the American academy have likewise consulted the annals of African American literature as they debate the meaning and representation of black being. Of these, I discuss, in turn and in brief, the work of Lucius Outlaw, Charles W. Mills, and Lewis Gordon. Of the many African Americanist literary theorists whose work adopts a philosophical perspective, I discuss two whose voices resonate well with the present project. The work of Hortense Spillers and Ronald A. T. Judy will, in crucial ways, bracket my discussion of African American philosophies of being expressed in literary culture, and their relation to (and reliance upon) the metaphorical.[1]

First, a return to Johnson. In *Being and Race*, Johnson defines phenomenology as a "philosophy of experience" that is grounded in the immanent rather than in the transcendent realm. For him, as we learned in the previous chapter, phenomenology is perceptual experience, and perception is an act. It is from this perspective that Johnson undertakes a phenomenological reading of African American literature and its literary history. That is, he sees African American literature as work that clarifies African American experience, and conveys the sense (the meaning) of that experience to a broad reading public that is inclusive of persons of various backgrounds.

"Our faith in fiction," Johnson begins, "comes from an ancient belief that language and literary art—all speaking and showing—clarify our experience" (3). For Johnson, the metaphorical aspect of this art is an "inherently existential [strategy] that allow[s] writers to pluck similarities from our experiences or to illuminate one object by reference to another by saying A *is* B" (6). Nonetheless, Johnson, in a Platonic mode and like many structuralist and poststructuralist theorists of the 1980s, remains rather skeptical of the role of metaphor in literary art, wondering whether it is a "mere illusion, a mind trick or trap that dangerously anthropomorphizes the world" (6). Yet, he observes by way of his reading of fellow novelist cum philosopher, William Gass, metaphor is "merely a means of fastening words to one another, not words to things." Even so, he lauds metaphor's capacity to provide, in Gass's words, " 'a consciousness electrified by beauty.'" Metaphor's "delights," he and Gass conclude, are " 'as wide as the mind is, and musicked deep with feeling'" (36).

Gass's notion of a metaphorical " 'consciousness electrified by beauty'" can be taken to constitute "historical beings," Johnson argues. That is, a consciousness that emerges from literature's aesthetics may be interpreted as a being grounded in an immanent temporality. In this way, the literary text may project a consciousness that engages with the reader in her own time, and even as time evolves our interactions with this consciousness evolve as well. One signal aspect of Johnson's thought in this respect resonates well with my own purpose: a reader may well encounter an historical being by way of philosophical expressions of consciousness. It matters less, as Johnson argues, that we engage a particular entity (whether country, region, or human subject) than that we perceive the gathering of experience and contemplation that is situated in consciousness-inflected lines of text. From our encounter with this gathering of meaning and sensibilities, the text, through its power of images—that is to say, through its metaphorical discourse—bodies forth meanings and understandings that we can take with us. To argue, as the present study does, that the black text works to convey black being through metaphorical constructions is, of course, not to argue that a racialized, proscribed flesh-and-blood being is conveyed to the reader through the material reality of the literary text or that such being's existence depends fully on the production of text, what Karla Holloway calls a scriptocentric perspective.[2] It is to say, however, that illimitable black being, such as that in favor of which Du Bois argues in "The Conservation of Races," is, as Johnson writes of the conveyance of historical entities, "so much in the way of perceptual experience that it is over rich, open-ended regarding its meaning, and thereby defies our [complete] understanding" (37). The sort of critical perspective I espouse regarding the capacity of metaphors to fulfill the task of creating meaning may render black being sublime, but it also underscores how metaphor bodies forth to the reader a meaning that can be grasped even if only partially when flesh-and-blood black being is indeed encountered. It should go without saying that this being is not at all monolithic, absolute, or static, but living, dynamic, and always in flux and evolving; it is, again, illimitable.[3]

Johnson's example of such phenomenology in writing is Richard Wright's *Native Son* (1940). For Johnson, *Native Son* is a phenomenological novel not because Wright writes Bigger into textual existence, but because it is rooted (following Wright's own poetics, as I discuss in chapter 7) in the black experience (13). In this novel, Wright has created, as Johnson so aptly puts it,

> a masterfully drawn *Lebenswelt*: we are made to see and experience meaning—the world—from the distorted perspective of a petty thief so mangled by oppression in its many forms that his only possibility for creative action is murder. . . . [Yet] *Native Son* remains more than anything else a phenomenological description of the black urban experience. Wright forces us to ask, "What is it like to be thoroughly manipulated by others?" He shifts from historical details of black poverty in Chicago to a startling use of poetry and metaphor—the white world, the racial Other, is presented to Bigger's ravaged consciousness as a natural force like snow, or a blizzard, or a storm; he projects himself into innumerable objects littering the black wasteland of his family— for example, the rat killed in the opening scene—and sees his guilt in the red-hot furnace where he has placed Mary Dalton's decapitated body. Page after page, we are forced to *interpret* everyday phenomena from Bigger's unsteady position in the world, a position of powerlessness, of Pavlovian reactions to whites who are godlike but "blind" to his inner life and humanity, a position where black life is experienced as being predestined for tragedy. (Italics in original 13)

If the whites Johnson mentions here are "godlike but 'blind' to [Bigger's] inner life and humanity," if they do not "see" that humanity with what Ralph Ellison called their "inner eyes," that is, eyes fashioned out of consciousness and thought, eyes in search of beings to embrace as fellow humans, then for these whites Bigger's inner life and humanity are nonexistent. His inner life and humanity, and by extension, he himself, constitute simply *non-being*. It is this negation against which Bigger rages. And thus there is an acute irony to one of Bigger's final articulations from his jailhouse cell: "But what I killed for, I *am!*"

That this statement, rendered as Bigger is condemned to death, is metaphorical, and that it is, further, an open tautology (because its meaning is both transparent and opaque), has not gained much attention from Wright's critics *as a conceptual metaphor* that poses a philosophical problem. Metaphors draw an equivalence between two entities: A is B. Bigger claims that he *is* that for which he killed: a free individual, at liberty from oppression, finally able to act and *do* ("they don't let us do *nothing*," Bigger had complained to one of his buddies early in the novel) with a sense of his own self-determination. If Bigger is not only the abrogated representative of these ideals (because he is their negation), but is also their living black embodiment, then the imminence of Bigger's execution at the novel's conclusion takes on the ironic symbolism of an oblation. Like Fred Daniels, the anti-hero of Wright's *The Man Who Lived Underground*, which I discuss in chapter 7, Bigger's execution makes of him a Christ figure whose metaphorical, poetic, and heuristic language carries the wealth of salvation, if only its vast import were grasped: if Bigger is not free, then neither is America; if Bigger is executed for his crimes, then his death—the negation of a negation—only leaves America with a false sense of consciousness. Bigger's last, desperate plea for understanding of his being is intended by Wright to form a bridge between Bigger, as the tragic, didactic (in the Aristotelian sense of didactic tragedy) example of black life who is *human* nonetheless, and Wright's readers, both black *and* white. Recall Wright's best known poem, "Between the World and Me" (1935). The poem demands with great skill the empathy of the reader, who, following the voice of the poet, is called to take the remains of a "sacrificed"—tarred, feathered, and immolated—black being into his or her own soul. All of this Wright accomplishes not through angry protest rhetoric, but through multiple and complex metaphors that raise the scene of a lynching before the eyes of the reader. With such compelling and eidetic metaphors, Wright instructs his reader to consider the violent realities of black life—and death—in the mid-1930s. Black death, by lawful execution or by an angry lynch mob, hangs over and stunts America's consciousness.

For a working-class African American readership, as Wright had argued in "Blueprint for Negro Writing," fictional stories such as Bigger's were meant to inspire and shape consciousness: if they could see in Bigger some aspect of themselves while divining the greater meaning of the story, they could be provoked to act against the yoke of oppression that held them firmly in their places. For white readers, Bigger's last words form an open and almost perversely captivating gateway to his humanity. Bigger does not plead his case, he states it: he is the freedom for which he has killed. If Bigger is not free, then neither is America. If Bigger is destined to die, then America should anticipate no less tragic a fate.

Wright writes black being after a fashion that challenges and deconstructs the status quo. As Johnson puts it, the status quo of Bigger's world is "Manichaean. To *be* is to be white. The Dalton's world is pure Being, a plenum, filled to overflowing with its own whiteness, while Bigger's world has a weedlike contingency—is, in fact, relative being" (14). Bigger's insistence upon his humanity, which comes in the form of a metaphorical equivalence between his life and the life he has taken, goes far in underscoring the revolutionary poetics of being Wright developed as his own. Johnson would contend that phenomenological prose—that which concerns itself it with what has been called "the black experience"—is charged with a poetics capable of "fling[ing] the reader of fiction toward revelation and unsealed vision" (33). That which reveals black being in pre-Civil Rights America is revolutionary; that which unseals our vision makes blackness visible.

However, the idea of the text as the transparent vessel of blackness has not gone unchallenged by critics and theorists, and well this should be the case. One might be justified in arguing, with Du Bois's concept metaphor of the veil as an ontological example, that black life prior to the Civil Rights Act of 1964 and the subsequent Voting Rights Act of 1965 required an "unveiling" before a white reading public largely unfamiliar with African American culture, history, and thought. (One is tempted to extend this date right up to the present. In the so-called "Age of Obama," when a man of African descent ascended to the American presidency, the American Supreme Court, under the leadership of Chief Justice John Roberts, nonetheless in 2013 stripped the Voting Rights Act of its most salient elements.) Even so, the prospect of the text as a transparent bearer of meaning has long been challenged, and the African American text has neither enjoyed nor demanded an exception, in spite of some arguments to the contrary during, for instance, the Black Aesthetic period (the 1960s). The major turn of the African American literary field toward poststructuralism and a new, critical historicism in African American thought is traced by Ronald A. T. Judy in his 1993 book, *(Dis)forming the American Canon*.

(Dis)forming the American Canon provides a concise history of African Americanist criticism and theory, and places particular stress on the decade

following the Black Aesthetic period. Beginning with a history of what Judy
calls "The Yale School," a school of criticism and theory led, principally, by
John Blassingame, Robert Stepto, and Henry L. Gates, Jr., Judy writes that
"their readings are exemplary of three central ideas that issued out of the
Yale school of Afro-American literary theory":

> First, their demonstrations that Afro-American literature can
> withstand critical scrutiny. Second, their demonstrations that
> close readings of Afro-American texts yield their linguistic (and
> cultural) wealth. And, they suggest that through sustained critical
> reading it becomes possible to delineate an Afro-American literary
> history as a field of substantial scholarship, to engage in a project
> of canon formation. The Yale school begins that delineation of
> its canon with the slave narratives, maintaining that the slave
> narrative was the archetype for all subsequent Afro-American
> literary forms. (18)

The Yale school thus "discovered in the slave narrative not only the
historical emergence of Afro-American literary history, but also the history
of Afro-American theorizing of experience" (19). Blassingame's work in
particular is of signal importance to Judy, who sees Blassingame's 1972 study
The Slave Community as the publication that set the slave narratives at the
center of "theoretical discussions on the historiography of the antebellum
South." This point is central to Gates's work, and Gates adds a second
point which is, according to Judy, "more subtly articulated and has to do with
the nature of historiography, with American literary theory's relationship, in
particular, to the concept of history" (33). Judy sketches this second point
in its relation to Blassingame's historicism.

Blassingame's work staged an intervention in the American
historiographical tradition, a tradition that had argued assiduously that
because most slave narratives were either edited by whites or dictated to
white amanuenses, they did not qualify as genuine autobiographies. "Even
when the editorial interpolation is minimal or nonexistent, the narratives are
discountable, because they are so wholly a form of deliberative discourse—
abolitionist propaganda—that they are too subjective to provide an accurate
account of 'historical reality'" (Judy 33). Blassingame interrupted this sort
of discourse on the slave narrative by using the narratives themselves as
documentary evidence of their veracity and historicity. What Blassingame
eventually achieved was nothing less than a "revolution in historiography" to
the minds of Gates and his collaborator, Charles T. Davis (34). Blassingame's

study demonstrated the specious nature of arguments maintaining that the slave narratives were too subjective to be taken as historical artifacts around which one could assemble a discourse of documentation. This was an especially important point, given what is now understood as the widespread subjective character of "mainstream" historiography. Instead, he centered the African American slave narrative/autobiography as a text that permits us access to the phenomenological perspective of the enslaved. For Blassingame, the slave narrative/autobiography represents what Judy calls "the enabling of the transcribing of experience, the writing of African American history, which is found 'in the black texts themselves,' in the recurring topoi and tropes which constitute the shared modes of figuration found in the slave narratives" (35–36).

Such an intervention into the praxis, theory, and philosophy of American history as Blassingame's is thus also an intervention into the philosophy of being itself. The philosophy of history is most often concerned with the history of thought, and thought, in spite of modern philosophy's surpassing of Descartes's *cogito*, is generally deemed the province of the human. In *The Philosophy of History* (1830–31), Hegel puts the matter thus: "The most general definition that can be given, is, that the Philosophy of History means nothing but the *thoughtful consideration of it.* Thought is, indeed, essential to humanity. It is this that distinguishes us from the brutes."[4]

Thought, it seems, could find its realization only in the costume and custom of writing. Judy decries this necessary linkage between thought and writing because it requires the symbiosis of writing and the human that essentially serves as the foundation of Gates's theory: the proof of humanity ("that which distinguishes us from the brutes," as Hegel put it) could be located only in writing. Thus writing took on an empirical and ontological status, and the writing of human history could do no less than contemplate and document the history of human thought. The collusion of thought (reason) and writing (reason's expression) would form the foundation of the West's idea of itself.

These considerations cast Blassingame's work on the slave narrative into even greater relief: Blassingame's intervention supplies a historiography and philosophy indelibly marked with figuration and metaphoricity. We have noted the importance of metaphor to Western metaphysics, but here we are granted absolute clarity on the role of metaphoricity in the African American literary tradition, a tradition that, over the past thirty or so years, has been taken up by contemporary African American philosophers as the scaffolding and bricks upon which a black or Africana philosophy is to be erected. Since

Blassingame argued that human agency founds the slave narrative, as genre and form, and, further, is located in the "linguistic structures of the slave narratives" themselves, it became necessary for theorists to examine African American literature for its qualities and functions, especially in terms of its use of figurative discourse. However, Judy argues, the agency that literary scholars (in particular) of the 1970s and 1980s identified in slave narratives has been discussed in terms of what he refers to as the "truncating effect of motto: canon formation" (37). Our theorizing of black agency (and perhaps here I might draw a provisional equivalence between Judy's usage of the term "agency," and my own usage of the term "being," since in my inquiry into the concept I am concerned as well with the centrality of action to being), analyzed during the years of America's culture wars, seems to have been hampered in the battle of criticism.

The work of Robert Stepto in *From Behind the Veil* (1979) is of signal importance in this regard, a work that falls short, according to Judy, because of its entrapment within the processes of canon formation that Stepto himself casts into question (38). Stepto presents the African American slave narrative "as a rhetorical intervention into the narrative Romantic historiography of American culture" (39). Here, Judy sees an opportunity for critique: "Because that designation is very limited, exclusively African American, the interpolation proves to be quickly and easily appropriated into the very instituting processes Stepto seeks to problematize. The dilemma of this particular critique is that in order to achieve a successful intervention into American literary scholarship, it articulates the same concept of the literal writing of culture informing Romanticism, historicism: the notion that the historiography of cultural production traces the historical emergence of a specific cultural identity" (38). Stepto's model seems not to challenge but to support the traditional historicism he purports to work against, Judy argues, given that it insists upon tracing "certain distinctly Afro-American cultural imperatives" back to definitive "roots" in the slave narratives (39).

Henry Louis Gates runs this same risk, Judy points out, but Judy writes that Gates averts danger by taking an alternative pathway. In Judy's reading, Gates recognizes the shortcomings of Stepto's theorizing, and instead theorizes that African American literary historiography emerges "concordantly with African American literature," an aesthetic enterprise that is shaped and guided by the perennial quest for self-conscious being and a free identity, which Ralph Ellison saw as the key to all American literature, not African American literature alone.

As I discuss at some length in chapter 1, Gates's theory is best known not by the motto of canon formation (though that was indeed a foremost thrust of his work during the period in question), but by his insistence that "the slave narrative represents blacks' attempt to *write themselves into being*." As Gates and Charles T. Davis put it in their introduction to *The Slave's Narrative* (1985), "What a curious idea: through the mastery of formal Western languages, the presupposition went, a black person could become a human being by an act of self-creation through the mastery of language. Accused of having no collective history by Hegel in 1813 [sic⁵], blacks responded by publishing hundreds of individual histories" (xxiii).

The slave narrative does not necessarily represent their accomplishment in attaining this goal, but rather their *attempt* to do so, in Gates's words. Gates understands, as he makes clear in *Figures in Black*, the distinction between a metaphysics of Being and human being as flesh and blood reality. But he also ponders the blurring of the line between these denotations: that persons of African descent were required to prove their very humanity by authoring literary works; that they, however provisionally, accepted such assessments of their lack of humanity by giving in to the "demand" to write; and that powerful conceptual metaphors promulgated in both scientific and social institutions, in fact, constrained them to do so. Gates writes that the

> black tradition's own concern with winning the war had led it not only to accept this arbitrary relationship [between literacy and humanity] but to embrace it, judging its own literature by a curious standard that derived from the social applications of the metaphors of the great chain of being, the idea of progress and the perfectibility of man, as well as the metaphor of capacity derived initially from eighteenth-century comparative studies of the anatomy of simian and human brains and then translated into a metaphor for intelligence and the artistic potential of a "race." (*Figures in Black* xxiv)

Gates laments what he sees as blacks' espousal of what is tantamount to their own negation, and, as I note in chapter 1, it is a critical stance that he has repeated in his various examinations of the origins of black culture and its tradition of literature. Yet for all of his pert attention to trickster figures (calling, at various moments in his work, a thinker of Frederick Douglass's immense stature a trickster, for instance⁶), here Gates does not allow that African American writers of earlier periods might have, quite simply, feigned submission to the literacy imperative in order to "psyche out," by way of deft linguistic play, their white judges. Nor does he concede that there might have existed in them the deep-seated desire for self-expression that strikes most who take on the mantle of artist (writer, poet, painter, sculptor, etc.), such that they feel compelled to give form to those thoughts that so possessed them. Equiano's narrative, to which I turn in the following chapter, makes clear at a number of points that he wrote not to prove his humanity, but because he believed his was an exemplary human story that carried a critical, even preordained, message to his reader.

Gates's work has been instructive and even formative in yet another fashion—his placing of the term "race" in quotation marks—a critical gesture that has not escaped the notice of practicing African American philosophers, even if their reference to it is by inference. In the 1985 collection *"Race," Writing, and Difference*, Gates argues that "[r]ace, as a meaningful criterion within the biological sciences, has long been recognized to be a fiction":

> When we speak of "the white race" or "the black race," "the Jewish race" or "the Aryan race," we speak in biological misnomers and, more generally, in metaphors. . . . Race has become a trope of ultimate, irreducible difference between cultures, linguistic groups, or adherents of specific belief systems which—more often than not—also have fundamentally opposed economic interests. Race is the ultimate trope of difference because it is so very arbitrary in its application. (4–5)

Such metaphorization of race, one that is closely related to the concepts of being Gates promulgates, is intellectually and ethically deficient for Lucius Outlaw, whose 1996 study, *Race and Philosophy*, is one case in point among philosophers grappling with the late-twentieth-century problem of race in relation to concepts of being. Outlaw, who takes W. E. B. Du Bois as an intellectual guide, argues that "raciation and ethnicization are facts of human evolutionary theory" (5). They may be socially contingent, but they are nonetheless "anthropologically necessary" to the organization of human society. Outlaw is discomfited by the contention of many scholars, among them Gates, that race is a social construction and this is so because there are so many obvious lived realities of race and racism. Yet Du Bois himself metaphorizes race, as I discuss in chapter 5, when he deems it the "most ingenious invention for human progress" ("Conservation" 817). Du Bois's metaphorization of race, which not only lends race a mappable social structure (in that it sets up two oppositional, logical poles whose antinomous interactions serve to define and debate the meaning and nature of race), also grants race—as a metaphorical term—a conceptual basis upon which it might be analyzed and, ultimately, deconstructed, as Du Bois does in "Conservation." Du Bois deconstructs race by performing a deep critical ontology of the concept and the Negro's place in nineteenth-century understandings of race. He does not simply dismiss race as a construction; rather, he begins his essay by criticizing those of his contemporaries who do so *uncritically*; he analyzes and strategizes around the concept of race even as he plans and calls for its abolition. For it is only by delving deeply into the history of race (as identity, concept, practice, limit, and construct) that one is able to transcend race (to move beyond its limits, such that black being shows itself to be illimitable), as Du Bois urges in the "Academy Creed" that concludes "The Conservation of Races." (He writes in the second paragraph of the "Creed," "We believe it the duty of the Americans of Negro descent, as a body, to maintain their race identity until this mission of the Negro people is accomplished, and the ideal of human brotherhood has become a practical possibility."[7])

Du Bois's insistence upon racial solidarity in the face of racial violence and discrimination provides the foundation for an argument such as that advanced by Tommie Shelby in *We Who Are Dark* (2005): that blackness, while insufficient as a moniker that could indicate essential and biological racial identity, may nonetheless be useful as the basis of a collective social activism and defense. Stuart Hall has similarly acknowledged the formations of such affiliation when he points out that blackness had been, in the 1970s, the umbrella under which any number of oppressed groups of people from diverse, non-white backgrounds in Great Britain could gather strength in numbers, in coalition, and in political and social solidarity against egregious forms of racism, capitalism, and oligarchy.[8]

Yet while Hall warns that such collectivities are as capable of nurturing essentialism as national powers have been ("diaspora, too, has been the site of some of the most closed narratives of identity known to human beings"[9]), Outlaw sees Du Bois arguing that races are bound together by common blood, that is, by biological descent, but that the variability of inheritable traits make identifying a race based on its physical features alone next to impossible. This is why, Outlaw argues, Du Bois turned to history and sociology to instruct him on the nature of racial grouping; that is, Du Bois, saw that the historical circumstances that a group's members enjoyed or, conversely, under which they labored, would serve to define them as a group because it bound them together in solidarity. They would, together as a group, defend the material and social gains they had made, or, again, together as a group, draw upon the strength of their numbers and collective effort to cast off oppression and insist upon a share of society's wealth and well-being.

Outlaw wants to establish a philosophical anthropology and social ontology that would allow him to understand and appreciate the "senses of belonging and of a shared destiny by which individuals are intimately connected to other individuals in ways that make for the constitution of particular kinds of social collectivities," which he calls "social-natural kinds." Races and ethnicities (or, "ethnies," as Outlaw calls them) are particular "'kinds' of collectivities; raciation and ethnicization the processes by which they are formed and maintained; raciality and ethnicity the interrelated sets of historically contingent and conditioned, socially defined, always varying and contestable physical and socio-cultural features relatively definitive of a race or ethnie" (7).

This position leads Outlaw to argue against those who see race as a construction, either simple or complex:

> Approaches of this sort fail to appreciate more fully varieties of kinds of *reals* and the full range of social realities. As a result, they help to impoverish social ontologies and thereby to impair the development of a social and political philosophy appropriate to a society that is diverse ethnically, racially, and culturally. As I have noted already, a major concern for me is the articulation of just such a philosophy supported by a combined social ontology and philosophical anthropology different in important ways from those that have been at the heart of modern liberal individualism: that is, revised to take seriously racial and ethnic groups in order to be a resource for praxes that might help us to realize social peace and harmony with justice. (8)

Thus, in Outlaw's argument, to say that race is a metaphor or a "biological misnomer" ("*Race,*" *Writing, and Difference* 4), and leave the matter there, interferes with and impedes the development of a social and political philosophy that can serve as the basis of a radical praxis intent upon uprooting injustice, including and especially racial and economic injustice. It also implies that to speak of race as metaphor is to ignore the historical realities of race; it is, in a significant way, an undergirding of liberalism's insistence upon a race-free society, but a society that ignores race in theory rather than in praxis. An important point to note here is that such a gesture accords with the insistence upon a "color-free society" that is one of the main tenets of mid-twentieth-century liberalism; further, it lends its rhetorical structure (albeit indirectly) to the discourses on the post-racial that are so compelling to the twenty-first-century American public today.

Outlaw ultimately upholds what he sees as Du Bois's insistence upon "conserving" races. He argues convincingly that race is a social reality that cannot simply be erased, placed in quotation marks, or deemed a social construct and thus done away with. It is a real problem of daily existence, and this is particularly true the world over of those social groups raced as something other than "white." The twentieth and twenty-first centuries have witnessed an "increasing frequency of conflicts tied to valorizations of differences among peoples that we characterize as 'races' and/or 'ethnic groups,'" and the horrors that take shape in race wars or wide-scale efforts at racial cleansing ought to alert us to the need to examine the questions of race and ethnicity with the closest attention we can manage, Outlaw writes. Citing the work of Daniel Patrick Moynihan (and echoing Hortense Spiller's 1987 critique of the Moynihan Report, and its perspective on "ethnicity" as "mythical time"[10]), Outlaw points out that modern liberalism had expected that racial divisions and, eventually, class divisions would melt away in a modern democracy. Such an expectation was "born in the philosophical anthropologies and political philosophies of modern European and American Enlightenments and nurtured in the centuries-old liberal-democratic, capitalist, and even socialist-communist revolutionary experiments with forming decidedly modern societies and nation-states. These legacies continue to serve as reservoirs of hope for many who would complete the realization of the promises of modernity," Outlaw concludes. "But it has not come to pass that physical and cultural differences among groups of peoples in terms of which they continue to be identified and to identify themselves, as races and ethnies have either ceased to exist or ceased to be taken as highly important in the organization of society [. . .]" (10).

Because such an overcoming has indeed not occurred, Outlaw intimates that the insistence upon erasing race from the American social lexicon (as in the work of Anthony Appiah), "may well come to have unintended effects that are too much of a kind with racial and ethnic cleansing in terms of their impacts on raciality and ethnicity as important means through which we construct and validate ourselves" (11). Just as we cannot will race out of social discourse, neither have we been successful in appealing to the reason of the global community as we seek to hold the excesses of racism in check: "Appeals to 'reason' have not been either an effective vaccine against the ravaging viruses of racism and invidious ethnocentrism or an antidote to the social ills they produce. In fact, both racism and invidious ethnocentrism are generally highly rationalized ventures. As was noted long before now, reason can be a whore who sleeps with anyone" (12).

Races must be seen as both biologically based and evolving, Outlaw argues. That is to say that while we might, ultimately, be able to trace any number of races to their origin (and possibly even a single origin, given the advances in the human biosciences), races must be seen as the "natural" (12), evolving groups that they are. Race groups are, at base, human groups, and humans, as "social animals" (13), must be recognized as association and affection seeking collectivities, groups "secured" by "loyalties [and] attachments that are contingent and variable, yet are necessary for any person to become fully human" (13).

This last phrasing is significant in light of the present study, because it underscores that for philosophers—and at times, even for Africana philosophers—individuals are not born human by virtue of being members of the species known as "homo sapiens." Rather, they are human by virtue of individual behavior, social and cultural associations, and, importantly, social and, in modern times, political recognition, whereby their standing as human beings is recognized, granted, and assured by a society, community, and polis that are themselves anchored in the broader political association that we call the nation-state. The definition of the human that I use is somewhat different, for it grants all homo sapiens the status of the human at birth, not by virtue of their material proof (in writing or otherwise) that they merit such standing. This definition of the human also flies in the face of the posthuman stance adopted by many in the schools of postmodernism and poststructuralism, who see the human, as a figure, so maligned by the thought and speculation of the Enlightenment that the category of the human must be set aside, cast into question, placed on a par with animals and plants, "seamlessly articulated with intelligent machines,"[11] and so on. In other words, what I imagine theorists of the posthuman to be about is an equivocation of categories of being, and thus a theory of identity that runs afoul of Aristotle's dictum against such blurring of ontological boundaries.

The philosopher Lewis Gordon might argue that the openness in Outlaw's perspective on racial groups permits a sort of existential freedom that he locates at the founding of possibility itself. But before going on to Gordon, I will turn to Charles W. Mills, whose 1998 book, *Blackness Visible: Essays on Philosophy and Race*, appears to provide a sort of commentary on that of Outlaw. Mills begins by making the case for a philosophical treatment of race, an argument that shares its thrust with that of Outlaw's perspective. Mills seems intent, however, on distinguishing his approach from that of Outlaw, at least in part. He writes that "[since] its emergence as a major social category several hundred years ago, race has paradigmatically been thought of as 'natural,' a biological fact about human beings, and the foundation of putatively ineluctable hierarchies of intelligence and moral character. The discrediting of old-fashioned racism of this sort has made a truism in liberal intellectual circles of a claim that once would have seemed quite revolutionary: that race does not really exist" (xiii). To pay philosophical attention to race, then, would appear to lend credence and authority to an "enterprise" that is not only "foredoomed" and "pointless" even if "harmless," but also one that "seem[s] to run the risk of becoming an inverted black version of traditional white-supremacist theory. So almost overnight race goes from being in the body to being in the head, and one shows one's liberal commitment to bringing about a color-blind society by acting as if it already exists, not seeing race at all, and congratulating oneself on one's lack of vision" (xiii).

Mills argues for a perspective on race that sees it simultaneously as both "real and unreal": "that race can be ontological without being biological, metaphysical without being physical, existential without being essential, shaping one's being without being in one's shape" (xiv). He intends to articulate a version of critical race theory, wherein the "critical" aspect of the work lies in the recognition that race is both a construction and something that "*exists* (and moves people)" (xiv). Thus for him, the aim of critical race theory should lie somewhere between Gates's constructionism and Outlaw's "conservationist" perspective. It should

> make plausible a social ontology that is neither essentialist, innate, nor transhistorical, but real enough for all that. And . . . the most illuminating framework for defending this claim is, literally, a global one: the thesis that European expansionism in its various forms—expropriation, slavery, colonialism, settlement—brings race into existence as a global social reality, with the single most important conceptual division historically being that between 'whites' and 'nonwhites.' Those termed *white* have generally had a civil, moral, and juridical standing that has lifted them above the other 'races.' They have been the expropriators; others have been the expropriated. They have been the slave owners; others have been the slaves. They have been the colonizers; others have been the colonized. . . . So one gets a formal ontological partitioning in the population of the planet, signified by 'race.'" (xiv)

Mills's argument here is echoed, in part, by Barnor Hesse, who insists upon a perspective on race, racism, and the post-racial that is framed by post-1945 history. Hesse writes that our understanding of race as a modern force must come from an understanding of the vast and ultimately world-transforming forces of colonialism and imperialism, without which we would not have come to know the current denotation of the word "race." European expansionism gives birth to modern concepts of race, Hesse argues.[12] Mills agrees:

> Indeed, Westerners *created* race in the first place, by demarcating themselves from other 'races,' bringing into existence a world with two poles, so it is doubly ironic that they should feign a hands-washing ignorance of these realities. Once the sociality and historicity of the term is recognized, the claim that philosophy, along with other, less lofty varieties of intellectual labor, is going to be influenced by race should seem less provocative and controversial. This claim does not imply any kind of biological determinism; rather, it entails a pervasive social construction, a set of positions in a global structure, for which race will be assigned a category that influences the socialization one receives, the life-world in which one moves, the experiences one has, the worldview one develops—in short, in an eminently recognizable and philosophically respectable phrase, one's *being and consciousness.*" (Italics in original xv)

Mills underscores the ways in which white being and consciousness have been privileged in white Western philosophical discourse and inquiry, in spite of its claim to be color-blind and impervious to racism. Privileged white being is simple to conceive if one allows oneself these obvious facts: "insofar as these [white] persons are conceived of as having their personhood uncontested, insofar as their moral prescriptions take for granted an already achieved full citizenship and a history of freedom—insofar, that is, as race is *not* an issue for them, then they are already tacitly positioned as white persons, culturally and cognitively European, racially privileged members of the West" (italics in original, xv).

From the perspective of Mills and, as he describes them, many of his African American students, Western philosophy is tainted by its transgression of its own moral preachments: philosophy claims to be race-free, but essentially is a philosophy intended to reflect upon the lives and experiences of free, propertied white men who regularly violate the human rights of men and women of African descent as well as, quite often, those of white women, even those of their own class. Mills puts the matter thus:

The impatience or indifference that I have sometimes detected in black students seems to derive in part from their sense that there is something strange in spending a whole course describing the logic of different moral ideals for example, without ever mentioning that *all of them* were systematically violated for blacks. So it is not merely that the ideal was not always attained, but that, more fundamentally, *this was never actually the ideal in the first place.* A lot of moral philosophy will then seem to be based on pretense, the claim that these were the principles that people strove to uphold, when in fact the real principles were the racially exclusivist ones. (Italics in original 4)

That is, people of African descent were erased from the scope of the Western philosophical project, which declared the essence of humanity to lie only within bodies housed in white skin. Blackness of skin made black humanity *invisible.* Mills describes such invisibility as the "experience of subpersonhood" (6).

The analysis of "subpersonhood" over and against "personhood" becomes for Mills the objective glue that holds (or should hold) all black philosophical enterprises together. It is useful to cite him at length here:

What is a (racial) subperson? (The term, of course, is a translation of the useful German *Untermensch.*) What are its specific differentiae? A subperson is not an inanimate object, like a stone, which has (except perhaps for some green theorists) zero moral status. Nor is it simply a nonhuman animal, which (again, before recent movements to defend 'animal rights') would have been regarded, depending on one's Kantian or Benthamite sympathies, as outside the moral community altogether, or at best as a member with a significantly lower utility-consuming coefficient. Rather, the peculiar status of a subperson is that it is an entity which, because of phenotype, seems (from, of course, the perspective of the categorizer) human in some respects but not in others. It is a human (or, if this word already seems normatively loaded, a humanoid) who, though adult, is not fully a person. And the tensions and internal contradictions in this concept capture the tensions and internal contradictions of the black experience in a white-supremacist society. To be an African-American was to be, in Aristotle's conceptualization, a

living tool, property with a soul, whose moral status was tugged
in different directions by the dehumanizing requirements of
slavery on the one hand, and the (grudging and sporadic) white
recognition of the objective properties blacks possessed on the
other, generating an insidious array of cognitive and moral splits
in both black and white consciousness. . . . This, then, is a more
illuminating starting point than the assumption that in general
all humans have been recognized as persons (the 'default mode,'
so to speak). In other words, one would be taking the historical
reality of a partitioned social ontology as the starting point rather
than the ideal abstraction of universal equality, qualified with an
embarrassed marginal asterisk or an endnote to say that there
were some exceptions. (6–7)

For this reason, that is, because the person of African descent
begins "free" life in the West with a completely different set of existential
dilemmas, all of them arising out of oppression, the basic tenets of Western
philosophy, if adopted out of hand without reshaping or reframing, will
have "little resonance" for her or him (7). Obviously, Du Bois, for instance,
found a number of resonances between his own thought and the ideas of
consciousness he read of in the work of William James, the ideals of religious
philosophy examined by Josiah Royce, and the ideals of philosophical
absolutism propounded by George Santayana. Yet he reworked these to fit
the particular situation of the Negro; that is to say that he did not reject
them out of hand (though many who see Du Bois as an elitist overly
influenced by the thought of white philosophers have argued that he should
have) in an effort to recreate the wheel, as it were. Similarly, Richard Wright
has written of his taking recourse to the ideas of James and the tenets of
European existentialism, if only to affirm the evolving philosophies of being
that he himself was spinning in his fiction and essays.[13]

The examples of Du Bois and Wright might be taken to underlie
the conception of what Mills terms the "Ellisonian *sum*." Making his scope
one of black and white, Mills argues that there are two sorts of selves
("*sums*") that one can identify in the history of Western thought on human
being: a Cartesian self with which most Euro-American philosophers will
be familiar, and an Ellisonian self that he imagines will be unfamiliar to
many of this same group. The Cartesian *sum* is faced with the question out
of which emerges all of modern Western epistemology, Mills writes: "what
can I know?" (8):

The Cartesian plight, represented as an allegedly universal predicament, and the foundationalist solution of knowledge of one's own existence thus become problematic, a kind of pivotal scene for a whole way of doing philosophy and one that involves a whole program of assumptions about the world and (taken-for-granted) normative claims about what is philosophically important. (8)

The Ellisonian *sum*, which Mills sees as emblematic of black being and black existence, takes shape in the face of a different epistemology, he argues. The "subordinated" individual, such as that represented in Ellison's *Invisible Man*, faces a wholly different set of questions when confronted with the query, "what can I know," and "who/what am I?" in the context of a globally-construed existence:

It could be said that only those most solidly attached to the world have the luxury of doubting its reality, whereas those whose attachment is more precarious, whose existence is dependent on the good will or ill temper of others, are those compelled to recognize that it exists. The first is a function of power, the second of subjection. If your daily existence is largely defined by oppression, by *forced* intercourse with the world, it is not going to occur to you that doubt about your oppressors' existence could in any way be a serious or pressing philosophical problem; this idea will simply seem frivolous, a perk of social privilege. (8)

The Ellisonian *sum* will thus be quite different from the Cartesian *sum*:

From the beginning it will be relational, not monadic; dialogic, not monologic: one is a subperson precisely because *others*—persons—have categorized one as such and have the power to enforce their categorization. African-American philosophy is thus inherently, definitionally *oppositional*, the philosophy produced by property that does not remain silent but insists on speaking and contesting its status. So it will be a *sum* that is metaphysical not in the Cartesian sense but in the sense of challenging a *social* ontology; not the consequent of a proof, but the beginning of an affirmation of one's self-worth, one's reality as a person, and one's militant insistence that others recognize it also. (Italics in original 9)

When Mills writes that the black *sum* is "not the consequent of a proof, but the beginning of an affirmation of one's self-worth," I take him to make yet another critical allusion to the discourse that surrounds Gates's contention that the "black tradition's own concern with winning the war had led it not only to accept this arbitrary relationship [between literacy and humanity] but to embrace it, judging its own literature by a curious standard that derived from the social applications of the metaphors of the great chain of being" (*Figures in Black* xxiv). Mills's position is analogous to my own when he argues that in the face of such opposition, the black tradition regularly and forcefully undertook a critical ontology of race that reaches its modern apotheosis in Du Bois's "The Conservation of Races": a critical ontology of race that critiques and deconstructs the genealogy that constitutes its constructedness. This sort of ontology requires not only thought, but action; not simply theory, but also praxis. Du Bois makes this clear in "Conservation," and a similar approach undergirds, I argue, the ontological metaphorics of *The Souls of Black Folk*.

Mills correctly reads the Ellisonian metaphor of invisibility—the Ellisonian *sum*—through its forebear in the Du Boisian metaphors of the veil and double consciousness, ontological metaphors that draw their strength from Du Bois's deep understanding of race's power of metaphoricity, which, *pace* Outlaw, I define in a way that acknowledges but ultimately differs from that of Gates. It is not the case that all or even most metaphors are weak or fanciful expressions of social realities; rather, such metaphors as those proffered by Du Bois, Ellison, and other writers I discuss capture and convey *concepts*, submit arguments, forge new epistemologies, and undertake, in deeply sedimented and highly complex expression, critical ontologies. This sort of metaphorical thought—which lies at the heart of the black philosophical tradition because it lies at the foundation of the black literary tradition—insists at every turn upon action of some sort in response to the knowledge conveyed via the conceptual metaphor in question. As Mills puts it, African American or black philosophy "develops out of the resistance to oppression." Thus it is "a practical and politically oriented philosophy that, long before Marx was born, sought to interpret the world correctly so as to better change it. . . . In a broad sense, virtually all African-American philosophy is 'political,' insofar as the insistence on one's black humanity in a racist world is itself a political act" (17).

Lewis Gordon agrees that black philosophy emerges from the "question of blackness" (5), and he, more pointedly than the other philosophers I have discussed this far, analyzes literature not as the proof of black humanity, but as a praxis intended to bring about freedom from oppression—freedom of the mind as well as the body. In *Existentia Africana* (2000), Gordon characterizes Africana thought as thinking that

> raises ironic self-reflective, metatheoretical questions. . . . Because of the emancipatory aims of Africana thought, . . . the activity of writing ascends here to the level of praxis. . . . Writing is one among many activities with creative universal potential, and it is the theorist's work not only to articulate this in the body of literature left behind by prior theorists, but also to draw out creative dimensions for subsequent generations, the effect of which, in each stage, is the complex symbiosis of epistemological, historical, and ontological possibilities. (3)

Again the ideas of agency and action take precedence in African American philosophy, but to underscore writing as a praxis intended to ensure freedom from oppression is to interrogate and challenge yet again the proposition that African Americans write themselves into existence—provide a proof of their humanity—through the composition of the text. Gordon makes clear that the oral tradition that extends from David Walker and Maria Stewart all the way through Angela Davis and Martin Luther King, Jr. (and beyond) involves a use of language that is purposefully crafted after a fashion that demonstrates its liberatory possibilities. Thus for Gordon it is the purposeful and creative use of language, through both aesthetic and conceptual means, that contributes to what C. L. R. James elsewhere refers to as "creative universality" (qtd. Gordon 3). And such "creative universality" is so central to African American (and Africana) philosophy "because it always raises *possibility*, constitutes freedom" (Gordon 3).

Freedom, embodied agency, and liberation are all problems of the human condition addressed by Africana existential philosophy, which Gordon calls a branch of Africana philosophy. The human condition gives rise to three recurring questions: "What am I/are we?" "What shall I/we do?" and "What shall I/we become?" The first question is one of identity; the second question is one of moral action; and the third question is one of purpose. These are all ontological interrogations that seek a certain sort of truth, and they are matters of teleological significance, Gordon tells us. Such questions are not reserved for persons who consider themselves to be modern beings, nor are they limited to persons who live relatively free from oppression. They extend, as Gordon points out and as I argue in chapter 6 when examining Du Bois's use of the Sorrow Songs in *The Souls of Black Folk*, even to those in bondage.

For those who might doubt the capacity of slaves for existential thought, Gordon, following the example of Equiano, Harper, Du Bois, and other forebears, supplies a ready response:

> I asked them if slaves did not wonder about freedom; suffer anguish; notice paradoxes of responsibility; have concerns of agency; tremors of broken sociality, or a burning desire for liberation. Do we not find struggles with these matters in the traditional West African proverbs and folktales that the slaves brought with them to the New World? And more, even if we do not turn to the historical experiences of slaves of African descent and the body of cultural resources indigenous to the African continent, there are also the various dialogical encounters between twentieth-century Africana theorists and European and Euro-American theorists. (7)

The perspective of the slave or the oppressed "free" person is, even so, a *perspective*, one situated in the world and in relation to the world. Situatedness, or "situation," should be understood here as "the lived context of concern." With regard to the argument under development in this study, Gordon's words serve us quite well:

> Implicit in the existential demand for recognizing the situation or lived context of Africana peoples' being-in-the-world is the question of value raised by the people who live that situation. A slave's situation can only be understood, for instance, through recognizing the fact that a slave experiences it; it is to regard the slave as a perspective in the world. (10)

Crafting a Poetics of Black Being: Du Bois's Philosophical Example

When W. E. B. Du Bois guides his reader into the inner recesses of the life of the slave and the slave's descendants, and when he poses the question, in the opening paragraph of "Of Our Spiritual Strivings," "How does it feel to be a problem?" he grants that the Negro's feelings in relation to that problem must be seen not as simple emotions, but as a noetic processes: as sites of intellection, such that structures of feeling are enabled to tell us what we know, to establish a black epistemology that is capable of answering ontological and existential questions. And in announcing—by way of conceptual metaphor as a constituent element of narrative description and argumentation—the existence of the color-line as a social and legal boundary that artificially demarcates non-being and being (since it separates black from white, subpersons, in Mills's terminology, from persons) while qualifying its rules, Du Bois challenges how we conceptualize the categories of racialized being that the color-line ostensibly makes intelligible. Du Bois conceived the metaphor of the color-line not only in response to the oppressive situation of his own day, but also in response to a long history of anti-black violence and discrimination. He therefore sets up an alternative ontology and an alternative epistemology that confront the American racial, political, and economic context. Such a creative strategy of responsive action resonates in Johnson's, Outlaw's, Gordon's, and Mills's thinking, which in each instance points out that a different frame of reference and perspective on the world such as that held by the oppressed subject necessarily calls for a different philosophy and a different way of articulating, categorizing, and judging knowledge. Du Bois calls forth and validates the long historicity of black folk, arguing that a history of enslavement and oppression does not leave the African outside of history, as Hegel claims. Rather it is still, indeed, a *history*.

By drawing on the archive of black historicity left to him by such early and diverse figures as Equiano, Phillis Wheatley, Frederick Douglass, and Alexander Crummell, by examining and theorizing the local and global experiences of blackness that obtained in his own day, and by insisting on the study of the Negro problems, as he had from the time he assumed the stewardship of the Atlanta University studies in 1897, Du Bois not only counters a false European and Euro-American universalism that equated whiteness with absolute being; he also develops a method of study and activism that *presupposes* black being, agency, consciousness, and freedom (in truth if not in fact under American slavery and Jim Crow), and in this way, as Gordon points out, he transforms the "epistemological expectations of inquiry" (93). Du Bois practices what Gordon calls an "epistemic openness," which recognizes that there is always more to know about a subject of inquiry, in this case, the American Negro.

Du Bois draws upon the epistemological possibilities of metaphor in devising the concept metaphors of the veil, the color-line, and double consciousness as metaphors supple enough not only to articulate the human condition of the American Negro (her situatedness in time and space) but also to respond to the particularities of her situation through concerted action shaped by her own perspective. Du Bois's use of conceptual metaphors makes clear that the historical question of black being and the role of language therein must even unto the present day be re-examined from a critical and creative perspective. Thus his work serves quite well as the prismatic fulcrum from which emerges, in a transhistorical fashion, the present inquiry into the poetics of black being.

Whither Blackness? Du Bois, Black Culture, and the Contemporaneity of Black Being

In light of Du Bois's work (rather than in its shadow[14]), the responsibility of the contemporary black creative intellectual (as Hortense Spillers has so aptly named her) compels her to respond to the specifics of the present time of "crisis" (in the humanities, in the University, in American social values, and in the global economy) and to those past moments of communal, social, institutional and national memory that constitute the present as well as the future. For each past moment of being at some point in our concept of time was once both present and future, and text allows us to reach back to those past moments to draw them forward into our own contemporaneity, even as we project our thoughts, actions, and intentions toward the future, toward the world to come.

The concept of contemporaneity and its relation to being has received wide philosophical treatment from Spillers and a number of other thinkers, and while my brief survey of its emphasis here cannot aspire to be comprehensive, the concept nonetheless demands some consideration in light of its relation to ideas of being, thought, and the lived context of concern. Søren Kierkegaard's view of contemporaneity, for instance, is intended to reject the linearity of Hegel's concept of time and history. Rather than Absolute Knowledge (Hegel) as the culmination of history and thought and the realization of consciousness through philosophical and, according to Mark C. Taylor, Christological mediation, Kierkegaard insists upon Absolute Paradox, such that consciousness never conceives of itself as a whole. Taylor puts it thus: "In the final analysis this essential difference in perspective explains why Hegel's pilgrim can come to feel at home in the world, while Kierkegaard's sojourner is forever an unsettled, rootless wanderer" (107). In another example of thinking on contemporaneity, the sociologist Karl Mannheim conceived of time as a "cumulation of discrete moments," and according to David Kettler and Volker Meja, "contemporaneity is one of the major suppositions" of his work (17). (Mannheim's concept of contemporaneity may aid in providing an apt and concise explanation for the existence of twenty-first-century anti-African American racism in what has been called the "post-racial"—but not "post-racist"—age of Obama.) Mannheim developed what Julius Stone describes as a concept of the contemporaneity of the non-contemporaneous: he held that certain contemporary social conditions have arisen from habits, attitudes, or social situations of bygone eras, and yet they coexist with habits, attitudes, and institutions that have arisen from present conditions. From a much more benign perspective, Gulnara Bakieva puts the matter thus:

> Contemporaneity is the present, which includes the past and the future. As a moment of the space-time continuum in a concentrated state, contemporaneity expresses both discreteness and endlessness. That is because history consists of a multitude of concrete historical and local contemporaneities.
>
> Contemporaneity is "here and now," while the past is "already" and the future is "later." History and human life go on between the "already" and the "later." Time is irreversible, and it runs from the past to the future. However, the past, present and future can be synchronized, thanks to social memory. . . . The being created by contemporaneity is the continuation of the past and the basis of [the] future. (v)

Each writer under examination in this study turns to social memory even as s/he engages and addresses the problems of his/her present day and plans for the future. Such is, as Balkieva notes, the mode of being in the world that is essential to modern humankind. In this light, the force of Jacques Derrida's "always already" emerges even more powerfully with respect to my work here: the past may never be left behind, for it, like the future, is always with us, ever and anon. Like Spillers's clarion call, Derrida's impassioned exordium in *Specters of Marx* (1994), at once stirring, compelling, and haunting, though aimed more broadly, calls us to a contemporaneous consideration of black being's past, present, and future:

> If I am getting ready to speak at length about ghosts, inheritance, and generations, generations of ghosts, which is to say about certain *others* who are not present, nor presently living, either to us, in us, or outside us, it is in the name of *justice*. Of justice where it is not yet, not yet *there*, where it is no longer, let us understand where it is no longer *present*, and where it will never be, no more than the law, reducible to laws or rights. It is necessary to speak *of the* ghost, indeed *to the* ghost and

with it, from the moment that no ethics, no politics, whether revolutionary or not, seems possible and thinkable and *just* that does not recognize in its principle the respect for those others who are no longer or for those others who are not yet *there*, presently living, whether they are already dead or not yet born. No justice . . . seems possible or thinkable without the principle of some *responsibility*, beyond all living present, within that which disjoins the living present, before the ghosts of those who are not yet born or who are already dead, be they victims of wars, political or other kinds of violence, nationalist, racist, colonialist, sexist, or other kinds of exterminations, victims of oppressions of capitalist imperialism or any of the forms of totalitarianism. Without this *non-contemporaneity with itself of the living present*, without that which secretly unhinges it, without this responsibility and this respect for justice concerning those who *are not there*, of those who are no longer or who are not yet *present and living*, what sense would there be to ask the question "where?" "where tomorrow?" "whither?" (*Specters of Marx* xviii, italics in original)[15]

It seems to me that Spillers usefully takes up the critical project of "whither" the direction of the question of black being, and "whither" the bent of African American theory and thought, as when she insists upon social memory and sociopolitical action via what she calls a "return to the idea of black culture."[16] Spillers's writing has long urged theorists and intellectuals to test the boundaries of disciplinary thinking even as one looks more intently into the recesses of one's own thoughts and practices. And so Spillers calls for transgression and displacement while inviting one to come home, after a fashion, an invitation to delve within that often takes, in mythological proportions, the shape of exilic wandering (in the sense that Édouard Glissant gives this notion[17]) and noetic descent. Such descent, if our philosophers are to be believed, is the only avenue by which we can reach a moment of clarity, overcoming, as it were, the particular opacity of our own conditions in order to attain to a critically revised sense of an open totality, a polyvalent universal: one that is creatively expansive, alternatively envisioned, and noetically rich. The synergy between gestures of descent and ascent in the end may serve as an analogy to the contemporaneity of time Derrida references: a delving deep into one's own intellectual habitation in order not only to place oneself meaningfully in the present of the universe, but also to commune with those others from times past and anticipate those others in times future who complement one's own being, who reflect one's humanity in their own. I read Hortense Spillers's 1994 riposte to Harold Cruse's *The Crisis of the Negro Intellectual*[18] (a piece that could now demand a post-date of its own, for two decades have now passed since its first appearance in *boundary 2*) in this sense, for it anticipates, in a number of ways, Spillers's more recent work in "The Idea of Black Culture" (2006). In my estimation, Spillers's thought in both pieces speaks ultimately to the broader importance that our consideration of metaphor and the poetics of being bears for the itinerary of African American literary theory, as I hope my brief discussion will show.

In "Crisis," Spillers offers both a rejoinder to Cruse's path-breaking book and an assessment of the work required of black intellectuals during the mid-1990s. The essay is striking for its address to black *creative* intellectuals, and by this moniker I take Spillers to speak to (even as she speaks for and with) a broad swath of black academics working in the post-Civil Rights climate of that decade, as the first wave of powerful, outspoken African American thinkers and cultural workers (Holloway, Gates, Outlaw, Baker, and many others) to have gained access to the so-called "mainstream" academy after the tidal wave of protest activism that marked the late 1960s. Such a "calling out" of creative African American writers and thinkers as Spillers puts forward had not been sounded since the deaths of Richard Wright (in 1960), W. E. B. Du Bois (in 1963), and James Baldwin (in 1987). Not without its own significance is the fact that Spillers's essay appeared in the months following Ralph Ellison's death in April 1994. It thus was her own critical moment of writing, her own creative habitation that she interrogated as she pondered the stretch of intellectual time that separated her temporality from that of Cruse.

Spillers was not alone in identifying 1994 as a moment of crisis in black American thought and activism, and this in spite of the accolades that the mainstream academy and public had showered on such literary lights as Toni Morrison and Rita Dove. Morrison was recipient of the Nobel Prize in literature in 1993; in that same year, Dove was named Poet Laureate of the United States. What is more, 1993 witnessed the publication of what has proved to be one of the most significant theoretical works of the decade: Paul Gilroy's *The Black Atlantic: Modernity and Double Consciousness*. Equally distinguished is Morrison's 1992 work of criticism, *Playing in the Dark: Whiteness and the Literary Imagination* (whose first chapter is titled, compellingly, "Black Matters," preparing the way, it would seem, for Cornel West's influential *Race Matters* the following year in 1993). While Morrison looks at figurations of blackness in modern white American texts, Gilroy takes up a much needed theoretical and historicist perspective on African

American cultural and intellectual expression in the age of modernity, a charge that he plunges into through the prism of Du Bois's concept metaphor of double consciousness. And I have already spoken at length of the contributions of Ronald A. T. Judy's work in *(Dis)forming the American Canon*, also published in 1993, to the critical discourse of the moment. In each case and to varying but significant degrees, these scholars' attention was drawn to the conceptual metaphorics at work in African American cultural production. Their voices, raised in unison with Spillers's, engaged with a great sense of urgency the work of the African American intellectual in Spillers's own moment of contemporaneity.

The convening of the "Race Matters" conference at Princeton University by Wahneema Lubiano and others in 1994 seemed likewise to rise to the task at hand. An influential collection of critical essays, *The House that Race Built*, published in 1997, resulted from the papers and discussions that took place in Princeton in 1994. The Princeton conference drew its inspiration from and followed in the considerable wake of West's *Race Matters*. West had, in his widely read book, insisted upon just such an expansive dialogue on race in America as would take place at Princeton the following year. And although Spillers does not appear among the roster of contributors to *The House that Race Built* (which includes pieces by West, Lubiano, and Morrison, among others) her work is undoubtedly in dialogue with them, offering a perspective that might best be described as that of the literary critic cum philosopher who turns her incisive gaze toward the responsibility of the "organic" black intellectual, even as she ponders the possibility that such a Gramscian notion could still be realized in the moment of late capitalism.

Foregrounding what she sees as the necessary task of her day, Spillers identifies Cruse's book as the first work since Du Bois's autobiographies to address specifically the role of the black intellectual in late-twentieth-century American society. For Spillers, W. E. B. Du Bois's autobiographies were

> themselves a demonstration of the project that the black creative intellectual might engage when he or she defines his/her auto-bios-graphe in the perspective of historical time and agency. Between Du Bois and Cruse, with the possible exceptions of Richard Wright and Ralph Ellison, who had both focused on the fictional writer's commitment and vocation, we had to wait awhile, as though poised, it seemed, for an apposite interpretive gesture at the close of an era of cataclysmic events between *Brown v. Board of Education* (Topeka) (1954) and the 1964 Civil

Rights legislation—the two punctualities that frame one of the most fateful decades of African-American cultural and historical apprenticeship in the United States. (*"The Crisis of the Negro Intellectual*: A Post-Date" 428).[19]

As she looks back to the time of Cruse's writing, Spillers is intent upon naming the dilemma of the contemporary African American intellectual by drawing into relation the writer's "auto-bios-graphe," which I take to refer to the expression of the self ("auto") and of one's existence ("bios") through writing ("graphe"), with historicity and embodied agency. She notes extensively the qualities that serve to differentiate her historical moment from those of Cruse and Du Bois. In the main, they have to do with such matters as the outsized African American prison population, America's drug culture, economic and educational inequities, the domestic and international appetite for violence, and rabid racism. "To call attention to these vital details is to indulge the litany of responses that is by now customary for the black creative intellectual," Spillers writes (431). Even so, it is a highly textured backdrop that Spillers insists requires an analytical and impassioned response. It requires the establishment of a "*total perspective* against which the work of the intellectual unfolds" (Italics in original 431).

In the wake of the Civil Rights movement, in light of the student uprisings and feminist agitations of the 1970s, Spillers contends that those black intellectuals who came "of age" during the 1980s have, at times, folded in the face of that decade's greatest challenges: urban blight and white flight as public schools were forced to desegregate; a declining American market; the breakdown of African American "communities"; and the white "backlash" against the gains of civil rights legislations, among other factors. Within this "maelstrom of forces," Spillers writes, "the black, upwardly mobile, well-educated subject has not only 'fled' the old neighborhood (in some cases, the old neighborhood isn't even there anymore!) but, just as importantly, has been *dispersed* across the social terrain to unwonted sites of work and calling" (433). In Spillers' view, what the creative black intellectual of the mid 1990s should realize is exactly where this leaves him or her, and what work she or he has to do. As Spillers puts it, the black intellectual should neither long for a lost mythological "community" whose collective, holistic identity could provide a curative for the loss of "home"; nor should she allow such overwhelming circumstances to leave her paralyzed "by guilt over one's relative success and profound delusion about one's capacity to lead the masses (of which, one supposes, it is certain she is not one!) out of their Babylon" (433). Rather, the black creative intellectual should contemplate the ground on which she stands, a site hallowed by the halls of the American academy, only recently opened broadly (though not fully) to those of darker hue. The "mainstream academy and its various ideological commitments" define the situatedness—the lived context of concern—of the black creative intellectual, the writer and thinker; indeed, those "progressive movements" that catapulted her to the heights of the ivory tower are under attack from well-funded conservative elements that are pushing back against progressive gains. Under this weight and under considerable siege, the black creative intellectual needs to consider what work is to be done *now*, Spillers argues.

Spillers brings her critique into the twenty-first century in "The Idea of Black Culture," a piece that I see in a continuum, a line of thought that extends from her 1994 intervention in the "Crisis" of black intellectualism. She names the problem of the twenty-first century in black critical studies, a crucial naming because critical black social discourse, as was proved at the emergence of what has come to be called the politics of postmodernism,[20] often directs the turning of theory. Spillers is intent upon analyzing black culture as a "conceptual object" and as a "practical devise [sic] toward the achievement of social transformation" (8). One would not be remiss in considering language and especially conceptual metaphorical language to be a foremost constituent of such a "conceptual object," given Spillers's working definition of "culture," which she shapes through readings of Herbert Marcuse and, in a gesture that parallels my own, Du Bois. What seems apparent at this point is that Spillers is concerned to address the idea of black culture as one that is capable of cultural "revolution." And indeed, the tracing of traces, faint and bold, of black culture might itself be considered a revolution in theory, if I may be pardoned for purloining the title of Julia Kristeva's *Revolution in Poetic Language* (1974, trans. 1984) in my phrasing. For Spillers, the very "idea of black culture" itself posits as a project whose aim is, in part, to undertake critical reflection on instances of "emergent social formation in *discourse*," and here, in my reading, both conceptual language and epistemology are flagged as *practices* that possess the capacity and potential of interventional *praxes*. It says that the *experience* of black being, expressed in various forms of culture (song, religion, dance, language, etc) carries within it the latent, but potent, promise of creative intellectual work. Again, then, in 2006 as in 1994, Spillers's attention to the work of black creative intellectuals comes clear; and here as she had some twelve years earlier, one finds Spillers tracing the history of black creative thought from the fervor of the 1960s to the upheavals of subsequent times.

Fred Moten's conclusion to "The Case of Blackness" (2008) provides an interesting rejoinder to my thoughts and Spillers's words. He writes that the "lived experience of blackness" (and he is here reading the critical questions of objectivity and subjectivity in the "early and late" Fanon) emerges as a "duty to appose the oppressor, to refrain from a certain performance of the labor of the negative, to avoid his economy of objectification and standing against, to run away from the snares of recognition" ("The Case of Blackness" 211). Moten reads the case of blackness in Fanon as one that opens the possibility of the recuperation of the human, even as it "[troubles]" such "rehabilitation." Blackness for him can and should impose a duty to "[refuse] the labor of the negative" (211). In a gesture that appears, at this point, to deviate from that of Gates and Judy,[21] a detour that in part reflects my own, Moten insists upon the positive and critical life force that might be exemplified in blackness, a life force that possesses the potential for change that is both social and cultural. This sort of ontology, which I have called a "critical ontology" (in Foucault's sense of this term), correlates in some ways with what Nahum Chandler has named a "para-ontology": it names the "transformative pressure blackness puts on philosophical concepts, categories, and methods" (Moten 215ff3). This sort of critical action accords with Spillers's idea of the revolutionary potential of black culture (if, according to her reading, black culture refuses the falseness of Western materialism and continues its long tradition of resistance and critique). Such is also central to the meaning(fulness) I want to grasp and hold on to as the living "thing" of my project, that is, the recuperation of black being, drawing it out of the fire of objectification and negation in which it has been immolated by some quarters of African Americanist thought. (The immolating gestures of such thought might be termed "post-black," but this is a question for another time.) Black being, relieved of certain falsities alive in "post-racialist" discourse, must nonetheless maintain a stringent exposition of global oppression, global capitalization and imperialism, nationalist racism, uncritical post-racialist discourses, racial "tolerance," post-modernist "mixed-race" thought of the sort that seems to lack a rigorous critique of the concept of race as it distances itself from it, and so on.[22]

In this light, Spillers's insistence on the value of black culture—that black culture can and should be considered as a conceptual field that is ripe for inquiry and that it can enable radical and even revolutionary thought and praxis—is of great importance to the sort of analysis of conceptual metaphors I undertake in this study, since language lies at the heart of our understanding of culture. Spillers casts the question of the idea of black culture as a "second level" stress that must follow an inquiry into the notion of culture more broadly defined. That is, as she writes, "before we can venture an idea about the 'idea of black culture,' we must reestablish an outlook on the 'idea of culture'" (10). To do so, she first turns to the work of Raymond Williams, who defines culture in terms of three " 'broad active categories of usage'" (11). First, culture is the " 'independent and abstract noun which describes a general process of intellectual, spiritual and aesthetic development.'" Second, culture indicates a " 'particular way of life, whether of a people, a period, or a group.'" And, finally, culture is that which " 'describes the works and practices of intellectual and especially artistic activity'" (11–12). Yet for all this, culture is "visible only in its effects, and its contents show forth a repertoire of implements, from the fantastic/ imaginal to the actual/material that splinter in pluralness and considerable variation. From this vantage, there are, perhaps, only [black] cultures" (12).

Many points arise for our consideration at this juncture. The simultaneous visibility and invisibility of (black) culture, for instance, and its striking relation to conceptual metaphors of the theoretical visibility and invisibility of black people are propounded in the work of Charles Mills. Blackness here is akin to the "accident" of fleshly appearance which makes it unequal to Aristotle's category of "substance" or "essence," even as it has been taken to be, since at least the Enlightenment, the very avatar of essentialized racial being. Spillers worries that a distinct notion of black culture has disappeared, having been absorbed into the state apparatuses that make cultural revolution improbable if not impossible.

This is a quite interesting assessment to make, since one could argue that the liberalism of the Enlightenment first differentiated whites from blacks, then demanded the "disappearance" of racial difference and particularly blackness, initially by writing black people out of the official documents of national belonging and recognition, then by making blackness the unnamable and infrahuman definition of whiteness, Americanness, and Europeanness themselves. Just as European and Euro-American thought "disappeared" blackness during the revolutionary era of nationalism and nascent capitalism, the postmodern era of late capitalism has yet again taken up a raceless ideal, postulating the "post-racial" black subject as that desired being whose difference is "absorbed" into the state apparatus of whiteness, while the "post-racialism" of *white* subjects has remained untheorized, un-desired, and outside of the popular and political imaginaries.

Spillers values culture in general, and black culture specifically, for its *"corrective potential"* (14), since it takes shape not only in its relation to what Marcuse called the " 'higher dimension of human autonomy and fulfillment,'" but also in its centrality to what he called civilization, which refers to " 'the realm of necessity, or socially necessary work and behavior'" (14). What this means for today's "cultural worker," for women and men who travail in what Du Bois called the "kingdom of culture," is that there is a critical intersection between "the imperatives of reading and the goad to action—in short, the defining dilemma of Du Bois's life and meditation" (15). This is, or at least should be, the end goal of the black cultural project, Spillers argues, again drawing Du Bois into discourse with Herbert Marcuse, whom he preceded in thought by a number of decades.

For Marcuse, the goal of the revolutionary cultural worker and the labor of *humanitas* consist in " 'modes of thought, imagination, expression essentially nonoperational and transcendent, transcending the established universe of behavior not toward a realm of ghosts and illusions, but toward historical possibilities'" (16). At the core of Marcuse's idea of *humanitas*, Spillers writes, is what he calls the " 'cognitive content'" of "the cultural oeuvres," which, when "set over and against operational modes of thought and behavior [favored by "the prevailing civilization in advanced industrial countries," that is, by the hegemon], would constitute and complement transformative aims analogous to the protocols of human reconstruction that Du Bois sketches throughout the body of *The Souls of Black Folk*" (16). While Marcuse argues that the so-called "high culture" of a society evolves into ideology that supports and makes possible the longevity of the hegemon, even as it neglects its responsibility of humanization and takes up, instead, the processes of civilization (which has the potential to colonize and oppress), the cultures of the working people and the oppressed, which, ironically, permit the reproduction of higher culture and civilization, may well serve as a site of respite that promises or makes possible revolution.

It is this site that Du Bois enters and into which he invites us when he analyzes the inner recesses of black life within what he metaphorically conceptualizes as the veil. This metaphorical, conceptual site, as Spillers argues, is the "space of the political" (20), a space of potentiality, potency, and action that black cultural workers of the twenty-first century must reclaim and cultivate as their own.

Thus, when Du Bois devises the metaphor of the veil to mark the threshold of this space, he devises no simple figuration of language, no languid ornament of speech to adorn and beautify a treasure of words. The metaphor of the veil, like the metaphors of the color-line and double consciousness, draws upon the history of black critical discourses whose traces and effects still resonated in Du Bois's day, drawing him into a communal interchange with such exemplary figures as Equiano and Harper. What is more, Du Bois's conceptual figurations, his folding of the onto-theological tropes favored by Equiano in his crusade for liberty and his re-memory of Harper's slave subject, whose life expressions Du Bois was instrumental in archiving, were formative modernist constructions of philosophical metaphorical discourse whose influence on the thought and poetics of such later writers as Wright and Ellison are palpable. This sort of metaphorical discourse reveals black being and ensures its viability, even as it analyzes, critiques, and resists the forced invisibility of the black subject. Such writing writes black being while refusing, as Moten cautions, the labor of the negative. The ethics of this poetics of being is an ethics of action, which emerges importantly (though not exclusively) from sites of consciousness and self-reflexion that one finds in text. The habitation of the veil is black being's inhabitation of the text, which names a poetics that remains vital in and ripe for the reading of African American literature. In Part II, I begin my series of theoretical readings by way of this poetics, commencing with Olaudah Equiano's eighteenth-century *Interesting Narrative*.

II

Reading the Poetics of Black Being
Before and After Du Bois

3

Being and Becoming

The Interesting Narrative of the Life of Olaudah Equiano, or Gustavus Vassa, the African

There are two remarkable and strikingly contrasting pieces—one visual and one inscribed, a duality of imagery and writing—that serve as equally significant paratexts to the 1789 classic, *The Interesting Narrative of Olaudah Equiano, or Gustavus Vassa, the African*, a memoir that is widely considered to be a founding text of the African American literary tradition. Equiano stands at the wellspring of this tradition not simply because his narrative represents a finely wrought modern subjectivity in a way that makes clear its relation to the formation of modern nation-states, but also for the powerful metaphorics with which he negotiates the competing discourses of church and state. From the opening pages of his text, Equiano informs the reader that his own being is forcibly formed in the crucible of such tensions, and that it is out of this abyss that his own sense of modern being must make itself known.

Indeed, Equiano uses what I have called metaphors of being in order to conceptualize his own existence with respect to the historical era during which he lived and, equally important, the agency he sought to foster and maintain. In this chapter, I consider Equiano's *Narrative* as the conceptual object he intended it to be. As I point out in chapter 2, the catalyst behind my approach may be located in Hortense Spillers's clarion call to black creative intellectuals.

In "The Idea of Black Culture," Spillers urges black intellectuals to reinvigorate their creative and critical practices with renewed attention to the vital details of black existence documented in what she calls the "auto-bios-graphe" of the black writer. I intend to analyze Equiano's *Narrative* as the sort of "conceptual object" and "practical devise [sic] toward the achievement

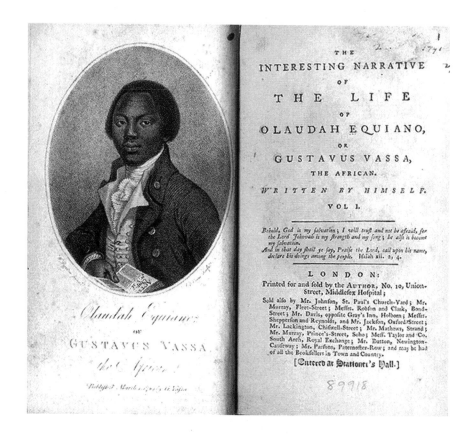

of social transformation" that Spillers deems the necessary focus of a useful and impactful critical discourse. Equiano's *Narrative* is located at that site where the traces of black culture have, over the past four decades, become more clearly legible to the theorist and historian. Thus it is with Equiano that I begin this study's analysis of the experience of black being as it is expressed through conceptual metaphors in African American literature.

As we shall see, the sort of metaphorical expression Equiano favors may be best described as onto-theological. At once secular and sacred in nature, Equiano's metaphors draw upon Biblical tropology even as he quite astutely expresses his sense of being-in-the-world as a modern man whose blackness enforces a perceptible distinction in his discourse. Here I am concerned, to borrow once again Nahum Chandler's instructive phrasing, to name the "transformative pressure" Equiano's metaphors of black being bring to bear upon modern "philosophical concepts, categories, and methods" (qtd. Moten 205ff3). Ingeniously, Equiano's use of the onto-theological in his metaphors of being emerges not through words alone, but also through visual culture. As Spillers might likewise say, such metaphorical expression as is exemplified in Equiano's work establishes the highly textured background so necessary to the contemporary black intellectual's work. It provides the context for Lewis Gordon's invaluable maxim that a "slave's situation can only be understood, for instance, through recognizing the fact that a slave experiences it; it is to regard the slave as a perspective in the world" (10). And certainly, as I have argued, the metaphorics that are so central to Du Bois's *The Souls of Black Folk* fully appreciate texts such as Equiano's as sites of intellection capable of inquiring into ontological and existential questions.

The ontological and existential questions between the secular and the sacred that characterize not only Equiano's era, but also his narrative are palpable even in his autobiography's prefatory material. For instance, Equiano makes his initial communication through his portrait, which serves as the frontispiece of his *Narrative*. He sits erect, his body turned slightly. He looks at us directly, but without, it seems, arrogance or hostility. His attire is that of an English gentleman, rather than an African: he sports a high-collar jacket, ruffled shirt, and fitted waistcoat. And his reading material bespeaks the status of one not only lettered, that is, literate, but also one who is a Christian. In his hand, he holds a Bible, open, fittingly, to the Book of Acts, which chronicles the adventures of the Apostles after Christ's death, just as Equiano's own book chronicles his exploits after the trauma of the Middle Passage.

In a compelling letter that follows this portrait and serves as both introduction to the text and as apology for faults the reader might find with his work, Equiano addresses the Lords and Commons of the Parliament of Great Britain:

> [The] chief design [of this Narrative] is to excite in your august assemblies a sense of compassion for the miseries which the Slave-Trade has entailed on my unfortunate countrymen. By the horrors of that trade was I first torn away from all the tender connexions that were naturally dear to my heart; but these, through the mysterious ways of Providence, I ought to regard as infinitely more than compensated by the introduction I have thence obtained to the knowledge of the Christian religion, and of a nation which, by its liberal sentiments, its humanity, the glorious freedom of its government, and its proficiency in arts and sciences, has exalted the dignity of human nature. I am

sensible I ought to entreat your pardon for addressing to you a work so wholly devoid of literary merit; but, as the production of an unlettered African, who is actuated by the hope of becoming an instrument towards the relief of his suffering countrymen, I trust that *such a man*, pleading in *such a cause*, will be acquitted of boldness and presumption. (italics in original, xxi)

The differences between the two pieces are both obvious and telling. While in the visual image, Equiano represents himself as a cultured African who, but for the color of his skin, closely resembles an Englishman, in his missive he describes himself as an "unlettered African" working simply to relieve the "suffering" of "his countrymen." Interesting also is Equiano's phrasing in his epistolary appeal to Parliament. He states that he was torn from his home and family by the horrors of the slave trade, and concludes that he "ought" to regard these "horrors" as "more than compensated" by his newfound knowledge of England and her culture (both her national character and her religious practice). Yet he does not state forthrightly and in an unequivocal manner that such culture *is* adequate compensation. Indeed, he allows that he "ought" to beg pardon for producing a work "so wholly devoid of literary merit," but he does not actually do so; he has no doubt—he "trusts"—that he "will be acquitted of boldness and presumption."

Equiano's phrasing in this letter is significant because it depends for its import and intent upon sedimented, metaphorical meanings at play in the English language, even as it reveals concepts of the moral and the ethical that are seminal not only to his own thought, but also to the thought of his time. Eighteenth-century usage of the verb "ought," for example, combined the preterite-present tense of the verb "owe," referring often to monetary indebtedness, with a sense of moral obligation. In using this verb, Equiano plumbs the depths of language—strategically, it seems to me, so as not to alienate his readers even as he challenges them—in an effort to refer simultaneously to the constraints of personal debt, and, by extension, human bondage—at the same time that he references the morality generally attributed to humanistic freedom by eighteenth-century philosophers such as Immanuel Kant and Jean-Jacques Rousseau. The sedimented meanings at work in the verb "owe"—along with Equiano's broader, sophisticated use throughout the *Narrative* of metaphorical language drawn largely from the Bible—allow him to contend with prevailing social and political precepts that he cites openly in his letter to Parliament: morality, religion, liberalism, freedom, humanism, and knowledge. These meanings sedimented in the verb "ought" are essentially dead metaphor that give the appearance of direct language, but that, nonetheless, impact the figurative sense of the language Equiano uses through their projection forward into his contemporary situation, one of bondage (indebtedness) and, eventually, freedom.

Theories of language that prevailed during Equiano's day called for direct and simple language of the sort that he only ostensibly employs in his letter, a language that eschewed gratuitous metaphorical flourishes even as it manifested complex layers of signification. Eighteenth-century views on figurative speech drew largely upon the sixteenth-century perspectives of the philosopher and rhetorician Peter Ramus. The "Ramist revolution," as it came to be called, required metaphorical constructions to function as arguments, as aspects of logic that shied away from esoteric signification. As Terence Hawkes[1] points out, the Ramist perspective demanded a shift from the "oral modes of drama" that obtained in Elizabethan literature, to the "literate mode of the printed book." Such could be seen as analogous to the shift from "an ancient world" to the "recognizably modern one" (30) Equiano inhabited and, to a good extent, exemplified. (Equiano's use of portraiture, of course, stood as an equally modern mode of expression, a point to which I return shortly in this section.) Samuel Johnson's *Dictionary* (1755), in contrast, Hawkes reminds us, stopped just short of defining metaphorical flourishes as "an abuse of language"; metaphorical expression could exhibit "'a great excellence in style,'" Dr. Johnson wrote, but it was, nonetheless, an ornamental aftereffect in the process of composition. It was, then, considered an excess of meaning, an embellishment of thought (32).

Rather than exhibit superfluous flourish, eighteenth-century modern expression was to be concise; since it was thought to serve as the outward appearance or costume of thought, it was generally required to be sober, modest, rational—as certainly befit language intended to represent the thought of the Age of Enlightenment—and, one cannot help but think, morally good. Meaning was not to be clouded by virtue of its performance in speech; it was not to be conveyed through individual speech acts, but through universally sanctioned repositories of knowledge, such as the dictionary and, ironically, the Bible. Certainly the Age of Reason was characterized in good measure by the rise of science, among other disciplines, and scholars generally agree that the rise of the nation-state during this era displaced the Church (Catholic, Anglican, and Protestant alike) as the foremost institutional organizing force in society. Yet the Church had not fully ceded its role as a pre-eminent guiding force at this point in Western history, and was still viewed by many as an institution whose doctrines put forward universally valid truths. In light of the contending forces at work between the church and the state, metaphors employed in eighteenth-century British literary and social discourse were required to deal in what was considered generally and universally acceptable to one, the other, or both institutions.

Terence Hawkes points out that such metaphors as these would "need no audience to 'complete' them, to respond to or join in with any thought-process that springs" (33) from the center of a culture that formed itself around ideals of national unity and Christian morality. Equiano exemplifies many aspects of this convention of metaphor in of his *Narrative*, so much so that a number of his reviewers commented on the sobriety of his prose even as they remarked the "interesting" picaresque nature of his life story and its narrative of spiritual conversion.[2] David Punter, in his 2007 book *Metaphor*, goes so far as to claim that eighteenth-century reception of Equiano's text was rooted not in Equiano's own crafted and purposeful metaphorical prose, but in the text itself as "a kind of metaphor" that accorded with currents in contemporary eighteenth-century social discourse, such as Christianity and freedom. He begins by wondering:

> One might ask why the word 'interesting' needs to be in [the title of Equiano's *Interesting Narrative*]: is it, perhaps, because otherwise the life of an ex-slave might indeed be deemed uninteresting? Is it indeed because the readership might have misgivings about the ability of an African to write a narrative, to give an account of himself, in any way that might be interesting to a white reader? The whole structure of Equiano's book is itself a kind of metaphor, because in it, he both recounts his life as a slave and gives some account of the circumstances under which he obtained his freedom, and of what followed from that; but it is simultaneously, in a way which may remind us of the four levels of classical Biblical interpretation, an account of his discovery of God, of his adoption of Christianity. We might then call this a narrative of redemption, which assumes a mythic or metaphorical structure taken over precisely from the culture of those masters whom Equiano is trying to evade. . . .[3]

Of course, the phrase "interesting narrative" appears in a number of titles that were published in the eighteenth and nineteenth centuries on both sides of the Atlantic.[4] In adopting it, Equiano follows a tropological convention of memoir and autobiography that has less to do with his racial identity (that is, whether a book written by a black man could be of interest to white readers, as Punter suggests), than with his intention to attract an intelligent and sympathetic audience to his text by way of a titular phrase well known to a transatlantic readership. It seems equally untenable that Equiano's entire text should be read as a metaphor because, in Punter's words, it "both recounts his life as a slave and gives some account of the circumstances under which he obtained his freedom." Equiano certainly accomplishes both of these goals in his autobiography, yet, complex though they may be, neither of these narrative strategies translates into metaphor at the level of discourse. And while I agree that Equiano's use of Biblical discourse, which I expound at length in the second section of this chapter, gets him closest to the hermeneutics of scriptural narration, I argue that Equiano's use of metaphor goes well beyond the narrative of redemption Punter underscores here.

This is so because although Equiano upholds the conventions of eighteenth-century narrative by adopting a plot structure that approximates secular myth and epic as well as the narrative strategies of Biblical texts—a point I take to be of inestimable importance to understanding Equiano's *Narrative*, as I discuss at length in the final section of this chapter—he also breaks these conventions when he essentially metaphorizes *himself*, not simply his text. As Equiano makes clear in his letter to Parliament, he clings to the hope that positive recognition of the meaning at play in his *Narrative* would, in his words, serve to "actuate" him, both as an individual—a subject in the modern world—and as a transfigured symbolic representation of Africans everywhere in the Old and New Worlds, for it is toward their freedom that he hopes to be an instrument. Equiano's faith in the power of writing to right social and moral wrongs impels him toward the public sphere via the medium of metaphor. Equiano writes that he believes his text to be "wholly devoid of literary merit" (xxi), yet this sort of modesty is itself a well-noted eighteenth-century convention. Equiano is concerned, through writing and specifically through sophisticated, complex metaphorical constructions that are both discursive and imagistic, with the disclosing of a subjectivity that is not self-doubting but self-assured, and that contends at once with the national and the spiritual in an effort to emerge as the embodiment of freedom.

From this perspective, I am interested in describing how Equiano accomplishes the disclosure of his being by devising a metaphorical discourse that interrogates the limits of his national identity, even as he takes advantage of a metaphorical, onto-theological language of the spiritual and the personal. Much has been made of Equiano's insistence upon literacy, his well-known trope of the talking book, and his activities as a slave overseer. Scholars have engaged in sustained debates over Equiano's origins and the possibilities for national belonging available to him during his era. What I am concerned to examine in greater detail is how Equiano profits from the intricacies of metaphorical language in his quest to give expression to his being, to make his being known to his readership. His language shows that he has inherited ways of thinking about and revealing or conveying being from two chief sources: Biblical discourse and a philosophical discourse on national belonging. In both Biblical language and nationalist theory (that is, philosophies and discourses on the nation-state that were taking shape during the era in which Equiano wrote), Equiano finds metaphors of being. In both the spiritual and the secular, he reveals the seeds of a polysemy that is driven by tropological constructions that served, to a great degree, as the motivity behind what it meant to be a modern subject in the late eighteenth century.

I grant that these notions of modernity are not always our own. However, the eighteenth-and early nineteenth-century thought of many philosophers of the nation-state and national identity who were Equiano's contemporaries, and against whose theories of subjectivity and racial oppression Equiano wrote, was substantiated, often contrary to their own explicitly stated intentions, by a language that could be read as that of a secular Christianity (this is especially so in the work of Immanuel Kant and Georg W. F. Hegel), or, at the very least, a secular morality (e.g., the essays of Joseph Addison and Richard Steele). Thus, the collocation of spiritual and nationalist metaphors at work in Equiano's text is not as oddly "pre-modern" as it might first appear. Spiritual metaphorical discourse is not senseless, as is sometimes assumed, and it is worthwhile to analyze this discourse in relation to philosophical metaphors of the nation because the sacred discourse Equiano champions lays claims to meaningfulness, to an ontological revelation of being and truth, and, importantly, to an ethics of moral humanistic action. My intention is to clarify the relation between the metaphorical discourse Equiano employs, and the referential dimension of his text, which serves to project his sense of being into the world about him. Equiano works to secure for himself a home in that world by encouraging his readers to undertake radical moral action that will ensure the abolition of slavery even as they, through an ethical, phenomenological practice of reading, "actuate" his being.

The Rhetoric of the Image: Being and Becoming in Equiano's Use of Portraiture

With these considerations in mind, I wish to return for a moment to my earlier discussion of Equiano's use of imagery and visual symbols in his portrait, in which one finds very much alive the sort of spiritual and nationalist discourses I discuss above. Equiano gives one the impression that he consciously uses the symbols of his portrait to convey his being toward the future even as he is absent from our own time. But what exactly constitutes an image, and what is the image's relationship to figurative language? W. J. T. Mitchell seems to speak directly to an analysis of Equiano's portrait when he compellingly argues that images "are not just a particular kind of sign, but something like an actor on the historical stage, a presence or character endowed with legendary status, a history that parallels and participates in the stories we tell ourselves about our own evolution from creatures 'made in the image' of a creator, to creatures who make themselves and their world in their own image" (*Iconology* 9). Taking these thoughts into account, if Equiano's image is a sign, then it functions by way of an inscription and conceptualization that could be described as spiritual. Further, by defining an image as a sign, Mitchell imparts to it the function of sound, as though the image were analogous to language and Equiano were speaking to us through it. Equiano's image would, then, employ a language, a rhetoric, as Roland Barthes maintains images do. The nature of the meaning it conveys could thus rightly be called linguistic, and its intention could be construed as that of a writer who, as Mitchell puts it with a Biblical trope of his own, makes himself and his "world in [his] own image." In other words, we may rightly read Equiano's image as a radical revisioning of and engagement with the world about him after a fashion that approximates the existential as well as the theological.

Equiano's portrait was initially rendered as a painting, completed by the miniaturist William Denton and subsequently reproduced in the engraving by Daniel Orme that is used as the frontispiece of the *Narrative*. Biographer Vincent Carretta writes that Equiano intentionally "chose [these two] artists to create and reproduce his likeness" (*Equiano the African* 280), and in so doing he thus creates his own image *purposefully*. A purposeful, intentional image, Barthes has argued, "immediately yields a first message whose substance is linguistic." It disseminates signifieds in a manner that is not easily mistaken because the signifieds of the intentional imagistic message "are formed *a priori* by certain attributes" of its subject ("Rhetoric of the Image" 33). If we consider further that the word *image* is linked etymologically to the root of the Latin word *imitari*, meaning "to imitate," or, in its Greek sense, mimesis or representation, then today's reader of the *Narrative* is faced not only with the question of the intentionality of Equiano's portrait, but also with the intentionality of representation at work in this image. Barthes argues that "the image is in a certain manner the *limit* of meaning," and yet it still "permits the consideration of a veritable ontology of the process of signification" (32, italics in original). In other words, Barthes insists that the image not only casts into relief its own system of meaning making, but also implies here, by using a term such as "ontology," or the study of being, in relation to "signification" and "image," that the process of meaning making in which the image facilitates an articulation of subjectivity, in the dual sense of "voicing" subjectivity (that is, an articulating "I" speaks subjectivity through the image), and projecting subjectivity toward a radically revisioned world through the intersection of two or more realms of experience, such as history and memory.

Barthes' definition of the image as a structure of language that permits an ontology of signification calls us to return to the likeness that Equiano provides us, and to look more closely at the elements that most importantly constitute its language and meaning: Equiano's European clothing, his appearance and bearing (that is, his body), his direct gaze into the eye of the painter and the reader, and the Bible he holds open for our perusal in a gesture that suggests an offering. The most significant aspects of this image are the body and the Bible, both of which may be read as textual and symbolic. Because Equiano's portrait also contains textual matter, we may rightly call it an image-text without contending that the Biblical writing simply intrudes upon the portrait or is, in some way, superfluous. On the contrary, the Biblical text seems to enhance the portrait in a number of ways by referring to a specific Biblical passage that will provide the reader with supplemental meaning. Like the letter it accompanies, the portrait does the work of prefatory material at the same time that it serves as paratextual material. I will say in brief before returning to this point later (and recalling the discussion of Charles W. Mills's work that I undertake in chapter 2) that Equiano's portrait, and specifically the image of his body, is in dialogic relation with the discourses of national identity most prevalent in his day. Further, it comments in a mediated fashion on Equiano's belief in the capacity of Biblical language to reveal truth and being, and prefaces Equiano's textual use of such language.

If we say that the portrait imparts a message whose substance is linguistic, then we should also consider the nature of its imagistic language, that is, whether its language is literal or figurative. Thus, we should be mindful of the iconicity or symbolism of the portrait. For our purposes, I will define an icon as a symbolic representation, and I will define a symbol as a figure that represents something other than what it is. Descending etymologically from the Greek *symballein*, symbol literally means "thrown together." A symbol collects and provisionally stabilizes social and linguistic meanings that are often themselves metaphorical and polysemic. Equiano uses his portrait to display for his reader a collection of visual symbols intended to convey a sensible image of himself; and the reader in turn uses the icons and symbols Equiano supplies in the portrait to form associations in his or her mind that ultimately gain expression in language. Equiano's body, his clothing, his gaze, and the Biblical text all take on iconic and symbolic functions, in that their meaning and value are derived from their context. And not simply the context provided by the details of the portrait, but also the context determined by the society in which Equiano lived and wrote. These aspects of the portrait might be read literally since they are each defined through the lexicon of Great Britain, that is, Great Britain's official dictionary. Yet the shift from a literal reading of these elements to a figurative one is necessitated by the intentional selection and arrangement of them. What stands out are the direct nature of Equiano's gaze, the propriety of his dress (which marks him as a member of the newly forming middle class and as a Westerner), the color of his skin (which, conversely, marks him as an outsider and a member of an enslaved class of people), and the text to which the Bible he offers us is open, Acts 4:12.

Recalling that one among the many aspects of metaphor is its movement from the literal to the figurative, these iconic and symbolic details of the portrait emerge as metaphorical elements that exist in a semiotic relationship with one another. Once we move past the "literal" attributes of the portrait (the red coat, the open book, etc.), we are then drawn to the metaphoric expression of the portrait via its symbols and the paradoxes these symbols seek implicitly to engage. For example, the color of Equiano's skin stands directly at odds with the manner of his dress. As I discuss in greater detail in the following section of this chapter, blackness was not generally taken to symbolize the civilization and culture that Equiano's clothing suggests. Neither does his blackness immediately indicate belonging to the Christian faith, as his offering of the Bible (as if it were he who was proselytizing) affirms. Yet Equiano's portrait seeks to appose these internal schisms of meaning through what can reasonably be called a logical disruption of conventional thought and a transposition of epistemological categories. Because symbolic representation can put forward contradictory elements that interfere with orthodox thought, the portrait possesses the power to elaborate what it represents and to extend beyond its own borders in the denotation of Equiano's subjectivity.

The portrait's rhetoric certainly supplements the written chronicle of Equiano's life, and therefore serves as a corollary of his expression of his being by setting forth an ontological program that is paired with a narrative of Equiano's written eyewitness accounts of historical events (for instance, the Transatlantic Slave Trade, battles of the Seven Years War, and a historic expedition to the North Pole), as well as personal events that constitute his individual experience. Pictorial modernity was imagined by Equiano and a number of other eighteenth-century African writers not in terms and themes of bodily fragments (as Linda Nochlin has so aptly shown with regard to the pictorial representations created by a number of eighteenth-century European artists[5]), but in terms of bodily wholeness, or at least the allusion thereto. The wholeness evoked by the portrait underscores the importance of constructing historical being through the pictorial medium. At the forefront of Equiano's intentionality as regards his portrait is the perseverance of his image for the benefit of future generations of readers. Thus, Equiano's past—memorialized in his autobiography through text and image—engages the future (our present) with vigor. Actuation (his "becoming" an Englishman, as he puts it, as well as an "instrument" of freedom for his enslaved African "brethren"), vision (Equiano's gaze), and the appearance of his body constitute the central metaphors of the portrait's visual rhetoric. To my mind, Equiano's portrait serves as paratextual matter, in that it is not superfluous, but serves as a portal that permits a more profound understanding of the metaphorics of his text.

Becoming and Belonging: National Desire and Spiritual Being in Equiano's Time

As with his portrait, the imagery of the personal is always interjected into the historical in the text of Equiano's *Narrative*, and he repeatedly engages our present by asking us to think with him as he draws upon the Bible in an effort to bestow a sense of order and meaning on the often chaotic journeys of his life. The Bible is the greatest literary influence on Equiano, and its metaphorical language regularly serves to answer the many ontological "whys" engendered by Equiano's life circumstances: Why is he a slave? Why is his life repeatedly spared while others perish?

In their engagement with such existential questions and in an extension of the imagistic, figurative language of his image, the metaphors Equiano draws from the Bible serve as the vehicles of the major ontological and epistemological thrust of the *Narrative*: Equiano uses them both to express and explain his reason for being, the significance of his individual existence, and the meaningfulness of his life in relation to the world. Indeed, the Bible seems to figure for Equiano as a national text with which modern subjects, and certainly his readers, were expected to identify and whose metaphors they would easily grasp. As Northrup Frye has argued convincingly, the Bible "set up an imaginative framework . . . within which Western literature had operated down to the eighteenth century and is to a certain extent still operating" (*Great Code* xi). It is, perhaps, the first great book of forgetting, wherein secular existence is methodically placed under erasure and replaced with the ideal of divine spiritual being.

However, traditional historicism grants little significance to Biblical language and writing, and instead grants secular nationalist discourse a much higher level of criticism. Homi Bhabha reminds us that traditional historicism generally grounds and gives force to the idea of national identity as an "empirical sociological category" (*The Location of Culture* 140), a holistic entity. Even so, the very idea of "nationness" also produces an ambivalence of being that becomes quite evident as one seeks to perform the act of "writing the nation," an act that is itself, Bhabha concludes, an "apparatus of symbolic power" that "produces a slippage of categories, like sexuality, class affiliation, territorial paranoia, or 'cultural difference'" (140). He invokes Frederic Jameson's argument that the very inscription of the individual story in writing outside of the "first world," meaning the West, is, by necessity, a species of national allegory in what Jameson calls "third world literature." Such an allegory entails a "laborious telling of the collectivity itself" even as it strives to tell the story of the individual (qtd. in Bhabha 140).

While Jameson's theory of the individual story as national allegory is seductive, for reasons that will become apparent over the course of our discussion here, this theory does not fully hold in Equiano's case. The national allegory is shifted or dislodged, largely because Equiano cannot begin his tale with a proper account of his origins, an artifice necessary to imagining national belonging. The violence of his displacement from Africa and his subsequent enslavement and loss of memory of his early childhood have the effect of barring him from any real appreciation of a fixed homeland in which to ground his own sense of ontological origins. It quickly becomes evident to the reader that Equiano's sense of belonging (which is regularly at work in autobiography—the writing and situating of a life) finds itself caught up in a continual process of transformation, or becoming. As we read the text, there is something in its composition that calls us to lend attention to evolving ideas of desire and "longing," an unspoken metaphor (Equiano does not directly employ it) within a word that his writing does evoke consistently: "belonging." "Long" and "belong" are, respectively, analogues of distance (desire and absence) and identification (selfhood and presence), and the metaphor consists in the process of meaning at work between these two words. In the *Narrative*, the tension between these poles of being gives rise to figural articulations of nation, race, and anagogy that work in tandem with the displacement Equiano experiences and the social death through which he perseveres. Subsequent to the violence of Equiano's enslavement, and his experiences of exile and errantry, the conception he works toward in his narrative is one of enlightened moral action, induced by a persistent—but unfulfilled—longing for "home" and mitigated by his desire for actuation through text.

We will take a further step in our understanding of the intersection of moral action—(what Equiano refers to in his letter to Parliament as being "actuated" by the reading of his text and adherence to the "instruction" (208) provided in his *Narrative*) and what I take to indicate a process of transformation, or "becoming," (an evolution of being that emerges from a longing for home, and a desire for "belonging") if we ask what, on the side of metaphors of actuation, can be considered as the counterpart to what, on the side of metaphors of home or belonging, is given as being in the eighteenth century life of an emancipated slave. We have already taken a step toward grasping a sense of the problem by questioning the correlation between personal and national narratives. The analysis that follows takes shape in the face of a vocabulary of reference, or origins, that is at work in the projection of concepts of nationhood in eighteenth-century prose, poetry, and philosophy. To be sure, authors of texts that propound such concepts—Hume, Kant, and others—intended to reflect their belief in an absolute, of which the nation-state was, Hegel argued early in the nineteenth century, the avatar and the Idea. Here I draw our attention to the concepts of morality, being, and the nation-state as each is articulated by way of metaphorical mediations in the work of European thinkers who were Equiano's contemporaries and who themselves commented on the possibilities of national belonging in relation to the limits of racial identity. A reflection upon these concepts as given within the world of philosophical text allows us to take a brief look at the concepts of being with which Equiano would contend and to which he would respond through image and text.

I have oriented my discussion in this section to reflect a passage of thought from broader European philosophical discourse that is highly dependent upon metaphors of the body and spirit, to the English public sphere. I will show how philosophical discourse and the discourse of the public sphere equally share in this dependence on metaphors of the body as concepts of national and racial identity are worked out in an age during which Western societies were rocked by the American, French, and Haitian revolutions. Enlightenment era thought such as that which I sample below is nonetheless characterized by a deep faith in human reason. It was also well agreed upon across national lines, such that thinkers like Kant, Hume, and Rousseau not only influenced one another, but were in fundamental agreement as to what were the pressing philosophical and social concerns of their day, in spite of their national differences. Amidst the era's revolutions in science and knowledge, Westerners and non-Westerners alike often experienced profound changes in social, political, and economic life even as they faced problems of moral uncertainty and feelings of alienation and social fragmentation. The fundamental metaphysical divisions that marked the philosophical thought of the era—reason vs. emotion, subjectivity (knowing subject) vs. objectivity (objects known in the world), freedom (moral autonomy) vs. nature (governed by natural laws), and mind (rational) vs. body (sensuous)—also stood as social challenges that demanded resolution. The pressing task was to ensure a unity of reason that did away with such schisms as these while safeguarding intellectual and social harmony. In short, a new relationship between mind and body had to be established, yet in all cases this relationship was predicated upon theories of racial difference and national identity.

Equiano entered this debate after a fashion that could in no way be considered insignificant. While Immanuel Kant and other speculative thinkers insisted, at least on the surface of things, upon a racialized secular philosophy of moral society in their attempts to achieve a rational and harmonious unity, Equiano—as a participant in the public sphere—worked to overcome the mind/body dualism by upholding the benefits of national identity even as he worked to elide racial difference by underscoring the importance of spiritual wisdom and earthly good works. His is a fascinating and complex approach: throughout the *Narrative*, Equiano argues that intellectual enlightenment, which, he states, has come to him through his introduction to English social principles, must be coupled with Christian works of faith in order to achieve actuation, and primary among these works must be, he makes clear, the abolition of slavery. The long and short of it is that he offers his account of his own life as an exemplar of this fundamental truth, and further challenges and engages his readers by calling upon them to "actuate" his being by acting upon the "jewels of instruction" he gives them in his text. Equiano uses onto-theological metaphors to provide a meaningful alternative to the racism and secularism of the Enlightenment, which deployed metaphorical discourses to insist upon lofty states of consciousness and morality even as they permitted and at times promoted the heinous immoralities of racism, xenophobia, and slavery.

To demonstrate my argument, I begin by turning to a few exemplary philosophical European texts that employ metaphor in an effort to make apparent the collective national subject as it was theorized in Equiano's time. I will present three in succession, followed by a discussion of the "sites" at which this subject becomes legible or recognizable. First, a selection from Jean-Jacques Rousseau's *The Geneva Manuscript* (1756):

> Instantly, in the place of the private person of each contracting party [that is, each individual entering into the "social contract"], this act of association produces a moral and collective body, composed of as many members as there are voices in the assembly, and to which the common self gives formal unity, life, and will. This public person, formed thus by the union of all the others, generally assumes the name body politic, which its members call *State* when it is passive, *Sovereign* when active, *Power* when comparing it to similar bodies. As for the members themselves, they take the name *People* collectively, and individually are called *Citizens* as members of the City or participants in the sovereign authority, and *Subjects* as subject to the laws of the State. But these terms, rarely used with complete precision, are often mistaken for one another, and it is enough to know how to distinguish them when the meaning of discourse so requires.[6]

The second text, from Immanuel Kant's *The Metaphysics of Morals* (1785), likewise presents a logic of metaphors in relation to national identity, but Kant constructs the individual's place in society primarily in terms of the *familiai*, rather than in relation to state power and the "social contract," as does Rousseau:

> The human beings who make up a nation can, as natives of the country, be represented as analogous to descendants from a common ancestry (*congeniti*) even if this is not in fact the case. But in an intellectual sense or for the purposes of right, they can be thought of as the offspring of a common mother (the

republic), constituting, as it were, a single family (*gens, natio*), whose members (the citizens) are all equal by birth. These citizens will not intermix with any neighboring people who live in a state of nature, but will consider them ignoble, even though such savages for their own part may regard themselves as superior on account of the lawless freedom they have chosen. The latter likewise constitute national groups, but they do not constitute states.[7]

And finally, the Scottish philosopher David Hume, who uses general metaphors of ontogenetic resemblance, writes in the 1754 version of "Of National Characters":

> Where a number of men are united into one political body, the occasions of their intercourse must be so frequent, for defence [sic], commerce, and government, that, together with the same speech or language, they must acquire a resemblance in their national manners, and have a common or national character, as well as a personal one, peculiar to each individual.[8]

The three texts I have chosen make use of metaphors—most of them bio-political metaphors, as in the "body politic," the "common self," the "common mother," or a "state of nature"—in order to describe the attributes of the nation-state, an "Idea," as Hegel calls it, that demands, in Rousseau's words, "unity, life, and will." Hence the discourse of the nation-state breathes life into the very idea of the national entity by way of ontological metaphors. It is in this way that nationalist discourse is able to imbue the idea of the nation with human characteristics while simultaneously insisting that the nation-state supersedes the wants and demands of the individual. Thus Rousseau may speak of the union of private persons as the "body politic." Kant may write that the members of the nation "can be thought of," or imagined, as "the offspring of a common mother (the republic)." And Hume may argue that the national character takes shape through frequent social intercourse, whereby citizens "acquire a resemblance in their manners." These sorts of ontological metaphors, with their sedimented and highly textured meanings, are examples of the widely grasped and conventional tropes of which Hawkes speaks in his periodization of metaphorical discourse.

Analysis of these tropes reveals that the discourse of the nation-state—inherently metaphorical—is intended to produce a reality of its own. It seeks to produce the effect of a collective consciousness, and it does so by way of metaphors of being that were widely understood and accepted, and thus required no undue intellectual effort on the part of the reader to complete them. Such a reality is highly dependent upon a physical discourse, one that treats nationalistic concepts through metaphors of bodies and selves. Thus the people become the body politic, the republic becomes the mother, and the citizens eventually come to resemble one another through repeated dynamic encounters characterized as borrowing and mimeticism, and by way of these processes, one comes to "belong," one "becomes" a member of the nation-state. Rousseau's recognition of the fluidity of the terms he uses and the need for contextual readings underscores how such discourse seeks to refigure reality by establishing some sort of simulacrum in order to make reality more navigable, more manageable, and, ironically, more "real." Nationalistic discourse such as that which we see here makes observations regarding the order of things; indeed, it devises its own processes, its own order, its own logic, and thus we are able to read this discourse comfortably within the framework of philosophical thought. The discourse of the nation-state—which is made manifest in what we call nationalism—responds to reality with ontological metaphors, and such metaphors ostensibly serve as the motored configurations of harmonious modern social being.

Further attention to the status of personhood in the writings of European philosophers who were Equiano's contemporaries easily convinces one that the *philosophes*, while deeply engaged in notions of personal and moral freedom within the boundaries of the nation-state, remained in a state of tension as regards the subject of racial slavery and its relation to the body politic. The denunciations of slavery by John Locke and the Baron de Montesquieu, for example, rarely went beyond the obvious in their analyses of the institution. The writings of Locke in particular adopt a double-sided stance on the issue: he condemns slavery on moral grounds, but not on economic, material grounds. Indeed, some philosophers held a personal stake in the financial interests of slavery. Peter Gay reminds us that "Locke's part in the establishment of the Carolina colonies, and his investments in the slave-trading monopoly, the Royal African Company, shows plainly enough that actual slavery did not trouble his conscience."[9] It is by now well known that Richard Steele, a founder of *The Tatler* and *The Spectator*, maintained a plantation in the West Indies. Trading in slaves and depending upon their labor and servitude for a life of comfort came to be commonplace among a number of presumably liberal writers and thinkers of the era, not least of whom is the celebrated American nationalist, revolutionist, and democratic philosopher, Thomas Jefferson.

By extension, then, racism and xenophobia are widely noted in their writings. Hume's well-known footnote, which was appended to the 1754 version of "Of National Characters," is echoed by Kant in *Observations on the Feeling of the Beautiful and Sublime* (1764), and provides an apt example. Hume expounds the concept of "nation" and national belonging in terms of the ethos of the national citizen. These collective and common characteristics arise from "moral causes . . . which are fitted to work on the mind as motives or reasons, and which render a peculiar set of manners habitual to us" (244). Accordingly, he argues, these characteristics are based upon mimesis, and it is in this way that the body politic comes to life: men convene to build commerce and prosperity, imitating their so-called superiors in order to spread ideas that would advance the national collective. As is the case in a number of Enlightenment-era writings on nationalism, the idea of race emerges as inextricably bound to the possibility of national belonging. And since, for Hume, the nation-state is predicated on an ability to mimic national norms, the power of xenophobia and racial exclusion largely forms the basis of national belonging. Blacks, Hume asserts in his note, are capable of only the meanest mimesis, and thus were precluded from membership:

> I am apt to suspect the negroes [sic], and in general all other species of men (for there are four or five different kinds) to be naturally inferior to the whites. There never was a civilized nation of any other complexion than white, nor even any individual eminent either in action or speculation. No ingenious manufactures amongst them, no arts, no sciences . . . Such a uniform and constant difference could not happen in so many countries and ages if nature had not made an original distinction betwixt these breeds of men. Not to mention our colonies, there are Negroe [sic] slaves dispersed all over Europe, of which none ever discovered any symptoms of ingenuity; tho' low people, without education, will start up amongst us, and distinguish themselves in every profession. In Jamaica indeed they talk of one negroe [sic] as a man of parts and learning; but tis likely he is admired for very slender accomplishments, like a parrot, who speaks a few words plainly. (252n1)

Hume's sentiments were influential on the thought of Immanuel Kant, who had long been an admirer of Hume's philosophical works. In *Observations on the Feeling of the Beautiful and the Sublime*, Kant paraphrases

Hume's sentiments so completely as he himself works to sort out the characteristics of various national groups that I need cite him only in brief: "The Negroes of Africa have by nature no feeling that rises above the trifling . . . So fundamental is the difference between these two races of man, and it appears to be as great in regard to mental capacities as in color."[10] He even goes so far as to say that the Negro's color rendered any idea s/he articulated "stupid," though he might otherwise have thought the utterance worthwhile had the voice been that of a white man. Here I will cite him at length:

> In the lands of the black, what better can one expect than what is found prevailing, namely the feminine sex in the deepest slavery? A despairing man is always a strict master over anyone weaker, just as with us that man is always a tyrant in the kitchen who outside his own house hardly dares to look anyone in the face. Of course, Father Labat[11] reports that a Negro carpenter, whom he reproached for haughty treatment toward his wives, answered: "You whites are indeed fools, for first you make great concessions toward your wives, and afterward you complain when they drive you mad." And it might be that there were something in this which perhaps deserved to be considered; but in short, this fellow was quite black from head to foot, a clear proof that what he said was stupid. (*Observations* 113)

Lost on Kant is the irony of his statement: given the horrific nature of slavery and the depths of whites' involvement in the slave trade, he fails to consider the depraved nature of the Europeans who set themselves up as "strict masters" over the Africans. His sardonic comments are intended, no doubt, to inject a bit of unfortunate racist humor into an essay that is full of similar misfortunes regarding "national" groups such as Arabs and the Chinese. Considering that such animosity as Kant's greeted the simple deductions of a black carpenter, we cannot doubt that the words of "a stranger" such as Equiano were met with skepticism if not out right disdain and disbelief, as is evidenced in a number of the letters Equiano appended to later editions of his text.[12] What is more striking is the certainty with which Kant and Hume deemed blacks to be incapable of both elevated thought and national belonging and, further, to be a threat to the cultural cohesion of the nation.

In light of this vein of philosophic thought, English writers in particular often warned their readers against the contagion of foreign elements—people as well as goods—entering the nation. For instance, the narrator of Richard Steele's "Brunetta and Phillis," a satirical sketch resembling a comedy of manners and appearing in the June 1, 1711 issue of *The Spectator*, provides his reader with a construction of the limits of English social standards, specifically those concerning contact between English citizens of the metropole and those living abroad in Britain's New World colonies. The story's most remarkable feature is a narrative voice that directs without seeming to do so. That the reader will willingly follow along and grasp his metaphorical intent Steele naturally assumes. He begins by telling the reader that Phillis and Brunetta were first childhood playmates and later adolescent rivals. Central to the story's message is that both girls were born in Cheapside, London, a prosperous neighborhood where a good number of merchants and shop owners lived and kept trade. The wealth of this class, which rose to prominence from the ashes of feudalism, likely made them fine targets for Steele. He himself was not of the aristocracy, though he secured financial comfort through a profitable first marriage to a woman whose property included the aforementioned Barbados plantation and its slave chattel. Steele, a one-time gazetteer to Queen Anne, had deeply immersed himself in Whig politics, and once a shift in the political winds came, took to composing moralizing pieces having to do with innocence and virtue. The moralistic thrust of "Brunetta and Phillis" comes in the piece's closing paragraphs, and vital to its point is that each woman, exquisitely beautiful but lacking in class and social grace, had married a West Indian planter and then moved to Barbados, a colony largely populated with African slaves. There, their rivalry grew in measure with the vulgar slave wealth to which they had become privy through marriage. Their competition finally consumed them:

> It would be endless to enumerate the many Occasions on which these irreconcileable [sic] Beauties laboured to excell each other; but in Process of Time it happened, that a Ship put into the Island consigned to a Friend of Phillis, who had Directions to give her the Refusal of all Goods for Apparel before Brunetta could be alarmed of their Arrival. He did so, and Phillis was dressed in few Days in a Brocade more gorgeous and costly than had ever before appeared in that Latitude. Brunetta languished at the Sight, and could by no Means come up to the Bravery of her Antagonist. She communicated her Anguish of Mind to a faithful Friend, who by an Interest in the Wife of Phillis's Merchant, procured a Remnant of the same Silk for Brunetta.

Phillis took Pains to appear in all publick Places where she
was sure to meet Brunetta; Brunetta was now prepared for the
Insult, and came to a publick Ball in a plain black Silk Mantua,
attended by a beautiful Negro Girl in a Petticoat of the same
Brocade with which Phillis was attired. This drew the Attention
of the whole Company, upon which the unhappy Phillis swooned
away, and was immediately conveyed to her House. As soon as
she came to herself she fled from her Husband's House, went
on board a Ship in the Road, and is now landed in inconsolable
Despair at Plymouth.[13]

The dialectic of body and apparel that is at issue in Equiano's portrait is
likewise at work in the story of Brunetta and Phillis. The hermeneutic woven

into this passage builds upon the relationship Steele had developed with his readership, which had come to anticipate his satirical brand of morality. The author pretends to be merely the narrator of a story he describes as "maelancholy," and there appears to be but one interpretation to be had here: the notions of honor and virtue at play in the competition of Brunetta and Phillis find their culmination in a lesson on communication through one's physical self-presentation in society. In brief, Steele speaks to the stylization of the female body, black as well as white. Brunetta conquers her rival not simply by donning a beautiful understated gown of elegance and high quality (wholly contrary to the tawdriness Steele describes as common to inhabitants of the West Indies, indicated by the inappropriateness of wearing a dress made of brocade—a heavy, rich fabric usually woven of silk, with an ornate raised pattern in gold or silver—in the heat of the Caribbean), but also by dressing her servant girl in a remnant of the brocade fabric from which Phillis's gown was made. The "company's" witnessing of this spectacle actually seals Phillis's undoing, and precipitates her hysteria—through which she, in the eyes of her public, actually regains some ground, as hysteria indicated to the eighteenth-century reader an attestation of feminine emotionalism and, thus, virtue. However, while the reader may hold Phillis in sympathy, Brunetta cleverly emerges as the victor by means of her manipulation of the body of her slave. Not only does the anonymous Negro girl wear the same brocade as Phillis; she wears it as a petticoat—an undergarment, yes, but one that figured prominently in eighteenth-century fashion. Petticoats were often worn visibly through an inverted V cut into the overgown. Brunetta raises herself, as mistress, above Phillis by demonstrating her financial ability to attire so richly her slave. In the scene portrayed by the painter above (Figure 1), the fabric is used not as a petticoat, but as a fully visible skirt, making the insult that much more impactful. Phillis's shame comes by way of an alchemy of fashion and style. In the eyes of the spectators, she is reduced to a level beneath that of the slave. Steele intends us to read her retreat to Plymouth (in "inconsolable Despair") as a condemnation of her vulgarity. And the humor of the piece consists in the insult of dressing a Negro attendant in a manner approximating the habit of an English lady.

While Steele's vignette is concerned with the manners of those who migrated to the Caribbean, Alexander Pope gives voice to his own anxieties regarding commodification and foreign contagion in *Windsor Forest* (1713). Pope, an associate of Steele and Joseph Addison who contributed pastoral poetry and prose to *The Spectator*, drew Equiano's attention largely through his translation of Homer's *Iliad*, published in 1720. Pope's translation of

Homer made the classical era poet accessible to eighteenth-century English readers, and was widely respected.[14] The significance of Pope's translation was certainly not lost upon Equiano, who cites it a number of times in his *Narrative*. Pope presented Homer's *Iliad* in a manner that underscored the virtues of dignity and morality. Likewise, Pope's topographical poem *Windsor Forest*, completed in the aftermath of the Treaty of Utrecht (1713), celebrates the moral peace that came with the granting of the Spanish Asiento to England.[15] Pope's preoccupation lies with outside forces that touch England's shore, and his concern over commercial and social exchange with the outside world comes through in these lines:

> The Time shall come, when free as Seas or Wind
> Unbounded *Thames* shall flow for all Mankind
> Whole Nations enter with each swelling Tyde,
> And Seas but join the Regions they divide;
> Earth's distant Ends our Glory shall behold,
> And the new World launch forth to seek the Old.
> Then Ships of uncouth Form shall stem the Tyde,
> And Feather'd People crowd my wealthy Side,
> And naked Youth and Painted Chiefs admire
> Our Speech, our Colour, and our strange Attire!
> Oh stretch thy reign, fair *Peace!* from Shore to Shore,
> Till Conquest cease, and Slav'ry be no more.[16]

In these lines, the freedom mentioned by Pope evokes an anxiety that is reflected in metaphors such as "ships of uncouth form," "stem the tyde," "feather'd people," "painted chiefs," and even "peace," which becomes a metaphor by virtue of the sentence in which Pope situates the word. The seas—analogized to the Thames—no longer separate nations or regions, but serve instead as relational spaces between the colony and the metropole. Pope's preoccupation with the immigration of outsiders and the importation of foreign goods into England mirrors that of Joseph Addison in "The Royal Exchange,"[17] but exhibits quite a bit more anxiety. Addison was fascinated by the variety of people and goods he encountered at the Exchange. He thanked merchants for all the wealth to which his eyes were privy. Of them he writes, "there are no more useful members in a commonwealth than merchants. They knit mankind together in mutual intercourse of good offices, distribute the gifts of nature, find work for the poor, add wealth to the rich, and magnificence to the great."[18] Pope's verse and Addison's prose alike depict a curious lack of violence in the amassing of empire. While both writings evidence the complexities that attend strategies to reconcile a moral economy with a financial one, of the two, Pope alone evinces such anxiety regarding commodification. His unease regarding the mixed benefits of the Asiento reveals concerns about foreigners who would thereafter have greater access to England. Pope expects that these outsiders—non-Europeans—will admire English "speech," "colour," and "attire." The savageness of the non-native is juxtaposed against the refined wealth of the English upper-class. The morality inherent in the cessation of war is at odds with the contagion that peaceful trade brings. And while Pope prays for the abolition of the slave trade, it is indeed this trade that has generated the great wealth he extols. Of the writers I discuss here, Steele seems most cognizant of the violence capitalism and imperialism impart to the human psyche. Not surprisingly, however, he lends more attention to the vulnerabilities of English national selfhood than to that of the colonized and the enslaved.

The juxtaposition of metropole and colony, master and slave, brings us back round to the question with which I began this section, regarding the intersection of becoming and belonging, of moral action and the desire for home or nation. In assembling a reading of texts drawn from philosophy, prose, and poetry, I have sought to address the ideological atmosphere of the public to which Equiano addressed himself. My conclusions take shape by force of the examples I have chosen, but these examples are fairly representative of the thought of Equiano's age. We might say as regards the first three texts by Rousseau, Kant, and Hume, that the prescriptions for reading inscribed within them orient the reader to the author in terms that recall the relation of master and slave: the author is one who knows, the reader is one who comes to know through the act of reading. No matter the fervent attention to freedom each writer evinces in the corpus of his writings, the reader is not left free through the act of engaging the text, but finds her- or himself bound to the metaphors of collectivity and national identity each text uses to define its purposes. Each sets itself up as a "normative" system, and only Rousseau, in a closing gesture, allows for the contingencies of context.

The next two examples, drawn from the philosophical writings of Hume and Kant, work to limn the contingencies that function within the metaphorical systems of their texts. In speaking of national characters and the possibility of national belonging, each is compelled to speak once more in figurative terms of the body and, specifically, in terms of those bodies that are not normative. Neither trusts the reader with interpretations; each provides rules of reading that determine the set of answers to questions that arise in relation to the text. Thus we find that through their metaphorical discourse on the national body, we are led to discover those bodies that do not matter, that are rendered abject.

The final examples, drawn from prose and poetry by Steele, Pope, and Addison, may be taken to underscore the strategy of persuasion. They seem, collectively, to effect a shift from the rhetoric of philosophy; the reader is now in a position of authority because she or he is called upon for interpretation. Yet these texts also assume a mediate position, for they demand reading practices that are neither purely rhetorical nor purely hermeneutical. Each calls for a specific sort of moral action alive in the discourse of the philosophers we have seen, and each gives evidence of a desire for the purity of the national collective that may only be achieved if one views the metaphorical nation as an actuated whole purged of racial contagion and impurity. The economies at work in Steele, Pope, and Addison may be the lever that, ironically, pries this whole open, for it is imperial desire—for slaves, for lands, for goods—that leaves the nation-state open to the contagion each of these writers fears. In this field of discourse, Equiano's narrative stands midway within a paradox, somewhere between the national being outlined by the philosophers and the national desire expounded by the writers.

Occupying a mediate space of discourse relieves Equiano of the weight of stasis we encounter in all but the writing of Rousseau. For the reader, Equiano's narrative consists in moving from a static notion of pastness to a dynamic, refigured image of the past that permits the possibility of actuation. Narrative in general serves as a phenomenological *telos* characterized by what Paul Ricoeur, following Edmund Husserl, calls "transcendence within immanence."[19] That is, it permits the writer a site within which to propound the development of a narrative voice that is, of course, bound to its structure (its genre, its plot, in short, the imaginative world constituted within the text), even as it imagines a reader to whom the text and the writer are directed and a text and author toward which the reader is inexorably drawn. In this way, the metaphorical meanings at work in the *Narrative* have the potential to overflow the boundaries of the page and blur temporal lines. While autobiographical narratives provide a phenomenological "home" for the writer—in that his or her thoughts, and the images and experiences related to such thought, abide with and are disclosed by way of the text—by engaging in the act of writing, Equiano projects himself and his past toward the future by assuming an act of reading. It is only through this second phenomenological act—that of the active assumption of and engagement with an imagined act of purposeful rather than passive reading—that both the *Narrative* and its author are actuated or assume the possibility of actuation *beyond* the limits of text. Equiano keeps alive a fragile hope that in the margins of secular reason, there may exist a realm of transcendent spiritual possibilities that can refashion and reorient the world of his readers. His text serves as a medium through which such possibilities might be achieved.

The acts of writing and reading that bring about the intersection of the worlds of both Equiano and his reader create what Toni Morrison has named (with her own apology for so provocative and decontextualized a term) a "third world." The "third world" Morrison describes functions in ways similar to the phenomenological *telos* described by Ricoeur: it is both "snug and open," with the potential to reveal the "interiority of the 'othered.'"[20] For Equiano, this sort of intersection discloses a site of intellection, yes, but it also functions as a catalyst toward actuation and action, where the void psychoanalytic theory names desire is recast as work. That Equiano never sacrifices himself to a detached or seemingly omniscient narrator in his text means that he is the central occupant of the *Narrative*; it is he, himself, who will encounter the reader when their two worlds collide. What strikes us is that through this encounter, he submits himself to the reader and the reader's world, and there he is refigured. It is he who is, as he states, "actuated by the hope of becoming an instrument towards the relief of his suffering countrymen" (xxi). Grasping faith and never losing hope, Equiano intends to write his way home.

Hope in Narrative: Equiano's Biblical Turn

We have now to discuss more fully how Equiano's hope for "actuation"—a tropological articulation appearing as simple, concrete language—comes to enrich the mediation of his text, such that the interweaving of history, memory, and imagination results in a metaphorics of being and becoming. I have alluded to this in discussing the relation—which I have cast into tension, in Equiano's case—of autobiography to national allegory. As I advance my reading of Equiano, I will borrow a key modality from Paul Ricoeur's argument in *Time and Narrative*: that the writing of history does not exclude inscriptions of a historical knowledge of being (an ontology of historical subjectivity). As Ricoeur insists, the writing of history is not something we add to history itself. History, rather, borrows the modes of literature: it "imitates in its own writing the types of emplotment handed down by our literary tradition" (*Time and Narrative* 185). Literature enables us to "read" ourselves *in* history, as critical elements of and actors in the unfolding of history, such that certain modes of relating historical events are rendered recognizably ontological through genres such as tragedy, comedy, and so forth. Writing in its many forms—e.g., autobiography, artistic expression, historiography—thus holds great implications for how writers view themselves as historical beings seeking to relate their experiences to the members of national bodies who regularly receive their work. Just as the writing of history produces the effect of writing a life, autobiography can enact the project of seeing the past. Autobiography, then, puts into play one of the most striking historical effects Aristotle, in the *Rhetoric*, ascribes to metaphor, that of "seeing as."

The historical, metaphorical effect of autobiography—where the writing of one's life story is understood to realize or "actuate" a mimetic project of historiography—should be read as such in studies of the reception and criticism of secular literature in England, in particular, which began in the eighteenth century as an aesthetic practice that bolstered nationalistic and patriotic pride. Such a measure was in order after the Glorious Revolution, which had set differing political factions at odds with one another. As Terry Eagleton reminds us and as we have seen in earlier examples, eighteenth-century "[English] literature did more than 'embody' certain social values. . . . [I]t was a vital instrument for their deeper entrenchment and wider dissemination."[21] Eagleton's words imply a phenomenology at work in the discipline of English literature. Mastering the English language in the eighteenth century meant exposure to broad ranges of British life: literature, religion, philosophy, history, the arts, and the sciences. As we have seen in our discussion of Hume, Kant, and Rousseau, mastery of the language, including its poetic and rhetorical forms, what Walter Benjamin refers to, in broader terms, as mimeticism,[22] emerges as absolutely necessary to any notion of unified national belonging.

Equiano's *Narrative* leads us toward this conclusion, but along the way takes a turn away from the secular national subject central to the philosophical discourse I have discussed, and toward a spiritual subject whose being emerges as "whole" and "actuated" through the coincidence of Christian good works and Christian faith or belief. We read of his immersion in the English Bible, which he treasures among his collection of books. We see in his writing a practice of intertextualism that draws from the writers of the Old Testament, from Homer and Milton, and from historians and abolitionists contemporary to his time, such as Anthony Benezet. His practice gives evidence of the phenomenology of reading that he portrays as central to his psychical development. In a much noted metaphor, Equiano longs to "talk to the books" that he had seen the naval officer Pascal and the young American Richard Baker reading. "Talking to the books," interacting with them (specifically, his Bible) and willfully enacting a collision of his own "real" sphere of being and the textual sphere of Biblical scripture will, Equiano seems certain, permit him access to history; it will allow him to "learn how all things," including he, himself, "had a beginning" (39).

In this second section of the chapter, I will show how Equiano participates—in a contestatory, critical, and counter-cultural fashion—in eighteenth-century Western discourse on being (and the origins of human being) by eschewing or revising a number of the West's central bio-political metaphors. These sorts of metaphors include those exemplified in writings by Kant and Rousseau; yet Equiano, in an even more striking intellectual and rhetorical move, specifically rejects metaphors that evince ideas of racial essentialism and national absolutism that appear in the work of these same leading Western philosophers. Of course, Equiano does construct metaphors that give voice to his anxieties about living as a black man in a white world, such as when he writes of his childhood disappointment when the darkness of his skin will not wash away, as if it were the soiled result of a full day at play with his little white companion, Mary. Some scholars have read this metaphor, as well as the metaphor of the talking book, as evidence that Equiano was ashamed of his blackness. But while Equiano's contemporary, Ukawsaw Gronniosaw, uses the trope of the talking book to convey his certainty that the book would not talk back to him because he is black and despised,[23] Equiano uses this metaphor to convey his awareness not only of the limits of his social and political knowledge (and thus he determines to gain greater enlightenment and understanding through textuality); this metaphor also, more importantly, conveys Equiano's understanding of the ways in which his own humanity was cast into oblivion in European epistemological metaphorics.

Instead of developing bio-political metaphors of national absolutism or racial essentialism, which would, from the perspective of Kant and others, resolve the dualism they saw plaguing eighteenth-century society, Equiano develops metaphors of the spirit as a way of working toward the achievement of historicized and actuated *human* being, and thus his is a discourse on critical humanism that runs against the grain of a deficient white Western humanism that casts black being as non-being. Equiano's gesture here is quite nuanced: if, in his portrait, he makes us aware of the schisms in his existence by way of visual symbols and metaphors—a black body in European dress, holding a Bible open to a passage that exhorts just works as the manifestation of Christian faith—in his *Narrative*, he works to negotiate these schisms through a relational, metaphorical, and spiritual discourse. His discourse underscores the central importance of understanding and enlightenment as a way of navigating the fragmented aspects of his existence, and as key to achieving historical, actuated being.

In his narration, Equiano's path toward enlightenment is not straight and linear, but unfolds in progressive stages, some of which are marked by incongruities and ambivalences. Equiano's initial turn to the Bible as the record of the historical origin of things becomes an object of desire for him in an almost fetishistic way. The literary effect of the holy book regularly draws his attention, so much so that he often puts himself in danger to keep his Bible, in particular among his other books, with him. His anxious desire for *the* sacred text of the West—and for the possibilities that the Bible's religion and spiritual discourse present for the critical *expression* of Equiano's own discourse on the human, a discourse that takes shape beyond (but not in ignorance of) binding narratives of nationalism and race— becomes evident, for example, when Equiano narrates how Pascal, angry at false rumors of Equiano's planned escape, determines to sell him without giving in to Equiano's "offer" to retrieve his books (central among them his Bible) from his quarters:

> The ship was up about half an hour, when my master ordered the barge to be manned; and all in an instant, without having before given me the least reason to suspect any thing of the matter, he forced me into the barge, saying, I was going to leave him, but he would take care I should not. I was so struck with the unexpectedness of this proceeding, that for some time I could not make a reply, only I made an offer to go for my books and chest of clothes, but he swore I should not move out of his sight; and if I did he would cut my throat, at the same time taking out his hangar. (64)

Eighteenth-century usage of "offer" includes a tropological or secondary sense in which the speaker employs "offer" to convey an intention. Judging from Pascal's angry, and, indeed, immoral response, Equiano's "offer" was not a request. It was an articulation of purpose and, according to the *Oxford English Dictionary*, a presumption of his "right" to collect his books and clothing. He quickly formulates a retort, further incensing Pascal: "[P]lucking up courage, I told him I was free, and he could not by law serve me so."[24]

Equiano's desire for his Bible and the other texts he felt he possessed[25] might be read in terms of the knowledge and the affirmation of human being he was certain they held. In this, there appears to be an ontological analogue—another metaphorical operation—at work, a point to which I shall return. Yet the erudition of origins Equiano attributes here to the books he constantly read seems symptomatic of the void in his own memory and history, which he determines to rewrite by keeping a journal of his travels and by writing the story of his life. Equiano commences his narrative by providing us with a history of his homeland, from which, by his own account, he was kidnapped in about 1756. It was sometime during the following two years, in 1757 or early during 1758, that he regularly witnessed Pascal and Dick Baker in the midst of reading. From these visions, and the subsequent refusal of the books to "answer [him]" when he "talked" to them (39), his longing for textual engagement and what he repeatedly refers to as "understanding" is born. Nonetheless, his "great curiosity to talk to the books" and to thus "learn how all things had a beginning" (39)—including he *himself*—appear strange when juxtaposed against the litany of detail we encounter in the first chapters of the narrative.

For example, in the early portion of the text, Equiano, through what he calls the "imperfect sketch" of his memory (14), provides his reader with a fairly detailed portrait of his village, Essaka. He is, of course, as he tells us in his notes to the text, indebted to the Quaker writer Anthony Benezet for those images of West African village life that elude his memory, but he does not rely upon Benezet for the narration of the particulars of his childhood experiences. Equiano was not born a peasant child, but was the favored son in a prominent family. He clearly recalls his training in agriculture and warfare as well as his mother's determination to "form [his] mind" (17). It is reasonable to conclude that the formation Equiano's mother provided him included teachings in Ibo cosmology and theology. Yet, after his baptism in 1759, which took place before certain religious epiphanies that actually sealed Equiano's conversion to Christianity later in life, he tells of being "wonderfully surprised to see the laws and rules of my country written almost exactly [in the Bible]; a circumstance which I believe tended to impress our manners and customs more deeply on my memory" (63). Equiano appears to *need* reading—and, in particular, reading in the sacred text of those people with whom he regularly came into contact—in order to secure the images of self and origins afloat on his memory. And he makes a point of repeatedly engaging Biblical scriptures in order not simply to provide literary effects of consciousness, but to permit a disclosure of his being, a disclosure that surpasses the raciology of his day as well as its attendant nationalist absolutism. Because Equiano's memory of his childhood origins is blurred, as an adult he reconstitutes his sense of origins through metaphorical borrowings. In this way, he reconstructs an image of himself—a bodily image as well as a spiritual, ekphrastic representation—that allows him to mark a *humanistic* entry point into the world, one that exceeds the limits of race and nation alike.

This gesture constitutes, it seems, a sort of textual "mirror stage." Of course, according to Jacques Lacan, the mirror stage does not provide subjectivity, but moves the child beyond a sense of fragmentation and toward a sense of bodily totality, wholeness. The mirror stage, in Equiano's case, is supplied by ekphrastic text and memory, and from these he pieces together early memories that provide him a foundation upon which to construct a sense of the origins of his *human* being, and thus a sense of *historical* being. Text, and specifically sacred text, provides him the security of knowledge of his origins in a way that discourses of national belonging cannot.

Sacred text, however, was often employed as an aspect of a mimetic process of identification that regularly served as the root of eighteenth- and early nineteenth-century nationalist discourse. Hegel, for instance, sought to merge the church and the nation-state through his brand of metaphysical philosophy. While Kant's hypothetical imperative, "So act as to treat humanity, whether in your own person or in another, always as an end, and never as only a means," seems an essential translation of Christ's admonition to "do unto others as you would have them do unto you," Kant nonetheless, on the surface at least, insisted upon a separation of church and state. Hegel, conversely, felt this to be implausible. Ricoeur reminds us that "Hegel no doubt did try to make philosophy a secularized form of theology. . . . The fact is that from the end of the first third of the nineteenth century on, everywhere [sic] substituted the word 'man'—or humanity, or the human spirit, or human culture—for Hegel's spirit, . . . we do not really know whether it is man or God" (203). Northrup Frye concurs, adding that if Karl Marx's spiritual father was Hegel, Hegel's spiritual father was Martin Luther, the sixteenth-century founder of the German Reformation (*Great Code* xx).

Though he did not seek to hide it under secular prose, as did many modern thinkers of his age, Equiano also looked to the sacred to justify and examine his own human existence and to bolster his sense of historical origins and belonging to a community of free human beings. The paradox in this is that the Bible, specifically the Old Testament, is a book about exile. It may provide, as Hegel perhaps intends, the root of the nation-state, but it also repeatedly tells stories of rootlessness and wandering—of exceeding and transgressing the limits and constraints of the nation-state—

not unlike the exilic journeying in which Equiano engages. On this point, Édouard Glissant, citing, among other texts, the Old Testament and the ever-important *Iliad*, convincingly argues:

> [T]he great founding books of communities, the Old Testament, the *Iliad*, the *Odyssey* . . . the *Aeneid*, or the African epics, were all books about exile and often errantry. This epic literature is amazingly prophetic. It tells of community, but, through relating the community's apparent failure or in any case its being surpassed, it tells of errantry as a temptation (the desire to go against the root) and, frequently, actually experienced. Within the collective books concerning the sacred and the notion of history lies the germ of the exact opposite of what they so loudly proclaim. . . . These are books about the collective consciousness, but they also introduce the unrest and suspense that allow the individual to discover himself there, whenever he himself becomes the issue. (*Poetics of Relation* 15)

Equiano appears to press this point home with his reader by citing not simply the Bible, but also by quoting at length from Milton's epic poem of celestial exile, *Paradise Lost* (1667) and by alluding repeatedly to Pope's translation of the *Iliad*, even as he asserts his certainty in a specifically African cosmology. At the same time, though, he also asserts his belief (by virtue of his readings in the Bible) that the history of the African Eboes before the transatlantic slave trade bears a "strong analogy" to that of the Jews before their dispersal, "particularly the patriarchs, while they were yet in that pastoral state which is described in Genesis—an analogy which alone would induce me to think that the one people had sprung from the other" (14). Here Equiano writes of a "pastoral state" that lies beyond the fast-forming cities of modernity, which served not only as the centers (metropoles) of empire, but also as the centers of nationalistic life. That Equiano draws an analogy between his people and the Jews means not only that he sees them both as diasporic people and exilic wanderers whose existence took shape beyond and in spite of the reach of nation and empire, but that he deems himself and his people to be "people of the book" (a very important matter for Christians in recognizing other people as belonging to God), and it is there that their allegiance lies. I would contend, however, that Equiano's metaphorical recourse to the Bible signifies even further: It allows him not only to express his sense of the human, but further to argue for a humanism that is free of both racism and nationalism. I will return to this point later.

Equiano's recourse to the Bible is also significant for discussions regarding the aptness of Christianity as a substitute religion for Equiano: because he saw many resemblances between the words of the Bible and the words he likely heard during his religious training in Africa,[26] Christianity and its tenets became more palatable to him, and he felt a certain comfort in looking to its texts not simply for examples of figurations he might adapt to his own ontological discourse, but also for a textual model for revealing and narrating his sense of being. As a significant aspect of his reading practice consisted in engagement with the Bible, and because the Bible is itself an archetype of Western literature, we may use Equiano's account of his development as a reader of sacred scripture to further our understanding of him as a writer of secular prose who uses language laden with spiritual metaphors to convey his sense of being.

In fact, the Biblical discourse at play in Equiano's *Narrative* seems to raise the existential efficacy of his text, in that the unfolding of his autobiography comes in tandem with his application of the Biblical sources he reads to the life writing he practices. One aspect of reading Equiano as a writer of prose, then, consists in identifying a sequence of spiritual phases that signal a dialectical progression of thought and metaphorical representation in his *Narrative*, not simply, as I have outlined, from reading to writing to being read, but also from servitude, to freedom and an apocalyptic discourse that insists upon "understanding," to, finally, an insistence upon action and actuation in his conception of historical being. He significantly relates this latter to his hope of "becoming" an instrument of enlightenment and emancipation.

Phases of Being: Biblical Metaphorics in Equiano's Narrative of Becoming

Equiano situates what I will call his "phases of being" in metaphorical language drawn variously from both the Old and New Testaments. For instance, he regularly takes advantage of the New Testament writers' sometimes tacit reference to the scriptures of the Old Testament, and thus he conceives of the Bible as a narrative unity that is to be navigated fluidly, in spite of its origin as a set of disparate and at times fragmented texts,[27] just as he fluidly navigates representations of his experiences drawn from disparate episodes of his history. We should note that the main characteristic of Equiano's use of the Bible lies not in his replication of the Bible's sequence of phases—from creation in the Book of Genesis to the apocalypse in the Book of Revelation—but in his extraction of specific forms of speech from these phases for use in his own narrative. His text does not end, for example, with an allusion to or citation from the apocalyptic theme of Revelation, as we might expect, but with a reference to the Book of Micah, which oscillates between a condemnation of the present sins of the people and an exposition of God's purpose in blessing them. Most importantly, Micah speaks of the return of Israel from exile; such a matter was not lost on Equiano, who regularly described himself as a stranger whose travels suggest a prolonged quest for home that was never relieved from wandering. Further, the passage Equiano quotes from Micah underscores the importance of actuation and action on the part of the reader and hearer of the word: "He hath shewed thee, O man, what *is* good; and what doth the Lord require of thee, but to do justly, and to love mercy, and to walk humbly with thy God?" (Micah 6:8; *Narrative* 205). As Equiano portrays his process of "becoming," he overtly plays upon the journey metaphor that is necessary to the travelogue, germane to the epic, and persistent throughout the Bible. He also plays subtly upon the notion that the Word must be the ethical person's traveling companion, and this he demonstrates by presenting us with a narrative that does not emerge *ex nihilo*, but from a specific historical context that requires—by the text's conclusion—responsive action: the reader and hearer of the word must also become a doer of the word. The *Narrative* directs us along *the way* to action; certainly not lost in this is the metaphor, in the Gospels, of Christ as "the way." And, as Christ states simply, the way to heaven is not only through him; *it is him* (John 14:6 reads "I am the way, the truth, and the life: no man cometh unto the Father, but by me"). Christ's words seem to provide an analogy for the actuation Equiano seeks through writing. His own actuated being is the simultaneously immanent and transcendent *telos* Equiano sets forth, at the *Narrative*'s beginning as well as its end, as that way by which the reader must pass.

I see six main phases at work in the sequence of Biblical metaphors Equiano employs in the *Narrative* as he works toward this concept of actuated being: exile; freedom and liminality; abjection; faith; conversion and salvation; and finally, actuation. Each phase seems to build and expand upon that which precedes it; there are instances of antinomy in the sequence, as in the juxtaposition of the abject and the establishment of faith, just as there are a number of instances in which the phases overlap. Yet in the main, Equiano uses a sequence of onto-theological metaphorics to convey a sense of unity in the disparate nature of his spiritual evolution, similar to the unity he takes for certain in the disparate books of Bible. I will discuss each in turn.

EXILE

The characteristics of the exile metaphor are noted early in the *Narrative*, as early as the paratextual material—the letters I discussed earlier in this chapter—Equiano appends to the work. His initial reference to exile through allusion to the Bible appears in chapter 2, as he tells of having been captured, then sold and resold by various traders and families as he is transported to the West Coast of Africa:

> I now began to think I was to be adopted into the family, and was beginning to be reconciled to my situation, and to forget by degrees my misfortunes, when all at once the delusion vanished; for, without the least previous knowledge, one morning early, while my dear master and companion was still asleep, I was awakened out of my reverie to fresh sorrow, and hurried away even among the uncircumcised. (24)

The passage from Ezekiel 32:32, to which Equiano's exilic metaphor here bears a strong resemblance, describes the uncircumcised as those whose hearts were closed to God. While throughout the Bible, reference to the uncircumcised could indicate Gentiles, it could also designate those who did not bear this ritual mark of God's covenant with Abraham. Ezekiel posits the uncircumcised as foreign captors in the guise of Egypt who, the prophet Ezekiel insists, will be overcome after having instigated the fall of Judah and bringing about the exile of the Israelites in Babylon. Ezekiel 32:32 reads:

> For I have caused my terror in the land of the living: and [Pharoah] shall be laid in the midst of the uncircumcised with them that are slain with the sword, even Pharoah and all his multitude, saith the Lord God.

Equiano's evocation of this passage appears obliquely to assign blame for his own exile not only to those European foreigners who fomented war, dispossession, displacement, and the taking of captives, but also to another obvious party of guilt, those African "brethren" who were his initial captors and from whom were drawn the great majority of the New World's slaves. The prophet Ezekiel prophesied against the revered lands of Judah and Jerusalem as well as the sinful Babylon and Egypt. Judah and Jerusalem were part of God's legacy to the Jews, and thus Ezekiel's chastising of them is of some importance, largely because it indicates that the captor as well as the captive bears some guilt, some responsibility for the situation of oppression and for rectifying that situation.

In referencing these passages early in his *Narrative*, Equiano commences his autobiographical account not with birth so much as misbirth, with exile rather than a rooted sense of home, and this is the fragmented genesis from which his *Narrative* grows and takes shape. Thus the chief point he makes early in the *Narrative* is not about beginning but belonging, that is, his longing to belong to a community of human beings. The first chapter's narrative moments in which Benezet's history aids Equiano in the reconstruction of his pre-exilic world (rather than the resurrection of a holistic memory), such that he is enabled to demonstrate to the reader the fraught foundations of his sense of being, are significant. Such detours to outside sources and the attendant restructuring of his world by way of textuality ("I saw the customs of my people written there [in the Bible]") allow Equiano recourse to a sense of being and spirituality. In short, through a metaphoric process of integration—the analogy Equiano draws between the patriarchs of the Bible and the elders of his village—Equiano carefully crafts a provisional unity of being that paradoxically conditions the remainder of his story. This paradox is quite visible in what I have here designated as the freedom phase, which commences in chapter 7 with allusions to images of the liminal.

FREEDOM AND THE LIMINAL

Chapters 3 through 6 of the *Narrative* elaborate the exile phase by giving accounts of Equiano's adventures at sea and his myriad descriptions of slavery's horrors. Though his baptism is narrated in chapter 4, that scene is not described with words of religious exaltation, but rather is presented in a matter of fact tone that makes it clear to the reader that Equiano's full conversion is yet to come. In giving an account of his freedom in chapter 7, however, Equiano pointedly alludes to three Biblical passages in order to convey, again through onto-theological metaphor, his fast belief in the miraculous powers of God as an emancipatory and protective force, and he does so in ways that are fully absent from the baptism scene.

When, for instance, Equiano presents Mr. King with forty pounds sterling and then, with the aid of his captain, convinces the good Quaker to accept the sum and set him at liberty, he elaborates his freedom story in this way:

These words of my master were like a voice from heaven to me; in an instant, all my trepidation was turned into unutterable bliss; and I most reverently bowed myself with gratitude, unable to express my feelings, but by the overflowing of my eyes, and a heart replete with thanks to God; while my true and worthy friend the captain congratulated us both with a peculiar degree of heartfelt pleasure. As soon as the first transports of my joy were over, and I had expressed my thanks to these my worthy friends in the best manner I was able, I rose with a heart full of affection and reverence, and left the room in order to obey my master's joyful mandate of going to the Register Office [where his manumission would be drawn up]. As I was leaving the house, I called to mind the words of the Psalmist, in the 126th Psalm, and like him, "I glorified God in my heart, in whom I trusted." These words had been impressed on my mind from the very day I was forced from Deptford to the present hour, and I now saw them, as I thought, fulfilled and verified. My imagination was all rapture as I flew to the Register Office: and in this respect, like the apostle Peter (whose deliverance from prison was so sudden and extraordinary, that he thought he was in a vision), I could scarcely believe I was awake.[28] (108)

The metaphors of plenitude and excess Equiano utters in response to his emancipation ("my imagination was all rapture," "the . . . transports of my joy," "the overflowing of my eyes," "unutterable bliss") are also metaphors of the liminal. His analogizing (yet another metaphorical turn) of his experience with that of Peter, one of Christ's first apostles who is generally regarded as the founder of the Christian Church, means that he now sees himself as one miraculously, providentially saved from a life of enslavement.[29] In Equiano's emancipatory dream-state, the Lord saves those in captivity and demonstrates that from their sorrows they shall reap great joys and prosperity. Though Equiano does not actually quote Psalms 126, which is referenced in the passage I excerpt above, it would have certainly suited well his intentions in this passage. For Psalms 126, which is attributed to David, reads, in part: "When the Lord turned again the captivity of Zion, we were like them that dream. Then our mouth was filled with laughter, and our tongue with singing: then said they among the heathen, The Lord hath done great things for them."

The use of the verb "turn" in this scripture refers to a reversal of the exiled condition of enslaved Zion, and indicates that for Equiano, the attainment of freedom from slavery not only relieves him from his sense of exile and moves him one step closer to the belonging he desires; it also underscores the centrality of Equiano's faith to his pursuit of human freedom, and indeed, the dream-state that is essential to this passage's imagery is likewise crucial to Equiano's representation of the evolution of his consciousness. Equiano uses these sorts of passages to convey to the reader the sublimity of his sentiments: that he fully understands the concept of freedom even though the power of verbal expression momentarily fails him when freedom comes. Kantian elements of the sublime are in effect here: Equiano's feelings of reverence and awe, his profound sense of respect, and the failure of language in the face of overpowering emotion are all aspects of what Kant describes in his *Critique of Judgment* as constituents of the sublime, through which, Kant argues, the individual tests the limits of reason, freedom, and meaning. While Kant contends that awareness of the sublime can teach one the benefits of sensuous experience (that supersensible moral freedom is something we can *think*, even if we cannot comprehend it fully), Equiano's sentiments in this passage point to a higher moral significance, one that at once encompasses and surpasses the racial and national identities so firmly entrenched in and definitive of Kant's own philosophy.

Equiano's emancipation scene demonstrates the centrality of de-racialized being, in that it is not concerned with the limits of "blackness" as such in the eighteenth century, nor is it simply concerned with meeting prerequisites that permit membership in the nation-state. Rather, he narrates scenes of self-conscious awareness and human being in one of the most important moments of his life. His intertextual strategies make use of a series of Biblical dialectics in the metaphorical passages he cites: from sowing to reaping, weeping to rejoicing, dreaming to waking, sleep to consciousness. Each of these dyads turns out to be a subset of the major metaphorical dialectic at play in the freedom/liminal phase: from symbolic death and exile in slavery to being and belonging in human and moral freedom. The transformational context of Equiano's message—his sense of not simply "becoming" an Englishman, but also, and more importantly, revealing the very fibers of his sense of being—is clear: faith in God brings about a change in one's situation, even a change as revolutionary as transfiguration, whereby Equiano intimates that his manumission is analogous to being taken up into the Rapture. The persistent association of such metaphorical dialectics of metamorphosis and becoming in the text indicates to what extent Equiano saw his manumission as being caught up with the notion of divine salvation—a passage through the way and being of Christ. It underscores as well Equiano's continuing emphasis upon liminal dream-states, which provide an opening for not simply an advance in understanding, but also an advance toward self-actualization.

We see the next significant metaphorical gesture in Equiano's figuration of the liminal most clearly in the textual space that marks the separation of the two volumes that constitute the first edition of the *Narrative*, falling between chapters 6 and 7 (but coming after chapter 7 in the ninth edition, to which I refer). It begins with citations of two Biblical books that make much of the intermediate nature of dreams—The Acts of the Apostles and the Book of Job. An early manuscript of the former gives the title simply as "Acts," written in Greek by the apostle Luke, who, through this writing, provides an important history of early Christianity. Rendered from the Greek *práxeis*, or praxis, and referring to the doings, transactions, and achievements of the followers of Christ, Acts begins with an account of the disembowelment of Judas Iscariot, who had betrayed Christ and was thus punished by death as the Twelve prayed in an upper room. It concludes with the Apostle Paul's arrest and subsequent preaching at Rome.

Significantly, the Book of Acts also depicts Paul's imprisonment aboard a ship that later shipwrecked on the island of Melita. As we have seen, in various chapters of the *Narrative*, Equiano is quick to draw an analogy between Paul's situation and his own. He, like Paul, had undergone a revolutionary spiritual conversion; just as the youthful Equiano had proven immune to the dangers of snakes (*Narrative* 13), Paul "felt no harm" in the wake of a venomous snake bite (Acts 28:5). Moreover, Paul's self-possession in the face of the storm, and his certainty that all the men (they numbered "two hundred threescore and sixteen souls") must remain with the ship (27:31, 37), is likewise echoed in Equiano's text. In the aftermath of a great storm, which he narrates in chapter 8, Equiano ultimately succeeds in dissuading his irresponsible captain (a different captain than he who had helped Equiano gain his freedom) from battening down the hatches; had the captain done so, he would have assured the death of the slaves held captive below deck. Equiano instead advises the crew to leave the hatches unlocked and stay with the ship, taking it upon himself to patch the broken area of the vessel and, by concerted efforts with three Negroes and a Dutch creole sailor (the ethnicity and racial identity of these men are significant for Equiano in underscoring the morality of people of color), he "brought all safe to the shore; so that out of thirty-two people, we lost none" (123). In so speaking, Equiano cannily echoes Luke's account of Paul's shipwreck, which Equiano cites directly in the liminal space separating the two volumes, a space in which Equiano describes a journey across the liminality of the sea: "And so it came to pass, that they escaped all safe to land" (Acts 27:44; Equiano 118). He also provides a visual illustration of a shipwreck in the Caribbean Isles by reproducing the 1767 painting, "Bahama Banks," which depicts Equiano's ship, the *Nancy*, caught in a hurricane. The *Nancy* would wreck on the notorious Bahama Banks, and Equiano's account of this shipwreck stands as yet another instance of ekphrasis in his *Narrative*, offering a verbal representation (or textual picture) of this visual representation.

As Equiano makes clear, the premonition of the shipwreck had come to him three separate times by way of dreams; in each instance, his dream was the same and was "fulfilled in every part." He "could not help looking upon [himself] as the principal instrument in effecting [the] deliverance" of his shipmates (123). Thus along with the metaphorical analogy between his shipwreck and Paul's is the interpretation of his dream, a hermeneutic principle in the gaining of wisdom and understanding. The most salient aspect of the verses Equiano cites includes the dream-like appearance before Paul of an angel who tells him that the shipwreck must occur, but that all the men must remain together in the ship, and that all of them would be saved.

Equiano's citations from Job in the space that marks the separation of the two volumes of the first edition of his *Narrative* continue this strand of liminal dream-work. He uses Job's story of trials and tribulations to aid him in making meaning of his own obstacles in life. Job's story follows a dialectical cycle in which Job and his companions, in the shadow of Job's affliction, debate the ways of wisdom. Job's loss of faith—something Equiano uses to foreshadow his own sense of abjection in the phase that follows his attention to the liminal—may be read as a scriptural opportunity that allows man to voice his frustrations and fears in the face of life's uncertainties. These sufferings are frequently interpreted by Equiano as divine gifts that eventually lead to greater enlightenment and wisdom.

The scriptural restoration of Job's wisdom represents an element of hope for Equiano, but Job does not gain it independently. Wisdom in the Bible does not always take shape in the actions of those who follow the road well-traveled, but often emerges from dream-states in which God or his angels visit man and relate prophecies. Wisdom—that is, understanding or knowledge paired with intellect rather than simple "factual" knowledge— emerges through interpretation from those spaces "in between," from liminal spaces and silences. Job, to whom Equiano refers in the aftermath of his references to the Book of Acts, must be convinced by his friends of the inappropriateness of his anger; the reasoned and wise voices in the verses Equiano cites are those of Job's friends Eliphaz and Elihu, not of Job himself.

In the first scripture, Eliphaz, who, along with Elihu, has come to be with Job in his grief, admonishes Job for railing against God, and tells him of insights that came to him in a dream. These amount to an admonition to trust in God's greatness, and to cease believing that "mortal man" may be "more just than God" (Job 4:17). Later in Job's story, Elihu takes up the thread of what comes to be an extended parable, stressing to Job that God often places man under duress so that he will be "enlightened with the light of the living" (Job 33: 30).

Equiano's cultivation of the metaphor of the liminal as directly applicable to his cultivation of wisdom and reason, of the dream-state as a site of revelation and of preparation for ethical or enlightened action,[30] is taken up once more in chapter 10, whose central preoccupation is an account of the author's conversion. At this point, Equiano has become disillusioned with England due to the racism he experiences there. In his quest for a place that he could truly call home—a home that he imagined as a national community of true believers—he scrutinizes the doctrines of the Quakers, the Roman Catholics, and even the Jews (151), whose fabled history he had early on in the *Narrative* analogized to that of his own people, the Eboes. The lack he senses in all of these peoples' observance of the Gospel leads him, surprisingly, to plan a move to Turkey. The Turks were, he reasoned, "in a safer way of salvation than my neighbors" (151). (Critics who often argue that Equiano desired whiteness above all else because he ultimately desired an English national identity and decided to settle in England rarely at the same time consider Equiano's pointed critique of English racism, nor do they imagine how we might have construed Equiano's actions had he indeed settled in Turkey among the Islamist Kurds, Arabs, and Turks.)

His provisional rejection of England was warranted by him in what he perceived to be a deliberate deception by Granville Sharp, the famed abolitionist with whom he had become acquainted. Even in the ninth edition of his text, Equiano does not lighten his criticism of Sharp, in spite of Sharp's cooperation with him in litigating the case of the slave ship *Zong* in 1783. In 1774, Equiano had engaged the attorney on behalf of a beleaguered friend, a free black cook named John Annis. Equiano had hopes that Sharp would secure Annis's release, for Annis had been captured and detained after refusing to go back to work for his employer, who lived in St. Kitts. Equiano's hopes were soon dashed; by his account, Sharp "proved unfaithful; he took my money, lost me many months employ, and did not the least good in the cause; and when the poor man [Annis] arrived at St. Kitt's [sic], he was, according to custom, staked to the ground with four pins through a cord, two on his wrists and two on his ancles [sic], was cut and flogged most unmercifully." He remained in this state "till kind death released him out of the hands of his tyrants" (153). During Annis's imprisonment, Equiano had felt tortured as well: he describes himself as being at once under the "convictions of sin" (153) and consumed by the thought of dying as a sinner. The admixture of his emotions and his trauma, as well as his feelings against Sharp and his grief over Annis's death, combined to convince him to leave England, for which he had, up to this point in the narrative, proclaimed an abiding love.

It may seem curious that Equiano experiences a crisis of faith in England at the very moment he explores the liminal as a source of wisdom and understanding. Yet in the midst of his angst, we can discern a tactical move at work in his recitation, in the midst of the angst he describes in chapter 10, of Ecclesiastes 1:9, which reads, "The thing that hath been, it is that which shall be; and that which is done is that which shall be done: and there is no new thing under the sun" (Equiano 153). Here Equiano quotes a Biblical chiasmus. From the Greek *chiasma*, or cross, and often symbolized by the uppercase letter "X," a chiasmus indicates an inverted state or condition, though usually one of symmetry and balance. Equiano's use of this particular chiasmus underscores his belief in divine predestination. Its certitude gives him comfort at a disturbing time of his life, a time when his sense of upheaval and homelessness seems most acute. Yet the Biblical chiasmus from Ecclesiastes—even with its sense of surety—is not so far from the liminal as it might first appear. It allows Equiano to attain a perspective upon the pastness of his history as well as the seeds of time, which assure individual and collective futures through growth and development. Thus, through his citation of a belief in the philosophic import of this passage, he gains an understanding of his present through an assumed cohesion of his past, which projects itself toward an unknown that is to come. Ecclesiastes, a book viewed by Biblical scholars as intriguingly confounding, may be said to be the Biblical text most concerned with the propounding of wisdom. And, as one would have it, the nature of Biblical wisdom is generally not the rendering of concrete knowledge, but of a fluid ability to deal with life's vicissitudes and contingencies. In this second aspect of the liminal phase, Equiano devalues the concrete nature of "knowing" in favor of the more fluid concept of "understanding."

ABJECTION

The liminal phase of Equiano's *Narrative* is not immediately followed by an emergence into a full state of being, as we might expect. Conversely, it prefaces a state of abjection into which Equiano feels himself to be plunged by virtue of the very wisdom the liminal has brought him. The abjection phase Equiano enters and narrates with such poignancy is the briefest in the sequence of phases. Coming in chapter 10 near the apotheosis of Equiano's sense and feeling of liminality, his feeling of degradation and utter humility sets in upon him in the wake of his friend John Annis's torturous death. While Annis was "staked to the ground with four pins through a cord" (153), Equiano was plagued by thoughts that his "state was worse than any man's," and he despondently prayed for his own death:

> I often wished for death, though, at the same time, convinced I was altogether unprepared for that awful summons: suffering much by villains in the late cause [of Annis's imprisonment and torture], and being much concerned about the state of my soul, these things (but particularly the latter) brought me very low; so that I became a burden to myself, and viewed all things around me as emptiness and vanity, which could give no satisfaction to a troubled conscience. [The] only comfort I then experienced was in reading the Holy Scriptures, where I saw that . . . what was appointed for me I must submit to. Thus I continued to travel in much heaviness, and frequently murmured against the Almighty, particularly in his providential dealings; and, awful to think! I began to blaspheme, and wished often to be any thing but a human being. (153)

Equiano makes clear that the dream states that provided him with a sense of enlightenment and wisdom also allowed him to recognize the state of depravity in which he lived. As Equiano tells it, it seems necessary that he fall to the depths of abjection before he can meaningfully and purposefully emerge from this state, secure his faith, and act upon that faith through good works. It is equally important to him that he express clearly to his reader what is at stake in his full conversion, namely his *being*.

Equiano's narration of his abject experience in relation to his sense of being is intensified by the only reference to the Book of Revelation that appears in the text. Revelation 6:16 appears at the final stage in his descent into a hellish existence, but also aptly paves the way for his account of his transcendence:

> In these severe conflicts the Lord answered me by awful "visions of the night, when deep sleep falleth upon men, in slumberings

upon the bed," Job xxxiii. 15. He was pleased, in much mercy, to give me to see, and in some measure understand, the great and awful scene of the Judgment-day, that "no unclean person, no unholy thing, can enter into the kingdom of God," Eph[esians], v. 5. I would then, if it had been possible, have changed my nature with the meanest worm on the earth, and was ready to say to the mountains and rocks, "fall on me," Rev[elation]. vi. 16. I then, in the greatest agony, requested the divine Creator, that he would grant me a small space of time to repent of my follies and vile iniquities, which I felt were grievous. The Lord, in his manifold mercies, was pleased to grant my request, and being yet in a state of time, the sense of God's mercies was so great on my mind when I awoke, that my strength entirely failed me for many minutes, and I was exceedingly weak. This was the first spiritual mercy I ever was sensible of, and being on praying ground, as soon as I recovered a little strength, and got out of bed and dressed myself I invoked heaven from my inmost soul, and fervently begged that God would never again permit me to blaspheme his most holy name. The Lord, who is long-suffering, and full of compassion to such poor rebels as we are, condescended to hear and answer. (153–54)

This is yet another metaphorical effect that is of signal importance in telling the reader of the centrality of his conversion to Christianity. Wisdom and understanding, communicated to Equiano through liminal dream states, lead to a painful self-conscious awareness that is absolutely essential to his sense of being. It also serves as a transition toward hope: Equiano's hopeful affirmation that the phase of abjection is not simply to be superseded, but serves to confirm the believer in his or her faith and prepares her or him to act meaningfully.

Equiano's triumphant hope is signaled in his rather esoteric reference to the Biblical metaphor, the "searcher of hearts":

I felt that I was altogether unholy, and saw clearly what a bad use I had made of the faculties I was endowed with: they were given me to glorify God with; I thought, therefore, I had better want them here, and enter into life eternal, than abuse them and be cast into hell fire. I prayed to be directed, if there were any holier persons than those with whom I was acquainted, that the Lord would point them out to me. I appealed to the searcher of hearts, whether I did not wish to love him more, and serve him better. (154)

Equiano draws the metaphor, the "searcher of hearts" from Paul's epistle to the Romans, 8:27, which reads: "And he that searcheth the hearts knoweth what is the mind of the Spirit; because he [the Spirit] maketh intercession for the saints according to the will of God." The eighth chapter of Romans speaks to the self-reflective and self-conscious hope of the Christian and the power of the Spirit, or Comforter, the central occupant of the New Testament sites of the liminal. The Holy Spirit is the Bible's "third person" who dwells in the interstice between heaven and earth, an agile, peripatetic inhabitant of both realms. It is this mobile Spirit that induces man to heteroglossia and glossolalia; that serves as the other self of Christ (John 14:16, 17); and that lives and works with and within men as the active agent of God. Thus, it is to this spirit that Equiano alludes in his quest to cast off the weight of abjection as he works to grasp more fully his faith, which requires, as he puts it, all the intellectual faculties with which he had been endowed. And it is faith, born out of desperate abjection, that emerges as the fulcrum of Equiano's spiritual rebirth.

FAITH

Equiano's faithful appeal to the Spirit serves as the central efficacy of his conversion narrative. It permits him to rise above the limits of abjection and move toward a fuller grasping of his faith. It also serves to intensify his vision of actuation, which has, as we have discussed, two levels: the level of actuation by hope in the word of God, and the level of actuation through the reception of his own text by a world of readers, which is a different sort of hope. The latter level is that of both a secondary identity symbolized by the reconstruction of his memory of Africa through his reading of the Bible (an act that appears as a salvific gesture of transcending oblivion, that is, escaping a complete loss of being), and the ultimate sense of being Equiano fashions by turning to his own book in the present of his day, the text he imbues with his own sense of being and which he hopes will be actualized in communication with a reader who will, through faith and good works, join the Christian abolitionist movement and work to the benefit of all humanity. The reestablishment of faith that takes place at the heart of chapter 10 includes references to each of these two levels, and Equiano, through his citation of Matthew 25:41,[31] which aids him in conveying his surety of God's judgment of any shortcomings in the final days, shores up his faith by considering himself to be a vital actor in the consummation of God's kingdom and in the liberation of all of God's children, regardless of race (158).

Remarkably, Equiano's depiction of his full grasping of faith begins with his engagement aboard a "ship called the *Hope*" (160), an aptly named vessel whose symbolic significance should not be lost on the reader. When he boards the *Hope* to take his post as steward, he is still in the grip of the abject: "confusion seized me, and I wished to be annihilated" (160). As Equiano sails for Cadiz, he reads deeply in the Scriptures. He recounts that he "wrestled hard with God in fervent prayers, who had declared in his word that he would hear the groanings and deep sighs of the poor in spirit" (161). Persisting in prayer and reading, Equiano recounts that he began to "meditate" upon the passage of Acts 4:12, the very passage to which he holds open his Bible in his frontispiece portrait: "Neither is there salvation in any other, for there is none other name under heaven given among men, whereby we must be saved." This passage is not only one of the most important verses one may cite from the New Testament, but is also of primary importance to interpreting the *Narrative*. Matthew 4:12 counts Christ as the cornerstone of the Christian church, the foundation upon which the faith of the faithful is built (Matt 4:11). Equiano also cites this passage, as I have mentioned, in his emancipation scene, and his meditation upon it at this later point in the *Narrative* tells the reader of what is perhaps not the second, but the third "life" of Equiano, who lives now as one freed not only from the bonds of earthly chattel slavery, but also from the bonds of eternal sin.

Matthew 4:12 echoes another verse of scripture that Equiano cites from Isaiah 12:2 and 4, which likewise prefaces the entire *Narrative* and is found on the title page: "Behold, God *is* my salvation; I will trust, and not be afraid: for the Lord Jehovah *is* my strength and *my* song; he is also become my salvation. . . . And in that day shall ye say, Praise the Lord, call upon his name, declare his doings among the people." As Equiano ponders this passage in the light of his life and experience, wondering whether he has lived a life sufficiently moral to justify his salvation, salvation indeed comes to him. Meditation upon this and other verses of faith, such as Isaiah 25:7, cited below, finally leads to his full conversion:

> I began to think I had lived a moral life, and that I had a proper ground to believe I had an interest in the divine favour; but still meditating on the subject, not knowing whether salvation was to be had partly for our own good deeds, or solely as the sovereign

gift of God:—in this deep consternation the Lord was pleased to break in upon my soul with his bright beams of heavenly light; and in an instant, as it were, removing the veil, and letting light into a dark place, Isa[iah]. xxv. 7. I saw clearly, with the eye of faith, the crucified Saviour bleeding on the cross on Mount Calvary: the Scriptures became an unsealed book. . . . It was given me at that time to know what it was to be born again. (162)

By the time Equiano reaches Cadiz aboard the *Hope*, his aspirations toward Christian faithfulness have been realized by way of his full conversion and salvation. And as the *Hope* returns from Cadiz to London, Equiano conveys to his reader a signal truth: that faith is confirmed only by doing good and moral works. Primary among these good works is, Equiano will have us know as he returns to the center of the British Empire, the abolition of the trans-Atlantic slave trade that had, indeed, held such an empire at the pinnacle of immoral and ahumanistic world power.

CONVERSION AND SALVATION

In retrospect, what I am calling Equiano's "third life,"[32] his renewed sense of being and of the importance of just works, convince him that every misfortune, every "providential circumstance" that had happened to him thus far in his life led to his experience of conversion and salvation. His conviction that through this mystical experience he is sealed in Christ's salvation is underscored in his recourse to the Biblical metaphor, "the earnest of the Spirit" (2 Cor 1:21–22 and 5:5; Equiano 162). The "earnest of the Spirit" is a significant metaphor: the Apostle Paul's usage of "the Spirit" so closely associates this aspect of the Holy Trinity with Christ that the two are, at times, practically identical in his discourse. If the Spirit is so closely correlated with the identity of Christ, whom the Spirit succeeds as a comforter on Earth, possessing and possessed by believers awaiting the rapture, then the metaphor "the earnest of the Spirit" serves as a metonym for the name of God's son, whose sacrifice "sealed" believers, that is, saved them in order that they might enter the Kingdom of God in the afterlife. As Equiano comes to recognize the persistent presence of the Holy Spirit in his former captivity, enslavement, and sense of abjection, time collapses for him in a scene of contemporaneity: "Now every leading providential circumstance that happened to me, from the day I was taken from my parents to that hour, was then, in my view, as if it had but just then occurred" (Equiano 162). The chief point made about salvation in these passages is that once salvation is assured, man is not only redeemed, but also enlightened. For Equiano, enlightenment is the primary benefit of salvation, represented by his imagery of lifted veils and rebirth, and mentioned, for instance, in his citation of Isaiah 25:7 (162): "And he will destroy in this mountain the face of the covering cast over all people, and the veil that is spread over all nations."

From this point of view, we can see how important it is that Equiano toggles between the Old Testament and the New in his discourse on salvation. His recourse to Isaiah suggests the basis for such oscillation: the name Isaiah, meaning salvation of Jehovah, is almost identical in meaning to the name Joshua, meaning Jehovah is salvation. In the New Testament, the name Joshua is rendered as Jesus; Jesus, in turn, is the name of the Messiah proclaimed by Isaiah. Thus the book of Isaiah and its references are seen by Biblical scholars as particularly powerful and prophetic. New Testament writers regularly hearkened to Isaiah, whose words became deeply engrained in English national culture. (Examples such as Milton's *Paradise Lost* (1667), itself an important influence on Equiano, and Handel's oratorio the *Messiah* (1741), a composition that shares a name and theme with Alexander Pope's poem of the same title, which appeared in the *Spectator* in 1712, come readily to mind.) Christ himself began his preaching ministry by reading from the sixty-first chapter of Isaiah, declaring himself to be the fulfillment of Isaiah's prophecy, and so the book is sealed in its prominence among the Christian faithful.[33]

Such Christian discourses of faith further intensify Equiano's experience of salvation. To express this experience, he gives metaphors having to do with the law of God, by which he is saved. The conveyance of God's word, in which Christ makes such metaphorical proclamations as "Verily, verily, I say unto thee, Except a man be born of water and of the Spirit, he cannot enter into the Kingdom of God" (John 3:5; Equiano 162), are interpreted by Equiano during his conversion experience as types of judgment and instruction. In John's Gospel, Christ uses the trope of rebirth by water and Spirit to challenge the ruler Nicodemus, and speaks of the entrance into the kingdom as a central mystery that distinguishes between persons of faith and those unfamiliar with "the way," that is, God's Word made flesh, Christ himself. In the same scene in which he cites this passage, Equiano also cites a proclamation from Psalms that confirms for him that the judgments of the Lord are to be desired more than any wealth he might amass for himself, "yea, more than much fine gold: sweeter also than honey and the honeycomb" (Ps 19:10; Equiano 162). One might imagine that included among the list of such less than desirable wealth would be the ownership of persons.

It seems clear for Equiano that entry into God's kingdom did not call for simple acceptance of the Gospel of Christ, but was achieved by way of embracing a mode of ethical living dictated by laws propounded in the Old Testament, and rearticulated and reified in the New Testament through Christ as the Word incarnate, such that an understanding of the import of these metaphors is both accomplished and manifested through action against slavery and actuation of free being on earth as well as in the afterlife. Paul's enigmatic phrase for the coming of the law reads: "For I was without the law once: but when the commandment came, sin revived, and I died" (Rom 7:9; Equiano 162). Equiano cites Paul's words in an effort to describe his own situation; that is, that as soon as the commandment of God's law was effected, he was rendered carnally dead because his sins were made apparent. As the Bible now appears to Equiano as an "unsealed book" (162), the force of God's law is made fresh. His "unlawful self" is executed, to be replaced by an incorporeal, transcendent self that has been saved and redeemed, such that his very body—and by extension, his text, which symbolizes his *inscribed*, immanent being—emerges as a mystery to be read and interpreted, and his soul—his transcendent being—stands out as an actuated entity. For example, his allusion in this scene to the Epistle to the Romans, concerned, in its entirety, to exhort God's people to feel reassured in his power, dovetails with his reference to a minor metaphor in I Samuel 7:12: "Then Samuel took a stone, and set it between Mizpeh and Shen, and called the name of it Ebenezer, saying Hitherto hath the Lord helped us." Equiano writes that he "set up [the Lord's] Ebenezer" (Ebenezer means literally "stone of help") and he could thus boast of his savior to the unsaved in whose midst he stood as a transfigured being (164). Salvation in the Bible is a comprehensive event in the life of the believer. Surveying it in Equiano's *Narrative*, it is an event that marks the *experience* of liminality and conviction, the *incorporation* of faith and wisdom, and moves them dialectically forward through the transformed *being* of Equiano himself.

ACTUATION

I will discuss the final phase, what I refer to as "actuation in praxis," after a manner that takes it to be dependent upon the others for the accomplishment of the metaphorical mode of meaning making Equiano employs in the text. Equiano is intent upon setting down his experiences and beliefs in writing. What he has experienced is, primarily, an understanding of the power of "the word," which has granted him the "true" sense of not only the Scriptures (in both the straightforward sense of that phrase as grounded in literacy, and in the metaphorical sense of that phrase as it refers to the body of Christ), but also of his own being. What he experiences by way of spiritual conversion through the Bible's teaching echoes his understanding of Christ as both "the Word" and "the way." That is, through "the Word," one is not only saved but also actuated, as Equiano points out in his conversion scene. And salvation comes not by faith alone, but also by works in a way that underscores the signification of his being as well as his text.

I will explain what I mean by this last line in these concluding paragraphs of this chapter. The general material of the final phase of Equiano's *Narrative* is the familiar ground of understanding and action: there is again the juxtaposition of the saved against the unsaved, and this portends rather heavily as Equiano differentiates between those of his readers who will refuse understanding and will thus forego salvation, and those who, by persisting in their faith and via engagement with the world around them, will be the saved agents of worldly transformation (164). My summary of the process is borne out in Equiano's multiple scriptural references near the end of chapter 10 (164): if we consider his scriptural bricolage in this chapter as a quilt of phrases that positions the reader to engage in future social action, we find that there is a participatory moment that, ideally, is engendered in the reader's mind as soon as she or he completes the text. The Bible's invitation to the reader—to which Equiano directs us—is one that ultimately has to do with being as it relates to new beginnings and existence: the New Testament concludes not with a prognostication on the "end," but with an invitation to behold God as he makes "all things new" (Rev 21:5) in a "new" world beyond the time of the present. Equiano likewise concludes his *Narrative* with a vision of creation and "work," which he had, earlier in the text, struggled to distinguish from "grace" (164). Just as the actuation phase of Equiano's *Narrative* is participatory, the concept of work is of significance. Equiano calls for the abolition of slavery, missionary work in Africa (193), and education for the former slaves (196).

He also, importantly, commends and "blesses" those Westerners who provide "liberal" support for the "oppressed negroes" (sic, 205), a commendation that he offers along with a reference to Job 30:25: "Did not I weep for him that was in trouble? was *not* my soul grieved for the poor?" The passage from Job is striking, as it results from two readings. First, one must place it in the light of Equiano's reference, on the same page, to Isaiah 32:8, which speaks to setting aright the deceit practiced by those in power. Isaiah 32:7–8 reads: "The instruments also of the churl are evil: he deviseth wicked devices to destroy the poor with lying words, even when the needy speaketh right. But the liberal deviseth liberal things; and by liberal things shall he stand." Thus Equiano refers to the liberals who shall rightly be called liberals, not those who practice deceit against the poor, yet proclaim themselves champions of the downtrodden. Equiano's citation from Job follows this after a disjointed fashion. Biblical scripture shows Job to be an upright man, yes, but also one filled with arrogance and self-righteousness. His friends Eliphaz and Elihu try to point this out to him, yet Job appears unaffected by their criticisms when he counters that he has always thought of the poor, that he has always championed the troubled (Job 30:25). There is a bit of conscious irony in Equiano's citation, which comes as he reviews for his reader the activities of the British legislature as regards slavery and the colonization of Africa, and this after, in his letter to Parliament, having praised the legislature for its "liberal sentiment" and moral compass (xxi). In a round about way, he exhorts the reader to be forthright and sincere in his or her dealings with Africans, to resist villainy and embrace the role of what the Bible calls the true "liberal." Quite a nuanced stance.

An Actuated Being

In the closing pages of his *Narrative*, Equiano uses the Book of Proverbs, also called the Book of Wisdom, to underscore his call for true liberals to carry out moral and just social works. Proverbs 11, 14, and 21, all of which are cited in the *Narrative*'s final chapter, insist upon the dialectical tension of sin and righteousness. Equiano's movement from these scriptures to the Book of Micah in the final passage of the *Narrative* provides an apt conclusion to his life story:

> My life and fortune have been extremely checquered, and my adventures various. Even those I have related are considerably abridged. If any incident in this little work should appear uninteresting and trifling to most readers, I can only say, as my excuse for mentioning it, that almost every event of my life made an impression on my mind, and influenced my conduct. I early accustomed myself to look at the hand of God in the minutest occurrence, and to learn from it a lesson of morality and religion; and in this light every circumstance I have related was to me of importance. After all, what makes any event important, unless by its observation we become better and wiser, and learn 'to do justly, to love mercy, and to walk humbly before God!'[34] To

those who are possessed of this spirit, there is scarcely any book or incident so trifling that does not afford some profit, while to others the experience of ages seems of no use; and even to pour out to them the treasures of wisdom is throwing the jewels of instruction away. (208)

I suggested earlier that the Bible's final book, the Book of Revelation, culminates in a gesture toward that which lies beyond itself. Citing the Book of Micah as his final reference to scripture, in lieu of Revelation, a more obvious choice for a religious writer aiming to reveal truth to his readers, represents a concerted strategy on Equiano's part. Biblical scholars view Micah as a significant book of the Hebrew Bible. It shifts dialectically between a condemnation of the present sins of the people, and an exposition of God's purpose in blessing them. Chapter 6 of Micah, from which Equiano cites, concerns condemnation; it threatens idolaters and those who oppress the powerless. As an allusion to Deuteronomy 10:12 (they read almost identically), the passage from Micah calls upon God's people to obey his laws not selectively, but completely. Micah goes beyond issuing injunctions against those who oppress and deal falsely with the powerless; it emphasizes the importance of Judah and Israel's return from exile.

By referring at the conclusion of his *Narrative* to the sense of exile that opens his text and that, through the preponderance of the autobiography, characterizes his sense of being, Equiano works to bring his account to a conclusion marked by a provisional unity of meaning. A call for morality, justice, and the end of exile are all subtended in the *Narrative*'s culmination by the practice, not simply the profession, of an ideal, rather than a false or incomplete, Christianity. At the end of his *Narrative*, wherein Equiano has inscribed the widely varied experiences of his life, he invites his reader to actuate the ideals of his Christian discourse by imbibing into their spirits and undertaking through their works the "jewels of instruction" he has granted them through a text replete with spiritual metaphors of his being.

～

If the Bible and its many metaphors eventuate in an archetype of literature, and Equiano looks to the fragmentary metaphors of the Bible to find how all things have an origin, then he certainly looks to it as inspiration for a discursive account of his own being and draws upon its metaphors accordingly. Equiano's autobiography should be seen as life-writing and as the protension of being: a disclosure of displaced but strident being that depends upon a practice of bricolage, in the sense that Lévi-Strauss gives that term. He pulls together a system of thought out of the bits and pieces of his experience and his reading, and this is the model he uses to convey his sense of being through image, text, and textuality. It is the language of the Bible that provides Equiano with words and metaphorical phrases with which to account for himself and to describe the parameters of his subjectivity. In that way, Equiano makes of his own text a talking book that does not bind his being to it or within it, but protends his being toward multiple horizons of readership. Refusing the indelible bond between being and textuality postulated by Western philosophy, Equiano nonetheless uses his autobiography to exhort, as does the Bible, readers to undertake morally responsible action, even as they actuate his very existence by engaging meaningfully with his text.

Equiano's *Narrative* puts forward this moralistic call during a period of history that marked the emergence of the nation-state and its philosophical and social discourses (as I discussed relative to the writings of Kant, Hume, Addison, Pope, and others). Before the nation-state rose to take its place as the guiding ideal of modern society, that role had been filled by the church, to which Equiano, as we see, pays full homage and fealty. Equiano's writing takes note of that which is involved in such a transition. We now understand better the ways in which Equiano's text may be called an event in the thinking of modern black being: his use of Biblical discourse and its many metaphors culminates in an onto-theological discourse upon the right aims of the only collective to which he felt he could belong: a universal humanism that exceeds and, indeed, critiques the limits of race and nation. For today's reader and as an event of thought, Equiano's text has affected history as well as the sort of historical consciousness that was lastingly propounded in nineteenth-century Hegelianism. Equiano worked to negotiate the gap between church, nation-state, and empire, to articulate a spiritual development of self-consciousness that would keep time with the development of a translocal, global spirit while, paradoxically, allowing for the expression of the particular and the realization of his being beyond the limits of race and text.

Equiano's exemplary negotiation of this paradoxical, metaphorical site of existence emerges as an iterable (or, repeatable) precedent, as we shall see in the forthcoming chapters. It is such iterability that founds the possibility of a poetics of black being. Equiano draws upon his experience and crafts his life story as useful testimony and instruction that, in turn, contribute to a revised, critical ontology of black being.

4

Remnants of Memory

Metaphor and Being in Frances E. W. Harper's *Sketches of Southern Life*

It's a kind of literary archeology: on the basis of some information and a little bit of guesswork you journey to a site to see what remains were left behind and to reconstruct the world that these remains imply. . . . [M]y reliance on the image—on the remains—in addition to recollection . . . yields up a kind of a truth. . . . [T]he image comes first and tells me what the "memory" is about.

—Toni Morrison, "The Site of Memory" (1987)

Neither the poem nor the song can intervene to save impossible testimony; on the contrary, it is testimony . . . that founds the possibility of the poem.

—Giorgio Agamben, *Remnants of Auschwitz: The Witness and the Archive* (1999)

That is why thinking holds to the
coming of what has been,
and is remembrance.
. . . .
But poetry that thinks is in truth
the topology of Being.
This topology tells Being the
whereabouts of its actual presence.

—Martin Heidegger, "The Thinker as Poet" (1947/1954)

If one project of contemporary literary theory is to submit the reading of nineteenth-century African American literature to a certain number of inquiries regarding metaphor and black being, then Frances Ellen Watkins Harper's *Sketches of Southern Life* (1872) serves as an exemplum to the present generation of scholars. Not only does Harper's work in this collection of poetry continue Equiano's use of spiritual metaphor as central to the expression of black being; it also paves the way for later quasi-secular expressions of black being such as those found in *The Souls of Black Folk*, *The Man Who Lived Underground*, and *Invisible Man*, works that are not usually discussed in light of Harper's poetics.

Even so, the poems collected in *Sketches of Southern Life*—specifically, those that constitute the "Aunt Chloe" cycle—have been invariably interpreted by critics as a crucial literary representation of the postbellum black vernacular subject. Harper's poetry was highly praised in its own time, and the century after Harper's *Sketches* appeared saw a line of early critics, led by James Weldon Johnson and J. Saunders Redding, who, though ambivalent about the value of the preponderance of Harper's verse and fiction, saw the Aunt Chloe poems as the incipit of black vernacular poetry, the cornerstone upon which later poets such as Paul Laurence Dunbar and Langston Hughes would build dialect verse and blues-infused metrical compositions.[1] Over the last twenty years, black feminist criticism—the line of Frances Smith Foster, Hazel Carby, and Melba Joyce Boyd—has founded its judgment on Harper's poetic and novelistic representations of pre- and post-Reconstruction life, her critique of sentimental white women's fiction, and her searing treatment of American racism and immorality.[2] These two lines coalesce in their attempts to limn Harper's role as a poet who projects the vernacular black subject into the realm of history. Yet it is black feminist criticism that has been more intent upon identifying Harper as central to the canon of great African American writers. Frances Smith Foster's work is indicative of this thrust. She explains that during Harper's postwar travels, Harper figured as an activist writer and race woman who "was especially interested in working with women and frequently conducted private sessions with them 'about their daughters, and about things connected with the welfare of the race.'" Harper's journeys throughout the Reconstruction South ended in 1871, the year before the appearance of *Sketches of Southern Life*—"a substantially original work that," as Smith Foster reminds us, "rendered in poetic form many of the scenes and characters [Harper] had encountered."[3] *Sketches* is, then, an act of historiography as well as an act of onto-theological metaphorics, and in this noetic convergence I see a clear connection between the projects of Equiano and those that would come from Du Bois, Hurston, Wright, and Ellison.

Equiano's autobiography, which I have just discussed, serves as a case in point. The writing of a life, as Equiano achieves in his *Narrative*, has long been recognized by contemporary scholars of poststructuralist and new historicist bent to be an act of historiography, and even of "critical historiography," to borrow a term from the work of Michel de Certeau.[4] In this way, Equiano not only wrote an account of his life that would forcefully (and counter to social convention) occupy the annals of history; he also gave an account of slave being from within the constraints of the peculiar institution. But while Equiano's act of critical historiography unfolds under the rubric of autobiography and thus makes numerous anticipated claims to "truth" and "transparency." Harper's critical historiography unfolds through versification, a concerted act of art and artifice that could be said to reveal "truth" of a certain sort (à la Morrison), as long as the qualification was not that its truth be "empirical," especially since herself Harper had never experienced slavery.

Harper, however, forges the "truth" of slave being through her art; her poetry reflects the lived experience of so many freed persons, and especially freedwomen, across the former slaves states, and they emerge in the forms of composite figures, Aunt Chloe most prominent among them. *Sketches* may thus be read as an "unauthorized," collective memoir that employs onto-theological metaphors as it gives witness to the being of the slave. It is a particular sort of "life writing" that, like Equiano's *Narrative* before it, is intended to challenge and revise the accepted discourse on Western humanism, expand the annals of Western history, and construct a world of humanity wherein black being is safe, at liberty, and, ideally, agency-driven.

However, most of the criticism on Harper's poems, even that which appeared during the 1980s when black feminist criticism began to crystalize its discourse, deals not with the onto-theological metaphorics that enliven her poetics, but, in a more pointed fashion, with either her politics, her feminism, or both. Patricia Liggins Hill's useful 1981 essay, " 'Let Me Make the Songs for the People': A Study of Frances Watkins Harper's Poetry," emphasizes the themes of uplift and feminism in all of Harper's poetry, including the Aunt Chloe poems. And while I certainly uphold her assertion that "Harper has helped to lay a sound aesthetic foundation upon which much of contemporary black poetry is based," close critical attention to those aesthetics is not given in her essay. More recently, Elizabeth Petrino's " 'We are a Rising People': Frances Harper's Radical Views on Class and Racial Equality in *Sketches of Southern Life*" (2005), also sees the poems in an act of "retelling history from the perspective of freedwomen," but strangely argues that Harper "refrains from dialect, thus rejecting stereotyped black voices."[5] This is, of course, a position with which I disagree in this chapter, because whether one calls Aunt Chloe's speech "vernacular" or not, in its time it was undoubtedly referred to (by Paul Lawrence Dunbar and later by James Weldon Johnson) as "dialect" poetry. This does not mean that Harper's portrayals may rightly be called "stereotypical," as I discuss quite to the contrary in this chapter. Finally, the fullest and most authoritative studies of Harper have been undertaken by Smith Foster and Boyd, both of whose pioneering work I note above. Boyd pays especially close attention to the metaphorics of Harper's *Sketches*; her substantive biographical work on Harper includes incisive expositional commentary on Harper's poetics. Amidst her groundbreaking studies of Harper's corpus, Smith Foster has detailed the thematics of Harper's Reconstruction-era poetry, and echoes in some ways my own attention to structure. My work in this chapter seeks to build on the foundation established by these critics by placing Harper in a genealogy of writers and thinkers whose literature employs onto-theological metaphors. I seek to examine these metaphors as vehicles for the expression and protension of black being.

In this chapter, I point out the ways in which Harper's metaphorics, not only at the level of the semantic, but also at the levels of structure and orality, permit her to construct an ontology of slave being as counter-cultural and as central to a critical, revisionist concept of the human. Harper's appearance as a focus of not only critical, but also, in this study, theoretical attention has, I argue, much to teach us. Not only does she exemplify a practice of historiography and onto-theological poetics that is aesthetic as well as activist in nature; she also provides us with a poetic structure that speaks as much meaning as her poetic metaphors themselves.

I suggest that it is the coincidence of Harper's vision of art and the ontological "truth" of black being that enables and gives voice to her poetic feminism and political activism (what I will here refer to as a translocal activism *avant la lettre*) in *Sketches of Southern Life*. Notwithstanding J. Saunders Redding's judgment that Harper's poetry is clumsy because it does not conform to the poetic conventions of its day, I demonstrate that Harper uses her poetic structure to declare a "newness" of both black being and black poetry. Harper has been criticized by Redding and others as a poet who was deficient in technique, but whose staying power came largely through her ability to read her work aloud before an audience, captivating and transporting them in the process. I submit that there are further important points to be considered here: that Harper's *techné* was not insufficient or foppishly amateurish, as Redding argues, but was, indeed, experimental. Harper knew well the technical achievements of her poetic and narrative models, which included her contemporaries Henry Wadsworth Longfellow and the abolitionist poet John Greenleaf Whittier. Moreover, she was part of an active and accomplished literary circle that included Harriet Beecher Stowe, Frederick Douglass, and Lydia Maria Child, and indeed was well their peer. In *Sketches* she sought to achieve a sort of symbolic representation of African American women that existed nowhere in the canon of American literature that preceded her. Even Harriet Jacobs' unparalleled achievement in critical autobiography (her 1861 narrative, *Incidents in the Life of a Slave Girl*) did not represent with great depth the African American vernacular subject. Harper would not only challenge the *techné* of her narrative models by insisting upon the metaphorical language of the black folk; she would also, through her own portrayal of slave women, counter the stereotypical image of the black woman as found in the most influential novel of her time, *Uncle Tom's Cabin* (1852), a point I discuss at length below.

Given her immersion in the literary conventions of her day,[6] one must simply consider that Harper felt some need to write beyond these conventions in order to represent compellingly and meaningfully the realities of slave being. Certainly, she must have felt that the experiences of the freedwomen with whom she visited during her tour of the Reconstruction South (between 1865 and 1871) would have been impoverished had their expression been forced to conform itself to that of free white women and their sentimental conventions of themes and narration. Harper's poetic structure, her *mythos* and *techné* all required refashioning if her poetry were to achieve the lofty goals she set for it. Out of Aunt Chloe's southern black metaphorics, Harper crafts a foundation for making black poetry—and black being—"new."

As I mention above, this new foundation would be buttressed by late nineteenth-century poets such as Paul Lawrence Dunbar, but the raising of its bones in the twentieth century would be undertaken in the poetry of Langston Hughes and the prose of Zora Neale Hurston as they, together among myriad other artists, crafted what came to be known as "New Negro" literature. Harper must certainly be seen as a foremother, if not indeed a mother of this literature, but such is not the only importance we are called upon to draw from her ontological metaphorics. Through it, Harper also helped erect a new nineteenth-century black feminism that took its cue not only from the lights of African American literary history that both preceded her and were of her own moment (e.g., Maria Stewart, Harriet Jacobs, Mary

Ann Shadd Cary, Charlotte Forten, Sojourner Truth, and Elizabeth Keckley, to name only a select few who were both feminist activists and writers/ memoirists). Her feminism also emerged out of an intellectual and social milieu that included such abolitionist and suffragist leaders as Douglass, Child, and William Wells Brown, among others.

Because *Sketches of Southern Life* emerges from this context and serves at once as poetry and an undeclared collective memoir (an alternative, critical historiography, the composite testimony of freed African Americans Harper met in the course of her postbellum travels), an examination of the Aunt Chloe poems through the layered framework of memory, metaphor, and being carries a certain significance. As I describe that layering, I shall imply its theory—a theory of onto-theological poetics practiced in tandem with a theory of history; an effort to discover an analogy for the task of the poet who seeks—in full understanding of the long genealogy to which Harper belongs, from Equiano and Phillis Wheatley, to Maria Stewart and David Walker, and on to Jacobs and Keckley—to act as a surrogate witness to historical and contemporary contexts of black being, and to, in turn, project such being toward a future world through the metaphorics of black vernacular expression.

The Evolution of Harper's Vernacular Poetry

In order to bring Harper's metaphorics into greater relief, in this section I will underscore the important play of sound and sense as it evolves in her poetry. Doing so will show how Harper's relationship with language allows her to approximate an ontology of slave being through poetic expression. I will discuss a number of Harper's signature poems that appear between the decades of 1854 and 1874. Harper wrote and published a great deal of poetry during these years. Not surprisingly, much of this poetry deals with the themes of freedom and slavery, women's rights, and labor. What is perhaps more striking is that during this period, the Aunt Chloe poems were the only ones among Harper's poems to make extended use of the slave's vernacular. Not only did this vernacular affect the "sound" of Harper's poetry, especially since she was often given to reading her poetry aloud before various audiences; it also affected the "sense" of her poetry, since black vernacular language is so often composed of syntactical and semiotic elements that result in fluid, multiple, and often ambiguous semantic meanings.

Discussing these poems—and the place of the Aunt Chloe poems among them—allows us to see more clearly the signification of black being through metaphorical language in Harper's oeuvre. And it allows us to see how and, perhaps, why Harper signifies black being quite differently in the Aunt Chloe cycle than in her other poetic compositions. Harper's poetics enjoin a poetics of being at work in African American literature since Equiano. And, as I discuss more pointedly in the final section of this chapter, her attention to an ontology of slave being resonates brilliantly with the ontology later at work in Du Bois's *The Souls of Black Folk*.

"The Slave Mother" (1854) is among Harper's best-known and most widely anthologized poems. Coming early in her poetic output, it is also among the most conventional in meter and imagery. It takes up the themes that characterize much of Harper's corpus: honorable motherhood; the indelible ties between mother and child; and the horrible ills of slavery. Harper eschews the popular meter of iambic pentameter in favor of alternating lines of verse written in iambic tetrameter and iambic trimeter. The first two lines of the opening stanza are written in iambic trimeter, and thus they are read quickly: "Heard you that shriek? It rose / So wildly on the air." The reader is thus plunged into the poem's narrative suspense, and emphasis is placed on these lines as conveying the central action around which the poem revolves. As we continue to engage Harper's lines of alternating meter, we are carried along by the relatively quick tempo of the poem, our eyes falling down the page until we reach the ultimate stanza, which concludes the narrative thus: "No marvel, then, these bitter shrieks / Disturb the listening air: / She is a mother, and her heart / Is breaking in despair." By moving us along so quickly, yet never relenting on the intensity of her message, Harper's use of meter works with the meaning, for while we are briefly uplifted by the poem's imagery in the seventh stanza ("His love has been a joyous light / That o'er her pathway smiled, / A fountain gushing ever new, / Amid life's desert wild"), we are swiftly carried along the stream of the slave mother's despair as the poem progresses. Harper forms this individual poem as a narrative whole, meant to impress upon the mind of the reader and the ear of the listener the dramatic image of the most heart-wrenching of America's childless mothers: the slave mother whose child is torn forcibly from her "circling arms."

While, as I mention above, early critics such as Redding critiqued Harper's technical skills, Harper does, in fact, craft her poems quite carefully. Her attention to craft is very much in evidence in "The Slave Mother," where she relates the first and last stanzas closely. Where the word "shriek" is singular in the first stanza, in the last, there are multiple "shrieks," as though the reader were confronted with a multitude of grieving slave mothers folded into a singular figure who stands as the symbolic avatar of all such mothers.

And while the first stanza is rendered in the past tense, the final one is rendered in the present. Such shifts in time and number work with the poem's meaning, and its effect is such that the reader is carried along in the poem's time and sounding, surrounded by the multitude of mothers it implies. However, any use of Biblical metaphor is fully absent from this particular piece. In its place, Harper renders metaphors of maternal and moral sentiment, the most striking of which comes in the fifth stanza:

> He is not hers, although she bore
> For him a mother's pains;
> He is not hers, although her blood
> Is coursing through his veins!

While the metaphors that enliven this stanza are not unusual, they do, in fact, speak directly to the reader the sentiments of Harper's maternal figure. Even so, this poem grants the slave mother power through pathos. Indeed, Harper relies upon the reader's sensibilities, for she neither depicts the slave mother in active resistance to her oppression (a strategy she did use to great effect in an earlier poem entitled "Eliza Harris," 1853, for instance), nor does she direct the reader toward a specific action by modeling action upon the narrator or the poetic figure.

Instead, Harper asks the reader to contemplate the scene before her or him, and in contemplating the scene she hopes the reader will not only broaden her or his understanding of what is at stake in the poem, but also the reader's stake in what is implicated in the poem's meaning. I would argue that while the poem deals deftly in conventions of sympathy (feeling for someone else), it does not fully engage the reader on the more intimate plane of empathy (feeling with someone else, or putting oneself in the other's place), a plane that might have been reached had Harper permitted the slave mother in the poem to speak directly to the reader, as she later allows Aunt Chloe to do. Thus while this poem appeals to the reader's morality, an appeal that is certainly not without merit, it does not, to the fullest extent possible, demonstrate the consciousness, or conscious being, of the slave.

Harper seems to work toward redressing this shortfall in "The Slave Mother: A Tale of the Ohio," published in 1856. The poem dramatizes the true story of Margaret Garner, whom Harper depicts as drawn toward the state of Ohio by the brightly shining "northern star." Garner's story is now well known, but required critical attention and interpretation as it was told and retold during Harper's lifetime and well beyond. After she fled to Ohio with her four children in search of freedom, Garner's quest was thwarted by the Fugitive Slave Law of 1850. As she faced recapture, Garner determined that her children would be better off in death than in a life of perpetual servitude.

The movement from the first-person voice of the poem's first five stanzas to the third person in the remaining eleven stanzas seems, in part, to obfuscate the slave consciousness that Harper seemed intent upon expressing. She does, in the eleventh stanza, revert again to the first person, but then only through the voice of the narrator. As with the earlier poem, it is the voice of the free narrator, rather than that of the enslaved being, that gives the most direct evidence of consciousness, though the slave mother's consciousness is represented through indirect dialogue. Indeed, Harper insists that Garner fulfilled her motherly duty toward her children: "I will save my precious children / From their darkly threatened doom, / I will hew their path to freedom / Through the portals of the tomb" (*A Brighter Coming Day* 85). Garner succeeded in killing one child, the infant, before she was subdued and captured. Harper closes the poem thus: "Sends this deed of fearful daring / Through my country's heart no thrill, / Do the icy hands of slavery / Every pure emotion chill? / Oh! If there is any honor, / Truth or justice in the land, / Will ye not, as men and Christians, / On the side of freedom stand?" Garner's American tragedy and Harper's appeal to American conscience make clear in this poem her own poetic consciousness, and alludes tantalizingly to that of Garner.

Harper, too, was personally affected by the passage of the Fugitive Slave Act. In its wake, her home state of Maryland passed a law in 1853 stating that any person of color who came into the state by way of its northern border could be sold into slavery. The Fugitive Slave Act was a threat to all free persons of color, North and South, because it put their liberty at risk. Harper's family, led by her Uncle William, left Baltimore for Canada, where he felt they would be safer. By Frances Smith Foster's account (in her introduction to *A Brighter Coming Day*), it is not clear why Harper did not go to Canada with them. Instead, Harper went only as far North as Ohio, where she took a position as an instructor at Union Seminary, a school founded in 1847 by the Conference of the African Methodist Episcopal (AME) Church. Effectively, Maryland's 1853 law meant that Harper could never go home again. She lived, as William Still pronounced her in his *The Underground Railroad* (1872), in "exile" (540), an exilic existence that draws her into relation not only with the subjects of her poetry, but with uprooted and exiled writers such as Equiano.

She published a poetic lamentation of her exile in 1857, "Bury Me in a Free Land," and as she did so she transformed the pain of her homelessness into a pointed social and political critique. The poem has impacted readers to the extent that it has become Harper's epitaph, thus it is quite central to any discussion of the evolution of Harper's poetics. Each of this work's eight quatrains develops a poetic statement that reinforces the poem's overall meaning, which is, in short, a call to abolition. The major devices that move the poem along are rhyme and repetition. The end rhyme scheme Harper uses is aabb; she employs both pure rhymes and slant rhymes. Pure rhymes make up the largest part of the rhyme scheme, existing in such pairs as "will/hill," "grave/slave," and "lash/gash." Slant rhymes, where sounds are closely related but not identical, come in such combinations as "bay/prey" and "high/by," and even these are quite close to pure rhymes. The rhyming combination of grave/slave repeats in the second stanza, and the word "slaves" closes the poem. Harper's use of repetition is dramatic, as she places a narrator in the text to convey a vividly imagined set of scenes. The most constant repetition in the poem, however, is a variation upon the first-person pronoun, "I." None of the stanzas lacks this pronoun. Stanzas two through four employ anaphora—they commence similarly: "I could not rest," "I could not sleep," "I could not rest." With each recurrence we are reminded of the poet's dying wish for peace in death, yet we are also compelled to examine that which conditions her wish: the prevalence of slavery in the land of her birth. Thus birth and death, being and non-being are juxtaposed; the recurrence of the "I" in the poem keeps us quite aware of the narrator's existence and subjectivity, and with each recurrence we are just as aware of the imminent proximity of her death. With each stanza, with each recurrence, a new aspect of her consciousness—which productively navigates the tension between life and death—is presented to dramatically different effect.

The decade that followed would see Harper moving into different intellectual territory, both literally and figuratively. In short order, the 1860s moved Harper quickly through significant phases of her adult life: she married in 1860, became a mother herself in 1862, and was widowed in 1864. Her marriage had constituted a pause (though not a complete cessation) in her public life. Now that she was widowed and left with her deceased husband's considerable debt, she took up fully once again her public work.

It may seem overly facile to conclude that with the close of the Civil War and Harper's subsequent tour of the South during the Reconstruction period came an even stronger sense of poetic consciousness on her part, but such does seem to be the case upon examination of the poems that she produced during this era. This conclusion is certainly borne out by an examination of the 1865 poem, "President Lincoln's Proclamation of

Freedom," a lyrical expression of hope for the future conveyed in both pure and slant rhymes as well as an emphasis upon black self-determination.

"President Lincoln's Proclamation of Freedom," is a composition of nine quatrains whose strongest structural characteristics are rhyme and repetition. The rhyme scheme is abcb. We have, of course, seen such a scheme in much poetry from Harper. However, in this poem Harper insists upon pure rhyming elements. The rhyming pairs of each quatrain are years/tears, bright/light, Caroline/shine, crime/time, key/free, light/light, dust/just, away/day, light/sight. The first thing we are led to notice is the absence of slant rhyme. Slant rhymes can be great innovations; they often insist upon the unexpected. Pure rhymes are clear and bold; they call attention to the poet's versification and intentions. The pure rhyming pairs are metronomes; they establish a pattern, both aural and visual. They are neither opposites, nor synonyms; by themselves, they establish no true sense of meaning. Their purpose appears to lie in their ability to call attention to the meaning that inheres in each stanza. In this way, they work in concert with the repetition of certain elements of the poem. The word "shall," which appears fifteen times in the poem, sharply underscores the poet's emphasis upon a determined future for the newly freed slaves. It appears in all but one stanza, and is connected to images of light and processes of enlightenment that, the poet intimates, attend emancipation. The metaphorical reference to "the sun-kissed brow of labor" should be read in light of Harper's poem "Free Labor," discussed below. Self-determination, freedom to participate as workers in the public marketplace, and the moral attributes of labor (through which one contributes to society), are all emphasized in the poem. The use of anaphora in the poem (coming primarily through the repetition of the phrase "It shall" in the first three stanzas) grants this piece the quality of an anthem. Though the anaphora breaks off in the middle of the poem, the rhythm reminds one of the strident tones of Julia Ward Howe's "The Battle Hymn of the Republic" (1862), itself modeled after "John Brown's Body" and the early African American camp song, "Say Brothers, Can You Meet Me?"[7]

Thus in this later poem that, like the Aunt Chloe cycle, appeared during Reconstruction, Harper employs the usual conventions of Western poetry in rhyme scheme, form, and voice while speaking to and of black being in ways that she generally did not before her southern tour. When compared with other of Harper's poetic figures that appeared during this period,[8] Aunt Chloe appears to be a symbolic maternal figure that not only served as a composite representation of the many freedwomen Harper spoke with and interviewed during her southern tour; she also appears to be a

literary figure whom Harper rescues from misrepresentation. Since Harper
had many times acknowledged the importance of Harriet Beecher Stowe's
Uncle Tom's Cabin, and had based one of her most important poems, "Eliza
Harris," upon a scene from Stowe's novel,⁹ it would not be a stretch to see
that Stowe's Aunt Chloe is multiply refashioned and recuperated in Harper's
poems. In Stowe's narrative, Aunt Chloe appears as a stereotypical "mammy"
figure, one with a good heart and good intentions, a dedicated wife and
mother, but also presented as central to the novel's comic relief. For instance,
when describing Aunt Chloe, Stowe writes:

> A round, black, shining face is hers, so glossy as to suggest that
> she might have been washed over with white of eggs, like one
> of her own tea rusks. Her whole plump countenance beams
> with satisfaction and contentment from under her well-starched
> turban. . . . A cook she certainly was, in the very bone and centre
> of her being. Not a chicken or turkey or duck in the barn-yard
> but looked grave when they saw her approaching, and seemed
> evidently to be reflecting on their latter end [. . .]. (66–67)

To make certain of the point—that of the stereotype—at work in
Stowe's novel, one need only note her description of Uncle Tom himself:
"He was a large, broad-chested powerfully-made man, of a full glossy
black, and a face whose truly African features were characterized by an
expression of grave and steady good sense, united with much kindliness and
benevolence" (68). Uncle Tom's blackness of skin and inveterate Christian
morality seem to be linked as cause and effect. Whenever he overheard his
children or other adult slaves complaining about their oppressed condition,
Tom chastised them with the greatest sense of moral superiority that Stowe
could manage to convey through him (and through his blackness). And
while Aunt Chloe appears to be equally dark, she does not match Tom in
morality. She is striking, however, for the dialect with which she speaks. The
following passage will suffice as an example of Chloe's everyday language
in Stowe's book:

> Here you, Mose and Pete! [Chloe exclaims, speaking to her own
> sons] get out de way, you niggers! Get away, Mericky, honey,—
> mammy'll give her baby some fin, by and by. Now, Mas'r George,
> you jest take off dem books, and set down now with my old
> man, and I'll take up de sausages, and have de first griddle full
> of cakes on your plates in less dan no time. (69)

Harper's revised image of Chloe is quite far from that provided by Stowe, a point that is confirmed by reading any of her Aunt Chloe poems. In "Aunt Chloe's Politics," for instance, the third poem in the series, Aunt Chloe emerges as a plainspoken moralist who speaks in the vernacular, but with none of the hyper-comedic and stereotypic characteristics with which Stowe over-burdens her own Chloe. As the composite sketch of wise African American women Harper encountered during her travels through the South, the Aunt Chloe who appears in this collection of poetry also undoubtedly serves as a model for Aunt Linda, a character who figures importantly in Harper's most accomplished work of fiction, *Iola Leroy: Or, Shadows Uplifted* (1892). It is reasonable to assume that a powerful literary representation of the women Harper encountered during her visits to the South, and who served collectively as the basis for the characters of Aunt Chloe and Aunt Linda, would not be served by the conventions of Harper's usual poetic style. While she maintains her use of iambic meter and alternating lines of three and four iambic feet in the Aunt Chloe poems, she seems to have relinquished her use of anaphora, traditional imagery of light, and other narrative techniques found in the earlier poetry I discuss above. In its place, we find the consistent metaphorical play of black vernacular speech.

As I discuss at length in the following section, Harper's Chloe uses metaphorical language that is ripe with such vernacular commonplaces as those Zora Neale Hurston would, in the 1934 essay "Characteristics of Negro Expression," term double descriptives (e.g., "mighty ugly," found in the first stanza and "honey-fugle," appearing in the second stanza). It is important to note that while these were commonplaces in the everyday speech of the African American working and former slave classes of Harper's day, and while they would appear to form the basis for what Hurston identified as metaphorical innovations that were "characteristic" of black vernacular, they were, in fact, ingenious innovations when employed in nineteenth-century Western poetic forms. In this way, their use set the tone for a new mode of expressing black being.

With her series of poems on Aunt Chloe, Harper won praise from even her harshest critics. J. Saunders Redding, who had roundly criticized her poems as lacking in force and originality, saw Harper's vernacular poems as groundbreaking. Harper had, Redding reluctantly admitted, anticipated Paul Laurence Dunbar's use of dialect and James Weldon Johnson's attention to folk speech. Further, she had done so without becoming ensnared in what Redding, Johnson, and others called the trap of dialect poetry. According to these critics, dialect poetry could do little more than express humor and pathos. Harper demonstrated the limitations of such criticism. In the Aunt

Chloe poems, she succeeded in moving beyond the limitations of dialect poetry as a literary convention, to its use as a site of ontological query and critique.

Between Metaphor and Black Being:
Aunt Chloe's Structure of Poetic Memory

How could she bear witness to what she'd never lived?

—Gayl Jones, *Corregidora* (1975)

This is poetry as illumination, for it is through poetry that we give name to those ideas which are—until the poem—nameless and formless, about to be birthed, but already felt. That distillation of experience from which true poetry springs births thought as dream births concept, as feeling births idea, as knowledge births (precedes) understanding.

—Audre Lorde, "Poetry is Not a Luxury" (1973)

I hope the foregoing and necessarily brief survey of Harper's vast poetic output—that appearing both before and after *Sketches of Southern Life*—has provided a framework for examining and understanding key elements of Harper's poetics, especially her insistence upon ontological and Biblical metaphors that distill black experience and give expression to black being. Such an aesthetic choice undoubtedly places Harper in the genealogy of African American ontological metaphorics that I map in this study, a genealogy that descends from Wheatley and Equiano through Du Bois, and on to Hurston, Wright, and Ellison. None of this is to argue that there is a singular black experience from which all African American poetics descends; instead, I argue that there are perceptible traces of ontological metaphorics that run across, between, through and underneath the widely varied works that establish an African American poetics of being. In the whole of her poems and as a significant contributor to this poetics, Harper accomplishes many things: the building of a new black feminism that takes its cue from and engages such outspoken female forebears as Maria Stewart; the inscription of a new black idiom, particularly confirmed in the poetry of Paul Lawrence Dunbar and the prose of Charles Chesnutt; and an insistence upon an activist poetic idiom, a gesture that was not recognized by early readers of Dunbar's poetry, but that is very much in line with Harper's intellectual milieu.

Yet for the contemporary critic and theorist, Harper does present additional challenges. She was, indeed, the sort of translocal activist extolled in contemporary critical discourse calling for a new critical humanism, or a "planetary humanism" (to borrow a term from the work of Paul Gilroy), and much of her poetry emerges from such activism. That is, as a translocal activist, she traveled far and wide in her antebellum efforts to abolish slavery and in her endeavors to rehabilitate the formerly enslaved after the Civil War. As Frances Smith Foster, Maryemma Graham,[10] Melba Boyd, and others have pointed out, after the war as well as before, Harper regularly put herself in bodily danger as she went from place to place, literally, from camp to camp, lecturing, teaching, and ministering to the poor and the displaced. It is during this journey of what Édouard Glissant would call "purposeful wandering"[11] that Harper set herself to work on attaining for the African American population not only women's rights and civil rights, but also, as would Du Bois and others after her, human rights. Harper's work shows us the ways in which attention to the black condition is also—necessarily— attention to the human condition. Thus in the Chloe poems, she opens her poetry to the truth of this condition in a practice of vernacular hermeneutics.

One difficulty that lies in reading the Chloe poems in particular is that the truth of the black condition during slavery was one riddled with trauma, and thus, as one finds in many of the main texts of trauma, any poetic act of remembering and testifying, of witnessing an event such as slavery, contains an impossibility, what Giorgio Agamben calls a "lacuna." It consists as much of memory as it does of that which is forgotten or repressed, a symbiotic representation of presence and absence. In his examination of the act of witnessing Auschwitz in narrative, for instance, Agamben argues that there is a discernible "structure of testimony," and that this structure evinces a reality that surpasses its "factual elements." For Agamben, "the aporia of Auschwitz is, indeed, the very aporia of historical knowledge: a non-coincidence between facts and truth, between verification and comprehension."[12]

Toni Morrison's account of her writerly practice in crafting narratives of black life during the era of slavery affirms this problematic:

> The crucial distinction for me is not the difference between fact and fiction, but the distinction between fact and truth. Because facts can exist without human intelligence, but truth cannot. So if I'm looking to find and expose a truth about the interior life of people who didn't write it (which doesn't mean that they didn't have it); if I'm trying to fill in the blanks that the slave

narratives left—to part the veil that was so frequently drawn, to
implement the stories that I heard—then the approach that's
most productive and most trustworthy for me is the recollection
that moves from the image to the text.[13]

The image of which Morrison speaks has implications for the partial
meaning transmitted to her through found memory, which itself results
from what she calls a "literary archeology": "the remains, so to speak, at
the archeological site . . . surface first, and they surface so vividly and so
compellingly that I acknowledge them as my route to a reconstruction of
a world, to an exploration of an interior life that was not written and to
the revelation of a kind of truth." This route allows her to explore "two
worlds—the actual and the possible."[14]

The problematic that Agamben and Morrison underscore seems to
function compellingly in poetry such as Harper's, which is driven by the
memory and witnessing of slavery, and whose structure appears to proffer
what I will call a topology of slave being. The phenomenological sense of
the word "topology" on which I draw defines it as the art of assisting the
memory by associating the thing to be remembered with some building or
place (either psychic or material) whose particulars are familiar. To refer
to the structure of Harper's Aunt Chloe poems as one that sets forth a
"topology of slave being" thus points out that the configuration of the
poems—that is, the structure of the poetic cycle—purposely sets forth an
anatomy of the slaves' existence through a witnessing of their experience.

Equipped with these insights, the critic discovers in Harper's text what
appears to be a "clearing," in Martin Heidegger's sense of the term,[15] a
site of revelation or unconcealment of truth and inner being not unlike
that which Morrison describes in her interactions with narratives of slavery.
Heidegger uses the image of a "clearing" as a metaphor that conveys to us
an idea of the process by which the work of art sets up a "world" that is
conceptual rather than imaginative. The work of art, he argues, engages in
a process of "presencing" that culminates in a "setting forth, a making."[16]
Yet simultaneous to this "setting forth," which is, for Heidegger, an act
of unveiling and a divulgence of truth, stands an active concealment that
resists presence doubly. The beings whose presence may be set forth in the
world of the work of art may resist such illumination (Heidegger calls this
concealment "refusal"); or a being may present him- or herself as other than
he or she is (concealment as "dissembling"). For Heidegger, "the open place
in the midst of beings, the clearing, is never a rigid stage with a permanently
raised curtain on which the play of beings runs its course. Rather, the

clearing happens only as this double concealment." It "grants and guarantees to us humans a passage to those beings that we ourselves are not." What is more, it grants us "access to the being that we ourselves are."[17] The Aunt Chloe poems collectively abide in this sort of narrative structure, one that emerges from a triple act of critical humanism: the archaeology of the slave's memory, the witnessing of slavery through poetry, and a poetic enunciation of subjectivity that seems determined to present a topology of slave being that is at once revelatory and concealing.

However, phenomenology is not often an approach taken by readers and critics of nineteenth-century women's writing, let alone African American women's writing of that period. Long has been the very act of recovering these works, some of which were completely lost or simply obscure, and others that were damned by short sighted criticism that was, at times, guided by early twentieth-century masculinist and sexist impulses, and/or, later, by the dictates of mid-twentieth-century Black Arts aesthetics. As I say at the outset of this chapter, it is only through the "search and recovery" work undertaken by women academics dedicated to listening to black women's voices that writers such as Harper have re-emerged into scholary and critical discourse.

Even so, these acts of vernacular hermeneutics, which may be seen as a species of phenomenology, play interestingly in Harper's poems. They allow Harper a modality by which to set the problematics of African American being forth into history, establishing a historicity to which the speech acts of Aunt Chloe bear witness. Chloe speaks in the stead of the slaves and freed persons who were—through illiteracy, absence, or death—unable to speak for themselves. However, as we shall see, her poetry does not put forth a full range of knowledge that grants the reader total access to what might be considered a holistic or transparent slave presence. The poems deal skillfully with those aspects of slave experience that can only be put forth as semiotic traces. Even so, the relative silence of the slave collective and the partiality of Chloe's speech acts do not augur a lack of subjectivity. On the contrary, Harper's negotiation of absence and presence in these poems calls for an alternative conception of being. We can see such a landscape of alternative concepts of being take shape in the fragmented metaphors of *Sketches of Southern Life*.

As the narrative proxy of the absent slave, Aunt Chloe provides poetic testimony that sets forth from the circular framework of the text. Six poems inhabit this circle. The first, whose title appears in all caps, "Aunt Chloe," is an introductory piece consisting of sixteen quatrains that set the themes advanced in the subsequent compositions. The titles of the poems that follow—"THE DELIVERANCE," "AUNT CHLOE'S POLITICS," "LEARNING TO READ," "CHURCH BUILDING," and "THE REUNION"—appear in a smaller font with what I will call title capitalization, such as you see here through the presence of typographical markers. Thus the reader is meant to comprehend them as evolving on a circular narrative plane that, though it approximates completeness, is suggestive of the sort of "clearing" Heidegger describes. These pieces declare their own version of absence and silence. They simultaneously reveal and dissemble even as Harper shapes them as metaphorical speech acts that set into motion an ontological itinerary of testimony. Taken together, the poems bear witness on behalf of those who cannot speak. They declare a relation between the impossibility of speech and the living subject, the survivor of slavery; they declare their own immanence even as they protend toward a possible world. The poems thus serve as Harper's articulation of a critical humanism, alternative concepts of subjectivity (which, in her historical moment, largely excluded persons of African descent), and her metaphorical archive of the slaves' being.

I begin my analysis of these poems by outlining the plan of the poetic cycle in an attempt to catalog the rich thematics of its lyric engagement. This inventory, which commences with an examination of the dual frame of the poetic cycle—the first and final poems—will permit us to return to a description of how the metaphorical processes of memory, witnessing, and being together emerge from a critical practice of historiography at work in the series of poems. They allow the critic to discover onto-theological metaphors of being or consciousness in the midst of a poetic lacuna.

We meet the eponymous narrator of the poems in the opening stanza of the first poem, "Aunt Chloe," and immediately become acquainted with her range of themes. Aunt Chloe can speak philosophically, or reach to the depths of pathos; her diction, in thought and voice, is almost always drawn from the rhetoric of the black folk—the beautiful poetry of the sacred, the aphoristic qualities of slave wit, the transition from thought to action evident in her verbalization of nouns, and so on. All emerge in this first poem, and all course through the cycle of poems, such that varying rhetorical moments not only penetrate and stand in relation to one another but also make an attempt at self-representation.

Within these *Sketches*, Harper essays to limn the world of Aunt Chloe and her episteme,[18] and in this way, her poems share, as numerous critics point out, constituent elements that characterize the slave narrative, though with some crucial changes. Indeed, the initial lines of the first poem do not proclaim the fact of birth that generally opens slave narratives ("I was

born"), but instead announces an intention of historiography and memory—
"I remember, well remember, / That dark and dreadful day"—an intention
that is, as the following lines reveal, at once individual and collective. (I
should note here that Equiano's narrative, an archetype of the eighteenth-
century slave autobiography, likewise does not begin with "I was born," but
rather with a proclamation of his thought and conviction: "I believe. . . .")
Chloe's effort of remembering indicates a simultaneous gesture toward an
idealist holistic history and a fragmentation of the psyche. Her traumatic
articulation of memory may be seen as a semiotic trace that allows both
her and the reader access to a historical past.[19]

In the first stanza, Chloe recalls the day her sons, Jakey and Ben,
were sold away to pay for her dead master's debt. And in the narration,
Chloe's autobiographical poem becomes poly-vocal: Chloe tells her own
story of loss, which carries within it cousin Milly's commiserations ("'Oh!
Chloe, I knows how you feel, / 'Cause I'se been through it all; / I thought
my poor old heart would break, / When master sold my Saul'") and Uncle
Jacob's ministrations ("'Just take your burden / To the blessed Master's
feet; / I takes all my troubles, Chloe, / Right unto the mercy-seat'").[20]
Considering the poem's title—"Aunt Chloe"—one is struck that this poem
presents not Chloe alone but also those of her set. She is introduced as an
individual encircled by an empathetic community that sadly informs her that
her children have been sold (SL, 117). This community, it seems, opens the
way for Chloe to communicate to the world beyond her own. In the face
of her loss, which she struggles to nurse "all alone," Aunt Chloe recalls that
she "wasted to a shadow, / And turned to skin and bone." But Uncle Jacob's
words "waked up" her "courage," after which she began "to pray." It is then
that "a something" begins to speak to her: "And it often seemed to whisper,
/ Chloe, trust and never fear, / You'll get justice in the kingdom, / If you
do not get it here" (118). This metaphorical "something" is characterized
in terms of prescience, a knowing founded on belief and faith even as its
articulation is disembodied. Not only are the first poem's speakers among the
living (Chloe and Milly) and the dead (Uncle Jacob). The voice that comes
to drive it, speaking without benefit of quotation marks, is the whispering,
spectral "something" that fortifies Chloe with a sense of hope that had
eluded her until the moment she turned to prayer. Chloe figures, then, not
as an independent person, but as one whose poetry shapes a dialogic matrix
of metaphorical, discursive forces that are both worldly and spiritual. In this
way, of course, Harper's poetry follows closely the example set by Equiano:
the navigation of the immanent and the transcendent in his attempt to reveal

his being. Harper's poetry demonstrates for us the continued significance of the onto-theological that nineteenth-century African American metaphorics inherits from the previous century.

In the poetic cycle, the connection between the first poem and the final one, "The Reunion," initially appears to be the conclusion the final poem provides. The title—"The Reunion"—indicates the coalescing of various elements into one body or whole, obliquely underscoring the ways in which Chloe's being is at stake. It is taken up with the return of Chloe's son, Jakey. Harper shows us Chloe as a free woman; while walking "down the street," she hears "a stranger asking / For Missis Chloe Fleet" (*SL*, 129).[21] The "stranger" turns out to be Jakey, and the scene of his reunion with his mother is related swiftly. Chloe's emotions run the gamut from laughter, to a remembrance of her distress at losing her sons ("My heart was awful sore"), to a sense of "comfort" and a longing for "peace" (130–31).

By virtue of the final poem's title, we expect that Chloe's lost family will be returned to her. However, Harper makes clear that peace has not come because Chloe has not yet reunited with her second son, Ben, who has married and now has three children. Once Ben and his family join Chloe and Jakey (" 'You must write to brother Benny / That he must come this fall, / And we'll make the cabin bigger, / And that will hold us all' "), Chloe hopes she will attain a certain tranquility that comes with the fulfilling of motherly and familial duty. " 'Tell him I want to see 'em all / Before my life do cease: / And then like good old Simeon, / I hope to die in peace' " (*SL*, 130–31).

The figurative reference to Simeon of the New Testament, who blessed the newborn savior Jesus in the Gospel of Luke, adds a layer of meaning to the conclusion of Harper's poetic cycle. The Apostle Luke depicts Simeon as a "just and devout" man who awaited "the consolation of Israel" and was possessed of "the Holy Ghost." Early Christians frequently sang his recitation, known generally as the "Song of Simeon," or "Nunc Dimittis," at Compline, or evening prayers; it indicated a fulfillment of God's promise—the advent of the Messiah, Christ, in whose coming Simeon believed and in whose imminence he had faith. Once Simeon had seen the baby Jesus, taken the child "up in his arms" and "blessed God," he declared that he could then depart earthly life "in peace, according to thy word: For mine eyes have seen thy salvation."[22] A close reading of the final poem implies the anatomy of the entire poetic cycle: the reunion of Chloe's family is analogized to Simeon's witnessing of the coming of the Messiah.

Chloe, of course, is no Simeon. As the first poem discloses (and again like Equiano before her), she has not been of devout nature throughout her life but learned the way of devotion through the teachings of an elder (in Chloe's case, Uncle Jacob) and her engagement with the otherworldly "something" given in the first poem as spirit. Harper's metaphorical evocation of the messianic advent symbolizes the restoration of faith and the unity of God's people, who are redeemed through the fulfillment of God's promise in his Word. It is important here to note, as we saw in our reading of Equiano in the previous chapter, the Christian belief that this fulfillment is possible only in the actuation and realization of God's Word made flesh; that is, human salvation comes only by way of the unified body of Christ, symbolized by God's Word (the Bible), and Christ's descent to earth is intended to deliver God's people. Harper's final poem, however, is hardly the act of perfection that its invocation of the Song of Simeon would lead some readers to infer. Chloe does not achieve wholeness. Instead, she envisions a death mediated by hope and longing. She can only hope for actuation, and can only desire the peace of Simeon; she cannot unproblematically obtain it.

Here I take Harper to be saying something fundamental about the situatedness of black being in the context of slavery, something that does, in fact, resonate with Equiano's hope that his readers will not cast away the "jewels of instruction" they should have obtained by reading his life story, but will instead embrace the lessons of his journey (his "way," again a reference to Christ as "the way" to salvation), and thus "actuate" his being. Chloe serves Harper as an ontological operator whose poetic force comes via her verisimilitude, as a metaphorical instrument in the struggle for being on the bio-political plane of slavery's aftermath. Harper makes clear in a number of instances that her work pursues a project of understanding through a balance of contemplation and action.[23] In the slave and post-slave contexts, what is at risk is black being, and Harper conveys these stakes through a sense of the significance of social virtue as a response to the trauma of slavery, and through a concern for moral action coupled with intellectual contemplation. Harper's historiography, presented to the reader as Chloe's act of remembering, gives evidence of this association between thinking, being, and doing. Harper conveys Chloe's experience (her history, her consciousness, her actions) in poetry; thus, the poem metaphorically constitutes Chloe's being and the problematics associated with black existence both during and after slavery.

If the final act of the poetic cycle—the postponement of Chloe's family reunion—is deferment, Chloe's being, by analogy, is effectively dissimulated: the final poem obscures the lacuna between memory and being, or history and being, the very gap that the cycle sets about negotiating. The cycle, in other words, embodies Chloe's fractured existence and thus works toward a topology of the nature of her being. If, then, we see in this sequence of poems an implicit depiction of Aunt Chloe's being as partial and dialogic, as formed by discourses that are both temporal and atemporal, that interchange with eras past and future, then we may also see in these fragmentary and dialogic interactions the basis of Chloe's epistemology, a way of knowing that responds to her present circumstances and fortifies her sense of being. Chloe's sense of being becomes evident in the poems that constitute the cycle.

One aspect of the tension between being and memory that characterizes Harper's poetic cycle is its contention with the transcendent: Chloe and her community seek to rise above, to transcend the constraints of both enslavement and newly—but not wholly—won freedom. Such is indicated by the salvific title of the second poem, "The Deliverance." This piece divides easily into five thematic parts that reflect the sweep of history and the ebb and flow of politics. In this poem, we note a theory of history that seems, upon initial perusal, to insist upon a striving toward transcendence and metaphysical wholeness. Ultimately, however, the poem underscores the immanent.

The first part, comprising stanzas one through fourteen, beyond introducing "Mistus" and her son Thomas, takes up the theme of war, a sort of trial by fire through which the slaves would have to pass before being delivered by freedom. In the second part, stanzas fifteen through twenty-seven, Uncle Jacob (then still living) seeks to reassure all the slaves, and effectively serves as a seer and spiritual advisor to Aunt Chloe. Part three, made up of stanzas twenty-eight through thirty-four, begins with the entry of the conquering Yankee troops into the South, upon whose appearance Chloe and the other slaves celebrate. Stanzas thirty-five through forty-three, making up the fourth part, chronicle the rise and fall of a number of American presidents: Abraham Lincoln, Andrew Johnson, and Ulysses S. Grant. With the mention of Grant in this section, Chloe pilots us through the thick of the Reconstruction years, and she is an effective guide. In addition to graphing the obvious point of Lincoln's assassination, she mentions what was widely known as Johnson's "swing around the circle"— an unsuccessful eighteen-day speaking tour in which he traveled through the Midwest and offered explanations of his policies—and notes Grant's (temporarily) successful move to break up the Ku Klux Klan.[24] In part five, the focus is on suffrage and, in particular, the role women play in keeping their husbands from corruption. The women depicted seem to take as part of their marriage vows a sort of moral-political responsibility to which they determinedly hold their husbands true, even at the risk of the marriage itself.

"The Deliverance" provides sedulous spadework for the remainder of the cycle. It is marked by a shift from the mystical and anagogic in parts one through three, to the political in parts four and five. We should be alert to Harper's establishment of a continuum here—from the metaphysical to the temporal, from transcendent freedom to immanent political exigencies. (In this way, I should say, she echoes Equiano, whose call to abolition, in tandem with his call to liberal Christianity, essentially constitutes a political discourse.) Harper's consideration of the slaves' temporalities continues in the next poem, "Aunt Chloe's Politics," which carries on the discussion of suffrage introduced in the second poem and urges responsible action under the Fifteenth Amendment. It is followed by "Learning to Read" and "Church Building," which together reflect two pillars of Harper's aesthetic philosophy.[25] First is the importance of the written word, specifically as it relates to the accessibility of sacred text and self-edification. (After Chloe learns to read hymns and the Bible at the age of sixty, she buys her own cabin: "And I felt as independent / As the queen upon her throne" [*SL*, 128]). Second is the import of religion itself. The practice of each—an investment in the intellectual as well as in the spiritual—serves to prepare Chloe for the final moment she narrates; the intellectual and the spiritual are the twin portals that lead to her reunion with her sons, Jakey and Ben, or at least this is what we are given to believe. However, that Chloe cannot consummate her poetic act—that she cannot fully achieve free subjectivity precisely because of her historical situation—is manifest not only in her family's failure to reunite, but also in Harper's, and thus Chloe's, inability to provide holistic testimony.

As author, Harper attempts to bear witness to Chloe's experience of slavery from a site that exceeds slavery's limits: a freeborn Southerner,[26] Harper had never had such experiences as those she sought to portray through poetry, though she would have been witness to them. Harper was born in the slave state of Maryland. Her hometown, Baltimore, a pro-slavery city, was populated with no fewer than 25,000 free African Americans in 1850, and 3,000 or fewer enslaved persons of African descent,[27] so Harper likely had many early experiences with the institution of slavery, although she did not live it herself. During her tour of the Reconstruction South, various conversations with freedwomen prepared Harper to undertake this metaphorical testimonial. Nonetheless, Harper is, by definition, an outsider who works to give voice to the lived experience of the black slave. If we follow Orlando Patterson here, we may read the fictional Chloe as inhabiting a space of social death from which Harper bids her speak.[28] Harper insists that Chloe bear witness from the inside of death, that she provide what

Agamben describes as "impossible testimony." Thus, the poetic cycle is actually a layered ontological narrative that permits Harper to create a character who serves as a witness to slavery and as a survivor of slavery's trauma.

However, it seems evident that Harper necessarily dissembles in her effort to present the truth of the slave's existence: Chloe's enunciation is essentially Harper's. Thus, there is a clear semiotic and rhetorical link between author and poetic witness: Chloe's testimony presupposes the lived experience of historical slave women and conveys it—in vernacular speech—as truth, thereby validating and certifying that experience. In her verse, Chloe renders the absence of the historical slave as presence, as being; she speaks in the name of an inability to speak, and thereby gains authority. As the source of Chloe's testimony, the absent slave is imaged/imagined as constitutively indeterminate. Chloe bears witness to the indeterminate nature of slave being. She permits the silenced to speak.

I am thinking of this textual permission as one wherein the ineffable does not embrace the exotic, but casts it off and demands full access to the concept of the human through the performance of speech. Chloe's speech act is an essential overcoming of the negative. It negates silence on three discernible levels of consciousness: that of the author (Harper); that of the witness, narrator, and survivor of slavery (Chloe); and that of the collectivity of silenced slaves (the paradoxical human/nonhuman, those who speak but do not speak for themselves, those who survive in representation though they might have perished). There is a way in which Harper, as a freeborn woman of color, and Chloe, as a freedwoman who, in Harper's poetic imagination, survives the terrors of slavery, are intertwined. Their fates and existences are interrelated; neither the freeborn and the freed nor the author and the narrator can be reduced to separate identities. They must be read as intimately related.[29]

The intimate relation between narrator and poet stands as a commentary on the moral necessity Harper resolved to convey to her reader. What I wish to explore further is the notion of Harper as the witness who works to "complete," in Agamben's terms, Chloe's testimony. Harper amasses scattered remnants of memory and arranges them in a poetic "whole" that is, nonetheless, fragmented: the poems refuse to present Chloe as a fully constituted presence who emerges from slavery's travails unmarked, perfect. Harper's act here is purposeful and comes by way of a number of refusals, which, following Heidegger, we may describe in terms of dissembling. Chloe speaks as one, when in fact she is many. She speaks for Harper as well as for slaves and freed persons. Her dissimulative voice makes testimony possible even as she (and thus Harper) omits pertinent facts of her history, such as the location from which she speaks, the dates during which she lives, and her parentage as well as that of her children. Chloe is, then, the uncommon slave narrator who refuses to substantiate and authorize her discourse with the conventional declaration that often commences with "I was born." Even as she refuses to cite her origins, she refuses a holistic ending. Such insistence upon indeterminacy is, to my way of thinking, also an insistence upon a specific moral, a critical humanism that emerges from the pen of a nineteenth-century African American feminist activist.

I see the remaining time in Chloe's text—the time Harper *does* narrate, the fragments of Chloe's existence she *does* give in poetry—as the motivity that advances the feminist and activist moral upon which Harper insists. The remaining time of the text may be seen as a projected world, projected toward the future as well as the past, and thus it coalesces with the present time of the reader in contemporaneity.[30] The poems exist as thought, productive thought in the time of the present. The role of thought and knowledge in the poems is of great importance. For instance, once emancipation comes, Aunt Chloe acquires literacy in spite of her advanced age of sixty, an achievement that should be seen in light of her longstanding desire before the war that all the slaves should gain and share knowledge even as they endured captivity:

> Our masters always tried to hide
> Book learning from our eyes;
> Knowledge did'nt agree with slavery—
> 'Twould make us all too wise.
> But some of us would try to steal
> A little from the book,
> And put the words together,
> And learn by hook or crook.
> (*SL*, 127)

The edification of the mind Chloe expounds here is paralleled in the poem "Church Building" by the building of a "meeting place" (*SL*, 129) where the slaves would edify their spirits as well as their minds. Both endeavors advance piecemeal: "book learning" is gained "by hook or crook"; the funds for the church grow as the former slaves "pinched, and scraped, and spared, / A little here and there" (129). As they pertain to the evolution of Chloe's being, these exemplary accomplishments, each presented as representative moral acts in the aftermath of oppression, serve to alleviate her solitude and to enact community. Yet they also, and this most importantly, perhaps, attest to the ontological "world" Harper seeks to reconstruct through memory and metaphor.

"Learning to Read" and "Church Building" underscore the centrality of thought in Chloe's poetry, not simply in its recourse to vernacular metaphors and its validation of literacy and self-improvement, but also in its very recollection of these undertakings—both Chloe's remembrance as well as Harper's memorializing of slave being through witnessing and a poetic structure intent upon recreating a world. Heidegger calls this type of thinking through an act of remembrance: "thinking holds to the / coming of what has been, and / is remembrance."[31] He relates this concept of time and memory to the function of poetry as a work of art. For Heidegger, the "nature of the work of art" is "the truth of beings setting itself to work":

> The work opens up a world and keeps it abidingly in force. To be a work means to set up a world. . . . World is never an object that stands before us and can be seen. World is the ever-nonobjective to which we are subject as long as the paths of birth and death, blessing and curse keep us transported into Being. Wherever those decisions of our history that relate to our very being are made, are taken up and abandoned by us, go unrecognized and are rediscovered by new inquiry, there the world *worlds*. [32]

In the Aunt Chloe cycle, the absent and the ineffable, enacted by way of dissembling and refusal, coalesce with an act of "worlding" through testimony and representation. I have said that the poems achieve historiography; they strive to archive a period of time that is accessible to us only through narrative. Harper's interviewing of slave women and her translation of their narratives into poetry make it possible to witness slavery from the inside, to enter an existence beyond our own; the poet grants us limited access to the inside of death, as it were, and partially preserves the voice of the witness. The poems serve as a modality that enables our imperfect observation of Chloe's inmost nature: Chloe—as being—is at stake in the poems. In situating Chloe's experience as a half-open portal to the existence and experiences of many historical slaves, Harper renders the poems absolutely necessary to our contemporary conceptions of slave being. The Aunt Chloe cycle puts into play a relation between poetry and being, vernacular speech and historical action. The poetic cycle is effectively a process of protension that extends Chloe's world to our own.

In Chloe as a constructed subject, we find, evoking Agamben's terms, a "field of forces always already traversed by the incandescent and historically determined currents of potentiality and impotentiality, of being able not to be and not being able not to be."[33] This is the risk of Chloe's poetic existence. As she translates Chloe's partial history into poetry, Harper disallows the mysticism we often attach to narratives of slavery. In some respects, twentieth- and twenty-first-century readers perceive the effort of the slave to speak her/his piece in one of two ways. First, the slave narrator often seems to us thwarted in his/her narrative attempts by the trauma of slavery; readings of slave narratives often convey a sense of awe in the face of what we deem ineffable acts forcefully existing between the lines of text given by the slave narrator. If this condition does not predispose us to a certain reception of the "silences" within the slave's text, then the conventions of nineteenth-century women's abolitionist writing, wherein it was considered improper to reveal the full horrors of slavery, may encourage us to accept the key omissions and aporia as natural to the text's conception and structure. It would seem that the intersection of the speech act and the historical archive in the Aunt Chloe poems calls for a different sort of reading than that to which we have become accustomed in our analyses of the slave's text.

Perhaps, as Agamben writes, the "relation between what is said and its taking place" will allow us to codify Chloe, as "the subject of enunciation," differentially. I take Agamben to echo Julia Kristeva in arguing that it is possible to "bracket," or identify, or determine, that which has been conveyed in an act of speech as an aspect of the historical context. Similarly, Agamben may take the "subject of enunciation" to refer to the individual who speaks, the "I" who enunciates. Either case refers to the gist of his conclusion that "the relation between language and its existence, between *langue* and its archive, demands subjectivity as that which, in its very impossibility of speech, bears witness to an impossibility of speech."[34] It is clear that language demands a subject (a living individual) in order to exist. Thus Chloe, as a subject deploying and deployed by metaphor, bears witness to the impossibility of the slave's testimony. For without Chloe as speaking subject, the slave's metaphorics, as well as his or her being, would suffer a death.

A Technology of Modern Black Being

"The Conservation of Races" as a Critical Ontology of Race

Little more than twenty-five years after *Sketches of Southern Life*, in the 1897 essay "The Conservation of Races," W. E. B. Du Bois took up the project of ontological metaphorics exemplified in Harper's work, and extended it toward the modernity of a new century. Even in our own day, modernity, through its apparatuses of the plantation and the slave ship, often works toward the erasure of slave being and the eradication of its contingencies; it seeks certainty and absolutism, such as it invests in the idea of the "whole," white subject. Harper counters the deficient humanism of the Enlightenment and its project of modernity, and puts in its place a vernacular hermeneutics that queries, represents, affirms, and protends black being toward our own time. As we have seen in chapter 4, Harper's Aunt Chloe, a vernacular, black subject, seeks redress through her own metaphorical enunciation and actually reconfigures the possibilities of poetry as existential potentiality. The Aunt Chloe poems are a re-instantiation of the contingent, a resurgence of the impossible: Chloe's speech act emerges from a caesura between being and nothingness. Harper refracts language through Chloe, and in doing so, she recasts a vision of how Chloe's being, as given in metaphor and as testimony to historical events, may (and must) be received. Thus, the Aunt Chloe cycle not only places before the reader the interstitial as productive of meaning and alternative subjectivity, but also serves to negate "impossible" black being.

Coming in the wake of Harper's poetics at the close of the nineteenth century, "The Conservation of Races," a work that continues to garner widespread critical attention in the twenty-first century, is perhaps most significant for its articulation of a revisionist theory of modern black being exactly twenty years after the end of Reconstruction. It is also significant for another reason, one not widely noted by Du Bois's critics, but which

I take up as a central aspect of the transhistorical thrust of my study: "Conservation" engages in a complex act of metaphorical conceptualization, which takes shape in tandem with its critical ontology of race and blackness. In doing so, Du Bois draws forward the ontological metaphorics at work in the writings of preceding generations of African-descended thinkers such as Harper and Equiano, and lays the foundation for the conceptual metaphors of modern black being that inspirit *The Souls of Black Folk*.

It is striking that "Conservation," which Du Bois presented at the March 1897 inaugural meeting of the American Negro Academy, appeared some five months before the essay, "Strivings of the Negro People." "Strivings," published in the August 1897 issue of the *Atlantic Monthly*, would be republished in 1903 with few changes as the first chapter of *The Souls of Black Folk*. In both "Conservation" and "Strivings," it becomes clear that the question of being, or, more specifically, modern black being that bore in 1897 upon the thought of Du Bois was whether human history could be revised from a global perspective that sought some mediation of the national as well as the racial. Du Bois essentially inquired whether the purview of history could be expanded from narrow nationalist and racist perspectives that excluded the Negro from the annals of modern existence, to a broader one that allowed for what Du Bois himself termed "human brotherhood," which Hannah Arendt would later refer to as "human plurality." My argument in this chapter is that Du Bois indeed undertook and achieved such a plural, global historiography of modern black being in "The Conservation of Races," one that sought to mediate and engage head-on the paradox of global humanity and particularized racial being through a concerted use of historical narrative and an understanding of the power of ontological metaphor. More to the central focus of this study, my reading of "Conservation" will demonstrate how Du Bois draws upon the onto-theological metaphorics exemplified in preceding generations of African American thought, secularizing them as he argues for a critically revised concept of the human. Moreover, as I will show in the following chapter, Du Bois's metaphorization of race in "Conservation" is taken up and refined in *The Souls of Black Folk*, where he adapts much of the sort of onto-theological and anagogic metaphors we see in Equiano and Harper to an ultra-modern and secular set of conceptual metaphors of black being: the veil, the color-line, and double consciousness.

As Du Bois lays the foundation for these conceptual metaphors in "The Conservation of Races," he touches upon most of the usual categories of American history—race, gender, class, national belonging, and so on—

yet ultimately forces their expansion through a nuanced critique. Fairly inaugurating a vista of eighty years of writing (his early writing was published in the 1880s while he was yet a student; he began writing professionally as an academic and activist in the mid-1890s; and he continued to publish and write up to the time of his death in 1963), Du Bois's thought both echoes and sounds against the themes that characterize the times in which he lived. It is a small wonder that his writing, even in its earliest stages, continues to engage us. Perhaps what we continue to respond to in Du Bois is his fervent, at times outraged, attention to the past, present, and future of global humanity, democracy, and justice. In "The Conservation of Races," his passion in writing conjoins metaphorical discourse and black being, prophecy and realism as he undertakes what I am calling a transhistorical, critical ontology of race, in the sense that Michel Foucault gives this term in "What is Enlightenment?" (1984). The sort of critical ontology Du Bois undertakes correlates with what Foucault would later describe as "an attitude, an ethos, a philosophical life in which the critique of what we are is at one and the same time the historical analysis of the limits that are imposed on us and an experiment with the possibility of "going beyond them" (50). Du Bois's critical ontology also advances what Spillers and Derrida more recently refer to as the necessity of ontological contemporaneity and agency, as I discuss in chapter 2. Du Bois's is an inquiry that concerns questions of being, historicity, and historiography, but it is also one that examines such questions while putting forward a considerable plan of action and redress.

The sort of critical ontology Du Bois employs to deconstruct the concept of race in "Conservation" also serves to analyze collective racial memory. Harper's work, as I discuss in the previous chapter, might be considered an outgrowth of such collective memory. And while poetry such as Harper's is of signal importance to our ability to theorize slave consciousness, Du Bois employs the processes of critical ontology, which in this instance unfolds by way of a historical analysis of the limits of race, in order to profit from an archaeology of the sort exemplified in Harper's testimony of black being. He analyzes black collective memory as constitutive of race, at the same time that he uses narrative to explain and deconstruct the idea of race as a metaphorical concept, and even to move beyond "race" as a limited category of being and toward a global, illimitable humanism.

In "The Conservation of Races," Du Bois's critical ontology narrates the experience of black social memory to tell stories not only of the varied African-descended peoples in far-flung places who constitute humanity wherever they abide, but of peoples the world over whose collective histories converge beyond the limits of racialization in a noetic space that he calls "human brotherhood." He tells of their mores and customs, their languages and sayings, their religions and cultural practices, their failings and progress. By telling and re-telling these stories of collective human being, as he does in "Conservation" and elsewhere, Du Bois's ontology makes clear that the operation of history works in tandem with the operation of national identity and the construction of racial identities, themselves evolutionary processes that, in modern times, provide a vantage point and a structuring principle through which the telling of history is regularly filtered. History and historiography, indelibly linked to the conceptualization of the human and thus to the question of being, are also intimately related to ideas of race and nation. Du Bois sought to highlight the dangers inherent in such intimacies through his critique in "Conservation."

Most, if not indeed all scholars of Du Bois's work recognize his historiographical intent[1] in "The Conservation of Races," but few acknowledge the ways in which the essay not only employs ontological metaphorics that critique the notions of race and nation as absolutist categories, but also, more to the point, the ways in which the metaphorization of race in "Conservation" in fact lays the groundwork for the major ontological metaphors that structure and bring to life Du Bois's chef d'oeuvre: *The Souls of Black Folk*. I argue for attention to Du Bois's metaphorization of race in "Conservation" because this essay is not one that exemplifies, in the words of Wilson J. Moses, the tenets of "classical black nationalism."[2] Instead, I will show how the essay deconstructs the categories of race that allow for and validate absolutist black nationalism as well as white supremacy. The message of "Conservation" is not one of racial or nationalist absolutism conveyed through straightforward and ordinary language. Instead, Du Bois introduces the reader to a set of metaphorical terms related to a specific vision and interpretation of the past and present that is concerned with, above all else, the articulation of a set of future possibilities. For example, in recalling, near the beginning of his text, the "hard limits of natural law" that give rise to the "practical difficulties of every day" (815), Du Bois seeks a description of the Negro's present reality that effects a useful and critical mimesis of his or her social condition. And this he does not through autobiography or poetry, as do Equiano and Harper respectively, but neither does he do it through the discipline he most intently practiced during the 1890s, sociology. Rather than presenting his readers with "scientific" facts, such as those he published in his 1897 study of Farmville, Virginia ("Conservation" lacks statistics, tables, graphs, and other visuals employed by Du Bois in much of his sociological work), Du Bois begins his critical ontology with a historical narrative, a sort of *muthos*[3] not wholly unlike that described by Aristotle in his *Poetics*. For instance, the first line of the essay reads, "The American Negro has always felt an intense personal interest in discussions as to the origins and destinies of races: primarily, because back of most discussions of race with which he is familiar, have lurked certain assumptions as to his natural abilities, as to his political, intellectual and moral status which he felt were wrong" (815). In my reading of this crucial entry point into the essay, a sort of narrative vestibule, if you will, where Du Bois situates and prepares his listeners and readers for the argument he will painstakingly elaborate, I see Du Bois framing this statement in a manner that is akin to the most recognizable form of *muthos*, that of the tragic, moral "hero" who seeks to embrace the ethical, while all along the forces of the cosmos have led him to a certain ironic and regrettable end: "He has, consequently, been led to deprecate and minimize race distinctions, to believe intensely that out of one blood God created all nations, and to speak of human brotherhood as though it were the possibility of an already dawning tomorrow" (815).

The elements of narrative are indeed here: the demiurge upon whose mythological shoulders rests the heavy responsibility for rendering all his creations as equal beings; the appeal to *humanitas* in the phrase "human brotherhood," a form of human virtue that calls for a balance of contemplation and action; the "dawning to-morrow," whose figurative presence in the sentence evokes images of a supreme heavenly being that guides understanding and ensures a future. What Du Bois argues, however, is that this masculine and "heroic" figure, as I will call him, must recognize that race, while invalid as a scientific concept, has deep and sustainable roots in social structures as well as in culturally central historical narratives. Thus, in spite of science's conclusion and Du Bois's pointed rejection of racial absolutism and its ills, he tells his audience not only that there does indeed exist a color-line, effected through social structures and enforced through white supremacist practices of racism the world over. We must also, he argues, recognize the existence of the color-line in the various manifestations it takes, whether in myths of racial absolutism that maintain a fiction of purity of blood, or in racial phenomenology that assigns racial essences by way of such questionable "sciences" as craniology, phrenology, and so on. Within its global context, in which it is very much alive, race continues to wield a vital, determinative force in American life, no matter the Negro's efforts at eradicating and transgressing its categories. Du Bois puts the matter thus:

The final word of science, so far, is that we have at least two, perhaps three, great families of human beings—the whites and Negroes, possibly the yellow race. That other races have arisen from the intermingling of the blood of these two. This broad division of the world's races which men like Huxley and Raetzel have introduced as more nearly true than the old five-race scheme of Blumenbach, is nothing more than an acknowledgement that, so far as purely physical characteristics are concerned, the differences between men do not explain all the differences of their history. It declares, as Darwin himself has said, that great as is the physical unlikeness of the various races of men their likenesses are greater, and upon this rests the whole scientific doctrine of Human Brotherhood.

Although the wonderful developments of human history teach that the grosser physical differences of color, hair and bone go but a short way toward explaining the different roles which groups of men have played in Human Progress, yet there are differences—subtle, delicate and elusive, though they may be—which have silently but definitely separated men into groups. While these subtle forces have generally followed the natural cleavage of common blood, descent and physical peculiarities, they have at other times swept across and ignored these. At all times, however, they have divided human beings into races, which, while they perhaps transcend scientific definition, nevertheless are clearly defined to the eye of the Historian and Sociologist. (816–817)

Early in his essay, then, Du Bois not only acknowledges the scientific doubt surrounding racial classification, but also takes the concept of "race" and places it beyond the realm of science and biology and under the auspices of history and sociology, two fields in which he himself was rigorously trained. His narration of the idea of "race" is as a concept deeply implicated by culture and inseparable from the historical processes that have empowered the rise of civilizations and nation-states.

When he goes on to call race the "most ingenious invention for human progress" (817), he therefore engages a number of discourses. First among these is the idea of modern "Human Progress" (816) itself, the idea that appears to stand as the analytic motivity of the essay. That is, the signal question of the role of Negroes in the modern era, how they would defend their freedom and, importantly, how they would advance in modern society, founds the impetus of "Conservation." For Du Bois, getting at the root of these questions demanded an analysis of the place of race in the history of "human philosophy" (815) and in the concept of "Human Progress" (816), a concept that always holds a significant rapport with the ideals of the Enlightenment, and the nationalist, materialist, and racist ideologies that emerge from the Age of Reason. Du Bois deems race to be a contrivance that emerged from this age, a figural phenomenon unmoored from empirical and biological evidence, yet anchored in a materialist modern American culture that depends upon the limitations of race for its progress among the community of nations. Modern American progress, materialist advancement, nationalist exclusions, and the "invention" of race were thus all of a piece and together occupied the crucible of Du Bois's analysis.

Du Bois's analysis yields the conclusion that race manifests a deceptive and elusive metaphoricity, and that this metaphoricity signifies more than simple figurative discourse. When Du Bois places race beyond the realm of scientific empiricism and critiques race as an invention that serves the doctrine of modern progress and nationalist exclusions postulated by the Enlightenment, he actually employs concepts that take shape by way of a forceful ontological metaphor in order to interrogate and deconstruct the metaphysical tradition that so strongly influenced his own intellectual formation. Race may be a "dead" metaphor, in the sense that Paul Ricoeur gives this term—that is, its metaphoricity may not be immediately recognizable, since it is taken to be a literal, concrete "fact" by racial absolutists—but it nonetheless exerts a long-lived and forceful influence over the everyday lives of modern people of African descent. That is, its metaphoricity is rarely ever recognized as such by the general public, though scholars such as Gates[4] have written of it in these terms; it is instead taken as a statement of empirical human reality.

When it came to race, Du Bois never quite managed to succumb to the teleology that his readings in the Enlightenment encouraged him to seek. The rise of the nation-state during the Enlightenment era and the concurrent ascent of scientific racism strongly impacted Du Bois's evolving concept of race in a way that forecasts more recent thought on the nexus of race and nation. Stephen Jay Gould, for instance, writes of how the work of Johann Blumenbach, long considered the father of the modern system of racial classification and cited by Du Bois in his essay, emerged at the moment when the modern American nation-state was being founded and its economy, largely built on the institution of slavery, was being theorized.[5] As in *The Souls of Black Folk*, "Conservation" proceeds via a metaphorical and symbolic analytic that tests the limits of these sorts of social formations by casting them as longstanding and grounded in history, but as nonetheless subject to changes that come about through social evolutionary processes.

As he probes these limits and after describing Americans and Negroes as conglomerate peoples, that is, as groups formed out of the exigencies of history and migrations (both forced and voluntary) rather than monolithic biological origins, Du Bois goes on to characterize the Negro as both an American and a Negro only to a certain point. Beyond this point, his identity is to be, for an ill-defined period of time and for reasons of political and social exigency, exclusively that of "Negro." Yet Du Bois concludes "Conservation" with an "Academy Creed" (and the word "creed" here is intended to refer to more than a set of beliefs; it is a set of principles intended to guide the future actions of the Academy) that underscores the ephemeral nature of such seemingly voluntary racial identities. Du Bois writes:

> We believe it the duty of the Americans of Negro descent, as a body, to *maintain* their race identity *until* this mission of the Negro people [to make a "contribution" to "civilization and humanity"] is accomplished, and the ideal of human brotherhood has become a practical possibility. (825, my emphasis)

In his examination of the American Negro subject in particular and the modern notion of race in general, Du Bois ends by describing the African American as existing in a state of liminality—a sort of "in-betweenness" that he will theorize to a greater extent in *Souls*. Du Bois sees the Negro as being able to shrug off his Americanness at will and adhere to a Negro identity, but only "until" African Americans have fulfilled what he sees as their obligation to contribute meaningfully to world civilization, and only until the threat of discrimination and annihilation based on race and color has itself been obliterated.

The crux of Du Bois's understanding of the metaphoricity of race lies not only in his analytic of race as an "ingenious" modern "invention," but also in his belief that the black racial identity that correlated with the concept of race could be "maintained" at will "until" the "mission of the Negro people" had been "accomplished." This is a point that critics in the vein of K. Anthony Appiah appear to overlook. If we interpret clearly Du Bois's theory of race in 1897 based on his own words and the hermeneutics of his narration (that is, if we seek to understand Du Bois's thought by immersing ourselves in the epistemological flow of his text), then there is little need to question his 1940 stance on biological determinism, as Appiah does in his well-known 1986 essay, "The Uncompleted Argument: Du Bois and the Illusion of Race."[6] Du Bois argues early on in "Conservation" that the metaphoricity of race is so liminal, so temporal that it may be cast off once a political and social prerogative has been attained. The temporality evident in Du Bois's final proclamation (in the "until" that he stresses in the "Academy Creed") makes it difficult to ascertain any clear meaning in his use of the term "race" as literal, biological fact. "Conservation" thus appears to function heuristically; it serves as an exemplary technology by which a critical ontology of race and blackness is performed using a hermeneutical process. The hermeneutics of race in "Conservation" never manifests itself as fully teleological and deterministic. If Du Bois is the quintessential dialectician that David Levering Lewis, Wilson J. Moses, and Anthony Appiah claim him to be,[7] he never quite arrives at a synthesis of his argument that will allow him to pronounce without hesitation a teleological and absolutist definition of race.

The argument is unfinished, as Appiah notes, but not because Du Bois cannot grasp that biological science was no basis for racial identification. Rather, he rejected the synthesis that would demand a fixed idea of race. The interpretation he advanced was a stratagem designed to dislocate race from its paradigmatic position in modern Western thought, an act of dislocation and metaphorical dislocution that would effectively throw into question the very concept of race, setting the stage for Du Bois's repeated attempts throughout his oeuvre to trouble an ostensibly stable definition of the meaning of race and color in the American social and political context. His metaphorization of race problematizes the collectivities of race and nation-state alike, probing notions of essentialism and particularism while noting the inherent volatility and instability of such ideas. In so doing, Du Bois's critical ontology intercedes between the dangers of racial particularism and the perils of an uncritical Western universalism.

Being in the Occasion of Discourse: "Conservation," Metaphor, and the Historical Narrative of Race

The argument I advance here does not seek to show that Du Bois's perspective on race was "right" and "non-essentialist," for I have elsewhere pointed out the ways in which a number of aspects of contemporary criticism has sought erroneously to identify a sense of biological determinism at work in the essay.[8] Here, I intend to show that the metaphoricity alive in Du Bois's articulations on race in "Conservation" not only reflects his understanding of the ambiguities of "race" itself, but that this metaphoricity also sets the stage for the development of the three major conceptual metaphors of being that guide and give intellectual substance to *The Souls of Black Folk*. At the meeting of what appear to be ambiguities and inconsistencies in Du Bois's thought, one often finds instead metaphorical contingencies of which Du Bois is fully aware and makes use as he works to give birth to new epistemologies and ontologies that shine forth upon the difficulties of black existence. Just as scholars have lately begun to recognize that early on in the evolution of his thought, Du Bois considered the color-line to be not simply an American phenomenon, but a global one, we should come to a fuller understanding of the ways in which his deployment of the metaphorics of race in "The Conservation of Races" prepares us for the metaphorics of black being in *Souls*.

There are three problematics set forth by the usual readings produced by critics of "Conservation," who generally read a tenor of racial absolutism into the essay, and these should be addressed as I move on to my purpose in this chapter. I identify them as problematics of racialized being, historical narrative, and conceptual metaphor. Each demands an exegesis of "The Conservation of Races," and together they converge to form an additional problematic at work in the essay. This additional problematic is textual, of course, but more specifically, we find it in greatest evidence when we give due consideration to the intellectual chain that draws together processes of thought, writing, reading, and hearing. These meet in Du Bois's occasion of discourse, in this instance, the convening of the American Negro Academy.

I have assigned to the occasion of the essay three senses, which I will introduce in turn. First, in much scholarly writing on this essay, critics have attached its meaning to the person of the speaker, namely, Du Bois. That is, the essay has been read as Du Bois's intimate occasion of self-expression; thus the character of the essay is often read as the character of Du Bois himself. Second is our consideration of the essay as a discursive event. The subject of the essay is brought to the forefront of the scene through Du Bois's version of historical narration. He seeks to describe, represent, and express the sense and meaning of race, nation, and black being at the close of the 1800s and the dawn of a new century. Thus, Du Bois seeks not only the engagement of an argument that is, as he demonstrates, open-ended and oriented toward the future, but, more importantly, he seeks an effect in the wake of his argument. He seeks an exchange—of speech and hearing, of information and intellection, of knowledge and action. The essay is the temporal occasion of this sort of coming together, whereby the codes of metaphorical language are employed in the service of political thought and the call for a specific sort of moral action.

Third is the temporality of this discourse. Du Bois draws upon a discourse that is historical in nature; that is, he draws upon certain metaphorical terms masquerading as concrete language—most important among them the idea of race itself—that pertain to the history of science, the history of societies across the world, and the ways in which these histories have been documented and narrated. These metaphors serve as the provisional unities upon which his own discourse is formed. In turn, they draw upon language as a system of signs, which serve as the fundamental elements of meaning and which give the illusion of timelessness, of being beyond history. Thus the metaphorical language Du Bois uses precedes him historically; he must draw it forth from the sediment of the past and, provisionally, anchor it in the present through the occasion of narration. Further, if he is to achieve the aims of his discourse, he must draw upon the unities and discontinuities of language in such a way that his discourse and the racialized being which is its subject may be projected toward the future in a gesture of contemporaneity, as I discuss in chapter 2.

There is in our reading of Du Bois's text a further problematic at work. First, we cannot fully re-situate Du Bois's oration in its original setting. Despite historical accounts of the evening in question, including Du Bois's own and that which I provide here, we cannot be fully certain of the manner in which Du Bois's interlocutors reacted to his discourse. That is to say that through our reading of the text, we are at a loss in any attempt to experience a common reality shared by the author and the auditors. We must instead rely upon historical representations of this, representations that grant us only a partial idea of the full levels of understanding achieved by the listeners. Second, we are at equal pains in attempting fully to situate "Conservation" in our own horizon of reading and hearing; in fact, we can no longer "hear" Du Bois. Thus the illocutionary aspects of his discourse, the tone and inflections he used to underscore or direct the meaning of words he articulated, are lost to us. We do not have these inflections for our own use as we interpret the essay. Likewise, we must strive to appreciate fully the nuanced sense of such words as "race," "nation," "progress," etc., in late nineteenth-century parlance. It is no understatement to say that the text requires a hermeneutical process to approach fuller understanding. "Conservation" is neither fiction nor poetry, but its language poses a similar sort of fundamental hermeneutic problem as these forms. In Du Bois's essay, metaphor, being, narrative, and the occasion of discourse, articulate one with the others, and this articulation forms the core of the hermeneutic problem one initially encounters in reading the piece.

We might be aided in our examination of this hermeneutical problem by drawing upon certain of Paul Ricoeur's broader theoretical propositions, in which he summarizes the arguments of John R. Searle and J. L. Austin, two linguistic philosophers who investigate discursive events similar to that enacted by Du Bois:

> The act of discourse, according to these authors, is constituted by a hierarchy of subordinated acts, distributed across three levels: 1) the level of the locutionary or propositional act: the act of saying; 2) the level of the illocutionary act (or force): that which we do in speaking; 3) the level of the perlocutionary act: that which we do by the fact that we speak. If I tell you to close the door, I am doing three things: I relate the predicate of action (close) to two arguments (you and the door); that is the act of saying. But I tell you this with the force of an order, and not of a contestation or a wish or a promise; that is the illocutionary act. Finally, I can provoke certain effects, such as fear, by the fact that I give you an order; these effects make of discourse a sort of stimulus that produces certain results; that is the perlocutionary act. . . . By its nature, it seems, discourse undergoes a process of exteriorization that moves it from thought to various forms of locution. (Ch 5, pg 14, ln 16–18: *"Du Texte à l'action"*)

What I wish to draw from Ricoeur here is that in its transformation from thought to text, discourse such as that which Du Bois proffers in "Conservation" is transformed into work or action. Ricoeur's position on this point is interesting: not unlike the distanciation Marx theorizes with regard to the product of man's labor, Ricoeur argues that there must exist a certain distance between the individual and the written text. This is because in the inscribing of discourse there exists a method of stylization by which thought becomes situated in text. Thus, according to Ricoeur, stylization exists in a dialectical relation with the occasion of discourse. Stylization indicates a sort of working of language wherein a writer such as Du Bois stands analogous to the artisan. He is no longer one who simply speaks: he is the artisan who "works" language (123). He is, as well, one who interprets language in order to convey thought in the occasion of discourse. Du Bois, then, provides the foundation for the hermeneutics of his text in the very structure of his work.

Does he thereby also provide the foundation for a hermeneutic of himself? In other words, in the occasion of discourse as work, does Du Bois willingly render himself as object, as he is so often appropriated by his contemporary reader?

It seems that a response to this question requires our consideration of two points. First, the hermeneutics of Du Bois's writing and tropology in "The Conservation of Races," to include further analysis of the occasion of discourse, marked by the 1897 convening of the American Negro Academy. Second, the perlocutionary act constituted by way of ontological metaphor in Du Bois's text, which stands to prompt his listener toward the embrace of certain points of belief, and, beyond this, to certain modes of being and action, articulated in the text of the essay as well as the "Academy Creed." These are, of course, two aspects of the poetics of being that I see at work throughout the tradition of African American literature, as I have argued thus far through the examples of Equiano and Harper. I will turn to the second point regarding the perlocutionary aspects of Du Bois's metaphorics in the next section of this chapter.

Along the lines of the first point, the relation of speech (or, *parole*) to writing is of some significance. Ricoeur and others have argued that writing does far more than fix speech into place (*From Text to Action* 124); more importantly, writing liberates the text from the author. In something of a New Critical fashion, Ricoeur insists that the text no longer bears the burden of intentions placed upon it by its author; textual existence and authorial psychology (or authorial signification) do not share the same fate. In other words, the author's text is displaced from his or her horizon, such that it may be re-situated and recontextualized in a new, more temporally immediate environment, namely, that of the reader. There, while it may not be heard in the author's own voice, it may indeed be analyzed: it may undergo a process of hermeneutical interpretation aimed at establishing understanding.

This is the sort of dialogic situation described by Mikhail Bakhtin, underscored by Hans-Georg Gadamer, and exemplified in Du Bois's text.[9] Ricoeur's notion of understanding is to a good extent informed by his readings in the work of Wilhelm Dilthey, with whom Du Bois took a graduate course during his graduate studies at the University of Berlin.[10] Dilthey's concept of understanding, Ricoeur argues, will not leave us ensnared in Dilthey's own romantic notions, nor will it leave us in the trappings of structuralism. Instead, we will find ourselves afoot in the "*monde du texte*," the world of the text. Ricoeur draws from Dilthey's often misunderstood notion of *befindlichkeit* (a way of understanding or feeling oneself situated in the world) the conclusion that understanding exists dialectically with being in a specific situation, as the projection of the most appropriate existential possibility with regard to the situation in which we find ourselves. Ricoeur's theory of the text adopts and adapts Dilthey's stance. What we are regularly called to do in interpreting a text is, he points out, to undertake an interpretation of a *"proposition de monde,"* a world proposition. That is, we are called to interpret the world we are capable of inhabiting, with the aim of projecting upon it an appropriate possibility. This is, in his words, what he calls "the world of the text, the world proper to this unique text" (*From Text to Action* 128).

Obviously, such a world may be envisioned with not a little of the chaos so aptly described by Equiano in his *Narrative*, and by Harper in *Sketches*, even if the aim in both writings is to mitigate such chaos by imposing upon it the myriad possibilities that emerge by way of one's vision and enactment of a critical humanism. Richard Wright in "The Man Who Lived Underground," and Ralph Ellison in *Invisible Man*, two texts I discuss in chapters 7 and 8 of this study, likewise seek to impose upon the world's chaos what Ellison calls a "pattern." As Ellison puts it, and as I shall expound later, "the mind that has conceived a plan of living must never lose sight of the chaos against which that pattern was conceived" (580–581).

I would suggest, then, that the poetics of black being Du Bois devises in "The Conservation of Races," the "plan of living" (to borrow another of Ellison's phrasings) he describes—Du Bois writes of "planning our movements, [and] guiding our future development" ("Conservation" 815)—is a plan envisioned against the background of the world's racist and nationalist chaos and projected upon a possible world. The "Creed" Du Bois proposes at the end of "Conservation" is likewise projected against a world of chaos and with hopes and belief in a better, race-less world to come. Such is clear in his stated belief that the Negro's "race identity" should be maintained only "until this mission" of a critical and lasting contribution to humanity has been "accomplished, and the ideal of human brotherhood has become a practical possibility" (825). Even so, as black being is clarified and protended a "pure," absolutist notion of black being is neither advocated nor dreamed of. Like Equiano and Harper before him, Du Bois's notion of black being is one whose "conflict within" (Ellison) must still be negotiated. Mae Henderson has written in "Speaking in Tongues," that "black women's writing" is distinguished by "the privileging (rather than repressing) of 'the other in ourselves'"[11] Revising and expanding this framework, I read in Du Bois's thought a model of African American ontological metaphorics that addresses a subject of whichever gender othered and "racialized" in the experience of being. It is this racialization, and its attendant economics and social strictures, that produces a white world in which black being is distorted and "dislocuted" (disarticulated, unsaid, and therefore cast as non-being). The black text and its ontological metaphorics create a space for a discourse with the "other that is within," as well as a discourse with the other Other.

In this way, it seems, the world of text in African American literature is homologous to the world in which we live. Those texts that interest me in this study act with the intent of bettering this world even as they render it mimetically (by way of representation with a difference). And I say this as I take into account the inability of the text to represent fully that to which it refers in the world about it. Of course, poetry and fiction present the greatest examples of writing in which the referent may readily disappear. Poetry is especially important in this regard, as, in many of its forms, poetic language works for the embellishment of speech and not for the elucidation of processes at work in the world outside of the text. However, as I have argued throughout this study in relation to African American literature, and specifically in poetry such as Harper's and in an essay such as Du Bois's, with their contestatory metaphorical language, ontological metaphorics in the African American literary tradition often work not only in service of their own aesthetics, but also subtly set before the reader and hearer the particulars of lived conditions, as well as the sensibilities of shared humanity, and an exhortation to act, ethically and responsibly, in light of that which one has read and understood.

A Technology of Black Being: "The Conservation of Races" as the Contested "Mediation by which We Understand Ourselves"

To gain an understanding before the text is, as Ricoeur has put it in more general terms, a functionary dimension of the notion of text. Beyond understanding Du Bois's text in itself, what I wish to call forth from Ricoeur's theory is the idea of the text as "the mediation by which we comprehend ourselves" (129). That is, I wish to propose viewing "Conservation" as the mediation—a technology—in this particular instance by which Du Bois intends that African Americans come to understand themselves as a world historical people with a meaningful future. Indeed, the two notions that most concern many present-generation readers of "Conservation"—that of race and nation—are notions that often come to us, as they came to the interlocutors of Du Bois's time, through text itself. Thus we, and they, come to understand the parameters of racialized and national being through the mediating and historicizing qualities of text or even the absence of text: we know that certain social and national groups have been situated (by the hegemon) quite low in the world chain of being because of, to cite one reason among many, their reliance upon orality rather than literacy. These groups are considered to be outside of history and thus ahistorical persons lacking the full qualities of historical being. As I have noted, the process of understanding promoted by Ricoeur holds at its core the problematic of alienation: we necessarily operate at a distance from the historical realities of race and nation, and can only approximate these realities through texts that represent them to us and thus allow us some access to a historicity that might otherwise retreat into oblivion. The texts that give us access to a reality not our own might be either oral or written, but the force of representation depends upon the textured nature of the narrative, a weaving usually accomplished through metaphorical innovations capable of setting past lives, experiences, and beings before us. They serve as dialectical points of interaction, as depositories of culture, inert but full of possibilities because they can bring us to a greater sense of ourselves. The text serves as a technology through which we may understand ourselves; it advances propositions and reveals potentials.

This point allows us to reach a provisional conclusion as we move to consider the perlocutionary aspects of "Conservation," a task I undertake in the following section: that in "Conservation," the world of text provides an opening onto the world of black being of Du Bois's time by way of reflection upon and analysis of the condition of a collective people; the world of text thus aids in collective comprehension. We may then also consider two additional points: the hermeneutics at work in Du Bois's philosophy of the language of race and nation, and the powerful force of textual situatedness itself. Doing so allows us to reflect upon the philosophical discourses that gave shape to the metaphorics of race and nation in Du Bois's time (and that still permeate our own temporality). It also allows us to account for the forces of society that frame and impact his discourse. It is from this point that we may return to *"la chose du texte,"* to the potentiality and perlocution of "Conservation." That is, what is it that the essay reveals, and what did it, in its own time, call upon its interlocutors to do? Further, what does it, in the time of the present, call upon us to do?

I have pointed out that what contemporary critics have often done in their readings of "Conservation" is to effect at least two substitutions. First, many have allowed or even called upon present-generation readers of the essay to take the place at once of the interlocutors with whom Du Bois interacted during the ANA meeting, and the readers who read the occasional pamphlet issued by the ANA later that year. The argument may certainly and reasonably be made that Du Bois intended his writing for posterity; yet the fact remains that he spoke to the contemporary situation of his audience and readers. Thus there is a process of displacement and decontextualization that the essay regularly undergoes in many approaches to it. This we must acknowledge and take into account.

Second and in an analogous fashion, the essay as scholars know it (from its useful reprint in the 1986 compendium, *Writings*, to its strangely truncated form in the 1999 Norton Critical Edition of *The Souls of Black Folk*) regularly stands in for the act of locution as well as for Du Bois himself. As I have mentioned, we often feel that by reading the essay, Du Bois speaks to us; likewise, we feel ourselves placed in an interpersonal relation of sorts, whereby we respond to him as he speaks. Through this relation, we assume that we know Du Bois as an individual, even though our knowledge of him is necessarily posthumous. It is, therefore, a necessarily imperfect discursive act, for he cannot respond to us. The case of "Conservation" is unlike that of "The Talented Tenth," where public backlash against the writing was striking, such that Du Bois took up the topic forty-five years after its initial publication in 1903, and then only to make his point more stringently and relentlessly. Most readers outside of the academy do not know "The Conservation of Races," but they do know "The Talented Tenth": it is a discursive metaphor that is often used to mark Du Bois as elitist. Du Bois, however, never revisited "Conservation." He never apologized for or revised his concept of race as stated there, not even in *Dusk of Dawn* (1940), where his major concern was to attempt an "autobiography of a race concept," and thus to speak of himself in symbolic terms that made plain the transformative power of race metaphors. In any case, among scholarly readers, "Conservation" has come to stand in for Du Bois without due consideration of the occasion of his discourse. In a sense, "The Conservation of Races" has functioned to "conserve" a certain version of Du Bois *himself* for academic posterity. In this way, the essay serves as a peculiar archive of social and intellectual memory and a repository of reconstituted being, such that critical tendencies have moved away from analysis of the material object of the text and its meanings towards a symbolic object that may be seen as theoretically constructed: Du Bois as symbol. Ironically, Du Bois's writing after 1900 encourages such gestures, for, as I discuss elsewhere more pointedly, he regularly makes of himself a symbol to be construed as representative of the experience of black people.

To counter such *ad hominem* tendencies, a structural analysis or close reading of the essay, where we move paragraph by paragraph through its sentences, phrases, and words, might allow us to discern categories of meaning in the text (for example, we may propose categories headed by such terms as "race" and "nation," and then chronicle their situated use in each instance in which they appear). However, it would seem that, in doing so, we would explain, not interpret, their use. Ricoeur's distinction between these critical processes is quite helpful here, and is worth quoting at length. He writes:

> To interpret . . . is to appropriate to ourselves here and now the intention of the text. In saying this, we are laid within the enclosure of Diltheyan 'understanding.' However, what we have just said regarding the semantic depths of the text to which structural analysis returns invites us to understand that the intention in which the aim of the text is not . . . the presumed intention of the author, the experience of the writer into which one may transport oneself, but what the text wills, what it wishes to say, for he or she who obeys its injunction. What the text wills is to place us within its meaning, that is to say—according to another acceptance of the word "meaning"—in the same direction. If, then, the intention is the intention of the text, and if this intention is the direction that it opens for thought, the semantic depths must be understood in a fundamentally dynamic manner. I will, then, say this: to explain is the disengaged structure, that is, the internal dependent relations that constitute elements of the text; to interpret is to take the path of thought opened by the text, to put oneself en route towards the orientation of the text. We are invited by this remark to correct our initial concept of interpretation and to seek, within the subjective operation of interpretation as an act upon the text, an objective operation of interpretation that would be the act of the text. (*Du Texte à l'action* 174–75, my translation)

Ricoeur's comments point up a central theoretical problem in our usual approaches to this text, in that what Du Bois works at in "Conservation" is the interpretation of social phenomena with the aim of advancing propositions regarding black historicity and black being. What we, as critics, often aim for when we discuss this essay is the explanation of his interpretation at the level of the noun ("race," "nation"), or at the level of the *ad hominem*. We assume we have no need of an interpretation of the dynamic semantic depths of his discourse. Du Bois's writing on race and nation will continue to vex us until we come to see it as a quintessential interpretation of language, history, and ideology, with all of the inevitable ambiguities and directions of these modes of thought.

The Interpretation of Black Historicity:
Reading "Conservation" in Context

One cannot, to be sure, demand of whole nations exceptional moral foresight and heroism; but a certain hard common-sense in facing the complicated phenomena of political life must be expected in every progressive people. In some respects, we as a nation seem to lack this; we have the somewhat inchoate idea that we are not destined to be harassed with great social questions, and that even if we are, and fail to answer them, the fault is with the question and not with us. Consequently, we often congratulate ourselves more on getting rid of a problem than on solving it. . . . The riddle of the Sphinx may be postponed, it may be answered evasively now; sometime it must be fully answered. It behooves the United States, therefore, in the interest of both scientific truth and of future social reform, carefully to study such chapters of her history as that of the suppression of the slave-trade. . . .

From this we may conclude that it behooves nations as well as men to do things at the very moment when they ought to be done.

—*Suppression of the African Slave-Trade*, 1896

If history is going to be scientific, if the record of human action is going to be set down with that accuracy and faithfulness of detail which will allow its use as a measuring rod and guidepost for the future of nations, there must be set some standards of ethics in research and in interpretation. If, on the other hand, we are going to use history for our pleasure and amusement, for inflating our national ego, and giving us a false but pleasurable sense of accomplishment, then we must give up the idea of history either as a science or as an art using the results of science, and admit frankly that we are using a version of historic fact in order to educate the new generation along the way we wish.

—*Black Reconstruction*, 1935

"The Conservation of Races" is one of a succession of Du Bois's writings that begins not only with a recognizable *muthos*, as I have noted, but also with a compelling historical imaginary into which we, as readers, are to delve in order to attain the sort of interpretive understanding Du Bois (as he makes clear in the above passage from *Black Reconstruction*) would have us seek. Du Bois gives us to understand that without such context, our work of interpreting the information he provides will be hindered. We are, then, called to extend our discussion of Du Bois's historical imaginary in "Conservation" by interpreting his own historical method and philosophy in "Conservation" in relation to a number of his other pre-1900 writings before going on to discuss the thought and work of other agents of the time.

Throughout his career, Du Bois regularly availed himself of many statements on the province of history and the nature of historiography. He also put his own theories of history into practice in nonfictional and creative texts alike, and in most all of his works, historical imaginary and historical prophecy commingle. In what I call Du Bois's historical imaginary, that set of metaphors, plots, narratives, and symbols through which Du Bois re-members a veritable succession of African American epistemes in the services of presenting the African American—as well as the white American—reading public with a tool with which to assemble a varying and fluid African American identity—the past may be recuperated and refigured, but it is always accounted for, such that it, in often symbolic ways, lends itself to the oracular. It points toward a viable political and social future. Du Bois's political vision was born of the marriage of history and desire, of the past confronted with the future expectations of the individual as well as the collective. In history, one finds the allure of origin; yet Du Bois denied to history the surety of hermeticism. For him, history resonated with the present, such that, to his mind, the historian was brother to the sociologist and the philosopher; each must listen for the resonances by which present conditions variously create themselves, as well as the implications such resonances hold for the future. In this way, Du Bois's discourse on racialized being effects a contemporaneity of the sort theorized by Derrida, Spillers, and Morrison (see chapter 2), reflecting specifically the injunction to act that is central to the intention of so many African American texts.

The following historical, political, and philosophical context can provide a framework for understanding key elements of Du Bois's poetics, including his privileging of the discourse of history in "Conservation," a privileging that firmly places Du Bois not only within a genealogy of African American ontological metaphorics, but at its center. It is with "Conservation" and *Souls* that one sees this metaphorics in the midst of its "secular turn," even as it retains traces of the anagogic that is so central to the writings of Equiano and Harper and that will re-emerge in *Souls*. I take Du Bois to insist throughout his oeuvre, and pointedly in early writings that reflect his philosophy of history, that history and historiography serve symbolic functions in Western society, such that they are linked through narrative to metaphor and black being.

Many of Du Bois's early writings, specifically "The Problem of Amusement" (1897), "The Negroes of Farmville, Virginia" (1898), "The Present Outlook for the Dark Races of Mankind" (1899), and *The Philadelphia Negro* (1899), open with a historical narrative that, in some cases, begins in the eighteenth century with a pointed discussion of the particular history of slavery.[12] This historical imaginary is significant because it points to Du Bois's acute interest in the dawning of modernity and in the rise of African American literature and historiography through the slaves' oral poetry in the Spirituals and the slaves' narratives, with their varying plots and turns, insistence upon the abolition of slavery, and inestimable lens into the nature of slave being as an early form of African American historiography.

For example, in one of his less-discussed but quite significant essays, "The Study of the Negro Problems" (1898), Du Bois points out that the final decade of the nineteenth century has been fertile for the observation of sociological phenomena resulting from the "peculiar institution" of slavery. He then provides a general definition of a "social problem": it is "the failure of an organized social group to realize its group ideals, through the inability to adapt a certain desired line of action to given conditions of life. . . . Thus a social problem is ever a relation between conditions and actions" (71). The Negro problem in particular, he writes, is a "plexus of social problems," subject to the vicissitudes and antinomies of history. Thus, he concludes, the

> points at which [Negroes] fail to be incorporated into this group life constitute the particular Negro problems which can be divided into two distinct but correlated parts, depending upon two facts: First—Negroes do not share the full national life because as a mass they have not reached a sufficiently high grade of culture. Secondly—they do not share the full national life because there has always existed in America a conviction—varying in intensity but always widespread—that people of Negro blood should not be admitted into the group life of the nation no matter what their condition might be. (72–73)

In this essay, as in "Conservation," Du Bois's use of the terms "race" and "nation" demands close attention, and should be compared to his usage of these terms in "The Present Outlook for the Darker Races of Mankind"

(1899). Race appears to be subservient to nation, though in "Conservation" (and he repeats this necessity in "The Study of the Negro Problems"), he argues that racial belonging must be privileged above national belonging with the goal of solving such problems through "race organization for common ends in economic or intellectual lines" (73). The problems often consist in the relation between the "modern state" (which is, at times for Du Bois, interchangeable with his use of "nation," but which undoubtedly refers to the modern nation-state), and the races that have historically inhabited that state. In the case of a diverse nation-state such as the United States, the population consists of various racial groups that are, for all practical purposes in Du Bois's time, largely separated/segregated from one another. Thus the racial groups, because of limited intergroup contact, may be referred to as nations themselves, even as they reside in a common modern state. As nationalist logic turns, race groups may be looked upon as national groups that may or may not enjoy the privileges and protections of a modern state.

In this respect, "Present Outlook" is of a piece with "Conservation": each employs the terms "race" and "nation" symbolically, such that the words become mediating social tropes that codify a certain historical imaginary and put into play a set of meanings approximating a holistic system through which one comes to "belong" to a group—a national group, a racial group, or both at once. What Du Bois appears to stress in his writing is that these tropes cannot be defined or even discussed independently of one another; they intersignify to such a great extent in the service of ostensibly stable institutional systems that function to exclude African Americans from the life of the country that they must be addressed with a great deal of agility, showing with certainty the interconnectedness of their meaning effects. As Du Bois employs them in his writings, tropological systems of race and nation go beyond language in providing an interpretive context for particular notions of belonging. They establish a narrative medium—an historical imaginary— through which collectives as well as individuals within a social group may look in search of one of the greatest benefits literature, broadly defined in a new historicist sense, can grant: the expression of one's very humanity.

When reading and interpreting "Conservation," then, we must speak of symbolic conventions of reading and writing, into which are inscribed a certain philosophy of history and being. Du Bois recounts history in each of his early writings in order to draw upon or identify its patterns and narrative codes that reflect the conditions of existence under which the African American people strive. He presents to his readers historical narratives that can both reflect and inform contemporary perceptions of social problems and that can, further, give shape to actions in response to these problems. What we must flesh out, then, is how we might draw upon Du Bois's philosophy of history, which I have elaborated through his historical imaginary, for the identification of patterns of metaphorical language, repeated imagery, narrativized plots, and the evaluation of historical contexts that have shaped perceptions of the idea of racialized being. Du Bois's construction of an historical imaginary of race is an evaluative framework, one that is logically prior to the choice he presents regarding racial identity and global, rather than national, belonging. Attention to these points alive in Du Bois's thought may lend a certain legibility and legitimation to the social action he suggests in response to the idea of race, and that is that, as he states in the "Academy Creed," black racial identity should be maintained only *until* the problem of racial and national belonging is resolved through a contribution to world culture and civilization. What the reader gains from Du Bois's historical imaginary is, then, the ephemerality of race as well as the sanction of committed social action, which he uses as a foundation for an inscription (for the future as well as the present) of a sense of subjectivity or being. Social acts and the act of writing may be seen, then, as the mediated outcome or product of a specific episteme and its symbolic codes.

Let us push this analysis of Du Bois's symbolic or mediated action further through an examination of the historical context out of which he wrote. If the intersignification of the symbolic codes in "Conservation" persist in compelling us, it is because the essay is a testament of history's texture of action. "Conservation" translates this history into cultural text.

Du Bois's statements on the role of history are many and vital. I have chosen two, given at the beginning of this section, which I will use as a guide to what I see as essential to understanding the historical imaginary of Du Bois's time. The seeming paradox of history and metaphor, though it may induce contestations that the two are unlikely related, can nonetheless tease us into thought with respect to "Conservation." What exists in Du Bois's historical imaginary that impinges upon both the occasion of his discourse and our reading of the text? Further, what serves, in our own horizon of reading, to draw us repeatedly to this essay?

An exposition of the ideas that mark the historical period in which "Conservation" was written may seem a bit too obvious as we work to respond to these questions. We know of the legends of the 1890s, of Booker T. Washington and Ida B. Wells, above all, of Frederick Douglass and Alexander Crummell, for whom Du Bois held great admiration. Yet even those who find nothing striking in these reflections on the times may consider these figures and the events that make them relevant to a greater understanding of "The Conservation of Races." My brief examination of the times derives from Du Bois's conclusion in "Propaganda of History" (1935) that history functions symbolically in society, such that it is linked to ideology. In other words, as he makes clear in "Conservation," attention to the history of an idea (such as race) can clarify the deeper meanings cloaked in these orders of thought. Historiography is largely concerned with processes of identity, identification, and belonging, three elements of metaphor itself. Metaphor is a process of naming, of identifying objects, persons, and events through semantic substitutions, and thus it is a process through which transpositions across orders of meaning take place. It is, however, also important to bear consistently in mind that the meaning of metaphor is not static, as a number of metaphor's critics have alleged, but dynamic and constantly in movement, as the etymology of metaphor, from the Greek for "transfer," makes clear. Noting this point takes us back round to the guiding metaphor of "Conservation," that race is "an ingenious invention for Progress," which, in turn, depends upon historiography for documentation as such. To elaborate this point, let us look back to the years that immediately precede the publication of Du Bois's essay.

The World's Columbian Exposition of 1893 marks a moment of great import in the last decade of the nineteenth century, and thus it may serve as an apt historical moment in which to note an early context for "Conservation." The Exposition took place in Chicago a scant twenty-eight years after the close of the Civil War, nine years after European interests carved up Africa to satisfy their hunger for colonial power at the Berlin Conference of 1884, and four years before the founding of the American Negro Academy. At the time of the Chicago World's Fair, as the Exposition is also known, Du Bois was in Berlin undertaking graduate studies abroad, yet he took note of its import. The architectural layout of the fair spoke its message to the world. The central attraction was the White City. True to its name, it comprised white buildings, which occupied the central area of the fairgrounds. It was, by design, the domain of upper-class white men, who used the venue to display wealth, military arms, and advanced technology. At the far end of the fairgrounds, the Midway Plaisance provided space for the exhibition of continental Africans and other non-European peoples (!), as well as German and Swiss villages. Separating the Midway from the White City was the Women's Building, which not only displayed artifacts documenting the progress white women had made in literature, art, and a number of other fields, but also boasted, after concerted appeals for space by Frederick Douglass, Ida B. Wells, and other African American leaders, the largest, though unofficial, exhibit mounted by African American men and women. Frances Ellen Watkins Harper attended the 1893 Fair, where she gave a speech entitled "Woman's Political Future"[13] before the World's Congress of Representative Women, a meeting held in conjunction with the Columbian Exposition. Christianity, temperance, family, and human rights are all themes that Harper forcefully exerts in this essay, which may be one of her finest.

Considering Harper's piece as an aspect of the historical context in which the "Conservation of Races" arose allows us to see how Harper's poetics as exemplified in her verse is connected to her political activism. Further, it allows us to trace a bridge of thought between Harper and Du Bois, who might otherwise appear to be less than political and social contemporaries. The Columbian Exposition was intended by American industrialists such as the steel magnate Andrew Carnegie to demonstrate America's progress and prowess since the Civil War. Carnegie considered world's fairs to be bloodless fields of international striving upon which each nation contended for artistic, scientific, and technological supremacy.[14] The fairs were also meant to be material displays of white men's social and political power. It is true that white women were allowed a building dedicated to the display of their work and advancement. Significantly, the Women's Building was designed by a woman architect, Sophia Hayden. Yet it has often been remarked that the very layout of the fairgrounds was meant to underscore the supremacy of white men in all realms of life: the Women's Building was situated at the edge of what was called the White City, and could be found near the entrance to the Midway Plaisance.

Home to displays of persons of color from around the world, largely those of colonized countries, the Midway also provided space for the amusement of visitors to the fair. While the White City displayed the height of technological knowledge and military might, the Midway granted one the leisure of observing that which was considered uncivilized. The linear arrangement of the fairgrounds—from the White City of men, to the Women's Building (which engirded and perhaps in some eyes feminized the entire Negro American exhibit) on the margins of the City, to the flamboyance of the Midway (where the people of color were themselves on display in makeshift villages and the like)—was yet another way of announcing the ideal order of things in America.

Harper begins her essay by subverting the assumption that lay at the center of the fair's organization: the dominant conviction that all serious cultural advancement was white and male. Because of their ability to contribute morally and spiritually to the advancement of the nation, women, she argues, remain central to not only American, but also global society. "[M]ind is more than matter," Harper insists, and because "the highest ideal" is "always the true real," woman, the possessor of true sentiment and knowledge, Harper seems to say, surpasses man in her intellectual purity. As a consequence, woman has the opportunity to lead the world to "grander discoveries" than those supposedly made by Christopher Columbus (436).

Of course, Harper's rhetorical posturing here is on point, as the World's Fair that year was held in honor of Columbus's "discovery" of America. (A dubious claim to discovery, as Native Americans had erected a civilization that was already thriving upon Columbus's arrival.) She insists that America was standing "on the threshold of woman's era" ("Woman's Political Future" 437), an era in which the cultural work of women would open a whole new world of cultural possibilities. It was up to women to build a stronger national character, not only through the rearing and educating of children (this is also made clear in Harper's poetry, as we have seen through her emphases on motherhood), but also through direct participation in the social sphere. As she asserts in the Aunt Chloe poems, Harper saw voting as supremely important, and she also called upon women to enter the work force and claim "at least some of the wealth monopolized by her stronger brother" (437). As her own life evidenced, Harper saw woman's future as flourishing beyond the sphere of the domestic. Indeed, she actively advocated the participation of women in political as well as economic realms, and called upon them to temper the avarice and immorality of some male leaders with what she referred to as the distinctive feminine virtues of temperance, Christianity, and universal human rights.

Harper's efforts to articulate an African American and female positionality was echoed in the work of Frederick Douglass and Ida B. Wells, who had fought to ensure exhibition space for the descendants of the slaves. In spite of Douglass's and Wells's efforts to ensure that African Americans would have space in which to represent themselves at the fair, the exposition's white male American organizers had well ensured their power and authority to define a multitude of identities upon an international stage. They were intent upon limiting as best they could the voices of African Americans, proposing "Colored American's Day," August 25, 1893, as a paltry offering that was rejected by many leaders of the black community. Wells and Douglass, who was himself given greater visibility at the fair because of his position as representative of Haiti, were a formidable but uneasy pair united in combating the heavy-handed exclusions of the organizers. They went to great lengths to publish and distribute a pamphlet of well-informed critical essays, entitled "The Reason Why the Colored American is not in the Columbian Exposition."[15] Douglass's moralistic chiding of American exclusionary practices in his introduction to the pamphlet was sustained by

Wells' more forceful rendering of statistics that illustrated the persistence of the awful American practice of lynching. Wells drew a crucial and heretofore unspoken analogy between the political terrorism represented by lynching and economic oppression, and repressive codes of sexuality and morality.

Douglass's death in 1895 left African Americans worried about who would succeed him in leadership. Wells had positioned herself admirably with her fiery editorials, forceful speeches, and international anti-lynching campaign, but she was outmaneuvered by the conciliatory message of Booker T. Washington, whose 1895 Atlanta Exposition Address secured his popularity among both Northern and Southern whites, and made his ascendancy inevitable. The fact that she was a woman undoubtedly was an issue; however, Wells continued to play a vital role in African American political life through her work in founding the National Association of Colored Women (NACW) in 1896, the same year of *Plessy v. Ferguson*, which upheld the constitutionality of "separate but equal" public facilities for blacks. Segregation manifestly had the support of the highest court in the nation. As United States citizens struggling for equal rights, African Americans found themselves in a perilous political position, grappling with the problem of national belonging in 1890s America at the same time that they worked to define themselves as a world-historical people demonstrating proof of their progress on the international stage of the World's Columbian Exposition.

Importantly, their actions in 1893 challenged the philosophy of world history advanced by the prominent German thinker, Georg W. F. Hegel, who had, in 1820 and again in 1830, delivered the influential set of lectures that would comprise his *Philosophy of History*.[16] Hegel commences his *Philosophy* by dismissing both North America (where his focus rested on the former colonies of the United States, deprecating Canada and Mexico as weak states that elicited no fear from the "North American Federation") as well as Africa, and for two different reasons. America is, Hegel writes, "the land of the future" (*Philosophy of History* 86): while it manifests a "prosperous state of things; an increase in industry and population civil order and firm freedom" (*sic*, 83–84), it is simply "a land of desire for all those who are weary of the historical lumber-room of old Europe" (86). As a "Land of the Future," Hegel continues, America "has no interest for us here, for, as regards *History*, our concern must be with that which has been and that which is. In regard to *Philosophy*, on the other hand, we have to do with that which (strictly speaking) is neither past nor future, but with that which *is*, which has an eternal existence—with Reason; and this is quite sufficient to occupy us" (87).

While America is deemed by Hegel to be the land of the future—unactualized, and thus irrationally positioned outside of his philosophy of history—Africa was to suffer a different fate in Hegel's analysis. Though its pastness suited well Hegel's requirements for *History*, Africa had, to his mind, remained "shut up" from the "rest of the World" (91). It lay "beyond the day of self-conscious history," "enveloped in the dark mantle of Night" due not only to its "tropical nature," but also its "geographical condition" (91). It thus displayed "no movement or development," no sense of present self-awareness and thus no Reason, and so Hegel concluded quickly that it had "no historical part in the World": "What we properly understand by Africa, is the Unhistorical, Undeveloped Spirit, still involved in the conditions of mere nature, which had to be presented here as only on the threshold of the World's History" (99).

Hegel's portrayal of Africa as "unhistorical," as a collective "undeveloped spirit" meant that, to his mind, Africa and Africans lacked the insight and self-reflexivity that constitute what Enlightenment- and Romantic-era philosophers referred to as self-consciousness, or self-conscious being: "In Negro life the characteristic point is the fact that consciousness has not yet attained to the realization of any substantial objective existence—as for example, God, or Law—in which he realizes his own being. This distinction between himself as an individual and the universality of his essential being, the African in the uniform, undeveloped oneness of his existence has not yet attained; so that the Knowledge of an absolute Being, an Other and a Higher than his individual self, is entirely wanting" (93). The African Spirit remained unrealized, Hegel argues, because in lieu of an organized religion, Africans practiced "sorcery" and superstition. And since they recognized no higher or supreme being, Hegel contends, they consequently demeaned themselves as degraded beings who indulge in a "perfect *contempt* for humanity." So intense is their degradation of human life, Hegel insists, that they practice tyranny and cannibalism with impunity, and they practice slavery in such a way as to outstrip even the European colonies in their viciousness. Hegel painted a dire, bloody, and highly suspect portrait of African brutality. He wrote, for example, that heads of African states "composed [solely] of women" took "captives in war" as husbands, casting away male children or pounding their own children with mortars, and using their blood to "besmear" and thus mystically empower themselves (italics in original, 97).

Hegel's overview of Africa's past went to great extents to rationalize leaving Africa outside of his philosophy of history. He in fact argued that because of the African's natural disdain for humanity, exemplified in their supposed blood-thirsty cruelty, Africans likewise devalued freedom, since freedom is "the essence of humanity" (99). Slavery thus came naturally to the African; bondage would, Hegel contended somewhat paradoxically, beneficially provide Africans with "a phase of advance from the merely isolated sensual existence—a phase of education—a mode of becoming participant in a higher morality and the culture connected with it" (99). Slavery, in other words, would allow Africans to advance toward European notions of being and self-conscious existence. Thus the abolition of slavery, Hegel argued, should be only gradual, a method that "is therefore wiser and more equitable than its sudden removal" (99).[17]

The Exposition's organizers addressed America's abolition of slavery—which had not come gradually, as Hegel counseled, but, through the cataclysm of Civil War—immediately yet obliquely. By denying African Americans space in the "white city" to document and exhibit their own history and progress, and by thus forcing them into a small, inadequate space provided by the Fair's Women's Committee, who were themselves forcibly limited in their participation in the Fair's organization, the white men at the Fair's helm tightly controlled representations of their version of America's redemption story. The Fair presented a concise, white masculinist narrative of how ably the young nation-state had rebounded from the desolation of its Civil War, only twenty-eight years earlier. America had managed not only the abolition of slavery, a major component of the American economy, but had also worked assiduously to emerge from the deep economic depression into which the South had subsequently fallen.

America had, in the language of Hegel's *Philosophy of History*, established itself as a political constituent of some importance in its present historical moment. The organizers highlighted the postbellum ideals of American nationalism and imperialism that had begun with the Mexican American War of 1847–1848 (and which would ultimately reach their nineteenth-century apotheosis in 1898 with the advent of the Spanish-American War, liberating Cuba from Spanish rule and granting America Guam, Puerto Rico, and the Philippines as territories). Late nineteenth-century American imperialism took the place of its official slave economy, which was in turn transformed into peonage, black codes, and Jim Crow laws. During this the Gilded Age, Manifest Destiny seemed indeed to be America's Destiny; immigration reached its peak as industrialization took root; the black codes that were the legacy of the Civil War were enforced to keep blacks "in their place" in the economic and social scheme of things; and Jim Crow rode high.

The decade during which Du Bois wrote "The Conservation of Races" was thus not exempt from the racist Hegelian historicism that had infected Western thought. It was a time of great social ferment for African

Americans as well as whites. Du Bois's brand of activism was not the only sort to take hold of the black social and cultural imagination. Black theater emerged during this period, and figures such as Will Marion Cook, the Johnson Brothers (Rosamond and James Weldon) and their collaborator Bob Cole, and Williams and Walker were popular performers. The coon song and ragtime were all the rage. Scott Joplin, whose "Maple Leaf Rag" was an instant hit in 1899, came into prominence, as did Ernest Hogan, the African American vaudevillian who in 1896 had written "All Coons Look Alike to Me," a minstrel song used in white shows. Charles Chesnutt and Paul Laurence Dunbar were major literary figures of the day, and Dunbar himself wrote lyrics for minstrel songs, co-authoring the one-act musical play, Clorindy, Or The Origin of the Cakewalk (1898) with Hogan. Antonín Dvorak came to America from his native Bohemia in late 1892 to serve as director of the newly-founded National Conservatory of Music in New York City, where he began to sketch out his Symphony in E Minor, popularly known as the "New World Symphony." Dvorak counted several African American composers among his students, including Will Marion Cook, and would later alternately both uphold Negro folk music as the future of an American school of composition, and flatly deny that he himself had been influenced by the Negro themes that were quite evident in his own work.

What is more, the 1890s in both America and Europe witnessed the rise of anarchy. Bombs, assassinations of major public figures (American President William McKinley would be murdered by an anarchist at the turn of the century at yet another fair, the 1901 Pan-American Exposition in Buffalo, NY), and political tracts calling for the overthrow of all government abounded. Labor organizing, widespread socialism (one of the most popular novels in the United States in the 1880s—to which Du Bois would often refer—was Edward Bellamy's Looking Backward: 2000–1887 (1888), a utopian nativist novel that advocated socialism and sold over one million copies), and progressivism became watch phrases as many were talking about reform. But in spite of widespread attention to social reform and progressive ideals and, indeed, despite the broad popularity of African American cultural forms such as those mentioned above, pseudoscientific doctrines of black inferiority continued to abound in the United States and Europe much as they had during the late eighteenth century, and they played a significant role in the confusing mix of progressive and regressive ideologies.

The inaugural gathering of the American Negro Academy was intended especially to counter regressive social discourses of the 1890s, but also to undergird and encourage the significant social and cultural advances African Americans had made since the Emancipation Proclamation was issued by

Lincoln in 1863. The orientation of the ANA, which Booker T. Washington had been invited to join, but whose membership he had declined, flew in the face of the Tuskegee principal's conservative dictates, and was indeed aimed at challenging Washington's materialist and complicitous solution for navigating the confusing times of the 1890s. Instead of calling for a sentiment of concession and accommodation among blacks, as Washington had done in his 1895 Atlanta Exposition Address, Du Bois's group demanded that blacks not be damned to continue their quest for freedom at the bottom rung of the social ladder, but that they instead be granted opportunities based on their ability and interests. Du Bois's paper opened the Academy meeting, but first I will turn briefly to Alexander Crummell's speech, which followed Du Bois's lecture on the meeting's program. It will provide us with further understanding of the ideological context that informed the thrust of the Academy's mission, as well as Du Bois's plain interest in guiding and shaping this mission.

After being duly elected founding president of the ANA (Du Bois was voted secretary), Alexander Crummell, an Episcopalian of some note who had published, among other works, a collection of sermons and essays entitled *The Future of Africa* in 1862 while on residency in Liberia, and the book *Africa and America* (1891), dealing with the condition of blacks in post-Reconstruction America, proceeded with a lecture entitled "Civilization, the Primal Need of the Race." Described as a manifesto of high culture by David Levering Lewis (1993, 170), Crummell's oration emphasized topics he treated at length in *Africa and America*, including the need for higher learning among Negroes, and for the study and production of literature, art, and philosophy, among other humanistic endeavors. He argued that the "special race problem of the Negro" in America was his "civilization" (1969, 3). Crummell felt that blacks in America were destined to attain a certain "place," or, that blacks were destined to attain a certain historicity, and that this place and historical being could not be reached "until we attain the role of civilization" (4). "To make men you need civilization; and what I mean by civilization is the action of exalted forces, both of God and man. For manhood is the most majestic thing in God's creation; and hence the demand for the very highest art in the shaping and moulding of human souls" (4). The "master-need" of the race was neither Washingtonian materialism nor a predisposition toward "blood and lineage as the root (source) of power and progress," Crummell argued; "the leader, the creative and organizing mind, is the master-need in all the societies of man" (4, 6). Crummell, in other words, was arguing not simply for self-conscious black being, but pointedly for self-conscious black manhood, a masculine-gendered self-reflexivity that would allow for the attainment of the sort of world historical being of which Hegel had declared all Africans incapable.

The emphasis on manhood, civilization, and historicity, and the de-emphasizing of "blood and lineage" as sources of "power and progress" preached by the elder scholar deserve further comment, for both are concepts that Du Bois revisits in "The Conservation of Races" and throughout the essays that comprise *The Souls of Black Folk*. Crummell defines civilization as "the action of exalted forces," very much akin to the higher Being Hegel deemed necessary for a philosophy of history, but the influence of racist pseudoscience and the doctrines of nationalism that abounded during the era in which he wrote added certain other connotations to the word. To be civilized was to be a man worthy of human rights, citizenship, and enfranchisement, and thus, as a construct, civilization held far-ranging connotations regarding race and sex. The ideal citizen was, of course, white, male, propertied, and monied. White manhood tended to define itself in relation to white womanhood—"true" womanhood—which demanded that a woman be pious, submissive, domestic, and chaste. Black male concepts of manhood in the nineteenth century operated in a somewhat, though not wholly, analogous fashion. Indeed, nineteenth-century black nationalism, as it was articulated by a number of prominent black men, depended heavily upon notions of ideal black manhood, and this manhood was, to a significant extent, modeled after an anxious white patriarchy, which demanded the subjugation of women in order to propagate itself. Crummell's essay "The Black Woman of the South: Her Neglects and Her Needs" (1883/1992) provides evidence of this stance. Harper, of course, openly dissented from this perspective, yet a good number of prominent African American women, Anna Julia Cooper among them, did not disagree with Crummell's paternal and patriarchal conclusions.

The white man, however, defined himself not in relation to white womanhood alone, but also in opposition to the sort of "man" he was not, specifically "the Negro" or "the Indian." The journalist Ray Stannard Baker, for example, in his essay "What is Lynching? A Study of Mob Justice, South and North" (1905), rendered a dubious argument against this practice by pointing out that in lynching blacks, the white man would become as savage as Negroes. What he seemed also to fear was that whites in Europe would look at American practices of lynching—savagery in a country that Hegel had judged unworthy of a philosophy of history just as the African continent ironically was—and deem them cause enough to withhold from America full membership among the community of nations. Even so, black men's desire to be viewed as vital components of the national body politic entailed their almost wholesale acceptance of Euro-American ideals of civilization. Furthermore, the idea of civilization extended itself to the domination of colonialism—the *mission civilatrice* of the French and the varying concepts of Manifest Destiny practiced by the Americans and the English, ideologies adopted by both Alexander Crummell and Edward Wilmot Blyden in their writings on Africa. Because the black masses as well as white women were generally considered to be less than civilized by their elite, both groups were to be dominated by those classes of white men who were more "evolved"; we see this clearly in the history of the 1893 Columbian Exposition. And while Social Darwinism itself did not initially arise as a measure through which African Americans and women were purposefully and specifically oppressed, racial theories of civilization came nonetheless into practice under its aegis. With these many events of the nineteenth-century's final decade in mind, let us again turn to the hermeneutics of "The Conservation of Races."

"Conservation" and the Hermeneutics of Race

The civilizationist overtones in "The Conservation of Races" are somewhat consistent with Alexander Crummell's philosophy, yet Du Bois is quite clear about the shortcomings of white civilizationism, and he articulates this through extended irony. Among the earliest of his serious ruminations on the peculiar situation of the black man in America, Du Bois begins his speech before Crummell and the ANA, as we have noted, by ostensibly building a case against the idea popular among the black elite that the notion of race should be set aside in favor of achieving universal brotherhood. The American Negro, he writes, has been

> led to deprecate and minimize race distinctions, to believe intensely that out of one blood God created all nations, and to speak of human brotherhood as though it were the possibility of an already dawning tomorrow. Nevertheless, in our calmer moments we must acknowledge that human beings are divided into races; that in this country the two most extreme types of the world's races have met, and the resulting problem as to the future relations of these types is not only of intense and living interest to us, but forms an epoch in the history of mankind. (815)

Du Bois's stated aim in the early portion of the essay is to encourage Crummell and other African American civic and academic leaders who were present—Kelly Miller, Archibald Grimké, and others to view the race "problem"—"the problem as to the future relation of these types" (815)—as the decisive factor that renders their present moment in history epochal and distinctive. In this reframing of the so-called Negro Problem, which, as we recall, Du Bois deems a plexus of social problems, he calls upon the members of the ANA to reconceptualize their understanding of race and to place the idea of race at a greater primacy than that of nation. The American Negro's zeal in minimizing the importance of race is naïve, Du Bois warns. History has been built on the race ideal, he argues, and black Americans, no less than members of other races, must come to terms with the importance of race and its function in the political and social machinery that undergirds national law and governs the interchange among nation-states. In his attempt to shed light on the meaning of race as a concept, we should recall that in his critical ontology of race Du Bois traces what he calls "the question of race in human philosophy," and thus he traces the force of a *concept* that comes to demarcate "our guiding lines and boundaries in the practical difficulties of every day" (815). Instead of emphasizing the maxim that "out of one blood God created all nations" and the already accepted universality of "human brotherhood" (this is the sort of humanism Du Bois's discourse in "Conservation" ultimately embraces), he first calls upon African Americans to recognize "the hard limits of natural law" (815), implicit within which are the limits of race. Within this frame of reference, which is superficially essentialist but manifestly ironic, Du Bois determines to interrogate "the real meaning of Race" (815), and its significance for the Negro people.

And what is this "real" meaning? A good deal of the difficulty scholars have generally encountered in untangling Du Bois's ideas on race lies not only in the varied accounts of the meaning and history of race as an idea (proffered, for example, by historians and scientists such as Thomas Gossett, Joel Williamson, William Stanton, Winthrop Jordan, and Stephen Jay Gould) and the place of this idea in Du Bois's thought (as analyzed by philosophers such as K. Anthony Appiah, Lucius Outlaw, and Robert Gooding-Williams). The difficulty is also evident in the inability of scholars of nationalism and race studies to come together on a definitive idea of the nation and to agree upon just what criteria grant groups of people the right to nationhood. Du Bois draws upon the exigencies of racialist and nationalist discourses as he limns the meaning of race in America, and the collusion of these two social, political, and economic forces demanded that he bring to bear upon philosophies of being the meaning of blackness in the modern world. This "strange meaning of being black" is, of course, Du Bois's central theme in *The Souls of Black Folk*, and this is one of the ways in which "Conservation" serves to prepare the way for *Souls*. Du Bois's critical ontology of the meaning of race in "Conservation" lays the foundations for and facilitates the concept metaphors of the color-line, the veil, and double consciousness that would lend depth and meaning to his later work on black being.

Grasping the implications for black being in "Conservation" thus requires further contextualization of Du Bois's ideas regarding black nationalism, his understanding of what it meant to belong to a national community, as well as the implications of being excluded from such membership on the basis of racial identity and/or color. We may accomplish this through a brief discussion of the wide-ranging discourses on nationalism. In *Nationalism*, first published in 1960, Elie Kedourie describes the movement as one of many ideological currents that responded to or reacted against the impersonal bureaucracy that governed groups of people (xv). Hans Kohn writes in *Nationalism: Its Meaning and History* (1965) that "Nationalities are the products of the living forces of history, and therefore fluctuating and never rigid. They are groups of the utmost complexity, and defy exact definition" (9). In *The God of Modernity* (1994), Josep Llobera stresses that nationalism does not encompass the same realities when applied globally. He limits the scope of his text to Western Europe, "the birthplace and lieu classique of nationalism" (ix–x). Paul James' *Nation Formation* (1996), focuses on what he calls the "structural subjectivities" that provide the foundation for nation building: "the body, space, and time. [. . .] The body relates to the nationalist emphasis upon organic metaphors such as the 'blood of the people'; space is relative to the emphasis on territoriality; and time is important to the cultural themes of historicity, tradition and primordial roots" (xiv). Paul Gilbert, in *The Philosophy of Nationalism* (1998), argues that nationalism may be thought of as the overt expression of the political beliefs on which the nation is founded. Conversely, Benedict Anderson, author of *Imagined Communities* (1991), maintains that nationalism must be understood as emerging not out of political ideologies, but out of the large cultural systems that preceded it, namely religious community and the dynastic realm (12). For Anderson as for many other scholars, the eighteenth century marks "not only the dawn and the age of nationalism but the dusk of religious modes of thought" (11). He defines the nation-state as "an imagined community—and imagined as both inherently limited and sovereign" (6). Anderson's text has taught us to understand nation-states as metaphorical constructions that are not ornamentations of language, but mimic the "hard limits of natural law" Du Bois underscores at the outset of his essay.

Like those of race, the metaphorics and mimesis that represent the "limits" of the nation-state through figurative language call us to see nationalism as both myth and symbolism, as an instrument that is both expressive of and crucial to the birth of modernity and modernist thought. The imprecision with which the concept is often discussed may contribute to a lack of understanding of Du Bois's usage of "race" in relation to "nation" in "The Conservation of Races." Within nationalist terminology there exist fine shades of meaning that are important to a fuller understanding of the concept of nationhood, yet none of these is hard and fast, in spite of nationalism's attempts to erect such limits. While the terms "nation," "state," and "nation-state" are often used interchangeably, there are subtle variations of which one must be aware and which may aid us in grasping Du Bois's intent when speaking of the invention of race and of an emerging black nation. A "nation" is usually characterized by its relatively large size and independent status, and may be thought of as a community of people composed of one or more nationalities or ethnicities. In this concept of the nation, pluralism is expected and is inherent to the body politic; common origin is not underscored in the classic idea of the nation, but emphasis is placed on the ability of the body politic, comprising peoples of varying nationalities, from which one might infer disparate ethnic and/or historic origins, to govern itself. A "state" may be defined as a politically organized body of people usually occupying a definite territory, especially one that is sovereign. Common origins or ethnicities are not germane to the definition of the state; rather, greater emphasis is placed on the occupation of a specific, autonomous geographical territory with recognized spatial boundaries. The concept of the "nation-state" stands apart from these definitions. The nation-state is that form of political organization under which a relatively homogeneous and theoretically historical people inhabits a sovereign state, especially a state containing one as opposed to several nationalities. The concept of the nation-state generally rules out notions of both pluralism and ethnicity. It demands the myth of a monolithic national culture, common origins, and homogeneity, promulgated through such metaphors as "the body politic" and "the blood of the people." In the West, the ideology of nationalism usually operates upon the postulates of the nation-state.

As Du Bois works at excavating the "meaning" of race in American and world history from this plethora of theories, we should recognize the emphasis he places on the power of language in general, and the metaphorics of the word "race" in particular, to do the work of politics, culture, and representation in such social structures as the nation-state. Whenever language does the work of culture, language becomes, as Julia Kristeva has noted, metaphoric.[18] It functions according to the laws of discursive logic in which truth is not necessarily that which is true, but that which is given the appearance and assurance of being true. As with his hermeneutics of the "meaning of being black" in *Souls*, in searching for "the real meaning of Race in "Conservation," Du Bois recognizes this metaphorical discursive logic and seeks, not only through the political organizing of such an institution as the American Negro Academy but also through writing—a discursive, perlocutionary and even illocutionary act (as I discuss above)—and by deconstructing racial and nationalist metaphors as well as the history of signification these metaphors are capable of evoking, to counter it. At the center of the question of race in America is the question of who belongs and who does not; who possesses the criteria that grant one "Americanness." When we speak of the relation of being and metaphor, we speak of an appurtenance to specific categories, and especially to categories of meaning, which are regularly transposed and transgressed in metaphorical operations. When it comes to metaphors of racialized being especially, there is, as Stuart Hall (1997) points out, no safety in the terminology of race, of difference, of nationalism.

Kristeva's conclusion regarding the metaphoricity of language as it is called upon to do the work of culture is manifested in the way Du Bois's discourse enacts a process of identification, whereby the signifier "black," or more specifically, the "Negro race," provides the basis for a political agenda intended to battle racist white nationalism. And nationalist ideology, as both an expression and consequence of modernity, is central to Du Bois's understanding of the evolution of racialist thought. This subject consistently reappears in his discourse and provides the foundation for his "unveiling" project in *The Souls of Black Folk*. Du Bois explores the meaning of race from a point of view that is both historical and contemporary to his time. In fact, Du Bois speaks of the "invention" of race in much the same way that Benedict Anderson speaks of the "invention" of the nation. Anderson writes that "nationness is the most universally legitimate value in the political life of our time," and argues in favor of viewing nationalism as a cultural artifact: "[T]he creation of these artefacts [sic] towards the end of the eighteenth century was the spontaneous distillation of a complex 'crossing' of discrete historical forces" (4). Du Bois's account of the development of the races into what he calls their current "morphological" states reflects these "crossings," and is aligned with the evolution of the nation-state's body politic. He traces its roots to "vast families" that merged to form the city-state, which, upon integrating with other geopolitical entities, contributed to the intermingling of what were then taken to be different racial types:

The age of nomadic tribes of closely related individuals represents the maximum of physical differences. They were practically vast families, and there were as many groups as families. As the families came together to form cities the physical differences lessened, purity of blood was replaced by the requirement of domicile, and all who lived within the city bounds came gradually to be regarded as members of the groups, i.e., there was a slight and slow breaking down of physical barriers. (819)

Du Bois describes the city-state, in loose and flexible terms, as a "practically vast" family whose members were related not simply by blood, but by culture, economics, and history: "This city became husbandmen, this, merchants, another warriors, and so on. The *ideals of life* for which the different cities struggled were different" (819, emphasis in original). The "crossings" narrated by the young professor are inherent to his understanding of the evolution of nations as well as races:

When at last cities began to coalesce into nations there was another breaking down of barriers which separated groups of men. The larger and broader differences disappeared, and the sociological and historical races of men began to approximate the present division of races as indicated by physical researches. At the same time the spiritual and physical differences of race groups which constituted the nations became deep and decisive. The English nation stood for constitutional liberty and commercial freedom; the German nation for science and philosophy; the Romance nations stood for literature and art, and the other race groups are striving, each in its own way, to develope [sic] for civilization its particular message, its particular ideal, which shall help to guide the world nearer and nearer that perfection of human life for which we all long, that "one far off Divine event." This has been the function of race differences up to the present time. What shall be its function in the future? (819)

Leaving aside Du Bois's opinion on the predilections of each nation to favor certain disciplines and sciences, the manner in which he explains how certain "race" groups, comprising the "sociological and historical races of men," functioned as nationalities which came to stand for ideals is significant. And his attempt at classifying American Negroes as a "nation," the first step in declaring them members of a legitimate "state" with rights to self-determination, makes the question one of urgency. Multiple levels of metaphorical discourses of being are thus at play. "American" denotes not only geography and bio-politics; as an "identity" it also results from the alchemy of nation-making, particularly the ideal of cultural assimilation, which discards old ethnic identities in favor of a new, unified, even symbolic one. "Negro" effects a process similar to that of "American." "Negroes" in nineteenth-century America were "new world blacks," separated from their homeland by the Middle Passage and the attendant history of slavery, and lumped together under a convenient signifier that distinguished them by not only, and not strictly, color of skin, but also by an African cultural heritage. This outwardly imposed signifier of identity dismissed the ethnic differences among blacks in the new world as unimportant to the order of things in plantation and post-plantation societies. The plural identity of the Negro American not only lays the foundation for an existence defined in terms of an historical void in the wake of slavery and colonialism; it provides for its structure. Thus, when one speaks of the "American Negro" in terms relevant to nation and race, one might characterize this expression, like the "cultural artifact" of nationalism, as belonging to the tradition of mythmaking or metaphorization. The very phrase "American Negro" conjures images of hybridity and plurality, and the imagined community of the nation and the invention of race emerge as the necessary determinants of the American Negro's identity.

To some degree, this aids in explaining the ambiguity present in Du Bois's text. In "Conservation," Du Bois endeavors, on the one hand, to dismantle received theories of racial pseudoscience that labeled blacks inferior and placed them at the bottom of the "great chain of being," and on the other hand, to establish some grounds upon which to valuate and perpetuate the very sort of nationalist discourse that sustained racialist theorizing. The loss of ethnicity experienced by the black subject during the crossing of the Middle Passage reconfigures this quest as a search for a nationality upon which a certain racial signification is bestowed from without. O. R. Dathorne writes that the "'Negro' becomes a figment of the imagination" (8), meaning that color, which is used as an ontological signifier denoting (connoting, as it were) racial identity, becomes a border that demarcates the rigid opposition of white and other. This is integral to the process of becoming a "new world black," and is indicative of the transmigration of the black body across the Atlantic on the journey towards a reconstruction of self and identity, a reconstruction now formed in a context of racial determinations that had, up to that point in history, remained relatively unthought. A significant factor in this process of transformation is the imbibing or ingestion of other cultures and cultural forms, and the adoption and adaptation of these forms for new and specific purposes of social survival and progress. The loss of ethnicity during the horrific voyage of the slave ship, and the artificial construction of borders of nationality and race cast the new world African as a member of a seemingly cohesive new social group, without ethnic differentiation among blacks. Dathorne refers to this process as the evolving of a collective, historical black American identity which, while tacitly recognizing its diverse constituent elements, positions Africa as the ancient, mythological center and foundation of this personality, what he calls "Afro-Americanitude." Following this argument, it was the new world that transformed historical Africans into New World or modern "Negroes," harnessing their various contradistinctions under one modern social indicator that nonetheless barred them from any real sense of Americanness. The terms "American" and "Negro," which function similarly as inventive and integrative forces of modernity, operate at odds one with the other.

It is in this way that the equivocation over the appropriateness of membership in the modern American nation-state regarding those deemed "outsiders" becomes evident in Du Bois's analysis of theories of race and nation. The concept of race and the corresponding concept of ethnicity, to which the term "Negro" is implicitly relevant, theoretically disallow among blacks the "othering" specific to the concept of the nation-state. That is to say that during Du Bois's time, there was a significant way in which the term Negro, or black, was used as a racial signifier that could also be employed, in counter-discourse, to aid folks in organizing under one political umbrella, to borrow phrasing from Stuart Hall. Thus the solidarity that emerges from Du Bois's analysis of a race identity—which I see as distinct from (though related to) the consciousness of black being—is, for blacks, preferable to allegiance to a nation-state that repudiates them. Blacks had a more difficult time assimilating not because of differences of ideals or even culture, and Du Bois makes this clear, but mainly because of differences of physicalities that were presumed, via discourses of racial pseudoscience, to represent a specific racial essence, itself taken to be an indicator of national belonging and of intellectual capacity. Therefore, when writing of the nation-state and acceptance into the national body, Du Bois found it first necessary to consider and examine strategems of identity rather than being. Doing so set the stage for entering into the question of being in *Souls*.

Strategic praxes of racial identity (e.g., coming together under a signifier of racial identification so as to carry out plans of political action through solidarity) constitute a key modality in Du Bois's analysis of race. He found examples of such solidarity in the activism of Harper, Douglass, and Wells. Du Bois's example claims that it is only through a critical ontology of race that one may grasp the "uses" of a black racial identity that can be employed subversively to test and break the limits of racist thinking and aggression.

Of course, there is a risk in Du Bois's effort at valuating a black identity by granting it primacy over the identity that comes through national belonging. In seeking to define and give shape to what he imagined to be an emerging black nation (emerging from the "races," just as other nations had), Du Bois's gestures were designed to further the illusion of homogeneity and unity among American blacks, and to underscore the force of social conflicts that were defined by racial differences. He lists "eight distinctly differentiated" historical races, which he names mainly in terms of nationality:

> They are the Slavs of eastern Europe, the Teutons of middle Europe, the English of Great Britain and America, the Romance nations of Southern and Western Europe, the Negroes of Africa and America, the Semitic people of Western Asia and Northern Africa, the Hindoos of Central Asia and the Mongolians of Eastern Asia. (817–18)

While Sterling Stuckey (1987) defends Du Bois's classification as an enthusiastic dismissal of racial categorization, it is unclear how Du Bois came to choose these eight as the major race groups. The minor ones—the "Esquimaux," the South Sea Islanders and the American Indians—figure less prominently, but are mentioned to underscore the fact that the larger races are, in fact, "far from homogeneous":

> The Slav includes the Czech, the Magyar, the Pole and the Russian; the Teuton includes the German, the Scandinavian and the Dutch; the English include the Scotch, the Irish and the conglomerate American. Under the Romance nations the widely-differing Frenchman, Italian, Sicilian and Spaniard are comprehended. The term Negro is, perhaps, the most indefinite of all, combining the Mulattoes and Zamboes of America and the Egyptians, Bantus, and Bushmen of Africa. Among the Hindoos are traces of widely differing nations, while the great Chinese, Tartar, Corean [sic] and Japanese families fall under one designation—Mongolian. (818)

Du Bois's declension of "races," which he names not as biological groups but as national groups, grants him the expansion and revision of racial terminology he seeks and permits him to define race as "a vast family of human beings, generally of common blood and language, always of common history, traditions and impulses, who are both voluntarily and involuntarily striving together for the accomplishment of certain more or less vividly conceived ideals of life" (817).

Du Bois certainly did not base his concept of race on any firm idea of biological determinism. What is more, his statement on race begs the question: how does it happen that within a "race" constituting a "vast family," some members are "involuntarily" striving toward a collective goal? How, in fact, are they constrained to do so if they are not bound by some inexorable duty toward the larger collective, enforceable by decree of the offices of the larger collective?

When Du Bois writes in "Conservation" of the nationalistic and racial attributes that consign the individual within the body politic and draw the line between the public citizen and the private individual, the examples he follows form the bedrock of nationalist Enlightenment thought of Equiano's time. For instance, the organicism evident in Du Bois's expostulations on race is central to Immanuel Kant's own definition of a nation. Du Bois maintains that the Negro race "*must* be inspired with the Divine faith of our black mothers, that out of the blood and dust of battle will march a victorious host, a mighty nation, a peculiar people, to speak to the nations of earth a Divine truth that shall make them free" ("Conservation" 823, italics in original). When we read Kant, whose writing grants us our germinal understanding of what a modern nation-state is, after reading Du Bois, the resonance between the two texts rings clearly. Kant writes in 1797:

> The human beings who make up a nation can, as natives of the country, be represented as analogous to descendants from a common ancestry (*congeniti*) even if this is not in fact the case. But in an intellectual sense or for the purposes of right, they can be thought of as the offspring of a common mother (the republic), constituting, as it were, a single family (*gens, natio*) whose members (the citizens) are all equal by birth. (Kant 1797/1985, 38)

Du Bois was quite familiar with Kant's particular brand of political philosophy, and writes in *The Autobiography* of having read Kant alone with George Santayana during his undergraduate years at Harvard (143). In Kant's theory, a group of human beings, though biologically unrelated, may be thought of as descending from a common "mother," which stands as a metaphor for the republic, or the nation, for the "purposes of right," that is, for the purposes of citizenship and protection under the law. Thus, men and women who have come together in order to establish a social and political bond may do so under a nexus of affinity or common spiritual conviction while lending themselves to a process with metaphoric, organicist connotations, including such abstract notions as "the blood of the people" and "the body politic." In other words, Kant "invents" a consanguineous racial relation among disparate groups of people in order to ensure the advance of the nation-state. In this light, Du Bois's recognition of the metaphoricity of race, that it is "the most ingenious invention for human progress," resounds with a portentous sort of relation in thought.

Metaphorical discourse stands at the heart of the history of speculative philosophy regarding nation-formation, and helps us see more clearly Du Bois's emphasis upon the historical "voluntary and involuntary strivings" of the American Negro. Jean-Jacques Rousseau, whom, as with Kant, we have already encountered in our discussion of Equiano, writes:

> Indeed, each individual can, as a man, have a private will contrary to or differing from the general will he has as a citizen. His absolute and independent existence can bring him to view what he owes the common cause as a free contribution, the loss of which will harm others less than its payment burdens him; and considering the moral person of the State as an imaginary being because it is not a man, he might wish to enjoy the rights of the citizen without wanting to fulfill the duties of a subject, an injustice whose spread would soon cause the ruin of the body politic. In order for the social contract not to be an ineffectual formula, therefore, the sovereign must have some guarantees, independent of the consent of the private individuals [. . .]. So the fundamental contract tacitly includes this engagement, which alone can give force to all the others: that whoever refuses to obey the general will shall be constrained to do so by the entire body. (24)

The public citizen and the private individual converge within Rousseau's social contract, where the private citizen submits him- or herself, or is constrained to submit by the general citizenry, to the greater good of the collective. For Rousseau, this gesture is crucial to the longevity of the body politic, and echoes Du Bois's conception of the black folk, who, as individual, racialized beings, are "voluntarily and involuntarily striving together for the accomplishment of certain more or less vividly conceived ideals of life" (817).

~

It would seem that in the year 2014, more than 200 years after Equiano presented us with his *Narrative*, more than one hundred years after the appearance of both Frances E. W. Harper's *Sketches* and W. E. B. Du Bois's *Souls*, more than sixty years after Ralph Ellison won the National Book Award for *Invisible Man*, and more than forty years after Asa Philip Randolph organized the great March on Washington that catapulted the Reverend Martin Luther King, Jr. to prominence, we would be finished with the idea of race, at least in biological terms. Scientists have told us repeatedly that there are greater differences within so-called racial groups than there are between them. Indeed, the Public Broadcasting Service (PBS) only a decade ago ran a series aimed at convincing its audience of the universality of human sisterhood and brotherhood. *In Race: The Power of an Illusion* (2000), a young African American girl was shown to have DNA that closely resembled, for example, that of a young Danish boy. The point to be taken was that race matters not, or at least not in a way that permits us to distinguish among people by classing them into racial groups that have, historically, fallen under the dictates of political and economic imperatives.

Race, however, does matter to some experts in the scientific world. Yet another PBS series aired the same year, this one entitled *The Mystery of the First Americans* (2000), focuses on the discovery of Kennewick Man. It points out that many scientists see the validity of race from the perspective of forensic anthropology, which assesses the reality of race by examining morphological differences among human beings. For them, the reality of race is evident in the bony traits of the mouth and cranium. A prominent nose, which is said to humidify air more efficiently in hot, humid climes, leads many anthropologists to the conclusion that racial differences coincide with specific climatic zones. They stress that such characteristics as the curliness of one's hair or the color of one's skin may not be quite so significant to a serologist who is primarily interested in questions of blood relation which may stretch across the boundaries of time and space. On this side of the argument, race is more than skin deep, and cannot be denied to satisfy the exigencies of political correctness. Thus, the question of race raised by Du Bois in his 1897 essay "The Conservation of Races" appears to be just as hotly under debate today as it was then.

I have argued that the ingredient most crucial to a successful reading of Du Bois's discourse on race is an awareness that this discourse is always mitigated by a metaphorical logic that is chiefly concerned with narratives of national belonging and racial identity, rather than being. Du Bois's critical ontology of race draws upon the upheavals of his own time as well as the long durée of metaphysical nationalist discourse, which employs a metaphorical, organicist language in order to overcome the schisms (such as those arising between the individual and the political collective) that were the bane of philosophical thought during the Enlightenment and Romantic periods.

There is much objection to analyzing the idea of race in terms of metaphor, and these objections arise when some conclude that metaphor is only figurative speech, both spoken and written, and that its importance ends when we are done examining florid poetry, or beautiful prose. However, I must agree with Stuart Hall when he deems metaphor to be an "absolutely deadly political [question]" (290). Du Bois's concept of race in "The Conservation of Races" is not only metaphorical and contingent; it is also political and activist. In proposing the categories of race and nation as not simply oppositional, but as coefficient, overlapping, and imprecise, that is, as possessing metaphorical qualities that escape concrete definition, and in problematizing the categories of manhood and civilization (for his reader if not for himself), Du Bois, in a sense, gives the "program" for subsequent work. As he puts it, he proposes an activist program for how race shall and should "function in the future" (819). In this light, "Conservation" may be interpreted as a preparation for an encounter with the being that lies within those raced as black. As a work of critical ontology that supplements the work of Harper, Douglass, and others even as it counters the outrageous claims of Hegel, "Conservation" refuses racial absolutism. Instead, it prepares us for the ontological metaphorics of the "meaning of being black" that comes forth in *Souls*. *The Souls of Black Folk*, a text constructed from and constituted by fragments—essays—is, like being black itself, plural and multiple in form, with each vignette, story, sociological tract, and historical rendering lacking the deep structure of a unified tome, composed of fragments and proliferating details that demand a certain "economy" of hermeneutical analysis. This economy is mediated by what I am calling a metaphorical poetics of black being, one that explores the very existential indeterminacy elaborated by Du Bois more than a century ago.

6

Habitations of the Veil

Souls, Figure, Form

Du Bois announces at the outset of *The Souls of Black Folk* that black being is conveyed metaphorically in the problematic, fragile, and, at times, capricious mediation of consciousnesses that prevails across the boundaries of race, language, and writing. It seems no accident, then, that the first word of the book's opening essay, which is entitled "Of Our Spiritual Strivings," is the word "Between." Du Bois writes:

> Between me and the other world there is ever an unasked question: unasked by some through feelings of delicacy; by others through the difficulty of rightly framing it. All, nevertheless, flutter round it. They approach me in a half-hesitant sort of way, eye me curiously or compassionately, and then, instead of saying directly, How does it feel to be a problem? they say, I know an excellent colored man in my town; or, I fought at Mechanicsville; or, Do not these Southern outrages make your blood boil? At these I smile, or am interested, or reduce the boiling to a simmer, as the occasion might require. To the real question, How does it feel to be a problem? I answer seldom a word. (363)

What occurs in this space "in between," what Nahum Chandler has termed a site of sedimentation (that which requires what I will call "thought-full" archaeological spading, giving due consideration to the thought processes that hold Du Bois's attention), is not the projection of an essence, presence, or particular frozen in time, and therefore static. Instead, we witness what Martin Heidegger would later theorize as the projection of a horizon of multiple existential possibilities. The linguistic structures we perceive through *The Souls of Black Folk* represent what the philosopher Clive Cazeaux has called "ontological conditions of experience" (85), and the very possibility

217

of our recognition or apprehension of the set of experiences Du Bois gives the reader across time requires powers of perceiving both similarities and dissimilarities as we strive to make sense of that which we have discerned. This power is, in Aristotle's terms, the power to grasp the import of metaphorical discourse. Heidegger, adapting Aristotle's perspective, calls it "the quiet power of the possible."

Drawing upon this relation of the metaphorical and the possible in his reading of Heidegger, Cazeaux writes that ontological metaphors—those philosophical metaphors that intimate or disclose being and subjectivity— could be said to recognize "that all concepts resonate with possible transpositions and, [as] such [bring] to the fore the world-making power of speaking" (Cazeaux 197). Cazeaux and the Shakesperean scholar Terence Hawkes both personify ontological metaphor (by identifying it as a site of subjective possibility) even as they describe it as an object of thought. Hawkes, for example, maintains that ontological metaphors "construct a reality from within themselves, and impose this on the world in which we live" (Hawkes 47). In deconstructionist terms, ontological metaphor, as that which insists upon the existential, may be said to engage with that which is beyond yet also included in language. "[O]ntological metaphor," Cazeaux writes, "structures experience as an openness to transposition [across categories of existence and meaning], an openness to movement between concepts, with the consequence that what belongs to one concept and what belongs to another cannot be taken for granted" (Cazeaux 197).

The movement of metaphor between and among such concepts and categories of meaning creates a nexus of relations and a fluid sort of knowledge. As Cazeaux points out, this sort of "metaphor necessarily opens itself to what is beyond metaphor" by posing a challenge to binary distinctions such as subject/object and presence/absence (198). As I have agrued, I see this sort of transposition at work in archetypal metaphors throughout the African American tradition, not only in such metaphors as the Veil, but also, for example, in Ralph Ellison's metaphor of invisibility, in the various vernacular metaphors developed by Frances Ellen Watkins Harper in the collection of poems, *Sketches of Southern Life*, and in Sojourner Truth's classic trope, "I sell the shadow to support the substance."

If one examines such "knowing" and "living" figures of language as they are embedded within the social and intellectual upheavals from which they emerge, and which they critique and clarify, one may readily see these metaphors as tropes that function at the level of discourse and that project being after a manner that is crucial. Ontological metaphors, as they are deployed within numerous African American texts, regularly do the work of epistemology and speculative thought that is so unyieldingly demanded by the social context in which the writer writes. The metaphors I examine in *Souls* point out the problem of language encountered by many African American writers, since the existing lexicons of their societies are often simply inadequate to the issues and questions they encounter in *being*—in lived experience. In response, many of these writers regularly make of ordinary language a purposive discourse intent upon establishing new meanings, and this is usually done through metaphorization. They put into play a discourse capable of conveying their lived experiences: discourses of existence and metaphor converge in their writings in an extratextual gesture toward the future, and, therefore, toward future horizons of readership. This chapter introduces a hermeneutics of these linguistic and textual structures of metaphor in Du Bois's text, and Du Bois's metaphors, in return, provide a critical framework for understanding ontological and epistemological figurations as they persist throughout the African American literary tradition.

∽

In the first section of this chapter, "Incipit and Exipit," I observe the way in which Du Bois establishes the groundwork of metaphor in the Forethought of his text, and the way in which he seeks to set the text in motion, to move from textuality to being, in the After-Thought of the work. To this end, I examine in these short, framing sections an anagogical template—dichotomized, for example, in the metaphorical phrases "bone of the bone and flesh of the flesh," and "God the Reader"—as it sets the stage for a narrative structure that renders metaphor ontological. In the long section that follows, titled "Poem and Paratext" (which is itself subdivided to provide a greater sense of organization), I focus on the poetic selections and bars of music drawn from the Spirituals that preface each essay of the book. In particular, I focus my attention on the ontological and epistemological metaphors at work in the paratexts of *Souls*—the poems and, especially, the Spirituals that serve as an aesthetic archive of black being. These paratexts, in collaboration with the essays they punctuate, go a long way toward documenting the historicity of African Americans as racialized beings, even as they also document the Negro's contributions to modern society. In this way, *Souls* is of a piece with "The Conservation of Races," in that it fulfills that essay's "Academy Creed" and moves the figure of the American Negro substantially along the path that leads to Du Bois's critically amended theory of universal brotherhood. As I discuss at length in the previous chapter, his revised humanism does not set aside the question of race in favor of a hurried and idealistic post-racialism that rejects the idea of race without considering and deconstructing its ideological content and realities (leaving whiteness and its powers untheorized and unchallenged). Rather, Du Bois analyzes racialized being as an object of thought, promulgating a revised notion of the human. In good measure, he accomplishes this influential critique by taking recourse to the poetic as a mode of thought and a propaedeutic of action. I discuss the Spirituals' and poems' varying relation to the philosophical, cultural, and linguistic content of the essays, and I examine the ways in which Du Bois draws out their historical and literary allusions in a gesture of contemporaneity that allows him to affirm the historicity of black being even as he works to protend black being beyond the limits of the text.

Incipit and Excipit

My concern with the relation of metaphor and being in *Souls* originates with what I see as the liturgical quality of the Forethought and the After-Thought of the text, which serve as framing elements that give shape to the collection as a whole. Certainly, Du Bois, in the Forethought, situates the groundwork of the text's ontological metaphorics even as he provides us a dutifully succinct introduction to the elements of his text, while the After-Thought concludes the work by insisting upon intersubjective connections and openings. In this way, the intellectual trajectory of the collection serves as an example of open-ended, relational poetics where, glossing Édouard Glissant, being is itself relation and "thought in reality spaces itself out into the world" (*Poetics of Relation* 1).

The first line of Du Bois's Forethought alerts the reader that she is about to embark upon a metaphorical journey that is at once experiential, ontological, and epistemological: "Herein lie buried many things which if read with patience may show the strange meaning of being black here in the dawning of the Twentieth Century. This meaning is not without interest to you, Gentle Reader; for the problem of the Twentieth Century is the problem of the color-line" (359). The peculiar stresses of Du Bois's phrasing—the shaping of what is, essentially, a philosophical inquiry into the nature of being black, of black *being* or existence—is essentially what lends power to this incipit. I resort to the somewhat abstruse term "incipit" because it conveys at once the image of a discursive and ontological starting point (that the text promises to provide a meaning or definition of blackness that heretofore was lacking), and a narrative genesis (that the full story of blackness is as yet untold). Further, and perhaps most importantly, the "incipit" evokes connotations of the liturgical, which is ultimately concerned with the public exchange of spiritual meaning that obtains in Du Bois's use of the Sorrow Songs throughout the book. Thus with the contemporaneity of the incipit, the text is grounded in the world about it, populated with souls as yet unknown. It is embedded in the social history and social tangle that likewise have formed the knot of the problem of the color-line.

In the incantatory lines of the Forethought, Du Bois imagines an invisible and ideal reader to whom he introduces this problem and these souls, a gesture that underscores the centrality of ontological concerns in our reading of *The Souls of Black Folk*. The practice by which a writer might address him- or herself to an imagined reader is hardly unconventional. Indeed, that the readership is unknown and unseen is largely taken as a given in many forms of fiction and creative non-fiction alike. Yet the quiet intensity with which Du Bois announces his intent certainly strikes the reader. The elements of the text that will provide the reader with meaning related to the problem are somehow buried within the text itself, and thus require archeological spading and, perhaps, epistemological reconstruction on the part of the reader. Du Bois requests that the reader "[study his] words with [him]," "forgive mistake and foible for sake of the faith and passion" that are in him, and seek diligently "the grain of truth hidden there." Presumably, an actual reader who would intuitively address *Souls* as Du Bois desired did not exist; thus, Du Bois works to interpellate the reader for whom he longs. It is with the unseen reader whose powers of discernment would allow him to enter with interest into the text that Du Bois wishes to hold a colloquy. There is an aspect of intimacy effected in the opening pages of the text: the "Gentle Reader" must trust the author; must peer within the veil at that "spiritual world" which is "sketched" only in "vague, uncertain outline" (359).

Yet the formulation of the Forethought belies its own sense of intimacy. What separates Du Bois from a close rapport with his reader—a generalized white reader, if we are to take into consideration Du Bois's own reflections on the authorial intent behind *Souls*[1]—is indeed the very blackness he addresses and claims as his own. And this he reveals not in the first sentence of the Forethought, but in the last: "And finally, need I add that I who speak here am bone of the bone and flesh of the flesh of them that live within the Veil?" (360). Thus Du Bois is the estranged "I" whose ontological being (metaphorized in his adaptation of Biblical metaphors of "flesh" and "bone") consigns him to the Veil, divorces him from conventional understandings of the Universal, and marks him as one with the Problem that is his subject.

Du Bois's use of the rhetorical "I" and his swift introduction of the metaphors of the color-line and the veil provide us with a paradigm of the text, even as the concept-metaphor of double consciousness goes fairly well unaddressed in both the Forethought and the After-Thought. We might say that although this latter concept lacks direct treatment in either the Forethought or After-Thought, Du Bois's rhetorical "I" is nonetheless indicative of the voice of double consciousness he assumes in his text. Indeed, as I have mentioned, it is only at the conclusion of the Forethought that one finds that Du Bois, too, is black. If we linger over the lines that precede the final one, we find that a certain critical distance has been assumed in his narrative voice. He speaks obliquely of "ten thousand thousand Americans" who inhabit the spiritual world he describes. He tells us that he has dedicated two chapters to describing "what Emancipation meant to *them*," not "us." He criticizes "candidly the leader who bears the chief burden of *his* race," rather than "my race" or "our race." Indeed, Du Bois's intention of raising the Veil, his movement within and without it, and his final declaration that his existence is grounded among the multitude of his subjects, mimics the nature of double consciousness.

If the narrator's function in the Forethought is to limn the metaphors of the veil and the color-line while performing the concept-metaphor of double consciousness, his function in the text's After-Thought, after having presented exempla depicting those souls held in oblivion, is to offer us a model of how to act upon that which we have read and experienced. In the narrator's words, the Gentle Reader has taken on the added identity of "God the Reader" (547), a God with whom the narrator seems to have established little intimacy, but with whom he contends as an opposing source of power and of possibility: "Hear my cry, O God the Reader; vouchsafe that this my book fall not still-born into the world-wilderness. Let there spring, Gentle One, from out its leaves vigor of thought and thoughtful deed to reap the harvest wonderful" (547). Du Bois's comments in the excipit—the closing liturgy—of his text are quite brief when compared with the length of the Forethought, yet they present an echo of sorts. Where the Forethought commences with the phrase "Herein lie," the After-Thought begins with the assonant refrain, "Hear my cry." In response to the narrative of experience of that which is buried—"Herein lie"—we are called to action as listeners—"Hear my cry." The alliteration of the closing sentence of the Forethought, containing the metaphorical phrase "bone of the bone and flesh of the flesh" is repeated in elements of the After-Thought: "thought and thoughtful deed," "tingle with truth," "drear day" and "turn the tangle straight." The closing emphasis in the Forethought upon a figuration of racial being—"bone of the bone and flesh of the flesh"—is countered with the After-Thought's figures of cognition ("thought and thoughtful deed"), feeling ("tingle with truth" and "drear day"), and action ("turn the tangle straight"). Today's reader may be surprised that Du Bois does not prescribe specific action in this text, as he had in the "The Conservation of Races." But there are equally great moments of meaning to be found, the narrator seems to say, in the suggestive metaphoric use of repetition in vowels, consonants, and syllables. And it is clear that Du Bois intended his book to carry out a worldly existence, to set forth the truth of black being, a task he had begun in "Conservation," and to induce the reader to act in light of this truth, thereby achieving a meaningful change in the socius.

Scholars of Du Bois's work have long agreed that an aspect of the power of *The Souls of Black Folk* lies in its revelatory gesture, in its insistence upon granting to a largely white readership an imperfect yet indispensable bird's-eye view of black life in America, at least in the text's own time of publication. But we should also underscore the phenomenology that is at work in the text and that obtains *through* metaphors that seek to protend the consciousness of black beings caught within the veil toward the world about them. Du Bois not only extends black being across the limits of writing; he also protends the black world within the veil across horizons of experience. In Du Bois's text, the black world *worlds*.

The relation of the black body and black being is a central concern in the *worlding* of *Souls*. I see *Souls* as an element of a philosophy of culture and society that holds as a transitional requirement the disclosure of the specific, racialized subjectivity of the African American. Yet its ultimate goal, as with "The Conservation of Races" before it, is the surpassing of such specificities in favor of a singular ideal: human brotherhood. The singularity of human brotherhood should not be confused with the ideal of the universal: what we might call singularity in Du Bois's work does not require a Hegelian embrace of the absolute—that is, the erasure of difference that Hegel deemed necessary to the constitution of the universal. Instead, the Du Boisian singularity of human brotherhood requires an intellectual nomadism across what Glissant has called the *chaos-world*; it requires the skillful navigation of an immensely differentiated and open-ended totality, an ability to spar with the chaotic and the absurd (and specifically the absurdity of racial essentialism), taking comfort in the experience of global relation.

In *Souls*, Du Bois insists upon the singularity of human brotherhood at the limits where precept and possibility meet. These limits are perhaps metaphorized most succinctly in the tropes of the veil and the color-line: Du Bois casts the veil as the mediation of black otherness through language; the color-line extends the workings of the veil through its simultaneous operation upon the plane of the global (the *chaos-world*) and the local (which in *Souls* takes shape in the geography of Tennessee and Georgia—with its blood-red soil and its legacy of violence and horror). If the veil delimits embodied black existence on the regional and national planes, the color-line serves as a trope that deterritorializes black being, as this being constitutes itself through relation. Existing in isolation within the veil while struggling within an open dialectic of recognition vis-à-vis the world of white folk, Du Bois describes black being as simultaneously self-constituent and co-constituent. Enduring isolation while striving for recognition, in *Souls* Du Bois—through metaphor—portrays black being as singularly human, the creative force behind the medium of its own expression.

Poem and Paratext: The African American Spiritual and the Strivings of Black Being

The metaphorics of black being that Du Bois expresses through the ontological and epistemological tropes of the color-line, the veil, and double consciousness are reinforced in the closing line of the Forethought, where, as I have mentioned, Du Bois's self-identification as "bone of the bone and flesh of the flesh of them that live within the Veil" reflects the persistent protension of black being through sound, allegory, allusion, and reference. As many scholars have noted, "bone of the bone and flesh of the flesh" is an alliterative and metaphorical phrase that revises Adam's words in the Biblical book of Genesis. Referring to Eve, whom God has just created as Adam's companion and "help meet" in the Garden of Eden, in this passage, Adam proclaims her to be of his own body. Du Bois uses Adam's determination of Eve as an elliptical nod toward his own subjectivity and sense of belonging, and thus embarks upon the beginning of a pervasive use of scriptural and autobiographical references throughout *Souls*. It is a way of communicating to his "ideal reader" the authenticity of his revelatory gesture in lifting the Veil. It also allows him to align himself with the community of black folk in the old-time tradition of Canonical allegory. Slave culture exhibited a tenacious fondness for the tales of the oppressed tribes of Israel, which constituted a downtrodden and ostracized Hebrew nation.[2] Blacks could readily identify with such suffering, and frequently adapted the tales of the Hebrews to fit their own circumstances, especially in the Spirituals.

In harking to the metaphorical phrase "bone of the bone and flesh of the flesh," Du Bois seems not only to analogize the situations of blacks and Jews (which he starkly contrasts throughout his economic analyses in *Souls*) and to extend the onto-theological metaphorics of Equiano and Harper into the twentieth century, but also to instantiate a modern African American mythopoetics that would provide a formative example for such future writers as Wright and Ellison to follow. That is to say that in drawing upon myth and poetic discourse through his use of the Spirituals and Biblical phraseology, Du Bois draws upon concepts of origins, of beginnings, and this provisional appeal to an originary identity appears to be what permits Du Bois's narrating of individual and collective black experience even in the wake of his dismissal of racial essentialism in "Conservation." When we consider that in *Souls* such an originary identity is strategically and mimetically reinforced in the bars of music that preface each essay, and that this identity is explicated and explored in the final chapter on the Sorrow Songs, we are certainly called to give deeper consideration than before to the musical and poetic paratexts of *Souls*.

∽

I will begin with Du Bois's own exposition of the nature and significance of the Sorrow Songs in the final chapter of *Souls*. His thoughts there provide us a greater understanding of what I see as his editorial intent not simply in choosing to place an example of these songs at the beginning of "each thought" (*Souls* 536), but also in selecting specific songs for their unique importance in the modern context. Immediately striking at the outset of "Of the Sorrow Songs" is that Du Bois claims the Spirituals as his own, that is, as part of his upbringing and his heritage. Our most popular image of Du Bois's familiarity with these songs is his description of hearing them sung in the South at Fisk and, later, Atlanta Universities. Undoubtedly, this is the image he most often proffers. Yet perhaps because of the migration of African Americans north to states such as Massachusetts, Du Bois's home state, or perhaps due to his own family's background, he knew them instinctively. They "came out of the South," he writes, "and yet at once I knew them as of me and of mine" (536).

Indeed, the Spirituals are said to have come out of the Carolina Sea Islands, a region characterized by insular retentions of African culture, which provided a nearly mythical, originary setting for the development and preservation of the Sorrow Songs. They date back to at least the seventeenth century in some instances, but what do the songs mean? Du

Bois asks. And his question resonates squarely with the "strange meaning of being black" that he sets out as his object of thought at the incipit of *Souls*. His answer: that the songs "are the articulate message of the slave to the world" (538), and in some ways this echoes his insistence, in "Of Our Spiritual Strivings," that "Negro blood" (a metaphor that I might, perhaps precipitously, analogize to black being) "has a message for the world" (365). The songs provide a "witness" to the life of the slave. They are not stories of the "careless and happy" servant, Du Bois avers; rather, they are "the music of an unhappy people, of the children of disappointment; they tell of death and suffering and unvoiced longing toward a truer world, of misty wanderings and hidden ways. The songs are indeed the sifting of centuries" (538). They are, then, revelatory of black being; more than simple musical expression, Du Bois calls us to see the songs as ontological and epistemological in nature.

As an example, Du Bois compares one of these songs of the ages that stretch toward a "truer world" beyond their own—a song passed down to him by his grandfather's grandmother, with its "primitive form and its intuitive meaning"—with the Spiritual "You May Bury Me in the East." Both of these songs are, he writes, expressive of "the voice of exile" (539). It seems that the abyss of exile and separation are, in Du Bois's estimation, at the heart of any reasonable interpretation of these Spirituals:

> Over the inner thoughts of the slaves and their relations one with another the shadow of fear ever hung, so that we get but glimpses here and there, and also with them, eloquent omissions and silences. Mother and child are sung, but seldom father; fugitive and weary wanderer call for pity and affection, but there is little of wooing and wedding; the rocks and the mountains are well-known, but home is unknown. (542)

Of interest to us, then, in our reading of these paratexts, is Du Bois's underscoring of the veiled "inner thoughts of the slaves" and of omission and silence as constitutive of the musical works. Not only are the songs the founding texts of the African American poetic—and hence, narrative—tradition; they also serve as the genesis of America's musical tradition, Du Bois argues, the one truly American cultural artifact in song.[3] What are we to say of a tradition built upon a foundation that—with its veils, gaps, and silences—constructs a foundation less than firm? What is Du Bois saying more broadly about American culture and identity at the very moment that he attends to "the strange meaning of being black"?

After a fashion, Du Bois casts us willy-nilly back upon ourselves. He is not less than his word when he, at the outset of the text, tells his reader that "Herein lie buried many things which, if read with patience, may show the strange meaning of being black here in the dawning of the Twentieth Century." This problem he poses is but an element of a greater concern, that of the color-line, which he has, throughout *Souls*, cast as a question of global proportions. Thus the situatedness of the Negro problem in its American context is drawn into immediate relation with the global problem of the color-line. And, by virtue of his conclusion, Du Bois identifies the Spirituals, collectively, with the problem—or, problematic—of the color-line.

The task Du Bois gives his ideal reader, then, is that of examining the nature of the Spirituals he evokes at the beginning of each essay, determining their collective and singular relation to the problem and to the metaphors Du Bois uses to convey his message. These, initially, at least, must be examined in relation to the additional paratextual elements that open the chapters—excerpts from the work of Lowell, Symons, and others—about which Du Bois says never a word. (The singular exception to this is the leading paratext of the final chapter, drawn from the Spiritual "Lay this Body Down," about which he does comment in "Of the Sorrow Songs.") Du Bois's silence here, his omission of any commentary on the works of European and Euro-American poetry and drama from which he draws, is, its seems, of moment. It is, I would argue, a further metaphor that Du Bois develops as a judgment on the America he so deftly takes to task through his use of the Sorrow Songs.

∾

Du Bois's consideration of the Sorrow Songs as a resource for social and political critique goes against the ways in which later twentieth-century commentators of the African American Spiritual generally defined the form. In the twentieth century, the Spiritual was usually classed as an expression of musicality, creativity, joy, or sorrow. It was widely described as having originated through the spontaneous composition of an individual or group close to nature. Thus our generalized image of the singers of Spirituals is of an intuitive (by contrast to "thinking," "thoughtful," or "critical") people whose songs reveal what Nathaniel Dett has called "a religious faith almost past understanding" (xi), as well as what even Du Bois refers to somewhat obliquely as the Negro's "fatalism" (543). Yet it is clear that, at the same time, Du Bois sees that many complex and intricate operations of belief must precede spiritual expressions of faith and fatalism, of placing trust, of the laws of causation. We have names for these sorts of operations: ideological, value-driven, and propositional. They are considered the underpinnings of faith, the foundations for adherence to principles or creeds, the motivity of primary judgment. Yet these are not the usual descriptors we evoke in speaking of the Spirituals.

Instead, the Spirituals have largely been considered the product of simple religious fervor, especially those that were created by the African-descended population of the United States *during* the age of slavery: more irrational than rational, more given to an ephemeral amelioration of slavery's deplorable conditions than to an articulate worldview. Being essentially poetry set to unwritten music, they are, deemed largely if not purely folkloric rather than epistemological. Since the Spirituals speak in doubled voice (frequently dubbed "primitive" in nature), and thus since they blithely recount the paradoxical, they seem unsound as epistemological activities and artifacts.

Thus the relation of these songs to what philosophers call "knowledge" or "critique" seems, on first approach, an uneasy one. This is the case not least because of the values that American society (indeed, Western society in general) has long placed upon distinctions of class, color, gender, race, and questions of national belonging. In short, because the singers of the Spirituals were slaves, and because these slaves were "black," the foundations of their knowledge were constantly placed into question.[4] Laws that emerged from a culture other than their own governed the science of epistemology. Although their songs appeared to reflect (even if in the veiled fashion that Du Bois describes in *Souls*) their ideas and beliefs regarding the world they created and inhabited, most accounts of these songs continue to emphasize the faith, fatalism, and spontaneity that is said to have guided their birth. The implication here is that the Spirituals are an unorganized form of expression, an outburst of feeling emerging from no system of thought or knowledge and therefore providing no possibility of a science of them.

There have been some exceptions to this convention. Zora Neale Hurston, whom we have already encountered, performed radical and broad interpretations of the Spirituals, refusing their label as Sorrow Songs and giving pointed attention to intonation, expression of feeling, and form. While she did attend to the metaphorics at work in the songs in her 1934 essay "Spirituals and Neo-Spirituals," she did not pursue an extended discussion of these metaphorics as either elements of a slave ontology or as aspects of social critique that approach the level of epistemology. More recently, Donald H. Matthews, in his well-argued book *Honoring the Ancestors* (1998), follows the lead of Du Bois in arguing that the Spirituals function as expressions of the desire for freedom and, what is more, that they are "replete with central metaphors that carry the most deeply held beliefs of the community" (53). Alexander Weheliye reads the Sorrow Songs, and, specifically, Du Bois's use of them in *Souls*, as uncanny textual elements that present a somewhat "uncrackable" code.[5] Weheliye assigns the Spirituals and their musical notations to a certain illegibility that, nonetheless, "calls upon the reader to imagine blackness sonically" ("The Grooves of Temporality" 320). Weheliye sees the Spirituals as profitably severed from their origins, such that they form the basis for our consideration of what he calls "sonic Afro-Modernity."

One could cite other critics who write compellingly on the Spirituals, but whose focus does not lie with the relation of metaphorics and ontology in the songs. (I am thinking here of the work of such scholars as Erskine Peters, Sterling Brown, and Jon Michael Spencer.[6]) Many critics have argued instead that the bars of music appearing (*sans* lyrics) in *Souls* not only contradict the poetic elements that preface each of Du Bois's essays, but also present a barrier to meaning-making in their own time.

I have considered the more or less progressive critical accounts of these songs: of the latent resistance and rebellion that may be ferreted out from their double voiced lyrics; of the hidden nature of them (that during slavery, they were not regularly performed within the hearing of whites); of their serial nature and their ubiquity (that they were repeatedly improvised, that they exist in various versions, and that they continued to be created after the abolition of slavery); of their supposed "primitiveness," naturalness, naïveté, and "tropicalness." I believe that these and other purported characteristics of the Spirituals (whether or not we agree with them) lead us to say something more about the thought Du Bois's chosen songs convey as they plot both ontology and epistemology. Within these songs, a scene is set wherein we may observe the generating of meaningful aesthetic forms by a collective people held captive against their will. I will be paying specific attention to how the singers order the inner structure of the Spirituals that appear in *Souls* to represent metaphorically the way in which the slaves' experiences give shape to their conception of existence. And I will consider the ways in which their metaphorical expressions of existence and consciousness relate to the central problematic of Du Bois's text: the "strange meaning of being black," or, the peculiar meaning of black being.

Inspiriting Time: The Spiritual and the Ontology of the Slave

The Spirituals that head each essay in *Souls* aim to bring the temporal into relation with the atemporal, that which is of this world (what Du Bois calls, in "Of the Passing of the First Born," "the narrow Now") into closer contact with the world that exists beyond the physical (what he calls, in the same essay, the "All-life" or the afterlife, a world that is not an abyss, but rather a "truer world" characterized by prescience and love). The songs seem not to unfold from the beginning of *Souls* to its end in a dialectical dénouement that achieves successively deeper exposition of a range of themes. Rather, the songs Du Bois chooses seem aimed at an exhaustive record of temporal/atemporal concerns regarding the slaves' *being*. They examine human experience under the weight of bondage in a way that aspires toward a breadth of perception: they take comfort in conveying that Christ alone knows and understands their strivings and troubles; they dwell a great deal on the dual themes of admonishment and encouragement, blindness and insight, and bondage and errantry; they forecast the apocalyptic tradition that pervades African American literature; and they establish the process of metaphorization that has since lain at the heart of great works of African American literary and cultural expression.

I will focus upon close readings of the paratexts, both the Spirituals and the verses of poetry, at times examining their traces throughout the essay each prefaces. I will conclude by reading the paratexts in relation to one another collectively and intertextually, positing Du Bois as an editor who amasses an anthology of meaningful paratextual elements that undertake a sort of social and philosophical "work." We might assume, at least in some preliminary way, that the major criteria for inclusion in the collection is the ability or potential of each paratext to contribute to Du Bois's exposition of "the strange meaning of being black." That is to say that we might assume that Du Bois selected each of these paratexts in light of what he perceived as their relation to an examination of the ontology and epistemology of black being, black consciousness. Such an approach will permit us to consider the *figura* at play in each of these paratexts as existing in relation to the major questions and problems Du Bois addresses in his text, and in relation to the major tropes he himself expounds.

∽

One conundrum that has regularly faced today's readers of *Souls* is the bars of music that represent the Spirituals in the text. It seems clear from Du Bois's prose that the ideal reader he construed was neither poor nor, exclusively, African American. Further, and this in spite of the sharp critique of middle-class money-getting that persists throughout *Souls'* pages, Du Bois certainly addressed himself to the burgeoning American middle-class, both North and South, and, almost just as certainly, the bars of piano music Du Bois presented to his reader found a ready audience. In the cultured, middle-class America of the late nineteenth and early twentieth centuries, the piano was not only a symbol of status and success; it also served to satisfy the middle-class's need to feel intellectually aware, to feel themselves a part of civilization. The piano was, as James Parakilas and others argue in *Piano Roles: A New History of the Piano* (2000), a central element in this attempt at cultural interaction: "the piano has always exhibited a unique power to act as a cultural go-between, as a medium through which social spheres that stood in opposition to each other could nonetheless nourish each other" (4). Indeed, pianos were so ubiquitous in nineteenth and early twentieth-century middle-class households that most genteel American families could boast ownership of one. Taking the novels of such African American writers as Sutton Griggs, James Weldon Johnson, and Jessie Fauset (e.g., *Imperium in Imperio* [1899], *The Autobiography of an Ex-Coloured Man* [1912/1927], *There is Confusion* [1924], and *Plum Bun* [1929]), as well as a number of photos of African American households included by Du Bois in his Exhibit of American Negroes (at the 1900 World's Fair in Paris), the same may be said of the genteel African American household. Throughout the country, an element central to a proper young woman's upbringing was an ability to play and sing as part of, say, a family's activities on a given Sunday afternoon. Thus any engaged reader might have carried Du Bois's little book directly to the piano that occupied the parlor, and request that the lady (or even the gentleman) of the house pick the notes out, however hesitantly.

Upon first encountering them, what a pianist unfamiliar with the fuller compositions of the Sorrow Songs might have had trouble placing are the specific measures that are reproduced in *Souls*. The bars of music Du Bois gives are drawn from various points of the Sorrow Songs. They confine themselves neither to the beginning of the compositions nor to their end, but appear to draw from that portion of the song that struck Du Bois most keenly. The curious reader at his or her piano might, of course, be perplexed in trying to place the notes. However, the music of the Spirituals, made widely known in the late nineteenth century by the Fisk Jubilee Singers and the Singers at Hampton Institute most notably, would likely have been familiar.

The "melody of these slave songs stirred the nation" in the 1830s, Du Bois writes (537). After the close of the Civil War, significant numbers of the songs were collected and set to music: *Slave Songs of the United States* (1867) by William Francis Allen, Charles Pickard Ware, and Lucy McKim Garrison, and J. B. T. Marsh's *The Story of the Jubilee Singers with Their Songs* (1877), are among the earliest, most popular tomes that included musical scores. (Thomas Wentworth Higginson's well-known memoir *Army Life in a Black Regiment*, published in 1867, gave only lyrics to selected songs.) Admittedly, the initial sales of *Slave Songs* were slow, yet the book is credited with instilling in Americans an interest in black culture that seems little abated.[7] Marsh's book fared far better: it came in the aftermath of the Jubilee Singer's international successes in the 1870s, and even capitalized on their popularity, immortalizing the Jubilee performers through brief biographies of each one as *The Story of the Jubilee Singers* underwent multiple printings and editions. The Jubilee songs, as the Spirituals also came to be known, became elements of late-nineteenth-century minstrel shows that, though secular, incorporated the Spirituals' religious sentiments and jocularized them for popular consumption. All of this is to say that the Spirituals, and their musical notations, were likely not as alienating to Du Bois's intended readership as we at times imagine.

Metaphors of Perceiving, Knowing, and Mourning: "Of Our Spiritual Strivings," "Of the Dawn of Freedom," and "Of Mr. Booker T. Washington and Others"

The first Spiritual given in *Souls*, and one of the most widely recognized Spirituals in the collection, is "Nobody Knows the Trouble I See." Du Bois draws upon the following lines:

> Nobody knows the trouble I see
> Nobody knows but Jesus

The lyrics of this song include verbs of perception and cognition that metaphorically draw together the limits of the physical and non-physical or metaphysical worlds: "seeing" trouble is itself a metaphor, although its use is so widespread as to occlude its metaphorical nature. Metaphors of perception and cognition akin to seeing and knowing—two human faculties ordinarily given as the "higher" senses—reappear as hearing and wakefulness, or awareness, in "My Lord, What a Mourning," which prefaces chapter 2 of *Souls* and includes the following lyrics in the refrain: "You'll hear the trumpet sound / To wake the nations underground." The latter song pays pointed attention to questions of the apocalypse—and thus, to questions of revolution—that prevail in the Book of Revelation (to which it refers [8:10]). Each of these songs is an early exercise in a self-reflexive and self-conscious poetic art: the composers' work of representing cognitive perceptions such as seeing and knowing, stand alongside other representations that characterize these songs, such as hearing and waking. In both cases, the impression is given that important intellectual phenomena have been noted, documented orally and aurally. And in both cases, the singers appear to contest the division between the faculties of perception as purely physical, and the more elevated faculties of the intellect and the spirit or soul. The remainder of the songs Du Bois quotes throughout the book, much like these first excerpts, works at collapsing notions of the physical and the metaphysical into that which can only be termed ontological, that which has to do with questions and transpositions of the meaning of being, or, more specifically, black being, across categories of human experience.

Black being is thus sublimely represented in the rhythms of the songs, which, as Nathaniel Dett has pointed out, may be compared to "that of the human pulse which is a series of throbs all of equal intensity" (xv). Commentators on the Spiritual from Du Bois to Dett to Johnson to Hurston have underscored the chromatic nature of the form, its insistence upon sounding notes in a scale both major and minor, tones and semitones, notes that are accidental and unexpected or abnormal in the scale in which they appear. Might we also not say, then, that the Spirituals are concerned with a chromatic form of thought in which the stories that fill the songs are made up in a way that renders vague their constructive invention, such that they merely appear instinctual? These songs lay out, through their chromatic scales, concerns attendant upon the paradox of living between two worlds—the seen and the unseen, the profane and the holy—and their lyrics attempt to master this paradox through sounds and metaphors that draw the two dissimilar realms into a syncretic sphere of resemblance and harmony.

If the Christ who reigns over the invisible sacred world understands the troubles of the slaves' profane "Now" in "Nobody Knows the Trouble I See," we are meant to believe that the slaves nonetheless knew a certain euphonic "rest" that consistently eludes the free narrator of Arthur Symon's "The Crying of Water," the poem that heads chapter 1 along with "Nobody Knows." The excerpt Du Bois provides reads thus:

O water, voice of my heart, crying in the sand,
    All night long crying with a mournful[8] cry,
As I lie and listen, and cannot understand,
    The voice of my heart in my side or the voice of the sea,
    O water, crying for rest, is it I, is it I?
    All night long the water is crying to me.

Unresting water, there shall never be rest
   Till the last moon droop and the last tide fail,
And the fire of the end begin to burn in the west;
        And the heart shall be weary and wonder and cry
  like the sea,
All life long crying without avail,
   As the water all night long is crying to me.

In this mournful poem we find doubled metaphors. The water is described in terms of an inscrutable voice, thus it is, to some extent, personified. This image of sound and opacity is carried further in that the water is the voice of the poet's heart. Thus when we come to the words "crying in the sand," we are no longer clear as to whether the poet is alluding to the extra-lingual sound of the ocean, which is clearly affecting him, or the equally extra-lingual sound of his own heart crying inconsolably within him. The poet himself is confused by the voice, and a weakness of the poem is that he does not clarify matters for his reader any more than he does for himself. Further, the syntax generated by the first line of the first stanza provides no possibility of clarification. We find only images that are hopelessly muddled and blurred, such that when the poet asks "is it I, is it I?" we have little idea of the genesis of the question, nor of the importance of its response. The object of the voice's query—understanding and rest—could likely be attained from a benevolent God, but it is not to the world beyond the physical one that the poet appeals. (The poem may rightly be called an ode, addressed as it is to the physical but inanimate water.) The poet sees that his ability to know the source and sense of the voice crying within and about him is in contention with the very world in which he lives. He seems powerless to grasp the import of unseen realities. The distinction between "The Crying of Water" and "Nobody Knows the Trouble I See" shows us that metaphorical constructions in many of the paratexts serve to navigate the boundary between two worlds in a fashion that echoes Du Bois's own trope of the color-line. Strikingly, the Symons poem is inadequate to this task in ways that do not beset the majority of the remainder of the European and Euro-American poems Du Bois chooses.

Moments such as these, which underscore the contingencies of the temporal while idealizing the image of a world beyond the present, predominate the paratextual elements of chapter 2, "Of the Dawn of Freedom." Du Bois opens the chapter with a stanza of a poem titled "The Present Crisis," written by James Russell Lowell in December 1844. Best known as an abolitionist, Lowell was also a poet, critic, essayist, diplomat, and editor, between 1876 and 1881, of the *Atlantic Monthly*. "The Present Crisis" was included by Du Bois's former Harvard professor, Albert Bushnell Hart, in his collection *American History Told by Contemporaries* (1901). Hart had earlier included two works by Lowell in his 1899 reader, *Source-Book of American History*. He obviously saw Lowell's work in general and this poem in particular as quite central to understanding American history and identity. It is likely that he discussed this poem, which is among the most cited of Lowell's works, with Du Bois either through academic work at Harvard during Du Bois's time there, or at some point afterwards. (Hart continued to maintain contact with Du Bois well after Du Bois had completed his doctorate at Harvard in 1895.)

A long poem of 18 stanzas, "The Present Crisis" is, like Lowell's later poem "A Satire on the Mexican War" (1846), framed as a response to American westward expansion coupled with some overt allusions to American slavery. Indeed, many anti-slavery agitators saw in the United States' push to annex the newly independent state of Texas along with Mexican and British territories in the west a desire to extend the reach of American slavery. Thus, Du Bois's choice of Lowell's poem resonates with the topic of his own essay, a critical history of the Freedmen's Bureau. Essentially, he uses the poem as an element of his elaboration of the twentieth-century "problem of the color-line," which he announces as the fulcrum of his "history from 1861 to 1872 so far as it relates to the American Negro" (372). He chooses the eighth stanza:

> Careless seems the great Avenger;
>   History's lessons but record
> One death-grapple in the darkness
>   'Twixt old systems and the Word;
> Truth forever on the scaffold,
>   Wrong forever on the throne;
> Yet that scaffold sways the future,
>   And behind the dim unknown
> Standeth God within the shadow
> Keeping watch above His own.

This stanza—the penultimate stanza of the poem—seems enigmatic, as it refers to an avenger not mentioned in prior stanzas of the poem. When we place this element within the context of the larger work and observe the poem's ideological evolution, we note that Du Bois's selection of this stanza appears to come in response to the Manichaean struggles to which Lowell exposes the reader throughout the poem. The poem opens with the idealist themes of freedom and prophecy; the second stanza onward marks the beginning of the themes of social strife and struggle that punctuate the remainder of the poem. The imagery initially vacillates between "hut and palace," or rich and poor, but ultimately between good and evil, past and future, truth and falsity. Where manhood is of importance in the first stanza, the birth of a man-child is central to the second stanza: "glad Truth's mightier man-child leaps beneath the Future's heart" (a metaphorical construction that Du Bois will echo in the essay "Of the Passing of the First Born"). The orientation the poet encourages is toward the future, when Truth shall prevail. There is a break between the second stanza and the first, and some sort of enhanced transition would seem to be in order. Yet Lowell does continue the imagery of the birth of a new Era, whose circumstances have yet to be fully revealed in the poem. In this period of change, nation will question nation, the old systems of the world will be tried and challenged, and the promise of a powerful new morality is evident.

In the third stanza, Lowell takes us immediately from the promise of a new age of Truth into the triumph of Evil from "continent to continent." Under the forces of Evil, the slave "cowers" and cries helplessly until his very tears unearth corpses. This sort of striking imagery continues in the fourth stanza as the poem unfolds: "mankind are one in spirit," "earth's electric circle," the "swift flash of right or wrong," and the "ocean-sundered fibres" of humanity. These redoubtable metaphors are sufficient to ameliorate the heavily moralistic tone of this stanza, and to render it interesting. Throughout the poem, Lowell develops the idea that the powers of human perception in one's own era are limited and thus deceiving. In spite of this "the soul is still oracular," he writes in tones that foreshadow Jean Toomer's modernist work, *Cane* (1923). It is "the Delphic cave within" (stanza nine).

In the final stanza of the poem, the writer asks the reader to take on, imaginatively, the mantle of the Pilgrim, to undertake a new voyage of freedom determined by the exigencies of his own day. It is interesting that he speaks of a "portal" to the future, an image that arguably alludes to his idea of the soul as "oracular" and "Delphic," that is, as a metaphorical and even epistemological counter-concept to the discourse of Manifest Destiny; indeed, he imagines an alternate path toward the furthering of civilization by way of crossing borders and encountering foreign cultures without domination. This final stanza reflects the message of Du Bois's essay.

In the penultimate stanza given to us by Du Bois in *Souls*, the poet concludes that God's vindication appears, at least, to strike the innocent along with the guilty, crossing categorical boundaries and transposing moral meaning. Further, he laments forthrightly that truth is always being tried and executed, while wrong is praised, exalted, and obeyed. The poet's use of "scaffold" draws upon its dual meaning as both a raised platform from which people were hung or otherwise executed, and as a raised platform used to erect new structures or to repair or decorate existing ones. Certainly the image of the scaffold as a platform of execution held some poignant meaning for Du Bois, as he likely first read this poem either at Fisk or at Harvard during a period that witnessed more than its share of lynchings. He must have been equally gratified at Lowell's doubling of the term, his use of it in two different lines with different semantic contexts. The second striking line comes in "One death-grapple in the darkness 'twixt old systems and the Word." The "Word" is a direct simultaneous allusion to Christ and the Bible, and it is between the Word and the world that the struggle recorded in man's history ensues.

"The Present Crisis" is followed by the Spiritual "My Lord What a Mo(u)rning," which Du Bois calls "the song of the End and the Beginning" in "The Sorrow Songs" (540). This is likely because of the alternate spellings given to "morning" and "mourning" in the song's title, and also refers to the lyrics and imagery of the swift cadences of this song. The lyrics to the measure Du Bois quotes read:

> My Lord, What a Mourning!
> My Lord, What a Mourning!
> When the Stars Begin to Fall!

As with many of Du Bois's selections, the quotation is drawn from the song's refrain. One could interpret the Spiritual as a song of Armageddon, the final battle foretold in the Book of Revelation (16:14–16). Lowell's poem could be read similarly, for if one turns to the scripture referenced in the Spiritual and reads of the seven vials that hold the last plagues of the earth, and of how these vials are emptied of their contents by the angels, bringing destruction to a world inhabited by the saved as well as the unrepentant, one might wonder about the indiscriminate way in which God seems to be wreaking havoc on the earth, in the Biblical book and in Lowell's poem alike. Yet the Spiritual appears to denote something more. Its surface rendition of a song of Armageddon and judgment belies what could be read as a call for revolution. Thus the phrase given in its lyrics, "To wake the nations underground": these lyrics are sung not by the chorus, but by its leader, and could not only refer to the dead buried in the earth who are to be raised in new life after the world's final battle, but could also be related to the black "nation within a nation" that is called upon by Du Bois, in this text, in "Conservation," and elsewhere, to stand and be recognized, to assert itself.

What seems crucial to keep in mind in reading the essay against the poem is that Du Bois's stated concern in chapter 2 is to give an account and critique of American government between "1861 and 1872 so far as it relates to the American Negro," and to provide an assessment of the workings of this government from the Negro's present point of view. Similarly, Lowell's poem is critical of the moral spirit of the nation in relation to its policies of slavery and war. The song, on the other hand, is concerned with the spiritual nations of the past/future (for the two are melded in the line "to wake the nations underground," a metaphor that presents an image of leagues of persons held in a sort of interim state from which they will be revived upon the falling of the stars) in relation to the strife of the present. The slave singers, in keeping, somewhat, with the moralistic figure of the slave that prevails in Lowell's poem, look to the righteous who sit at "God's right hand" as the struggle begins. The song's fearsome metaphors—morning/mourning, falling stars, God's right hand, nations underground—find their parallel movement not least in the conclusion of "Of the Dawn of Freedom," where Du Bois images an apocalyptic figure "veiled and bowed," the "tainted air" that "broods fear," and the awesome "duty and deed" of the new century. What should be underscored here is that each element of chapter 2 exacts critical judgment in the face of moral dishonesty; indeed, Du Bois demonstrates the very unfree nature of American democracy as it concerns not only the Negro, but also whites.

In other Spirituals Du Bois excerpts, we find that metaphor not only gains mastery over the relation between the physical and metaphysical worlds, but also conveys a sense of cognitive dominion, the "second-sight" and power of prophecy Du Bois credits to the Negro race in general. However, following Du Bois's reasoning, such knowledge prevails due to racism, and results in the double-consciousness that forms the major theory of identity at work in *Souls*.

The hymn of admonition, "A Great Camp-Meeting in the Promised Land" (also known under the title "Walk Together, Children"), appears to be one such Spiritual; it seems to have been chosen for its potential to respond to the tensions produced through double-consciousness. "A Great Camp-

Meeting" prefaces chapter 3 of *Souls*, "Of Mr. Booker T. Washington and Others." Du Bois chooses bars ten through sixteen, whose lyrics read thus:

> Going to mourn and never tire
> Mourn and never tire
> Mourn and never tire

This hymn provides a lyrical transition from the chapter it follows; this is especially apparent in the repetition of the word "mourn," which appears in both "A Great Camp-Meeting" and "My Lord, What a Mourning," yet carries different connotations. "My Lord, What a Mourning" indicates a new beginning, with both aspects of mo(u)rning at work: "morning" as indicative of a new beginning, and "mourning" as indicative of repentance, and hence a new beginning of a different sort. What the lyrics of "A Great Camp-Meeting" alone cannot convey, and what sets it apart from "My Lord What a Mo(u)rning," is the insistent crescendo of the music, which culminates in a striking minor cadence that hangs upon the listener's ear and there repeats. The clause "O, walk together, children" generates the rest of the song, which is serially punctuated with the phrase "Don't you get weary." Of the Spirituals Du Bois chooses for *Souls*, this piece, along with "Bright Sparkles in the Churchyard" (which prefaces chapter 7, "Of the Black Belt"), is among the lengthiest. Versions transcribed by Nathaniel Dett (*Religious Folk-Songs of the Negro* 26) and John Wesley Work (*American Negro Songs and Spirituals* 143) both give the line "Don't you get weary" as the response of the chorus to the leader's solo, while the verse that Du Bois selects, "Going to mourn and never tire," rendered in a striking flatted seventh chord, is noted as the repeating refrain. It is to be sung in "crescendo animando" (Dett 26), rendered in its repetition with increasing force of tone and an expanding liveliness.

The song's most salient characteristic—that of the reprise, of repetition with a difference—is also marked by the peculiarity of its terminology. Work writes that the "term 'mourn' in the Spirituals has a special meaning—a sort of weird hum, and is applied to one of the features of church worship. The term 'mourner' was given to a sinner attending 'revivals' or camp meetings who anticipated joining the church" (145). In considering what sort of metaphor "mourn" turns out to be, one ought to consider that Du Bois excerpts the "mourning" reprise of "A Great Camp-Meeting" not only and not even specifically as an element of his well-known rebuke of Washington. It functions more overtly as a rebuke of those duty-bound African American men he simultaneously extols and takes to task in chapter 3. Washington is not the only "mourner," or sinner whose calling bears reprising because it risks going unheard. Archibald Grimké, Kelly Miller, and a number of other African American men who, along with Du Bois, had founded the American Negro Academy (which Washington had declined to join) were themselves admonished in the Spiritual's ascendant cadence of doubled metaphor: a tropological canto of mourning, repetition, and redemption.

Like the other songs we've discussed thus far, "A Great Camp-Meeting" holds certain resonances with the verse it follows. In this instance, Du Bois chooses from the second canto of Lord Byron's *Childe Harold's Pilgrimage*, published in its entirety between 1812 and 1818. The poem, an autobiographical narrative in which the poet and Harold are, at some points, hardly distinguishable, renders an unequivocal statement regarding freedom and manhood, from which Du Bois cites:

> From birth till death enslaved; in word, in deed, unmanned!
> . . . .
> Hereditary bondsmen! Know ye not
> Who would be free must themselves strike the blow?

A fuller exposition of the connection between this poetic statement—specifically the clause "in word, in deed, unmanned!"—and the import of "Of Mr. Booker T. Washington and Others" must await another occasion. What seems evident at this point is that the Spiritual and the poem alike provide Du Bois the opportunity to model an idea, seized from a larger frame of reference and transformed into a concise aphorism on civil liberty and civil rights. If we limit ourselves simply to the excerpts Du Bois provides, we can see something important about the relation of this poem and song that is, in fact, paradigmatic of the majority of poem/song pairings that we see in *Souls*. "A Great Camp-Meeting" and the other Spirituals I discuss are not, as has generally been said of the Spirituals in *Souls*, contrapuntal to the poem they follow. Indeed, this Spiritual says not simply something different but something further. Byron, in *Childe Harold II*, laments Greece's loss of independence, and his mourning, like that of the Spiritual singers, is not merely aesthetic. His poem narrates his travels in the Balkan Peninsula; he notes with something akin to horror the varied skin colors of Greece's new inhabitants, which include Moors and Nubians as well as Turks. And he is not above composing a song that mocks the invading soldier, whom he depicts as lusting after the "fair face" of the Greek maiden whose father has just been slain ("I love the fair face of the maid in her youth, / Her caresses shall lull me, her music shall soothe; / Let her bring from the chamber her many-toned lyre, / And sing us a song on the fall of her sire."⁹) For Byron, the Greek controlled by Ottoman rule is not simply colonized, but, more pointedly, enslaved. Byron is much aggrieved to see the seat of "world civilization" held firmly in the hands of a non-Christian empire of dark peoples. Hence his concluding line of stanza 74, where he writes with palpable frustration, "From birth till death enslaved; in word, in deed, unmanned!"

When the poet continues, "Hereditary bondsmen! Know ye not / Who would be free themselves must strike the blow?" it should not escape the reader's notice that this line from *Childe Harold* was used as an epigraph by Frederick Douglass in Part IV of his 1853 novella, *The Heroic Slave*,¹⁰ and thus the poetic excerpt is linked even more closely to the import of Du Bois's essay. As I point out in chapter 5, Douglass's death in 1895 left a vacuum in leadership among African Americans; importantly, "Of Mr. Booker T. Washington" undertakes a genealogy of this leadership, and a staunch critique of the man who assumed the mantle of Douglass's power and influence upon Douglass's death. The response of the Spiritual rings, then, even more sharply, not in contradiction but in cooperation: "Going to mourn and never tire." That the Spiritual singers employ the flatted seventh in this lyric clause brings it sharply to the attention of the listener. The word "mourn," means not only, as I have mentioned, to lament, but to repent of one's sins and to live as one redeemed. In the Christian sense, this means to live, act, talk, and walk in the way of the redeemed who traverse the earth. In affirmation of the song leader's call for communal unity and direction ("O walk together, children"), the choral response is a promise of unending effort and striving. Du Bois thus uses Byron's poem as an ironic and unlikely allegory: the Negro people, colonized, like the Greeks, as a "nation within a nation," will not await redress by others, nor will they conciliate, as Washington had unsatisfactorily suggested. They themselves will strike the blow; they will "mourn and never tire."

Metaphors of Journeying and Insight:
"Of the Meaning of Progress," "Of the Wings of Atalanta," and "Of the Training of Black Men"

Chapters 4, 5, and 6 of *Souls* are each concerned with the quest for self-edification through education and life experience. In the paratexts to chapter 4, "Of the Meaning of Progress," Du Bois continues to lay stress on the imperative of casting off oppression. He cites a passage, given below, from

Friedrich von Schiller's, *The Maid of Orleans* (1801), a play that revised Jeanne d'Arc's story with great empathy, with the sort of feeling of humanness that seems innate to the poets and thinkers of German romanticism. It is undoubtedly an early example of the use of drama in exploring the human psyche. In the excerpt Du Bois presents, Jeanne (whom Schiller renames Johanna) agonizes over her decision to allow a military foe to live. This passage gives evidence of Johanna's ambivalence regarding her own humanity, as manifested in her sudden "love" for Lionel, the English opponent whom she cannot slay even as she bests him during their combat, and her divinity, which comes from the angelic presence that has visited her. She concludes that she was much happier as a simple shepherdess; indeed, that she was much better suited to the pasture than to the palace. In her stead she surmises that God should have chosen one of his cherubim, whose immortality would keep it from all sentimentality. In stark opposition, she paints herself as a "tender woman," with "the frail soul of [a] shepherd maid" (410), who is hardly fit for the field of battle:

> Wouldst thou proclaim thy high command
> Make choice of those who, free from sin,
> In thy eternal mansions stand;
> Send forth thy flaming cherubim!
> Immortal ones, thy law they keep,
> They do not feel, they do not weep!
> Choose not a tender woman's aid,
> Not the frail soul of shepherd maid! (410)

This passage marks the beginning, not the culmination, of Johanna's crisis: the critical point in the play actually comes later when her father denounces her as a witch before the king and his court (Act 5 Sc 1). Johanna does not speak in her own defense when this accusation is made, and is thus banished from the court that had shortly before showered her with praise. As she subsequently tells Raimond, her erstwhile suitor, she believed that God had spoken to the court through her father's voice, and sees herself as justly vulnerable to attack precisely because of her human fallibility, that is, her love for Lionel. She thus resigns herself to death as she is taken captive by the English. The play ends with Johanna having been vindicated: she escapes from her captors by heroically and mysteriously rending asunder the chains that bind her, and leads the victorious battle against the oppressor. Yet in spite of this, her death is the apotheosis of the play. In Schiller's revision, she dies not in the flame of the heretic's stake, but on the field of war.

By choosing this excerpt and coupling it with the Spiritual "My Way's Cloudy," Du Bois underscores to the reader that the thrust of his essay concerns the woman's ordeal in society, how she might insightfully take her place and define her role, how she might contribute to the uplift of the Negro race. The historical Jeanne d'Arc seems a bit far from Schiller's imagination, yet it is clear that he wished to refashion her memory into one wherein she would die the death of a national heroine—a woman warrior— rather than an apostate. At the same time there exist resonances between the Spiritual Du Bois chooses and the play he excerpts: the Spiritual singers, like Johanna, called upon the angels in times of spiritual blindness; and the collective singers and the singular Johanna alike raised prayers in the service of national salvation. Moreover, the trajectory of each piece is a teleological journey of moral enlightenment. Indeed, the focus in the Spiritual is on the *way*, the metaphysical journey through Christ to the all-knowing and all-powerful God, and thus, one might say more obliquely, the focus in these two paratexts, as Du Bois makes clear in his title of chapter 4, is upon "Progress."

The Spiritual and the play provide meaning cooperatively through progressive symbols and broad metaphors, yet they also, in their excerpted fragments, point up the incompleteness that is often a casualty of theories and discourses on the meaning of progress. In the Schiller fragment, we find that Johanna is lost in contemplation of the contention that exists between feminine love and moral duty. The excerpt of "My Way's Cloudy" opens with the cry "O brethren, my way," and trails off in the midst of the refrain: "my way's cloudy, my way. . . ." Here, the aphoristic character of earlier paratextual pairings ("The Crying of Water" / "Nobody Knows," "The Present Crisis" / "My Lord, What a Mourning," and *Childe Harold's Pilgrimage* / "Walk Together, Children") seems lost. The excerpts of chapter 4 do not produce concise axioms of knowing and seeing, hearing and awareness, or freedom and perseverance. Du Bois has actually trimmed away the portions of the chapter's paratexts that grant allusions to these epistemological tags: he shows Johanna in her weakness rather than in her strength; he allows the singers' music to trail off into incertitude rather than demonstrate its complete belief in the metaphors of the "promised land" and "the fire in the East" that characterize the symbolism of the song. I believe that this purposeful incompleteness serves to complement the thrust of the motive behind Du Bois's essay, the meaning and "measure" (414) of progress, while at the same time serving to underscore the motivity of *Souls* as a textual whole: the openness and lack of totality characterizing the "strange meaning of being black." (This seems certainly the case when one reads the closing lines of this chapter—"Thus sadly musing, I rode to Nashville in the Jim

Crow car" [414]—and again those coming in the midst of chapter 6 of *Dusk of Dawn*—"I recognize it quite easily and with full legal sanction; the black man is a person who must ride "Jim Crow" in Georgia" [666]—in light of Du Bois's contention in "Conservation" that race is "the vastest and most ingenious invention for human progress" [817].)

This incertitude and contingency serve as a transitional introduction to the chapters and paratexts that follow. "Howard at Atlanta," the poem that prefaces chapter 5, "Of the Wings of Atalanta," returns to the axiomatic and aphoristic qualities that the quotation from Schiller lacks. It seems most obviously suited to the essay it accompanies in its reference to the city of Atlanta. And upon first reading and hearing, the accompanying Spiritual, "Oh, The Rocks and the Mountains," seems related mainly to the essay, not at all to the poem. However, on closer examination, the relationship of the two comes clearer.

Whittier's idea in "Howard at Atlanta" is to comment upon the moral fitness of the newly freed slaves for citizenry. He composed the poem in 1869, after the end of the Civil War but before the end of Reconstruction. The poem's true hero is not the man of its title—Union Army General O. O. Howard—but the little black boy elegized in stanza seven of the poem, which Du Bois chooses as his paratext. By the time *Souls* was written, the historical "black boy of Atlanta" was well known to Du Bois: he was the former slave Richard Robert Wright, Sr., who lived between 1855 and 1947. Wright became famous once General Howard's enthusiasm for and appreciation of his spirited response to Howard's inquiries became widely known. Whittier's encomium immortalized Wright, though it left him unnamed. As the poem is fairly short, we may quote it in full:

> Right in the track where Sherman
>   Ploughed his red furrow,
> Out of the narrow cabin,
>   Up from the cellar's burrow,
> Gathered the little black people,
>   With freedom newly dowered,
> Where, beside their Northern teacher,
>   Stood the soldier, Howard.
>
> He listened and heard the children
>   Of the poor and long-enslavèd
> Reading the words of Jesus,
>   Singing the songs of David.

Behold!—the dumb lips speaking,
　　The blind eyes seeing!
Bones of the Prophet's vision
　　Warmed into being!

Transformed he saw them passing
　　Their new life's portal!
Almost it seemed the mortal
Put on the immortal.
No more with the beasts of burden,
　　No more with stone and clod,
But crowned with glory and honor
　　In the image of God!

There was the human chattel
　　Its manhood taking;
There, in each dark, bronze statue,
　　A soul was waking!
The man of many battles,
　　With tears his eyelids pressing,
Stretched over those dusky foreheads
　　His one-armed blessing.

And he said: "Who hears can never
　　Fear for or doubt you;
What shall I tell the children
Up North about you?"
　　Then ran around a whisper, a murmur,
　　　Some answer devising;
And a little boy stood up: "General,
　　Tell 'em we're rising!"

O black boy of Atlanta!
　　But half was spoken:
The slave's chains and the master's
　　Alike are broken.
The one curse of the races
　　Held both in tether:
They are rising,—all are rising,
　　The black and white together!

O brave men and fair women!
Ill comes of hate and scorning:
Shall the dark faces only
Be turned to morning?—
Make Time your sole avenger,
All healing, all redressing;
Meet Fate half-way, and make it
A joy and blessing!

After emancipation, and profiting from his unexpected fame, Wright went on to graduate from Atlanta University (from which he also earned a master's degree). As a graduate, he frequently accompanied the university's president, Edmund Asa Ware, on fundraising trips, during which he was billed as "the black boy of Atlanta" (*The Booker T. Washington Papers* 114). An adherent to the thought and policies of Booker T. Washington, Wright went on to become, in 1889, the first president of Georgia State Industrial College in Savannah. He was active in the Republican Party, which at that time in history was the party of most African American voters, as it was the party of the "great emancipator" Abraham Lincoln, and was at that historical moment more amenable than the Democratic Party to African Americans' desire for social parity and civil rights. Wright often made his political thoughts known through a newspaper he purchased and published in Augusta, Georgia, which he ironically called *The States Rights Sentinel*.[11]

Wright's visibility, and his friendship with Washington, brought him to the attention of President McKinley, who sought to appoint him to the post of minister to Liberia in 1898, the year of the Spanish-American War. Wright declined the offer. However, his political and social prominence would nonetheless bring him to Du Bois's attention, especially as Du Bois later became a friend to and collaborator with Wright's son, Richard R. Wright, Jr., a young sociologist, in 1906. (Wright Jr.'s dissertation, *The Negro in Pennsylvania: A Study in Economic History*, was completed in 1911 at the University of Pennsylvania, and was published in 1912 by the A.M.E. Book Concern. It seems certain that this study was fundamentally influenced by Du Bois's pioneering 1899 work of urban sociology, *The Philadelphia Negro*.)

In light of this, "Howard at Atlanta" was no simple poem for Du Bois. Though Whittier, a well-known abolitionist and Quaker, had dedicated much of his poetic output to such themes as the plight of the Negro, the labor question, and social reform, his prosody in this piece is neither regular nor remarkable. Indeed, the poem's rhythm, when read aloud, emerges as uneven and awkward. And to the twenty-first-century ear, such lines as "the little black people" and "those dusky foreheads" sound, at best, condescending. The poet's effusion over their "dumb lips speaking" and their "blind eyes seeing" lessen the reader's conviction that Whittier had full confidence in the humanity and social equality of his subjects. This doubt is only reinforced by the lines of stanza five: "There was the human chattel / Its manhood taking; / There, in each dark, bronze statue, / A soul was waking." The poet seems convinced that the gift of Lincoln—coming through the act of Emancipation—had "transformed" the slaves from "beasts of burden" to beings ". . . crowned with glory and honor / In the image of God!" (stanza four), that they possessed little humanity before that "transformational" moment. In fact, Whittier's poem as a whole focuses not on Wright's reply to Howard—"General, / Tell 'em we're rising"—a remark that is replete with black agency, but on the white poet's more inclusive reply to his reader: "They are rising—all are rising— / The black and white together." Similarly, the child's optimistic remarks are not among the lines Du Bois cites in his paratext.[12] Instead, he evokes the voice of the white poet, whose tone is moralistic and corrective:

> O black boy of Atlanta!
>   But half was spoken:
> The slave's chains and the master's
>   Alike are broken.
> The one curse of the races
>   Held both in tether:
> They are rising,—all are rising,
>   The black and white together!

We must then consider a number of points: the fame of Whittier's poem must be coupled with Wright's own fame, which was assured by the time of the publication of *The Souls of Black Folk*. It seems evident that for Du Bois, the absent and unnamed figure of Wright, known to many of his readers, black and white alike, would serve as an apt and symbolic central figure of a moralistic tale of the South, rendered through the myth of the hunter Atalanta. Wright's adherence to the policies of Washington,[13] whom Du Bois takes to task in good measure in chapter 3 of *Souls*, also lends another contextual layer to our reading of the poetic excerpt. Du Bois continues beyond chapter 3 to address Washington's program of vocational education and material prosperity in his critique of the city of Atlanta, employing terms that evoke Marxian sociology. Ultimately in "Of the Wings of Atalanta," Du Bois calls for the imagining of a new day, a future wherein wealth (such as that preached by Washington and secured by Wright) would be neither "the end and aim of politics," nor "the legal tender for law and order," nor "the ideal of the Public School" (417). "Of the Wings of Atalanta" is among the briefest chapters of *Souls*, yet its economic analysis of the South is among the most pointed and concise.

As with other chapters, chapter 5 negotiates critically the actual and the notional, and this mediation is metaphorically reinforced by the Spiritual that heads the chapter, "Oh, The Rocks and the Mountains." The refrain goes as follows:

> O the rocks and the mountains shall all flee away
> And you shall have a new hiding place that day.

This part is sung by a duet:

> Sinner, sinner, give up your heart to God

And the chorus joins in on the final line:

> And you shall have a new hiding place that day.

Du Bois's excerpt gives the reader only measures four, five, and six, whose lyrics are elements of the refrain: "And you shall have a new hiding place that day." In his essay, Du Bois argues that the panacea of wealth will no longer hold the imagination of the South—black or white (and this in accord with the last two lines of the excerpt he provides from Whittier's "Howard at Atlanta"). The "new hiding place" of the Spiritual will be attained only by "founding Right on righteousness and Truth on the unhampered search for Truth" (423). It seems also to refer to the "coming wings" of the South (*Souls* 421), by which Du Bois means to signify the proper higher education of the rising black middle class—an education that focuses upon their humanity rather than their purses. The Spiritual resonates with the metaphor of the veil in its use of a Biblical passage from the book of Isaiah that speaks of wings of the Seraphim that veil the angel's face and provide a hiding place and a path away from the ills of the world (*Isaiah* 6:2).

As prefatory material for chapter 6, "Of the Training of Black Men," which expands the critique of political economy and the educational and moral philosophy of chapter 5, Du Bois draws upon the opening bars of the Spiritual "March On," the lyrical excerpt from which reads, "Way over in Egypt land, you shall gain the victory." Unlike many of his other Spiritual excerpts, this line alternates between the leader and the chorus, with the leader singing the first clause ("Way over in Egypt land"), and the chorus picking up the second ("you shall gain the victory"). The lyrics refer to Egypt, also known as the land of Ham, Noah's son and father of Canaan. In pro-slavery discourse, the "peculiar institution" was regularly justified by deeming it a result of the "curse of Canaan," which came about after Ham had witnessed his father Noah's inebriated nakedness. When Noah emerged from his drunken stupor to discover that his son had seen him unclothed, he imprecated Ham's son Canaan: "Cursed be Canaan; a servant of servants shall he be unto his brethren" (Gen. 9:25).

Of course, there was much wrong in the logic of slavery's adherents: Noah specifically cursed Canaan in retribution for his father's sin; he made no mention of Canaan's offspring. Even if he had, the genealogy presented in the Bible gives Canaan as the father of the ancient Palestinians,[14] who themselves later fell under the domination of the invading Israelites, to whom the land of Canaan had been promised by God, and then again under the control of the Egyptians during the late Bronze Age, around 1500 BC. Thus, there existed some confusion in the thought of pro-slavery Christians, who confounded Canaan's curse and Ham's standing as progenitor of the darker races. For in addition to Canaan, Ham had also fathered Cush (the forefather of Ethiopia), Mizraim (the ancestor of Egypt) and Phut (the forebear of Sudan). Logically, if one wishes to read Noah's anger against Ham as a support for American (rather than Hebrew) slavery, then the Bible would have had to document a curse against one of these African primogenitors, not the Semitic one. The singers of "March On" appear to ignore this fact in order to strengthen analogies between their own situation of enslavement and that of the Israelites under Egypt.

The Spiritual is preceded by an excerpt from *The Rubaiyat*, written by the Persian poet Omar Khayyam and translated by Edward FitzGerald. It was first published anonymously in 1859, and remains a widely cited work in English poetry. The quatrain proclaims the freedom of the soul in the face of the body's earthly shackles; its lines build upon the lyrical foundation of "March On":

> Why, if the Soul can fling the Dust aside,
> And Naked on the Air of Heaven ride,
>   Were't not a shame—were't not a Shame for him
> In this clay carcase crippled to abide?

Just as the poet encourages the disembodied human soul to ride naked "on the Air of Heaven," the embattled slave is buoyed by the Spiritual singers with the encouragement to "march on" through the dust of a land that has, in the history of the Israelite and the slave in their differing circumstances, become synonymous with harsh bondage and the daily toil of life. Du Bois returns to this imagery in the final paragraph of the essay, where he maintains that his place of intellectual and social dwelling is "above the Veil," upon a "high Pisgah, between Philistine and Amalekite" (438). The Biblical metaphors here are multiple: it was Moses, son of an enslaved Israelite and husband to an Ethiopian woman, who sighted the Promised Land from the heights of Pisgah once he had led the Israelites to safety. Du Bois, in marking his habitation as being above the Veil and in drawing the metaphor of the Veil into relation with the Biblical symbol of the mount of Pisgah, claims for himself the insight of the prophet. Further, in posing a challenge to his reader, he conveys once more his solidarity with the mass of black folk, who, like him, possess the power of prescience: "Are you so afraid lest peering from this high Pisgah . . . we sight the Promised Land?" (438).

Metaphors of the Temporal and the Atemporal:
"Of the Black Belt," "Of the Quest of the Golden Fleece,"
and "Of the Sons of Master and Man"

Chapters 7, 8, and 9 are the most sociological chapters in *Souls*, and concern themselves, in part at least, with the relation of the temporal world (a world that can be observed and categorized by way of a critical, scientific gaze), and the world that exists beyond the physical one in which human beings live (a world constructed and attained through the imagination). There is more to say about the paratexts from chapter 6 in relation to the one that heralds "Of the Black Belt." There, for the first time in *Souls*, the incipient poetic paratext is not drawn from the poetry of Europe or America, but from the poetry of the Bible, to which Du Bois alludes throughout *Souls* in his own use of Biblical metaphors in the Forethought and the After-Thought, as well as in his citations from the Spirituals. He chooses for his first Biblical paratext one of the most confounding texts in the Bible, the Song of Solomon, also referred to as the Canticle of Canticles. Biblical scholars are often bemused by this book because of its subject matter. It is quite obviously a love poem, erotic in some aspects and sensuous throughout. Thus scholars have struggled to make sense of its place not only in the King James Version of the Bible, but also in the arrangement of the Megillot.

    In the Hebrew Bible, the Megillot is composed of five scrolls: the Song of Solomon, Ruth, Lamentations, Ecclesiastes, and Esther. Historically, each scroll has been read in liturgies celebrating annual Jewish festivals. The

festal scroll for Passover, Song of Solomon, is also a metaphorical song of
liberation: it memorializes the exodus of the Jews from Egypt under the
guidance of Moses (thereby linking the passage from Song of Solomon
to the previous essay in a way that is not immediately obvious); and it
commemorates the sparing of their first born on the eve of the exodus.
Most interpretations of the Song of Solomon have read it as allegorical
and dramatic: the apparent love story given in a dialogue between a man
and a woman is seen as an allegory of and testament to God's love for the
Hebrews, to whom the slaves regularly analogized their own situation of
bondage. In Christian thought, the book is understood as an allegory of
Christ's love for the church.

When Du Bois gives a passage from Song of Solomon as an
introductory paratext to "Of the Black Belt," we are immediately reminded
of those paratextual elements that introduce chapter 6, "Of the Training
of Black Men." The Spiritual "March On" especially relates to the exodus
of the Jews and the securing of their freedom from enslavement; and the
culmination of that chapter, where Du Bois metaphorically evokes the last
days of Moses as God shows him the Promised Land from the heights of
Pisgah, links the eve of the exodus, elicited by the reading of the Song of
Solomon, with its apogee in God's unveiling of Canaan. All of this is related
specifically to Du Bois's own metaphor of the Veil, with its implications
of insight, prophecy, and knowledge, and its direct relation to the texts of
Moses.

These seem in clear ways concomitant of the Spiritual that accompanies
the poem from the Canticles, "Bright Sparkles in the Churchyard." "Bright
Sparkles" is among the most complex of the spiritual compositions Du Bois
cites: it calls for parts sung by a duo of soprano and tenor, by a trio of first
and second sopranos along with an alto, by a quartet, and by a chorus. Du
Bois describes it as a "maze-like medley" (540); he seems to have seen the
song as a musical miscellany, and indeed it appears so. The song puts forward
a movement of themes: it begins with both a wish and an affirmation of
the wish's fulfillment:

> May the Lord—He *will* be glad of me
> May the Lord—He *will* be glad of me
> May the Lord—He *will* be glad of me
> In-a heaven, He'll rejoice

From this verse and a related refrain, both of which are sung
antiphonally, the song moves to a duo of soprano and tenor. Here the

lyrics give the impression of being unrelated to those of the first verse. The unison and harmony with which this verse is expressed is expanded as it is repeated by a quartet:

> Bright sparkles in the churchyard
> Give light unto the tomb
> Bright summer, spring's over
> Sweet flowers in their bloom

"Bright Sparkles" is sung at Easter time, which generally coincides with Passover. Thus, there is a sort of synergy created by the pairing of the Biblical verse from Song of Solomon and the Spiritual in relation to the sociological essay Du Bois pens. His essay on Georgia—"the black belt"—names the area as "historic ground" (439). It stands as the "centre of the Negro problem" that so vexed sociologists, including Du Bois himself. Dougherty County, which was the subject of an earlier sociological study by Du Bois, stands at the west end of the black belt, and was once called the "Egypt of the Confederacy" (*Souls* 449). Yet the imagery here is reversed. In Du Bois's analysis of the Egypt of the South, the Jew is no longer slave, but legatee of the former slave system. Jews are, in a twist of irony, the beneficiaries of the New World Egypt which has, in turn, become their land of promise: "The Jew is the heir of the slave-baron in Dougherty; and as we ride westward, by wide stretching cornfields and stubby orchards of peach and pear, we see on all sides within the circle of dark forest a Land of Canaan" (450).

Each of these poetic and musical paratexts appears to weave a tapestry of meaning, and Du Bois extends this intertwining in chapter 8, "Of the Quest of the Golden Fleece," returning once again to the apocalyptic scene of the Book of Revelation and underscoring that somehow, chapters 6, 7, and 8 are of a piece. The poem "The Brute" (1901), which prefaces chapter 8 and accompanies the elusive Spiritual "Children, You'll be Called On" (a song that is not widely anthologized), is an imagistic and allegorical poem about the pitfalls of industrialism in the modern age. In this way, the poem again takes up the concerns Du Bois addresses in chapter 5, "Of the Wings of Atalanta." As Du Bois does in that chapter, the poem's author, William Vaughn Moody, eventually ends on a positive note, with a strident hope in the future that is tempered by an undertone of wariness and circumspection. And like Du Bois's 1911 novel that bears a similar name—*The Quest of the Silver Fleece*—chapter 8 is a reflection upon both the political economy of the southern American context, as well as the sociological practice Du Bois felt sure would render apparent the elemental features and effects of that political economy. For this, he argues, real contact with the people of the South is required. As in the essay, "Sociology Hesitant" (c. 1904), Du Bois asserts at length that wholesale arguments and generalizations about black society and culture are not simply feckless, but also counterproductive. What is demanded is a redressal of the havoc that had been wreaked by the South's industrial modern economy, which was responsible for many ills that abounded in the African American community, including the destabilization of the African American family. The undermining of the black family in fact meant the erosion of the sort of national group that Du Bois (in "Conservation" and elsewhere) deemed necessary for the progress and elevation of black folk.

Throughout this chapter and permeating *Souls* in general is Du Bois's underscoring of the southern merchant as a thorn that exasperates the so-called Negro Problem. The rise of the southern merchant after the feudalism of American slavery introduced in the South—just as it had in modern Europe—a new and different type of slavery. For modern Europe, the problem was encapsulated in what Karl Marx defined as "wage slavery." For the American South, the problem was concisely stipulated by Du Bois as the "slavery of debt" (466). The images Du Bois found in Moody's poem fold neatly into the sociological work of "Of the Quest of the Golden Fleece," and here we must consider the function Du Bois was convinced sociology should carry out. For Du Bois, the value in sociological work lay in its concern with political economy, from which the more significant sociological studies descended.[15] Thus for him, any consideration of the state of society in which African Americans found themselves in the early twentieth century had to be concerned also with the state of the economy. Moody's poem serves these ends. Du Bois's excerpt of it reads:

But the Brute said in his breast, "Till the mills I grind have ceased,
The riches shall be dust of dust, dry ashes be the feast!
On the strong and cunning few
Cynic favors I will strew;
I will stuff their maw with overplus until their spirit dies;
From the patient and the low
I will take the joys they know;
They shall hunger after vanities and still an-hungered go.
Madness shall be on the people, ghastly jealousies arise;
Brother's blood shall cry on brother up the dead and empty skies."

With poetry such as this, Moody is said to have anticipated the generation of modernist poets who came after him, including T. S. Eliot.

Moody was doubtlessly in Du Bois's general acquaintance, as he graduated from Harvard in 1893 (two years before Du Bois would) and was, until a few years later, an instructor of English there. Robert Morss Lovett, a classmate whom Du Bois deemed to be "perhaps the closest white student friend [he] made at Harvard" (*Autobiography* 288), wrote of Moody as an intellectually powerful and aesthetically gifted poet whose "reputation [passed] into eclipse" (Lovett 463) through a brain tumor that struck him down in 1910 at the age of 41. Eliot entered Harvard in 1906; Moody had, by this time, left Harvard for the University of Chicago, where he and Lovett both served on the English faculty. By 1906, Moody was nationally noted for his poetry, and his most popular work—a prose play entitled *The Great Divide*—was published during Eliot's freshman year. Eliot's *The Waste Land*, which appeared in 1922, featured a sweeping, desolate urban landscape marred by the ravages of world war. Similarly, Moody's poem, from which Eliot's prosody profits, might be called a millenarian anti-encomium expressing hesitant hope in what was often a brutish modern economic and social terrain. Yet, as a poet expressing himself well before the Great War, he evinced a good deal more faith in the potential of the modern industrial era than did Eliot. Of the two, Eliot emerges by far as the more quixotic, trusting in the emancipatory gospel of poetry even as he disparaged modern industry in song.

Although himself a poet, Du Bois could little afford to trust so singularly in the power of poetry. Well before Eliot's interests turned to sociology during the 1930s, Du Bois assiduously advanced a theory of society that drew upon sociology, anagogy, and political economy as well as the poetic. Moody's hesitant optimism, his feral poetic imagery, and his ultimate faith in the moral rectitude of men[16] suited well Du Bois's insistence upon holding the protagonists of power to the test of fire. There is a way in which the image of the Brute portrayed by Moody may be likened to the Beast that wreaks havoc in the final book of the Bible, Revelation—a text to which Du Bois repeatedly alludes in *Souls* as well as in a number of his other creative writings. (See, for example, the apocalyptic themes at work in *Darkwater: Voices from within the Veil* (1920); "The Revelation of Saint Orgne the Damned" (1938); and the dénouement of *Dark Princess: A Romance*, published in 1928.) Both creatures are emblematic of systemic evil or oppression: the Biblical beast is taken by some as symbolic of Roman tyranny against Christians; and the monster conjured by Moody takes the shape of a creative/destructive modern force not unlike that which populated the imagination of Friedrich Nietzsche.

In fact, if we take the thrust of "Of the Quest of the Golden Fleece" as a guide to our analysis, we see that it is precisely the humanistic potential that lay underutilized and half dormant in modern political economy that appealed to Du Bois. In addition to his commentary on modern sociology, there are three other threads of thought that suffuse the essay: the black family, the white Southern merchant, and what Du Bois characterizes as the widening schism between "master and man," which reached its nadir in the Sam Hose affair of 1899. Du Bois wrote early on that the instability of the black family unit was indubitably the legacy of slavery (460–461). It is, he avers, economic in cause (461). Thus, the challenges faced by the black family had much to do with the problem of the white merchant, who filled the vacuum of power left by the Southern "aristocrat" after the fall of the South. The white merchant ushered in a different kind of slavery, which took the shape of peonage and "lawless oppression" (468) against African American families.

One might read in the intersection between the Jubilee evoked in the Spiritual, the apocalypse implicit in Moody's poem, and the chasm between the burgeoning white middle class and a black underclass the image of an afterlife, an "all-life," as Du Bois puts it in "Of the Passing of the First Born." The apocalyptic tones of Moody's poem, in as much as they allude to the Book of Revelation, have to do not simply with the world's end, but also with the making of life anew. Thus its verses are apt as allusions to the modern forces of creation and destruction. At the end of the Book of Revelation, the earth is harvested of all non-believers, and their blood courses through the city in an image of vines pulverized in a winepress. It is as though city and country are melded; indeed, Du Bois's imagery in chapter 8 begins with a rural field of golden cotton likened to the prized fleece sought by Jason, and it ends with an admonition to urban planners that the antidote for their ills might well lie beyond the city walls in the fields from which the dragons of peonage and oppression spring (474).

Such metaphors are evocative of the Spiritual, "Children, You'll be Called On," with its references to marching in the field of battle, rejoicing in the Jubilee, and the prospects of an after-life or after-world that has seen the end of earthly warfare. Etymologically descending from the Hebrew, the word Jubilee originally referred to a ram's horn with which good news was announced by a sounding; its sense later came to be associated with a wild cry or shout proclaiming freedom and restoration. The Spiritual also resonates with the *Book of Jubilees*, a set of fragments found among the Dead Sea Scrolls; though originally written in Biblical Hebrew, the book is preserved in an Ethiopic (classical Ge'ez) translation, and retells the history of Israel from the creation until Moses's ascent to Mt. Sinai (well before his viewing of the Promised Land from Mt. Pisgah). Thus "Children, You'll be Called On" might be seen—like Moody's poem—to allude to destruction in the face of evil. And, complementing "Of the Quest of the Golden Fleece," it evokes images of re-creation in its hope for the future, temporal as well as non-temporal.

Du Bois's probing of the soft underbelly of Southern politics, economics, and the widening chasm these discourses produced continues in chapter 9 of *Souls*, "Of the Sons of Master and Man." Here the chasm made apparent in the previous chapter is explored with the intent of blurring its edges. This is the argument Du Bois announces to the reader through the paratext drawn from Elizabeth Barrett Browning's mid-nineteenth-century poem, "A Vision of Poets." A bit of background on this poem will help us see the place Barrett Browning's work in general, and this poem in particular, holds in Du Bois's thought, for the poetry of Barrett Browning, like that of Tennyson, appears frequently as paratexts throughout Du Bois's oeuvre.

"A Vision of Poets" (1844) was published at a time when Lowell, Whittier, Tennyson, and other poets included in *Souls* were at the height of their profession. By the mid-nineteenth century, Barrett Browning was likewise considered to be among the foremost poets living and writing. Undoubtedly, Du Bois was quite familiar with her work, and this is evident in his choice to cite two of her poems as epigraphs to chapters 9 and 13 in *Souls*. "A Vision of Poets" combines the traditions of nineteenth-century lyric and narrative poetry in its depiction of an unlauded pilgrim-poet disaffected by a society that does not appreciate or recognize the worth of his gift. In a poem of 1005 lines and 335 triplets, Barrett Browning guides her poet through a nocturnal journey of dream-induced enlightenment. The insight of truth that the poet gains comes by transgressing a number of boundaries: life and death, symbolized in the poem by the juxtaposition of sleeping and waking; good and evil; light and darkness; ascent and descent; and temporal existence and its atemporal counterpart. As the angels of the poem aver, truth is known only through an experiential knowledge of suffering. Similarly and equally ironic, Barrett Browning writes unsparingly, "life is perfected by death" (stanzas 309 and 335).

The sufferings of the poet are described in salvific terms: his drinking from the pools of water are described in the poem as a "baptism" (l. 551), depicting the poet's journey not only as Christ-like but also as a process of renewal and rebirth. It is thus a bit surprising when we find—years later in the poem's narrative time—that the poet has died of his social, psychic, and emotional wounds. We witness, then, the martyrdom of the truth seeker, a trope that is wholly striking in light of the peregrinations of the narrator of *Souls*, Du Bois's poet-pilgrim/poet-prophet, who traverses the leaves of the text and dialectically situates himself simultaneously within the spheres of the temporal and atemporal worlds in varied human form (narrating the lives of John, Burghardt, Crummell, Josie, and Du Bois himself).

This sort of rupturing of narrative frames, where the various essays of *Souls* form a set of concentric rings whose theme is, after all, a quest and search for meaning, what Du Bois refers to as the "strivings" of the souls of black folk, effects an openness that is operant through the book. It is an openness that functions morally, for it is at base an insistence upon *freedom*, democratic freedom and the possibilities that emerge from what Du Bois refers to, in "Sociology Hesitant" as "chance."

It is through this insight that Barrett Browning advises the pilgrim-poet and all others who submit themselves to the vicissitudes of the demiurge, that the separation of the two spheres of understanding—the conscious and the unconscious—establishes a false limit of knowledge thanks to which we pretend to grasp fully the import of this or that. The limits of the two spheres must be transgressed in the pursuit of truth and knowledge, she insists. This point Barrett Browning makes clearly in the first triplet of the "Conclusion" to "A Vision of Poets," and it is this triplet that Du Bois chooses for his epigraph to chapter 9, "Of the Sons of Masters and Man":

> Life treads on life, and heart on heart
> We press too close in church and mart
> To keep a dream or grave apart

Here Barrett Browning's poet extols the idea of "chance" that Du Bois discusses at length in "Sociology Hesitant": the chance, or possibilities, that emerge from the contact of social groups. In "Of the Sons of Master and Man," Du Bois describes this social intercourse as the "world-old phenomenon" of the global contact of "diverse races of men" (475). Such a widespread occurrence may be beneficially studied in the American South, Du Bois insists, and, after a fashion, such is the thrust of *The Souls of Black Folk*: the situating of the Negro not simply within the American social plane, but, more importantly, within the plane of the global. Thus in the poetic excerpt, he at once announces his intent to effect a rapprochement of the global and the local. Much of what he sets about arguing here emerges from what he sees as the reciprocity of racism and socioeconomic disparities. The color-line is produced by this reciprocity; racism and class discrimination act as structural agents that produce "race," which, as we have seen, Du Bois defines in "The Conservation of Races" (1897) as a "most ingenious invention" for the effecting of progress.

When we consider the lines of the "Conclusion" in light of these points as well as those lines that close the poem—"Knowledge by suffering entereth / And Life is perfected by Death"—we gain the clear sense that Barrett Browning is intent upon blurring the boundaries of knowledge, even at the cost of the alienation the creative individual may inevitably experience. In this case, such alienation is endured by the poet-pilgrim, who determines to know and to be known.

The Spiritual Du Bois chooses to preface chapter 9, entitled "I'm a Rolling," echoes the alienation of the poet-pilgrim who figures prominently in Barrett Browning's poem, and who calls out—in anguish—for the comfort of community and recognition. The singer of the Spiritual does likewise:

> I'm a rolling, I'm a rolling
> I'm a rolling thro' an unfriendly world
> I'm a rolling, I'm a rolling thro' an unfriendly world
>
> O brothers, wont you help me,
> O brothers, wont you help me to pray?
> O brothers wont you help me
> Wont you help me in the service of the Lord?

It is the final line of the song, and its return to the song's beginning in exact time, that Du Bois cites as a musical paratext to the essay:

> Wont you help me in the service of the Lord?
> I'm a rolling, I'm a rolling

Du Bois seems also to place the excerpt from the Spiritual into relation with the poetic lines that close chapter 9, which are drawn from Tennyson's famous poem, "In Memoriam A.H.H." (1850), a poem that Du Bois cites in a number of his works. It hardly seems pure coincidence that Barrett Browning likewise uses Tennyson's "In Memoriam" as an epigraph for "A Vision of Poets":

> That mind and soul according well,
> May make one music as before,
> But vaster.

In Tennyson's verse, where the poet mourns the loss of his friend, ponders the values of the temporal, and imagines the mysteries of the non-material world, there is a transgression of boundaries that echoes the Spiritual's, Du Bois's, and Barrett Browning's gestures of contravening the categories of human knowing through experience, melding or blurring, for instance, body and mind, or mind and soul (that is, reasoning and thought vs. spirituality and intuition). There is much of this at work in the poem; and this sort of working draws this poetic paratext into relation with the poem from Browning as well as the Spiritual.

The Fundamental Mythopoetics of Metaphor in African American Religion: "Of the Faith of the Fathers"

Chapter 10 of *Souls*, "Of the Faith of the Fathers," appears to be a transitional chapter between the section it follows and that which it prefaces. In poetic terms, it might be seen as an *enjambement*: it has the mixed effect of broaching a new topic—African American religious practice—at the same time that it pushes forward its exposition of the radical newness of black being in the modern era. This is accomplished in two ways in this chapter. First, Du Bois presents the reader with a popular poem drawn from a poetic stage play by William Sharp (writing under the pseudonym Fiona Macleod); and then he presents the reader with an archetypal Negro Spiritual, "Steal Away," thereby signaling the central importance of this chapter and its paratexts. In terms of the structure of *Souls*, chapter 10 serves as prefatory material for the three chapters that follow it, and provides a critical framework for what would prove to be Du Bois's longstanding practice of coupling anagogy (a specialized form of allegorical representation that allows a reader to interpret spiritual and even eschatological meanings in a text) and auto/biography (whereby the authorial self and a discursive other are represented through narrative allegory—the authorial "I" regularly posits an other, whose life circumstances permit the author to expound upon a set of problems that are social, political, racial in nature). A life story is thus set up for critical discussion and analysis; often in Du Bois's writing practice, the biographical self and the authorial self merge in ways that may be described as at once anagogical and metaphysical (or, onto-theological, as with Equiano and Harper). A discussion of the background for this chapter may help us better understand its import, for it would seem that this is the best way to explicate the oddest choice of the poetic paratexts Du Bois chooses, "Dim Face of Beauty."

Three years before "Of the Faith of the Fathers" appeared as part of *The Souls of Black Folk*, W. E. B. Du Bois traveled by transatlantic steamship to Paris, France in June, 1900. There, he oversaw the installation of his decidedly successful Exhibit on American Negroes at the Exposition Universelle, that year's world's fair. Du Bois would write very little about his time in Paris,[17] yet it is clear that the event held a good deal of significance for him, for it provided him—and American Negroes as a group—an international stage upon which to demonstrate the advances and development of their culture, education, social customs and structure, intellectual output, and, indeed, the very diversity of what was called the Negro "type."

The success of the Exposition buoyed Du Bois as he left Paris for London, where the July 1900 Pan-African Conference, organized by the Trinidadian barrister Henry Sylvester Williams and of which Du Bois himself served as secretary, would take place. As biographer David Levering Lewis puts it, Du Bois finally found himself within a broad international circle of the black intellectual elite. Among the elite in attendance at the Conference was one of the most celebrated men of African descent in England, the composer Samuel Coleridge-Taylor. Due to the widespread success of Samuel Coleridge-Taylor's early work in the 1890s, Du Bois knew well of Coleridge-Taylor's intellectual and creative output, and made his initial acquaintance during the Pan-African Conference. Subsequently, Coleridge-Taylor and his wife, Jessie, befriended the prominent African American scholar, who was, as was so often his wont, traveling without his own wife. They enjoyed his company on a number of occasions, and invited him to their home, where they made him comfortable and prepared him a meal. Together, the three were in attendance at the Crystal Palace, where Samuel Coleridge-Taylor conducted the full *Hiawatha* suite, which had premiered, in its entirety, earlier that year.[18] Du Bois tells the story of the Crystal Palace performance and of his time with the Coleridge-Taylors in his essay, "The Immortal Child," a critical biography of Coleridge-Taylor that Du Bois uses to extol the absolute necessity of black progeny. It was published in the 1920 collection of essays, short stories, and poetry entitled *Darkwater*.

Du Bois's interest in Coleridge-Taylor's *Hiawatha* helps explain his choice of "Dim Face of Beauty" as a paratext in *Souls*. Based on Henry Wadsworth Longfellow's book-length poem, *The Song of Hiawatha* (1855), a legend-based folk epic that held great appeal for Samuel Coleridge-Taylor (as it certainly did for Antonín Dvorak), yet frustrated earlier composers who had sought to put it to music, Coleridge-Taylor's *Hiawatha* trilogy holds some affinity with other epic-like musical performances of its time, including—importantly, I will argue—William Sharp's poetic-drama, *The House of Usna* (1900). It is from Sharp's work, which I see as an indirect allusion to the creativity of Coleridge-Taylor, that Du Bois draws the poetic paratext for chapter 10, "Of the Faith of the Fathers." Du Bois uses a poem set to music and performed in the second scene of Sharp's one-act play. Its title is "Dim Face of Beauty":

> Dim face of Beauty haunting all the world,
>> "Fair face of Beauty" all too fair to see,
> Where the lost stars adown the heavens are hurled,—
>> There, there alone for thee
>> May white peace be,
>
> . . . .
> Beauty, sad face of Beauty, Mystery, Wonder,
>> What are these dreams to foolish babbling men
> Who cry with little noises 'neath the thunder
>> Of Ages ground to sand,
>> To a little sand.

Though Samuel Coleridge-Taylor would not visit America until the year after Du Bois's *Souls* appeared in print, William Sharp visited the United States in 1889 and 1890, during Du Bois's undergraduate years at Harvard. New York served as his home base; there he was the guest of the poet and critic Edmund C. Stedman and his wife. He spent time with W. D. Howells, a certain Professor Wright of Harvard University, and a historian by the last name of Windsor (*Memoir* 153). He also spent time with Arthur Sherburne Hardy, author of *Passe Rose*,[19] and he met with a number of editors: Richard W. Gilder, poet and editor of *Century Magazine*; Henry Mills Alden of *Harpers Magazine*; and the poet-critic Richard Henry Stoddard. During his time in the States, Sharp was elected an honorary member of the Century Club and the Players Club. He made a lasting impression upon the students at Harvard, who would dedicate an issue of the *Harvard Monthly* to his work in 1903. And while he was in the United States, he made the acquaintance of Thomas A. Janvier, author of *Colour Studies* (1885), a collection of sketches of life in Mexico and Greenwich Village.

On first glance, the excerpt from Sharp's work and the Spiritual, "Steal Away," which serves as the second paratext of the chapter, have little in common; they certainly seem distant from any consideration of the creativity of Coleridge-Taylor. Indeed, there is little in "Dim Face of Beauty" that makes it appear immediately significant to Du Bois's essay, "Of the Faith of the Fathers," in any way. Yet the number of historical events that place Coleridge-Taylor's *Hiawatha* trilogy into some relation with *The House of Usna*, coupled with the fact that Du Bois, seemingly intent upon choosing poetry from the Euro-American tradition as paratexts for all but the final chapter of *Souls*, pairs this poem with one of the most important Spirituals in the African American canon, compel the attention of the reader. This becomes even more apparent through an examination of the relation—historical, intellectual, and artistic—between Sharp and Coleridge-Taylor. The two men are, of course, of the same historical moment. More than this, though, they were members of intellectual and artistic circles that frequently intersected and overlapped. Both men, for example, were close friends of the poet Alfred Noyes, who would, ironically, pen eulogies to each man upon his death. (Noyes's elegy to Coleridge-Taylor is engraved on his elaborate marble headstone at Bandon Hill Cemetery in the London Borough of Sutton.) Both men were also acquaintances of the poet Robert Browning, husband to Elizabeth Barrett Browning, who is cited, intertextually, twice in *Souls*; although it was rumored in Browning's own time that he was a Jew (such a belief was explored and then dismissed by William Sharp, who nonetheless noted in Browning's mannerism idiosyncrasies that he generalized to Jews as a group[20]), Browning was partly of African descent, his grandmother having been a Creole from the West Indies. And, finally, the closeness of the dates on which the two works debuted is striking: the full *Hiawatha* trilogy debuted to critical praise on March 22, 1900, while *The House of Usna* premiered during the following month.

These are not the only coincidences that obtain in the lives and work of these two men. Like the *Hiawatha* trilogy, *The House of Usna* draws upon myth and legend in order not only to speak the national narrative of a people, but also to give voice to a people's collective desire. A one-act play in three scenes, *The House of Usna* was first performed by The Stage Society, of which William Sharp himself was president. It was published under Sharp's pen name, Fiona Macleod, first by the *Fortnightly Review* in the months following its premier, and later in book form by Heinemann of London in 1900. *The House of Usna* was intended to form a part of a series of plays that Sharp would title *The Theatre of the Soul* or *The Psychic Drama*.[21] Only in 1903 did the play appear in book form in the United States, a bit too late for it to be of influence in Du Bois's writing of the *Souls of Black Folk*, but its earlier run in the *Fortnightly Review* or the 1900 Heineman edition might have been of some importance to the initial version of "Of the Faith of the Fathers," which was published as "The Religion of the American

Negro" in 1900 in the December issue of the periodical *New World*.[22] It is likely that Du Bois became acquainted with this play and with the excerpt he quotes in *Souls* during his time in London in June of 1900, when he met Samuel Coleridge-Taylor and attended the Pan-African Conference during the months prior to publishing "The Religion of the American Negro."[23] It is also likely that the subject matter of the Hiawatha trilogy, steeped deeply as it was in lore and legend, made feasible for Du Bois his use of *The House of Usna* as a paratext for chapter 10.

Now that we understand a bit better the import of the play and its possible attraction for Du Bois, let us focus on elements of the play in order to situate properly the excerpt Du Bois chooses and determine its relation to the essay and the Spiritual. For our purposes, we may limit our discussion to the primary characters of the play: Concobar Macnessa, the king of Ulster and founder of the "Red Branch" (a forerunner of the Arthurian legend that grounds yet another paratext of *Souls*, *Idylls of the King*, by Alfred, Lord Tennyson, which prefaces chapter 12, "Of Alexander Crummell"); and Deirdre, the great object of Concobar's affection, reputed to be the greatest beauty in all of Ireland. Deirdre did not return Concobar's love, and instead rebuffed him openly and eloped with her lover, Naysha, one of the sons of the House of Usna and Concobar's nephew. Deirdre, Naysha, and his two brothers ran away to the Scottish wilderness to escape Concobar's vengeance. Sharp's drama is set in the year following the exaction of Concobar's murderous revenge against Naysha and his brothers. Concobar had long schemed to rid himself of the sons of Usna and had imagined that doing so would permit him to secure Deirdre's affections. However, upon learning of Naysha's death, Deirdre, too, dies (differing versions of the legend tell of her suicide by various means, or of her willing herself to death through grief).

Herbert Fackler sees the play as focusing upon "the effects of Concobar's treachery . . . and the repetition of a cycle of love and death in which Concobar has participated" (187). Fackler also points out that there are at least two levels of meaning at work in the play. On the first level, we find "a dream of the effects of love, revenge, remorse, and loss of the object of desire on a number of noble characters." And on the second level, we encounter "a universal pattern re-created in a cyclical manner, indicating the extent to which the action portrayed may be interpreted as a cultural archetype" (187).

The archetypal aspects of the play may explain its widespread appeal. A number of its poetic elements, including "Dim Face of Beauty," were reprinted in later collections of Sharp's works, and give evidence of the popularity of this poem, which, in the play, is rendered as a song. Thus, "Dim Face of Beauty," sung in the second scene of *The House of Usna* by Maine, a Norse prince and part of Concobar's retinue, might be read critically alongside the "master-song," "Steal Away," which serves as the second paratext to chapter 10.

At issue in "Of the Faith of the Fathers" is Du Bois's argument that black religion is at a critical stage at the turn of the twentieth century.[24] This is due not least to the times in which he wrote. The anarchical atmosphere that I discuss at length in the preceding chapter still tinged the era in which *Souls* appeared.[25] Further, there was the so-called "Negro Problem" of which Du Bois would write extensively in his 1903 essay "The Talented Tenth,"[26] and which occupied a good deal of his attention in *Souls* and elsewhere. American Negroes, Du Bois tells us, are compelled constantly to "discuss the 'Negro Problem,'—must live, move, and have their *being* in it, and interpret all else in its light or darkness" (my italics 501–502). The "problem," rendered as an ontological metaphor here and elsewhere in Du Bois's writings ("'How does it feel to be a problem?' Du Bois writes rhetorically in the opening paragraph of *Souls*), touched upon their innermost lives, including their religious beliefs, which prescribed, in good measure, their interpretation of the world in which they lived. The constraints of the Negro Problem served as the founding condition of double-consciousness, Du Bois argues. He describes the Negro's double-consciousness not only in racial and national terms in this essay, but also in historical terms that recall his definition of race in "The Conservation of Races." He writes:

> From the double life every American Negro must live, as a Negro and as an American, as swept on by the current of the nineteenth while struggling in the eddies of the fifteenth century—from this must arise a painful self-consciousness, an almost morbid sense of personality and a moral hesitancy which is fatal to self-confidence. (502)

The reference to the fifteenth century in this citation is surely a reference to the early time of the Middle Passage, an event situated in the episteme of the early modern period. Compare this point to Du Bois's mention (in chapter 12, "Of Alexander Crummell") of the nineteenth century as the first century in which "we began to descry in others that transfigured spark of divinity which we call Myself" (514), that is, when anagogical interpretation merged with modern views of selfhood to produce what we today call individual subjectivity. Selfhood, self-consciousness, and being are all of signal importance to the crux of this essay. How, then, might we see such concepts at work in the essay's paratexts?

As to the relation of the essay's concepts to its paratexts, one should note the dichotomy Du Bois sketches between the northern and southern Negroes, and their respective religious practices. Life in the South has rendered a Negro group that is pretentious and hypocritical in nature, and overly eager to compromise, Du Bois argues in tones that recall his criticism of Booker T. Washington; opposed to them are the northern Negroes, whom Du Bois deems to be of rebellious and radical character. Such a dichotomy may readily reflect upon the divergent characters at play in both the drama and the song that introduce chapter 10. "Dim Face of Beauty" bespeaks a tragedy of madness and radicalism, all played out against the backdrop of Irish national desire and a battle for supreme power. "Steal Away" speaks to the influence of black abolitionism that Du Bois considers formative of the thought of the slave (500–501). While "Dim Face of Beauty" is sung in the aftermath of horrific murders and the senseless death of a nation's beauty, "Steal Away" may be sung either as an act of spiritual submission and fatalism (the song could be read as a paean to death), or as an act of social and political defiance, a radical denial of the institution of slavery and a recognition of burgeoning modern self-consciousness (the song was regularly sung in advance of slave escapes). This point appears to reflect what Du Bois implies earlier in the book: that black being is at once resurgent and under threat of social erasure, and that this dualism is, in part, constitutive of the problem of double-consciousness.

In fact, "Steal Away" appears to characterize the shift in black consciousness that Du Bois sees taking place between two songs he cites in "Of the Faith of the Fathers." For the first, he gives the following lines, sung by slave "bards" (500) in prophetic tones:

> Children, we all shall be free
> When the Lord shall appear!

These lines indicate for Du Bois a "deep religious fatalism" that developed side by side with the sensibilities of "the martyr" (500), practically a stance of submission that is countered by what he sees as the more daring, abolitionist nature of the song "O Freedom," a Spiritual that is well known to today's reader:

> O Freedom, O Freedom, O Freedom over me!
> Before I'll be a slave

I'll be buried in my grave
And go home to my Lord
And be free. (501)

Unlike the lines from the prior song, this latter indicates for Du Bois the extent to which "Negro religion" transformed itself from a "fatalistic faith" (500) that led to a lack of subjectivity, to a radical "dream of Abolition" (501) whose insistence upon freedom provides the basis for modern black being. Du Bois would later revise his stance on the early passiveness of the slave in the face of a battle for his or her own emancipation.[27] Yet it is clear that in 1900 and 1903, he saw the dialectical aspects between the fatalism of early black religion and the radicalism of nineteenth-century abolition as productive of a crisis in black religion in his own time. This crisis had to do with the modernity of black life, which was, as Du Bois saw it, a double, contradictory, and conflicted life. After a fashion, Du Bois would argue, the dilemma of the American Negro is no more and no less a quintessentially modern dilemma, shaped by anarchist and radical thought coupled with social upheaval. It is "simply the writhing of the age translated into black,—the triumph of the Lie which to-day, with its false culture, faces the hideousness of the anarchist assassin" (503).

The northern Negro, arguably in closer touch with the "soul-life" of the "great modern nation" (501) than the Negro of the South, was thus also much more prone to radicalism than his or her southern counterpart. Yet the southern Negro does not escape Du Bois's judgment either, for s/he is prone to sycophancy, to "hypocritical compromise" (503). Even so, the black southern "proletariat," as Du Bois strikingly calls them (and thus, acknowledges their own revolutionary potential in spite of their fatalism and lack of subjectivity), are also prone to use deception against their conquerors, much as the rebellious South worked to deceive its stronger counterpart, the North. It is reflective of the global situation or condition of persons of African descent: "Nor is this situation peculiar to the Southern United States—is it not rather the only method by which undeveloped races have gained the right to share modern culture? The price of culture is a Lie" (504). If the price of culture is a lie, then so is the price of modern civilization, and, indeed, of the modern-nation state itself, given the processes of memory and forgetting—that is, revisionist historicism—that must be marshaled and engaged for nation formation to take place. Modern nationalism requires the forgetting of disparate histories in order to effect the coherence of a national people. Such "cohesion" rarely, in fact, bonds a people together, and it is the schisms in this union that Du Bois seems determined to expose.

If the northern Negro has been labeled a radical, it is, in part, Du Bois intimates, because s/he has been driven from the land s/he considers to be home, the South of his or her "birthright" (504), with all the images and implications that follow and pertain to such a term. (Consider the title "Steal Away" in this light—that not only are slaves taking their own freedom by force, but they are commenting—critically and sardonically—on the fact that they must "take" their freedom by "stealing" their own bodies and heading North.) Intellectually awakened to "new-found freedom" (504), a freedom that Du Bois appears to deem undemocratic because it is, in some way, forced, the northern Negro thus finds him/herself as unfree as his or her southern counterpart. These two extremes, and the proletarian "mass of millions" that fall between them, will, one day, sweep out of their refashioned chains, Du Bois cautions, leaving their irons broken in the dust as they move, en masse, in terrifying splendor, toward the goal of freedom.

Of course, this sort of interpretation may elicit a number of responses. Certainly we might see in this dichotomy of sycophancy and radicalism a reflection of the dichotomy of reason (North and South) Du Bois takes such great pains to explicate in "Of the Faith of the Fathers." It should not be lost on the reader that the Celtic legend that is crystallized in "Dim Face of Beauty" is akin to the theological mythopoetics that structures many of the Spirituals, whose beauty Du Bois describes in the opening lines of chapter 10 as coming to him *dimly* across the fields" in a "cadence of song,—soft, thrilling, powerful" (emphasis added, 493). Such a background lends itself to the power the songs exert as regards the nationalism of black people in America. (And I mean by such "nationalism" a fragile cultural cohesion as that described by Du Bois in this chapter, one delicately but purposely forged by slaves who descended from disparate ethno-linguistic groups (mainly) in West Africa. We might say that the eighteenth- and nineteenth-century subjectivities fashioned by American Negroes were birthed by the eddying waters of the Middle Passage, which Du Bois also references in "Of the Faith of the Fathers.") Certainly the radicalness of Concobar Macnessa, whose vengeance upon his lost love, Deirdre, resulted not only in her death but also in his own unending remorse, is meant to reflect upon the radicalness of the Northern Negro Du Bois describes in less than flattering terms in the essay, whose rash actions surely result in loss and contrition. On the other hand, the spiritual, reflective nature of the Southern Negro, who, through an agency that Du Bois nonetheless characterizes as deceitful and tactical, "steals" him or herself away from the plantation and indeed, from the turn-of-the-twentieth-century South, which, even in Du Bois's time of writing, serves as a prison and a place of violence. We might also say, given Du Bois's naming of "Steal Away" as an archetypal musico-narrative, that he too sees that the song has much to do with the wrenching of subjectivity from the dehumanizing conditions of slavery, the snatching of one's own being from the grip of social death, and, thus, an insistence upon life by the slave him or herself. Therefore, "Steal Away," the archetypal musico-narrative of the black American experience, symbolizes the willful forging of identity out of ignominy (in the Latin sense of this word, indicating namelessness and anonymity). It is the insistence upon self-determination, upon the condition of being even as non-being has been imposed, in an over-determined fashion, from without.

The Soul's Biography: Metaphors of Transition and Transcendence in "Of the Passing of the First Born," "Of Alexander Crummell," and "Of the Coming of John"

"Dim Face of Beauty," and "Steal Away" also resonate with paratexts that preface chapters 11, 12, and 13 of *Souls*, for the flight of black souls from the world of the living into the eternity of the after life assumes the focus of these chapters. In 1905, William Sharp, author of "Dim Face of Beauty," edited a collection of poetry by Charles Algernon Swinburne. He included in this collection the 1864 poem, "Itylus," the poetic paratext to chapter 11 of *Souls*, "Of the Passing of the First Born." Du Bois's use of the poem works in accord with the meditative posture generally demanded of readers of lyric poetry; indeed, Swinburne's melding of the dramatic monologue with lyric qualities in this poem provides Du Bois a language in which to eulogize his son, Burghardt, who died of dysentery in 1899. Though today's critical readers often castigate Du Bois for what they consider his insensitivity in neglecting, for example, to focus upon his wife's grief rather than his own (Du Bois does not even name his wife, Nina, in the essay, but neither does he mention his son's name, a point most critics overlook), "Of the Passing of the First Born"—at times rendered as an extended prose poem, a dramatic monologue of sorts—establishes a window through which we, along with Du Bois's contemporary reader, gaze in upon the scene of his contemplative grief and come to know a further, angst-ridden aspect of black being at the turn of the century.

Swinburne, an associate of Dante Gabriel Rosetti during his college days, won early praise from Alfred, Lord Tennyson (another of Du Bois's favorite poets) for his 1865 drama *Atalanta in Calydon*, with which Du Bois was likely familiar, since it echoed his own interest in the figure of Atalanta (as we see in chapter 5 of *Souls*). "Itylus" is one of Swinburne's best poems, though in his time he was criticized for the piece's anti-theism. There are at least two versions of the Itylus story that Swinburne might have used as a basis for his poem, and that thus indirectly impact the meaning at work in Du Bois's text. The first comes from the Greek myth of Aedon, the daughter of Padareus, and wife of Zethus. Aedon envied her sister-in-law Niobe for her many children and plotted to kill one of them. By mistake, she slew her own child, Itylus, and mourned for him in such an awful way that the gods transformed her into a nightingale. This story is to be compared with that of Procne and Philomela. Ovid's version of this myth comes in Book Six of the *Metamorphosis*. After marrying Tereus, the King of Thrace and a descendant of Mars, Procne, the princess of Athens, soon gave birth to their first child, Itylus. She longed for the company of her sister, Philomela, and sent Tereus to Athens to fetch her. Tereus, lustful, was immediately taken with Philomela, so much so that as soon as they returned to Thrace, he imprisoned and raped her, cutting out her tongue afterwards to keep his misdeed a secret. Tereus convinced Procne that her sister had died during the return voyage, and a year passed before Philomela managed to get a message to Procne that she was alive and held captive. Procne, filled with rage, liberated her sister during the carnival season. To avenge her, Procne determined to slay Itylus, whose innocent and youthful face seemed to her filled with the omen of his father's vile behavior. After Procne ran her dagger through the boy's heart, Philomela, mute, drew a cutlass across his throat. The women together cut the boy to bits, and served him to his father, who unknowingly consumed him during a ritual feast. Upon learning of the source of his repast, and sick that his body now served as Itylus's "sepulchral tomb" (*Metamorphosis* 1021), Tereus pursued both sisters, intending to kill them, and they were changed by the gods into birds—Procne a swallow, and Philomela a nightingale—to aid their escape. (Others argue that the metamorphoses were reversed: Procne a nightingale, and Philomela a swallow.) Tereus was likewise transformed. In some legends he became a harpoo; in others, a hawk.

Swinburne appears closer to the story of Procne than that of Aedon, for Procne's tale is much more sinister. Yet he absolves one sister—Philomela—at the expense of Procne, when both sisters acted murderously in Ovid's tale. The maternal violence of Itylus's sacrifice is subsumed in Swinburne's poem, and instead of a lamentation of a regrettable marriage and infanticide, the poem turns into a mournful elegy on the death of Itylus. Du Bois excerpts the final stanza of the poem as an element of his own elegy to Burghardt, leaving aside any hints of the mother's culpability. The excerpt he give reads as follows:

O sister, sister, thy first-begotten,
The hands that cling and the feet that follow,
The voice of the child's blood crying yet,
Who hath remembered me? who hath forgotten?
Thou hast forgotten, O summer swallow,
But the world shall end when I forget.

In the excerpt, which deals not with Itylus's murder but with its aftermath, Procne would be the forgetful swallow, and Philomela the moralistic, self-aware nightingale. In any case, the import of the full poem, with its sedimented references to Tereus's carnal feast and Procne and Philomela's infanticide, would be ill-matched to the meaning at work in Du Bois's essay. It is more so the mournful qualities of the single stanza of the poem Du Bois chooses, full of sonic import conveyed by way of repetition, alliteration, complex metaphorical phrases, and grief-ridden imagery, about which I will say more shortly, that powerfully complement his elegy of his son. No aspect of Procne's maternal guilt should be taken to reflect upon Du Bois's wife, Nina, since the essay clearly portrays her as the most perfect of mothers, devoting herself fully to the child's life and mourning piteously his death.

Nina is, in fact, emblematic of the ideal maternal figure referenced in Du Bois's use of the Spiritual, "I Hope My Mother Will Be There." This composition, Du Bois tells us in "The Sorrow Songs," developed later in the history of the Jubilee songs. He provides bars from the first two lines of the Spiritual as a paratext: "I hope my mother will be there / In that beautiful world on high." The lyrics portray the mother as the child's greatest hope in the afterlife: the desire to see her "in that beautiful world on high" assuages the earthly pain of young slaves grown old, many of whom had been separated from their mothers as children.

In Du Bois's text, the lyrics of the song are not the living child's address to the absent mother, but the deceased child's address to the mother tragically left behind, whose eventual passage to the world beyond the present is likened, by way of metaphor, to a salvific transformation of being in the full lyrics to the song: "With palms of victory / crowns of glory you shall wear / In that beautiful world on high." The metaphor "palms of victory" alludes to the victorious entry of Christ into the holy city of Jerusalem, an event noted by each of the writers of the Gospels. Three of the four Gospels refer to branches of trees laid before Christ as he made his way into the city on the back of a donkey: John alone specifies that the branches were from palm trees (12:13). Similarly, the metaphor "crowns of glory" carries deep signification. Not only was a crown of thorns placed upon Christ's head at his crucifixion, to ridicule him for proclaiming himself the son of God even as he was proven mortal through his crucifixion; a crown, as part of the raiment of a king or queen, would be bestowed upon each of the righteous in the afterlife, according to the slaves' theology (a notion also reflected in the song "I Shall Wear a Golden Crown"). The "crowns of glory" referred to in this Spiritual thus allude not only to the rewards of life after trials upon the earth, but also to the transfigured existence in which "glory" itself is set to culminate, "the changing of the bodies of the saints to the likeness of their glorified Lord," as given in Philippians 3:20–21: "For our conversation is in heaven; from whence also we look for the Savior, the Lord Jesus Christ: who shall change our vile body, that it may be fashioned like unto his glorious body, according to the working whereby he is able even to subdue all things unto himself."

Through the Spiritual and the poem alike, the body of Burghardt emerges as central to the metaphorics of the essay, in that the racialized black body of Du Bois's infant child serves to critique the processes of the color-line that, in effect, brought about his death. Du Bois presages the terrible outcomes of these processes through the intimate discourse of a father's fears for his child soon after he is born:

> I held him in my arms after we had sped far away to our Southern home,—held him, and glanced at the hot red soil of Georgia and the breathless city of a hundred hills, and felt a vague unrest. Why was his hair tinted with gold? An evil omen was golden hair in my life. Why had not the brown of his eyes crushed out and killed the blue?—for brown were his father's eyes, and his father's father's. And thus in the Land of the Color-line I saw, as it fell across my baby, the shadow of the Veil. (507)

The "evil omen" of "golden hair" (which resonates interestingly with the evil omen that Itylus's mother read in his smooth, seemingly innocent face); the potential of brown eyes to crush out and kill the blue; the color-line falling ominously across his baby—all constitute bodily metaphors—subsumed under the master concept-metaphor of "the Veil"—that allow Du Bois to intensify his understanding of the power always at work in racist contexts. Set alongside geographical metaphors such as "the hot red soil of Georgia" and "the breathless city of a hundred hills," Du Bois demonstrates to his reader that what lies beneath the smooth surface of such metaphors is the truth of reality as men and women of color live it daily, across class and gender differences. He gives us to know that it is the post-Reconstruction social context—with its violent racism and Jim Crow social policies—that kills Burghardt, as violently and as mercilessly as if the child had been taken forcibly from his bed and lynched.

Du Bois's use of biography to critique the color-line and the processes of double-consciousness continues in chapter 12, "Of Alexander Crummell," which draws its poetic paratext from Tennyson's *Idylls of the King in Twelve Books* (1859–1885). Du Bois cites lines 457–461:

> Then from the Dawn it seemed there came, but faint
> As from beyond the limit of the world,
> Like the last echo born of a great cry,
> Sounds, as if some fair city were one voice
> Around a king returning from his wars.

This stanza is accompanied by bars from yet another archetypal Spiritual, "Swing Low, Sweet Chariot." Du Bois chooses bars of music accompanying these lines:

> Swing low, sweet chariot
> Coming for to carry me home.
> Swing low, sweet chariot . . .

We shall turn first to the Spiritual before giving our attention to Tennyson's poem. Harry Burleigh writes that the lines of the Spiritual refer to the "translation" of the prophet Elijah into heaven, depicted in 2 Kings 2:11 of the King James Version of the Bible: "And it came to pass, as they still went on, and talked, that, behold, there appeared a chariot of fire, and horses of fire, and parted them both asunder; and Elijah went up by a whirlwind into heaven." Elijah, the Old Testament prophet, was a defender of the supreme God against competing Canaanite and Phoenician cults. In fact, Elijah emerges as one of the most important of the major prophets: in the time of the New Testament, John the Baptist took pains to clarify to the people that he was neither the Messiah, Elijah, nor "the Prophet,"[28] for Elijah was expected to return to the earth, and is said, in the Gospel of Mark, to have witnessed the transfiguration of Jesus along with Moses.[29]

Du Bois, who takes Crummell as his biographical subject in this chapter, immediately draws the image of Crummell as analogous to that of the Biblical prophet Elijah as well as the Arthurian legend of King Arthur. His reference to Elijah in a paratext to his brief biography of Crummell underscores the luminosity of Crummell's character and legacy to Du Bois's mind; and the fact that Elijah was expected to return to earth and continue his work as a prophet lends added longevity to the legacy of Crummell, whose soul, upon his death, "fled like a flame across the Seas" (520).

The Tennyson paratext Du Bois uses is drawn from the section of *Idylls of the King* known as "The Passing of Arthur," whose title resonates with "Of the Passing of the First Born." Arthur was a legendary king of Britain, and stories of his life and the Round Table of knights he formed were written by Crétien de Troye, Malory, and other medieval writers. Tennyson, whose *Idylls* spearheaded the revival of interest in the Arthurian legend in the nineteenth century and was itself enormously popular, also developed the form known as the "English Idyl" (spelled with one "l"), in which luxurious vignettes of the English countryside and landscape were combined with "relaxed debate" of current social issues. Indeed, *Idylls*, which was both prefaced by and concluded with poems addressed to Queen Victoria, served to reinforce an image of a perfect monarchy that ruled over an ever-expanding British empire. Beyond the political, as Tennyson put it, "My meaning was spiritual. I only took the legendary stories of the Round Table as illustrations. Arthur was allegorical to me. I intended him to represent the Ideal in the Soul of Man coming into contact with the warring elements of the flesh."[30] In this way, we should readily see Tennyson's poetic paratext as one of a piece with that of William Sharp, another commentator on the temperament of the monarchy, the value of Scottish and Irish heritage, and the perfection of ideals.

Tennyson was hailed as the successor to Keats and Shelley, and his work anticipated the themes of the French Symbolists of the 1880s as well as the symbolism of Arthur Symons, whose poem, "The Crying of Water" prefaces chapter 1 of *Souls*. He and Robert Browning are credited with developing a use of the "dramatic monologue" in their poetry, which grants the poem a polyphonic quality by revealing not only the thought of the poet but also the viewpoint of the impersonated character. This technique likely draws its influence from Shakespeare and evolves out of the soliloquy, of which Du Bois gives an example when he cites, in this same chapter, the soliloquy from *Hamlet* (iii.i 69–73). The scene ends more militantly (or perhaps, more melancholically) than an isolated reading of Du Bois's excerpt shows. Du Bois chooses to fold a fragment of the soliloquy into his own prose, rendering it dialogic: as he recounts Crummell's sense of dejection when suffering one of the many scenes of humiliation he endured as a young man of color seeking to undertake meaningful work in modern society. The *Hamlet* fragment flows out of Du Bois's description of Crummell's state of mind in the wake of Bishop Onderdonk's rejection of him (517–518):

Then the full weight of his burden fell upon him. The rich walls wheeled away, and before him lay the cold rough moor winding on through life, cut in twain by one thick granite ridge,—here, the Valley of Humiliation; yonder, the Valley of the Shadow of Death. And I know not which be darker,—no, not I. But this I know: in yonder Vale of the Humble stand to-day a million swarthy men, who willingly would

> ". . . bear the whips and scorns of time,
> The oppressor's wrong, the proud man's contumely,
> The pangs of despised love, the law's delay,
> The insolence of office, and the spurns
> That patient merit of the unworthy takes, . . ."

The passage from *Hamlet* ends with lines Du Bois chooses not to quote:

> When he himself might his quietus make
> With a bare bodkin?

Whether one reads the tone of the passage as militant or melancholic (suicidal), the echoes of death that resound through this passage likewise echo in the paratext from Tennyson, in the essay's repeated references to the "Valley of the Shadow of Death," in "Swing Low, Sweet Chariot," and in the very trajectory of Crummell's life. When the Episcopal priest Crummell is denied full entrée to Bishop Onderdonk's diocese, he faces the Valley of Humiliation (to which Du Bois also refers more obliquely as the "Vale of the Humble"—these two monikers are etymologically related to one another; they come from the Latin "humil-," meaning "low" or "lowly"). Du Bois writes: "You might have noted only the physical dying, the shattered frame and hacking cough; but in that soul lay deeper death than that" (518), that is, yet another valley through which Crummell was to pass.

The reference recalls distinctly Tennyson's depiction of King Arthur's slow course to death, the long durée of his passing away. Indeed, the three chapters that precede the final essay on the Sorrow Songs are each about such moral rectitude as Arthur's folding violently in the face of the world's harshness and misrecognition. Burghardt loved innocently and without regard to color before the constraints of the color-line itself brought about his death. John Jones of chapter 13 not only seeks to edify his community in the face of severe social constraints, but also to defend his sister valiantly against rape by a white man. Alexander Crummell, an upstanding, moral young priest, is bewildered in the shadows of the world's racial vicissitudes, which dimmed his emerging hopes and left in their stead what Du Bois describes as three dismal temptations: Hate, Death, and Doubt. These and the "Sacrifice of Humiliation" brought Crummell near to dying more than once. But, Du Bois writes, "The Valley of the Shadow of Death" gave Crummell back to the world, as it gives back only a few of its wanderers—sage prophets or knights errant, we might say, with a nod toward the Spiritual singers in their evocation of the prophet Elijah, and to Tennyson in his allegorical depiction of King Arthur. Du Bois uses a number of metaphorical images to underscore this movement between life and death: there is the figure of the gate in the Spiritual, in the Arthurian epic, as well as in the essay's conclusion; and there is also the figure of the whirling wind, which moves from West to East.

The link between the whirl of life and the valley of death intimated in the biography of Crummell is articulated explicitly by the Spiritual singers, who, in evoking Elijah's translation into heaven by a whirlwind, aid Du Bois's metaphorical allusions in the final lines of the essay. There, he depicts Crummell sitting beside a gate whose hinges are rusty and will not hold. The word "gate" appears only twice in "Of Alexander Crummell," both times at the culmination of the chapter, but in Biblical phraseology the gateway to a city was generally the site of judgment by a king or a judicial body. In Greek legends, which influence Arthurian literature such as Tennyson's, the gate metaphor was evoked as an imagistic conduit of true and false dreams. The *Oxford English Dictionary* defines a gate as a way, path, or road, and underscores that the word often alludes metaphorically to a journey or course of action. Thus, we might also speak of the journey metaphor as it gives shape to the Burghardt, Crummell, and John essays (and even to *The Souls of Black Folk* as a whole): each essay chronicles a life from beginning to end, marking its innocence, its knowing (a loss of innocence), and its tragedy, actions, and hope.

Such imagery holds a clear connection with the metaphor of the gate as portal, and the analogous motif of the journey: Crummell is depicted as a pilgrim, a wayfarer in the world, one who is simply passing through and whose nature it is, or so it seems at least, to feel quite alone and without home in this world. In some way, Du Bois brings this motif to fruition in the final chapter of *Souls*, "Of the Sorrow Songs," when he writes of exile, of weary travelers, of the foreign tongue of his great-grandmother, and of the hidden and at times esoteric epistemology of the slave. For "Swing Low, Sweet Chariot," the musical paratext of "Of Alexander Crummell," likewise conveys images of air, portals, and bodies of water; its figurative language hearkens to broad metaphors of transition that serve to categorize the narrower figures of wind, gates, and the sea. The wind, the gate, and the sea each provide imagery that evokes ideas of transformation and progression. None of them indicates stasis; rather, each alerts the reader to the inevitability of change and chance. The sea and the wind in particular, used as metaphors for and symbols of sublimity, are elemental tropes that recur in the text. This is, then, an underexamined figure at work throughout the book and throughout the African American literary tradition, for *Souls* is, in its entirety, about movement, psychic as well as physical, and about how, to my mind at least, all of these things have quite a bit to do with what black being, black existence, signifies, with the meaning sedimented within seemingly uncomplicated and straightforward narratives of black life.[31]

The paratexts to chapter 13, "Of the Coming of John," are of some significance, not least in their relation to the Spiritual that serves as paratext to "Of Alexander Crummell." First, the title of the essay plays on the idea of the coming of Christ, thus imputing to the title character, John Jones, a salvific quality. Indeed, as we see by the end of Du Bois's narrative, much of which is fictional save some similarities to the setting of the town of Altamaha Park, Georgia, which sits on the Altamaha River featured in the story, John Jones is indeed a Christ-like being whose sacrifice by lynching at the end of the story provides the narrative tragedy. The title of the story also evokes the name of John the Baptist, whose regular habit of baptizing converts in the waters of the river Jordan reinforces Du Bois's imagery of the sea in his fictional biography of the life of John of Altamaha.

More than this, Du Bois's use of the name John resounds with that of Elijah, who figures prominently in the Spiritual "Swing Low," which prefaces "Of Alexander Crummell." John the Baptist and the prophet Elijah alike preached by the River Jordan, and while John baptized converts to his teachings in Jordan's waters, Elijah, as I have mentioned, defended the monotheism of his God and, like Moses, parted the waters of the Jordan. The Jordan is arguably the most sacred river of Christendom, not least because Christ was baptized by John in its waters.[32] Baptisms John performed in flowing waters such as those of the Jordan would have been understood as the cleansing away of severe forms of uncleanness; such cleansings were intended to bring about forgiveness and repentance. Thus, John's baptisms mediated divine forgiveness and forecasted the coming of a beneficent savior who would both judge and restore Israel. The implications of this are eschatological (having to do with the final judgment and end of the world) as well as apocalyptic (that is, revelatory of a new beginning after this ultimate destruction, such as is foretold in the Book of Revelation).

Elizabeth Barrett Browning's poem "A Romance of the Ganges" (1838), the paratext to "The Coming of John," reinforces the important motif of the river, which thus becomes allegorical. Du Bois cites these lines (521):

> What bring they 'neath the midnight,
> Beside the River-sea?
> They bring the human heart wherein
> No nightly calm can be;
> That droppeth never with the wind,
> Nor drieth with the dew;
> Oh, calm it God! thy calm is broad
> To cover spirits too.
> The river floweth on.

The fuller poem is about love lost, about the strains and ambivalences of friendship, about life and death and the sites of each. Central to the poem's imagery is the Ganges River, holy in the Hindu faith and continuously flowing. Even so, time and memory seem not so swiftly carried along its waves, for Luti, the poem's heroine, still dwells upon the anguish of her father's death as poignantly as the more recent betrayal of her lover. Du Bois takes the tragic imagery of the river-sea from the poem and transforms it into that of the sea in "Of the Coming of John": the "moving men" of New York city, who "reminded John of the sea" (525); the "music of Lohengrin's swan" whose force caused John's heart to sink "below the waters, even as the sea-sand sinks by the shores of the Altamaha, only to be lifted again with that last ethereal wail of the swan that quivered and faded away into the sky"; John's solitary walk down to the sea in mournful realization that the people of Altamaha not only misunderstand him, but, more importantly, are not in accord with the plan of uplift he has envisioned (530); and, finally the sea-side as the site of white John's assault upon black John's sister, Jennie, as well as black John's retributive murder of white John (535). It is toward the sea that John turns as the lynch mob, which he pities rather than despises, descends upon him. As the mob approaches, he hums "Song of the Bride," again from Wagner's Lohengrin. Du Bois alters the libretto to fit his intent: "Freudig gefürht, ziehet dahin" ("Joyfully led, move along").[33] It seems, then, that although John is resigned to his death, he also sees his own death as sacrificial, and thus as entailing a necessary resurrection and renewed life in a day yet to come (a day when those forces that work to constrain him will no longer have power over him). Philosophical as to his fate but looking joyfully to the same "world beyond" that called Alexander

Crummell's soul and embraced that of baby Burghardt, John can easily be envisioned as a spirit baptized in the waters of the Altamaha and resurrected in the spirit-world beyond its sandy shores.

Likewise, the reader easily imagines the Spiritual that prefaces John's story as a meaningful alternative to Wagner's "Song of the Bride." This is especially so as one reads the slave singers' apocalyptic lyrics that accompany the bars of music Du Bois excerpts from "You May Bury Me in the East":

> You may bury me in the East
> You may bury me in the West
> But I'll hear the trumpet sound
> In that morning

The trumpet of the slaves' song refers to the centrally important figure of the trumpet in the Book of Revelation. Trumpets were sounded by angels at the opening of each of the seven seals. The opening of the first six of these were followed by horrific plagues, while the seventh proclaimed the power of God's kingdom (Rev 11:15–19). Later in this final book of the Bible, after we read of the casting out of Satan and the defeat of the beast, the appearance of New Jerusalem is allegorized as "a bride adorned for her husband" (Rev 21:2). This metaphor alluded to in the Spiritual resonates directly with the imagery of *Lohengrin*, but goes further in its connotations. It conveys to the listener that God would not be less than his word: he would preserve the humble but faithful man, even if he be a slave, through the restoration of God's kingdom. The body of the slave, the song gives us to know, may be buried in the temporal world, on ground holy or profane; but the slave's soul will rise in that "great getting up morning," and will ascend to a heavenly realm of peace, love, and redemption. When coupled with the essay and read alongside the reference to *Lohengrin*, "You May Bury Me in the East" signals to the reader John's honor, heroism, and redemptive qualities. It is also a powerful, poetic condemnation of the Jim Crow South.

Navigating the Undulating Waters of Being:
The Spirituals and the Possibilities of Metaphor

Any study of the Spirituals must begin and end in the realm or sphere in which these songs were developed and continue to exist, the realm Aristotle calls nature, and that we, in our more recent historical moment, call "reality," the existential plane that includes not only the physical world in which we live, but also the human condition of this world. Nature is itself a principle of change, Aristotle tells us, and human beings existing in a state of change can navigate its undulating waters through acts of consciousness, such as thought and art, that evidence an awareness of one's condition. It is such awareness that founds the possibility of agency and freedom. Such awareness also founds the possibility of the Spirituals.

These states of awareness, or acts of the mind that Du Bois refers to as the inner life of the slave, center upon imagination because imagination permits not reality, but an insight into reality. Freedom, which was habitually sung by the Spiritual singers, comes only through an understanding and interpretation of one's own condition, such that through understanding one's current state of existence, one can imagine—and in turn, bring into reality—a different state of being. The Spiritual singers' primary obedience was not to the state of enslavement and oppression in which they found themselves, but to the revolution in imagination that permitted them to arrest and redirect reality. The minimum requirement of such imagination, so to speak, is metaphor, the ability to, as Aristotle put it, "see as," to place reality before one's own eyes as well as the eyes of others, to project oneself toward an ideal world yet to come, and to imagine a cognitive bridge that spans the distance between what is and what is to be. It is from this site of metaphorical imagination that the slaves' songs sprung. They lived in a place not their own, and, even more to the point, their bodies were not their own in the illogic of their day. And thus their psychic resistance often came through metaphorization: the doubled meaning of words and phrases; the transposition of meaning across epistemological categories; the rendering of allegory and myth; the simultaneity of abstraction and concretization in imagery; and the rendering of narrative through silence and repetitive sound (such as ritual omission and repeated moans rather than transparent words with quite obvious meanings).

The theoretical postulate of Du Bois's use of these songs in *Souls*, along with his belles lettres essays and widely known citations of European and Euro-American poetry, is a world of metaphor, where the poets'—in this case, the Spiritual singers'—imagination engages the world of reality around them with a dual aim. First, they aimed to affect and redirect reality through their intellectual engagement with it. Second, they aimed to give voice to their own being through a poetry of "revelation." Certainly, this has to do with the apocalyptic meanings at work in many of the Spirituals Du Bois chooses for his reader. But we should also be careful to point out that the Spirituals' apocalyptic discourse is not so much nihilistic or fatalistic as it is expansive, visionary, and unorthodox: regularly, their musical discourse drew upon accepted notions of time and space to further expound an ideal and infinite world beyond the one generally given as "real." It repeats metaphors of hearing and perception that make clear the slaves' intention to achieve in each song a unique expression (through lyrics as well as sound, pitch, harmony, cadence, and so on), and to force the listener to attempt a commensurate act of apprehension that leads to an understanding of the breadth and plurality of human being, a movement toward the plural ideal of "human brotherhood," as Du Bois calls it in "The Conservation of Races" and elsewhere.

The meaning of black being, Du Bois says clearly throughout *Souls*'s many and important metaphors, is identical to the meaning of human being. Thus the Spirituals Du Bois gives the reader of *The Souls of Black Folk* do not simply found an aesthetic tradition that Du Bois calls truly American; they also, in their attempt to place before the listener a reality not his or her own, place before the listener the self-conscious beings that he or she is not. As a result, Du Bois presents to his reader not a set of anonymous spiritual fatalists, but a collective of essential, thinking poets.

7

Symbolic Wrights

The Poetics of Being Underground

Incipit

And there in that great iron city, that impersonal, mechanical city, amid the steam, the smoke, the snowy winds, the blistering suns; there in that self-conscious city, that city so deadly dramatic and stimulating, we caught whispers of the meanings that life could have, and we were pushed and hounded by facts much too big for us. Migrants like us were driven and pursued, in the manner of characters in a Greek play, down the path of defeat; but luck must have been with us, for we somehow survived; and, for those of us who did not come through, we are trying to do the bidding of Hamlet who admonished Horatio:

> If thou didst ever hold me in thy heart,
> Absent thee from felicity awhile,
> And in this harsh world draw thy breath in pain,
> To tell my story. [*Hamlet* Act 5 Sc. 2]

—Richard Wright's Introduction to *Black Metropolis*, 1945

It is fitting that Wright himself should provide the incipit for the work of this chapter. For in the epigraph above, drawn from his introduction to Horace Cayton and St Clair Drake's *Black Metropolis* (1945), Wright is deeply concerned with a similar metaphorics of chaos and cosmos, apertures and closings, heights and depths, and beginnings and endings that occupy me throughout this study. Wright was one of the greatest interlocutors on the modern implications of such dialectical oppositions, especially as they occur in the arena of political discourse and novelistic representation. As in his best known work of fiction, *Native Son* (1940), Wright's narratives gave birth to a broad new way of conceptualizing modern black life in

281

America; indeed, *Native Son*'s greatest explicit claim is that Bigger Thomas, the novel's tragic protagonist, is himself the scion of modern America and its split human condition. Thus as a metaphor, Bigger represents not black America alone, but America itself, replete with its ambivalences, paradoxes, ironies, and cataclysms. Bigger is America's natural and native son.

Yet even as much of our criticism has focused primarily on the ideological problems Wright raises in his fiction and especially in *Native Son*, there remains a need for further criticism focusing upon the workings of Wright's poetics in *The Man Who Lived Underground* (1944). In the wealth of literature on Wright, the main features of his poetics certainly have not gone unnoticed by critics,[1] yet most writers have focused upon *Native Son*, of course, with a second majority looking at his later fiction, especially *The Outsider* (1953). New critical interest in Wright's poetry is fast emerging. However, the fundamental innovation that Wright's poetics represents in this novella, which is, of late, woefully under-studied,[2] its differential relation to similar poetics found throughout the African American canon, and its potential for subversive action and knowledge have not yet received sufficient attention in the scholarship. In drawing our attention to Wright's poetics, I do not mean to underscore simply the structural and formal elements at work in his mode of art, but the affective force of his tropes, and the symbolic exchange he establishes between the conceptual metaphors he creates and the world beyond his texts. Wright himself calls our attention to such matters of the text when he opines, in "Blueprint for Negro Writing" (1937), that the "image and emotion" of literature "possess a logic of their own" (1410). Like Equiano, Harper, and Du Bois before him, he insists that affect and imagery—including figures of language—are capable of granting form, meaning, and access to a new and better world.

The novella *The Man Who Lived Underground*, paradoxically points the way to life in such a world through the complexity of its philosophical metaphors. In considering the novella, this chapter examines a characteristic element of Wright's poetics and the central metaphor of this story: the habitation of the chthonian world. This trope has, of course, attracted the attention of many of Wright's critics, most of whom, however, see it as Wright's bleak and pessimistic judgment of the world's sorry state of affairs.[3] My approach differs from this perspective. I see Wright's fundamental metaphor of psychic and bodily descent as emblematic of the ways in which archetypal tropes of death and life, guilt and freedom, time and space, memory and oblivion, and dreaming and waking facilitate the text's demand for a new and better world. Wright's novella underscores the value he places upon the exactness and complexity of the metaphorical image in narrative, and the relation between metaphorical images and the words used to convey them. Thus, as he, in the words of Shakespeare, draws his breath in pain to tell the story of the underground man, the task he sets before the reader is that of discerning the affinities of metaphorical language and human being, even as they are condensed in the weathered patina of the tragic anti-hero. The tonal images and sedimented emotions of *The Man Who Lived Underground* form a tropological stream of discourse in which the novella not only probes its own status as a work of art, but also demonstrates the ways in which Wright's theory and practice of metaphor touch on and contribute to broader philosophical issues of the crises of social belonging, the liminality of black existence, and the historicity of black being.

Of course, as I have shown, the use of ontological metaphorics takes place throughout the tradition of African American poetry and prose alike. In this study, I consider it as unfolding not in the *pursuit* of being (as has often been argued by such noted scholars as Henry Louis Gates, Jr., in *Figures in Black* (1987) and in *The Signifying Monkey* (1988), that is, that African Americans have used inventive metaphorical strategies to "write themselves into existence" and to "prove" their humanity, and thereby they establish or enter into historicity), but in the sociopolitical *revelation* of black being, or black being-in-the-world, to adapt the Heideggerian sense of this phrase to my purpose, such that the always already being of African Americans is granted, even the always already of their so-called racial difference. In *The Souls of Black Folk*, as we have seen, Du Bois metaphorically uses bars of music to preface each of his essays as a representation of black being, even though they also constitute an instantiation of silence. Human expression is transfigured into silence in Du Bois's text, yet this silence signifies both literally (as "visible music") and metaphorically, by way of absent lyrics. The bars of music function as graphemes that call us to a recognition of language, to an engagement with language. And thus, drawing upon the ontological a bit further here, being, not simply as particularity but also as existential thought in relation with the present as well as future worlds, inhabits this language.

In using bars of music to represent the Spirituals and, thus, the thought of the slave regarding her present and future conditions, Du Bois does not pursue or bestow being through his prose. Rather, he reveals its always already existence by thinking and sharing the poetics of the slaves with his reader. Ethical work is done through this gesture in *Souls*, for how can one grasp the truth of being writ large if one denies the existence of black being there within the veil? Sociopolitical work is done as well: Du Bois demonstrates how the slave and post-slave populations project their being toward the world through the art of metaphor.

Here, then, we must see the Spirituals not simply as ecstatic religious expression, but as an ek-static[4] instance of allegorical thinking. Allegorical thought, a species of metaphorical thinking, is also hermeneutical engagement, a thinking and an interpretation that have to do with a sustained engagement with worldly concerns, existential concerns. In this way, the Spirituals have much to do with an afterlife, yes; but they also have much to do with a critical concern for the world in which the slaves lived, and the world they themselves envisioned and created.

It must be said that Richard Wright had little understanding of the poetics of the Spirituals in the way I read them here. For Wright, the Spirituals provided fertile ground for the exposition of a pre-modern culture that must be overcome and surpassed.[5] He saw little of the modern possibilities—intellectual as well as political—that Du Bois saw in the Spirituals. Instead, Wright proffers them in *The Man Who Lived Underground* as evidence of a collective people's guilt. This point will require some explanation.

It is true that Richard Wright, in "Blueprint for Negro Writing," considered African American expression, including folklore, Spirituals, and the blues, to be a font of "racial wisdom" (1405), and he believed that Negro culture stemmed from the black church and African American folklore. Yet he also felt that, since the Civil War, the black church had functioned as an inadequate and even deceptive "antidote for suffering and denial" (1404). While he allows that black religion constituted an important element of early black radicalism and nationalism, Wright argued that Negroes of his own day were still apt to look to the church as the source of "their only sense of the whole universe, [their] only relation to society and mind" and their "only guide to personal dignity" (1404). Such over-dependence upon black religion and black folklore for the development of the Negro's *weltanschauung* is as manifest in black nationalism as it is in black institutions such as "a Negro church, a Negro press, a Negro social world, a Negro sporting world, a Negro business world, a Negro school system; in short, a Negro way of life in America," Wright insists (1406). Though African Americans did not ask for these separate social institutions, Wright states, they are compelled to accept them as integral aspects of a way of life that has been forced upon them by the oppressive social and political systems of the southern United States, especially.

Wright reiterates that African American writers must, in turn, embrace black nationalism and its constituent elements—including religious expression—as organic to black existence in America, but they must do so only with an eye toward transcending them. He argues:

Negro writers must accept the nationalist implications of their lives, not in order to encourage them, but in order to change and transcend them. They must accept the concept of nationalism because, in order to transcend it, they must possess and understand it. And a national spirit in Negro writing means a nationalism carrying the highest possible pitch of social consciousness. It means a nationalism that knows its origins, its limitations; that is aware of the dangers of its position; that knows its ultimate aims are unrealizable within the framework of capitalist America; a nationalism whose reason for being lies in the simple fact of self-possession and in the consciousness of the interdependence of people in modern society. (1406)

Though the black folk were full of potential as a natural proletariat, black folk were also guilty in Wright's mind because they refused the power of choice that was endemic to modern freedom: they could choose to move beyond nationalism; they could choose a broader form of thought. Instead, in Wright's view, they had refused the self-consciousness and awareness that Du Bois seems to accept as intrinsic to the black folk expression that founds black nationalism itself, at least in Wright's genealogy of the concept. Wright argued that black folk expression, especially in the Spirituals, was not a simple stage along the way to transcending an overly simplistic black nationalism, but that black folk expression in the Spirituals and other vernacular forms could, at the same time, be tapped as a source for the transcendence of the worldly limits of racism and oppression, a way of attaining, however tenuously, a state of psychic freedom and the realities of bodily freedom. Du Bois, too, recognized the signal importance of folk expression in American culture, but refused to call for its sublimation,[6] as did a number of his contemporaries, including James Weldon Johnson.[7] Du Bois, having completed his exposition of the Spirituals in the final chapter of *Souls*, links them directly to the cause of democracy. He sees them as cultural expressions that could help obliterate the global color-line that is one of the central foci of his critique. This is why, perhaps, we note that sharp shift in tone near the conclusion of *The Souls of Black Folk*, when Du Bois, after providing one of the earliest critical treatments of the Spirituals, which are indeed songs of freedom, in both the spiritual and moral senses of this term,[8] abruptly and brashly interrogates whites' supposed sole possession of freedom, which they ensured by claiming a racially exclusive national identity. "Your country? How came it yours?" Du Bois queries incisively, before launching a searing critique of American national history, in which

African Americans and their cultural expressions played a central and definitive role. The conclusion of his strident exposition is the articulation of a radical vision of democracy.

Wright, of course, did not note Du Bois's revisionist perspective on the Spirituals in "Blueprint." Yet his erstwhile protégé, Ralph Ellison, for whom *The Man Who Lived Underground* would be instructive as a model and as thematic inspiration, forcefully takes up Du Bois's attention to the intersections of black folk culture and radical democracy when he raises a similar question regarding freedom in his 1952 novel, *Invisible Man*. There, his concern for freedom is expressed through metaphors of ideal democracy, but his approach, too, contrasts sharply with Wright's. The invisible man's quip, "I yam what I am" (266), and his forging in the very crucible of black folk culture that is so important yet so seemingly dispensable to Wright, call us to a greater consideration of the historicity of black being and its continual efforts to make itself known even as it stretches forth toward an ideal world to come. Black being, as such, has had to contend with processes of objectification that arose in the early modern period, a period contemporary to the rise of Western imperialism in the fifteenth century, and that extends through the modern Civil Rights movement of the mid-twentieth century to our own day. Embodiedness, and the phenomenology of the black body, are issues in constant question in the work of each of these writers and thus they are frequently at the center of a poetics of being in African American culture and African American metaphorical constructions.

For metaphor, as Aristotle has taught us in the *Poetics*, sets before the eyes an image that relates the reality in which being is situated; it permits the grasping of the dissimilar within the similar, a transgression of categories of identity and a deviance from established sets of knowledge. Such oppositionality is false, of course, as the othering of the black body in particular takes place via the exigencies and dictates of white Western capital and political power. Wright makes clear his awareness of this point in "Blueprint." Yet Wright, like Du Bois before him and Ellison after him, employs metaphor in an effort to establish a rapport with the white Western reader (though he does not readily admit this point) and to commune with the reader of African descent by way of a subject/object paradigm quite familiar to the American reader (with whiteness occupying a position of subjectivity and knowing, and blackness relegated to an antithetical position of objecthood and inscrutability). And while Wright, unlike writers such as Du Bois, does not suggest to the reader a clear path of action as black being is revealed, he nonetheless offers her or him an ironic and subversive portrait of conscious black being and an alternative pathway to ideal humanism.

I suggest that the alternate pathway Wright offers is hewn subtly out of his antagonistic relationship to black folk culture and black folk expression. It is no simple thing that Wright's works remain compelling to the present generation of readers. I would argue that this is so because Wright's novels, essays, short stories, and novellas (to say nothing of his poetry) present to the reader a disturbing but crystal clear (if not at times purposely hyperbolic) portrait of the journey of black being in mid-twentieth century America. Whereas the fiction of Zora Neale Hurston (whose writing Wright disparaged) might have provided her reader inspiration for living, Wright shows his reader the clear path to death. In Wright's narratives, this pathway is littered with his protagonists' choices, which in most instances of Wright's fiction—the so-called later Wright in exile as well as the early Wright who wrote about the South from his perch in the urban North— disallow the freedom for which the protagonists dearly yearn. The wages of guilt, that is, the recompense for a refusal of consciousness, comprise the lesson one draws from Wright's fiction, but this is a lesson the reader must learn on his or her own. Wright does not specify how we must act, that is, in what ways we should demonstrate our care and concern for others through ethical action, as do canonical figures throughout the African American literary tradition, including the eighteenth-century autobiographer Olaudah Equiano, the nineteenth-century poet and novelist and activist Frances Ellen Watkins Harper, and the scholar Du Bois. Yet we, as did the protest agents of the 1960s who embraced Wright's work unequivocally, know that we must. Wright's greatest gift to us is such knowledge.

The grounds for an agency-based knowledge such as that Wright limns are firmly situated in a poetics of underground life: one must immerse oneself in the consciousness of the underground in order to grasp the global consciousness that comes with freedom. In *The Man Who Lived Underground*, Wright's poetics take shape through metaphors of chaos and cosmos, two oppositional, ontological tropes of understanding whose boundaries Wright transgresses even as he transposes the categories' content. Chaos becomes cosmos in Wright's revisionist text, and it then serves as the basis for revisionist and revolutionary thinking. By consequence, cosmos is shown to be not only inadequate, but also deceptive. That Wright's underground visionary, Fred Daniels, is remanded to death even as he seeks to emerge from his underground space seems pure tragedy and ahumanist, but a careful reading of the story reveals its affective intention: Wright intends that the reader become outraged, and if we gauge carefully the outcomes he intends his work to inspire, outrage, in turn, is transfigured into an ethical emotion, an expression of concern and care for freedom and for conscious being.

Mapping Black Ontology and Black Freedom:
"Blueprint for Negro Writing" in Context

I have said that one sees clearly Wright's concern for the ethics of emotion and freedom in literature in the 1937 essay, "Blueprint for Negro Writing." "Blueprint" follows other early attempts by writers such as Frances E. W. Harper ("Christianity," 1855), James Weldon Johnson (Preface to the *Book of American Negro Poetry*, 1922), and W. E. B. Du Bois ("Criteria of Negro Art," 1926) to articulate a poetics of African American literature and to outline the function of this literature in relation to black existence in American society, and it is instructive to contextualize Wright's stance within this genealogy of thinkers. Doing so will permit us to restore to Wright's essay the critical contexts he so neatly and purposefully strips away. It permits us to see Wright's criticism emerging not *ex nihilo*, as he so often portrayed it, but out of a vibrant critical debate over the function and poetics of black writing in America dating back at least to the mid-nineteenth century. And it allows us to frame Wright's ambivalent relationship to African American folk culture in a critical and historical light so that we might see more clearly the workings of folk expression and black spirituality in *The Man Who Lived Underground*. Such insight is indispensable to grasping the meaning at play in the narrative.

Early among African American thinkers on poetics is Harper, for whom philosophy and science are subservient to Christian ideals that she feels are the motive force behind her creative process. Both "have paused amid their speculative researches and wondrous revelations, to gain wisdom from [Christianity's] teachings and knowledge from her precepts." They "may bring their abstruse researches," but they are simply "idle tales compared to the truths of Christianity" (42). Christianity, which comes to be expanded to religion in general in this essay, "lifts the veil," "triumphs over" death, and "gazes upon the glorious palaces of God" as it instructs the individual in ways of being (42–43).

Harper might seem quite far from Wright's poetics, but as a theorist of the relationship between religion and literature, and as one of the most significant nineteenth-century writers to draw upon black folk expression for her poetry, a consideration of her thought is crucial. What becomes important in reading Harper here is a recognition of her willingness to abstract from the Christian faith and religion in general the "Word of God"—itself a metaphor for being, as it refers to both the written text of the Bible and the Bible made flesh in the body of Christ—which she privileges as "unique and pre-eminent" (43). Harper believed in the power of the Word, that is, the original and divine Word of God coupled with the potential of black vernacular (as she demonstrates in her Aunt Chloe poems, the focus of chapter 4 of this study) to provide humans with enlightenment and understanding. She exhibits none of Plato's angst regarding the likelihood of deception in vernacular language's representation of divine inspiration, and none of Wright's concern that black religiosity must be surpassed. Instead, she imagines this Word as aided by the Holy Spirit, who, it would seem, acts as a medium for those divinely inspired poets and orators who speak God's Word on earth. As a poet, Harper saw herself as receptive to the Holy Spirit, who gives shape to her literature and her poetic discourse. "Poetry has culled [Christianity's] fairest flowers and wreathed her softest, to bind her Author's 'bleeding brow'" (40). "Literature [may bring] her elegance, with the toils of the pen, and the labors of the pencil" (42), but literature without religion, without God, is, Harper says firmly, form without content, shadow without substance. The divine word is the only begetter of her earthly verse.

If we see "Christianity" as a statement of Harper's aesthetics, the essay morphs before our eyes from a fundamentalist riff on the glories of the Christian faith to an extended meditation on the powers of the Word, both sacred and secular. Harper's poetics and "amateur" ethnography, her collecting of the stories of Civil War–era black women and her translation of these stories into narrative, polyphonic verse that is shaped by black folk expression, reflects the relation she sees between black religion, the Word of God, and black vernacular speech. Literature, then, is an artifact that carries out a sacred and perhaps even ritualistic purpose—it aids humans as an intermediary, a buffer of sorts between the hostile world in which we exist and have our being, and the ideal world of divine sanctuary that we strive for through action and imagination. It is a way of seizing power and making meaning by imposing a form upon the chaos of the known world at the same time that it allows us to grant comprehensible form to our own wants and desires for a world to come.

In this light, Harper's poetics, exemplified in such representations of African American Christian religious practices as we see in the Aunt Chloe poems, seem in abstruse ways to be aligned with Wright's conclusion that black struggles for freedom during the antebellum period took place via the struggle for religious expression. Such contention "on the plantations between 1820–60," Wright asserts, regularly "assumed the form of a struggle for human rights" (1404). Seen through this lens, Harper's focus upon religious expression and ideals is not as deeply rooted in bourgeois middle-class thought as it first appears to many critics of her work. In fact, it is deeply invested in a vision of conscious being, ideal humanism, and, as Wright puts it, human rights.

James Weldon Johnson's critical Preface to his anthology, the *Book of American Negro Poetry* (1922), is likewise undoubtedly concerned with human rights, but reflects none of the deep belief in religion that marks Harper's poetics. It has become famous in no small measure due to the breadth of the poetry Johnson references there, but also as a result of the force with which he puts forth his poetics of African American music and literature. The Preface contains a range of literary and cultural criticism; it appeared 10 years after the initial publication of Johnson's *Autobiography of an Ex-Coloured Man* (1912/1927), a novel whose exploration of black cultural and vernacular forms, as well as its interrogation of black embodiedness and the phenomenology of race, is in discourse with Du Bois's *Souls*, and Wright's *The Man Who Lived Underground*, as well as Ellison's *Invisible Man*. Johnson's Preface boasts his best known prognostication of the future of African American poetics, a prognostication Wright likely took issue with through his oblique references to unnamed black critics going "a-begging" ("Blueprint" 1403) to white critics and readers. Johnson writes:

> The final measure of the greatness of all peoples is the amount and standard of the literature and art they have produced. The world does not know that a people is great until that people produces great literature and art. No people that has produced great literature and art has ever been looked upon by the world as distinctly inferior. (9)

Johnson was, of course, a race man, a proponent of black social freedom and equality who might be considered tangentially affiliated with the early twentieth-century cadre of black nationalists to whom Wright refers in "Blueprint." He held the firm belief that "the only things artistic that have yet sprung from American soil and been universally acknowledged as distinctive American products" (10) had arisen from the creative minds of the African American folk. He was not alone in his opinion that the great original art of African Americans would bolster them in their quest for a secure place in the American social sphere, nor was he this idea's best known proponent. W. E. B. Du Bois had written much the same in his 1903 classic *The Souls of Black Folk*, a text that shaped both the *Autobiography* and Johnson's Preface. In *Souls*, Du Bois opines that the African American "gift of story and song"—folk-songs in general and particularly the Spirituals—"the rhythmic cry of the slave—stands today not simply as the sole American music, but as the most beautiful expression of human experience born this side the seas [sic]" (545; 537). "It remains," Du Bois continues, "the singular spiritual heritage of the nation and the greatest gift of the Negro people" (537). Two decades later, in the 1926 piece "Criteria of Negro Art," Du Bois, who, along with the Jamaican immigrant Marcus Garvey, was known as a leading black nationalist and pan-Africanist, would underscore his earlier argument regarding the importance of black poetics as a matter of life or death by boldly stating that "until the art of the black folk compells [sic] recognition they will not be rated as human" (1002).[9]

The recognition of black being was thus closely aligned with a poetics of literature in the thought of Du Bois and Johnson, each of whom rooted their poetics in a valuation of vernacular cultural forms such as the Spirituals. The production and recognition of art and literature based on these vernacular artifacts was, for each of them, part of a larger political program whose goal was a concern for black existence, social equality, freedom, and the eventual abolition of racial distinctions. In his Preface, Johnson is quite careful to articulate these goals by way of literary and cultural poetics. In this respect, his political bent was not far afield from that of the English critic F. R. Leavis, who argued that the great tradition of English literature served as an intellectual clearing house of English common identity.[10] We often think of Johnson and the small number of other early African American critics as caught in a lonely but mighty struggle to make high art out of a black folk culture that was seen by so-called mainstream society as constituting nonsense. What we just as often forget or overlook is that, as is clear in the thought of Leavis and is demonstrated in the use of the Spirituals by Du Bois and Johnson, as well as in Harper's valuing of religion and black vernacular speech, folk expression in general was often viewed as a rich resource for modernist aesthetics by writers across Europe and America, black and white alike.

Many modernists were alarmed by the excesses of the industrial revolution and its decimation of soulful, traditional modes of being. Just as T. S. Eliot lays bare the heart of this malaise in his magnum opus, *The Waste Land* (1922), Wright gets at the marrow of this fear by showing the reader the effects of the soulless city on a black underclass in *The Man Who Lived Underground*. The effects are sobering and horrifying. Wright exacts a powerful critique of modern existence; he, no less than Leavis, lays the foundation for cultural studies in his insistence that literature must bear a direct connection to other fields of study and discourses that work to convey the difficulties of the human condition, including philosophy, history, and political theory. And in spite of his insistence that black folk thought and its corollary black nationalist impulses be surpassed, he saw in the complex structures of black folk culture—including religion—a rich resource upon which the black writer and artist could and should draw. The writer who "seeks to function within his race as a purposeful agent has a serious responsibility," Wright argues. He must develop a complex consciousness that recognizes and responds to the global nature of life. This consciousness must draw upon the interaction between the local and the universal; it must "[draw] for its strength upon the fluid lore of a great people, and [mould] this lore with the concepts that move and direct the forces of history today" (1407). Wright averred that the writer could shepherd readers through a radical experience of deep moral self-interrogation by drawing upon and reshaping familiar and rich vernacular forms that were ripe for the cause, and that through the experience of reading works that were intellectually engaged and morally invested, people would examine their own lives and their own positionalities. They would, in turn, be compelled to *act* thoughtfully—with care and concern—through an engagement with literature.

The idea of literary studies as a site of deep engagement with the world was, as Robert J. C. Young notes, "a self-consciously political activity from the start" (*Torn Halves* 104). Du Bois, we recall, had said as much in 1897 when he argued, in "The Conservation of Races," an essay that is widely read as the most stringent articulation of Du Bois's black nationalist sentiments, that the establishment of an African American aesthetic tradition—a "Negro school of literature and art," as he termed it (822)—needed to be guided by the race's "representative" men, such as those of the American Negro Academy. Johnson was only 15 years of age at the time Du Bois presented "Conservation" as the Academy's inaugural address and was thus far too young for membership. Nonetheless, he aligns himself with the ideals of the Academy when, in his Preface, he argues for a poetics whereby "the colored poet in the United States" would "express the *racial spirit* by symbols from within rather than by symbols from without" (Preface 41; my italics). Intrinsic symbols would, for Johnson, provide the touchstone from which black being—the mind, the intellect, as well as the body—would stretch forward to engage through the language of metaphor an often hostile white world.

Wright's "Blueprint for Negro Writing," coming some 11 years after Du Bois's "Criteria of Negro Art" (1926) and appearing just as the Harlem Renaissance was coming firmly to a close (the year Zora Neale Hurston's *Their Eyes Were Watching God* appeared[11]), diverged from the ideas regarding the expression of being through literature expounded by Du Bois. In "Blueprint," Wright seems either blissfully unaware or stubbornly ignorant of Du Bois's "The Conservation of Races," which calls for the establishment of the very black social institutions that Wright lists in "Blueprint" as being overly dependent upon African American religion. And like Wright after him, Du Bois always intended that these separate institutions be abolished as soon as "the ideal of human brotherhood"—the global humanism that was so important to Wright—was realistically possible and attainable. Wright and Du Bois alike called for solidarity among African Americans, a higher consciousness and a critically revised understanding of humanism. The major weakness of Richard Wright's "Blueprint" is that he never discusses analytically the work of black writers and critics whom he was quick to disparage. He makes of the black literary tradition a *tabula rasa* that, or so it seems, only he and those who followed his poetic dictates could fill with art and meaning.

Once he had cleared the horizon of thinkers who came before him, Wright charged the emerging black writer with guiding and shaping the black collective consciousness, and this even as he called upon Negroes to transcend the particularities of black nationalism. Black nationalism, though useful as a social strategy, was to be "transcended" as blacks progressed toward a higher ideal, Wright argued. The writings of the Harlem Renaissance and earlier periods had failed in this regard, at least to Wright's mind. This literature had "been confined to humble novels, poems, and plays," written by "prim and decorous ambassadors who went a-begging to white America," desperately hoping to "show that the Negro was not inferior, that he was human, and that he had a life comparable to that of other people" ("Blueprint" 1403). Instead of writing to white America, as Wright perhaps saw Harper, Johnson, and even Du Bois doing, black writers should have addressed their texts to a black reading audience in order to lead them toward a higher consciousness. The workers of the black community would have been ideal readers of this writing, Wright argues. Since they "[lack] the handicaps of false ambition and property, they have access to a wide social vision and a deep social consciousness. They display a greater freedom and initiative in pushing their claims upon civilization than even do the petty bourgeoisie. Their organizations show greater strength, adaptability, and efficiency than any other group or class in society" (1403–1404). Indeed, black workers constitute not the lumpen element of society; they are to be regarded as a veritable proletariat capable of effecting social change. Black writers have not taken advantage of the position in which their art places them, Wright stresses. They have neither taken up their duty as writers, nor have they formed useful alliances with black workers.

Nonetheless, in arguing that Negro art stems from the black church and black folklore, Wright, without acknowledging that he is doing so, places himself squarely within a genealogy of thought that includes Harper, Du

Bois, Johnson, and others. Yet he feels, in ways that Harper, Du Bois, and Johnson do not, that the black church is also a false "antidote for suffering and denial"; he sees the church, in vulgar Marxist fashion, as the opiate of the people, a social sedative that is counter-productive to liberation. He elaborates:

> In the absence of fixed and nourishing forms of culture, the Negro has a folklore which embodies the memories and hopes of his struggle for freedom. Not yet caught in paint or stone, and as yet but feebly depicted in the poem and novel, the Negroes' most powerful images of hope and despair still remain in the fluid state of daily speech . . . Negro folklore contains, in a measure that puts to shame more deliberate forms of Negro expression, the collective sense of Negro life in America. Let those who shy at the nationalist implications of Negro life look at this body of folklore, living and powerful, which arose out of a unified sense of a common life and a common fate. Here are those vital beginnings of a recognition of value in life as it is *lived*, a recognition that marks the emergence of a new culture in the shell of the old. And at the moment this process starts, at the moment when a people begin to realize a *meaning* in their suffering, the civilization that engenders that suffering is doomed. (italics in original, 1405)

Wright evinces a good deal of ambivalence on this point, or so it seems. Recognizing the power of a folk expression he (like Jean Toomer before him) seems certain is doomed to die, Wright nonetheless calls upon the black writer to make use of the power that emanates from the black vernacular, to use it to guide and enlighten black people, to give them some sense of what it means to live and exist, to *be*. Black nationalism, though a natural and temporarily necessary outgrowth of black folklore, paradoxically works against the enlightenment Wright calls for in this essay. His understanding of the parameters of black nationalism seems, on first look, contradictory. He writes that although black nationalism is reflected in all of black culture, and especially in black folklore, this folklore is not fixed; it acts from within "the fluid state of daily speech" (1405), the black vernacular. In spite of this, Wright appears comfortable in asserting that black nationalist ideas themselves arose from a seemingly stable, "unified sense of common life and a common fate" contained in black folklore. These nationalist notions form the foundation of black social "recognition" of the "value in life as it is *lived*"; it points to the black folk's recognition of the "*meaning* in their suffering." When this nationalism gains traction, when it gains in social currency, the civilization that "engenders that suffering is doomed" (emphasis in original, 1405), Wright warns. American capitalism is, of course, at the heart of that doomed civilization—Wright makes this clear. Yet, black nationalism, however much it may present a countermeasure against capitalism, is a stage of thought that must be surpassed through the higher intellection made possible by an art that emerges from the roots of black nationalism: black folk culture.

Wright's argument seems fairly circuitous unless the reader and writer can join in to take it a bit further. The writer who "seeks to function within his race as a purposeful agent has a serious responsibility" in Wright's eyes: s/he must depict a complex consciousness that recognizes and responds to the global nature of life, a global humanism, if you will. Wright's opinion that the writer should not simply present a mimetic portrait of black folk culture, but should instead reshape and present it for purposeful consumption by the reader seems to be what lies behind his rejection of Hurston's realistic, ethnographic representation of black folk culture in *Their Eyes Were Watching God*.

Wright makes clear that Marxism is only a beginning toward the goal of black freedom; it will aid the black writer to realize "his role as a creator of the world" (1407); but it cannot encompass all of life. Life is of great importance to Wright as an intrinsic symbolic concept, perhaps as that inner symbol of which Johnson wrote. Life must be "lived"; experience must be privileged over theory and should even be seen as giving shape to theory. One might go so far as to say that the reshaping of experience into the useful, subversive form Wright envisions *constitutes* theory.[12] Theory, then, must be presented as life experience on the page; life must be shown to be acted out (through dramatic sequences representing thought and speech) by way of the character's individual will. And this individual will must act in relation to the experience of the collective, and of the global community in which that collective resides. It is interesting, however, that while Wright promotes the notion of "faith" (the writer "possesses the potential cunning to steal into the inmost recesses of the human heart, because he can create the myths and symbols that inspire a faith in life," 1407), his own early writing seems to express a sort of tragic sterility that likewise coalesces with his theory. The writer who thus "steals away" not into the closet where he might converse with his Lord (as said in the Spirituals), but into the human heart where he might converse with humankind, "may expect either to be consigned to oblivion or to be recognized for the valued agent he is" (1407). We find such an anomaly of tragedy—the dialectic of oblivion and recognition—at work in *The Man Who Lived Underground*, where Fred Daniels' purposeful descent into an underground, chaotic space of oblivion forever seals his fate even as it paradoxically reveals his consciousness.

With all of the requirements of Wright's poetics, with his call to mold traditional expressions such as folklore even as one does away with tradition, with his recognition of the largess/largeness of the human heart even as he sentences his protagonist to death, theory does come to be of signal importance. For theory, speculation, questioning, and wonderment provide the materials with which to build a "human world" such as Wright envisions. The poetics of being that emerge from Wright's modernist angst is tinged with hope and intention. And it is built upon a belief in the ability of literature to do the world's work. It sees literature as doing more than reproducing the world in writing: literature is able to grant meaning to a new and better world. If, as Wright insists, the writer's function is to guide and enlighten, and if part of his or her responsibility is to carry out this task while at once responding to and transcending the nationalism of black people, we must ask ourselves how well and in what way Wright accomplishes the task he essentially sets before himself in *The Man Who Lived Underground*.

Being Underground

The Man Who Lived Underground was written in 1942 but did not fully appear in print until 1944, when a version of it was published in an anthology entitled *Cross Section*, edited by the novelist and poet Edwin Seaver.[13] Wright begins his novella *in medias res*, and the use of this narrative device allows him to render conceptions of time in complex foldings, such as flashback, narrative reminiscence, and forgetting. Just as we are not quite certain of the crime of the protagonist, Fred Daniels, as the story opens, neither are we immediately aware of the exact geographical setting or of the protagonist's race. We know simply that he is running through an urban space, that he is caught between impending danger and uncertain refuge (1437). He quickly decides to lower himself into a manhole, and in doing so, he crosses the first threshold of the narrative. Daniels at once transgresses and comes to inhabit the limits that separate the cosmos—the world aboveground—from chaos—the underground realm that becomes his provisional home.

The chaotic underground space of the novella is a geographical metaphor of gape and rift. In Wright's story, it is hardly the amorphous and random primordial mass described in the Classical-era writings of Ovid.

Rather, Wright adheres more closely to the image of the underground given in Hesiod's *Theogony*, which classes the abyss as the site of the world's origins. Whereas the civilized world aboveground takes the name Cosmos and is characterized by the rule of order, the underground world is given the name Chaos, which precedes the existence and appearance of the Cosmos. Chaos begets Cosmos, and thus is something of a pre-universe, a pre-condition for the ordering of knowledge to which the Cosmos gives rise and which it in turn bestows upon the civilized world. Whereas some aspects of postmodern theory, for example, that of Gilles Deleuze,[14] have tended to underscore the continuity between these two realms rather than their opposition, the modernist Wright seems intent upon underscoring the dissonance between these worlds and the falseness of the Cosmos. At the same time, he critiques the notion of the modern cosmopolitan writ large (a point on which I expound below), in so far as this concept is founded on Enlightenment-era notions of material value and global economic exchange. In the underground space of the novella, we find instead numerous processes through which Wright represents the repercussions of modern life on black being: the interrelation of Cosmos and Chaos with reason and madness; the chaotic interplay of memory and dreams; and the compression of time and space. Essentially, Wright situates his anti-hero within the structure of ontological myth, wherein Fred Daniels is compelled to define the nature of his existence and the ultimate reality of things. Daniels may be seen as an iconoclast and a deconstructionist, as he regularly subverts the ontological assumptions of the world above ground. Indeed, Daniels' descent into the underground world may be likened (ironically, given Wright's rejection of religion) to a Christian rite of passage; as with baptism, Daniels' immersion into an underground "sea" of chaotically flowing, putrid water is intended to affect and transform his mode of being. His descent is a metaphorical gesture in its religious signification, and thus in its relation to African American folk thought and expression. It may be read as a regression into the womb of mother earth. But his descent also constitutes dissent and resistance; through it, Daniels "becomes" a self-aware artist, a man possessed of self-consciousness. It is because of his descent that Daniels emerges with a revised and critical ontology. But certainly, his rite of passage does not confer upon him the power to conquer death. At the novella's conclusion, Daniels' murder by the police, the corrupt enforcers of the order of the Cosmos, remands him permanently to the chaotic oblivion of art and shadows. He is not permitted to re-emerge, and therein lies the tragedy of his life and existence.

Wright's tragic and ironic anti-hero is not unlike Ralph Ellison's invisible man, as I mention above. The affinity between the two protagonists is clear, given Wright's depiction of a man who descends into an underground

space from which he designs an intuitive plan for his life and his mode
of being. The invisible man and Fred Daniels alike are concerned with an
ethical love and care for those in their community who cannot "see" and
do not "know" with each character's own sensible acuity. Unfortunately for
Wright's protagonist, whose struggle is both continuous and finite and who
is thus, like Bigger Thomas, stricken with a type of double-consciousness
and existential "guilt," he emerges from his underground space only to
be consigned to it in death after a fashion that resonates with Wright's
dictates in "Blueprint": the artist always risks oblivion even as he strives for
recognition. It is as if the space from which the underground man plans
represents both freedom and enslavement, being and non-being; in the final
scene, his remanding into the underground space of enslavement/freedom is
made permanent by the trajectory of the bullet fired from the policeman's
gun. The main character's life is a tragedy, but it is also rendered absurd.

In a sense, the absurdity of the narrative results from the transformation
of the "real" world aboveground into the false or insufficient double of the
underground world. For Daniels, it seems, the originary Chaos of underground
life begets the Cosmos of the upper world, and reality is deemed the prosthesis
of originary chaos. Thus the underground world where he lives serves as
the ironic origin from which he divines the truth of being, a truth he longs
to share with the realm he considers to be distorted by the "dead world
of sunshine" (1451). "Reality," then, is surreal; so, then, is Daniels' ontology.
In a way, the relation between truth and the surreal (the truth of living
underground and the surreal stagings of life above ground) is analogous to
the relation between truth and fiction. The realm aboveground is contaminated
with a deceptive light that promises knowledge—a species of happiness and
security—but grants none at all, at least not in Daniels' most recent experience.
In other words, Wright renders Daniels as a primal poet in a savage city, not
unlike that poet who, in Plato's imagination, posed a threat to the order (the
cosmology) of the Republic, and must be banished by the guardians of that
city. Daniels' art poses a threat because through it, he promises to bring into
being a thing that, prior to his descent, was simply non-being.

I see Wright doing a number of things with this sort of opposition
between ascent and descent, between being and nothingness. After a fashion,
Daniels may be seen as an analogue of the poets—Homer and others—
Plato wished to banish from his ideal Republic. Afraid that poets were
unduly capable of evoking in human beings feelings that could disrupt the
status quo, Plato argued that poets ought to be surveilled and controlled.
Deception, not only through poetry, but also through other sorts of aesthetic

representations, is the danger the Republic's guardians should beware, a warning Plato conveys through his allegory of the cave. Yet while Plato's cave is nonetheless free of poets (there are no poets depicted in the cave, only hapless prisoners unable to discern between truth and falseness), Daniels, who emerges in the story as an improbable poet of the chthonian realm, descends into the underground where he encounters not the deception of shadows narrated by Plato, but the enlightenment of darkness. For him, the cave becomes a locus of insight where he sees more clearly, more truthfully than in the blinding light of the city. By situating the locus of Daniels' existence in an underground space beneath the modern city, Wright insists that we meditate upon the problem of life and black being at its outer limits. And because Wright renders the city and its entrails as veritable characters in the story, arguably those characters with whom Fred Daniels most regularly communes, the anatomy of the city itself, its geography, emerges as yet another guiding metaphor of the novella.

On the question of such a metaphor of geography, I am drawn to the work that David Harvey has done placing into relation geography, anthropology, and history as signifiers in the modern world. In his essay "Cosmopolitanism and the Banality of Geographical Evils" (2000), Harvey points out that in Immanuel Kant's theory of geography, geography and anthropology function as "the necessary conditions of all practical application of knowledge to the material world" (532). Kant felt that "geography, together with anthropology, defined the conditions of possibility of all knowledge and that such knowledge was the necessary preparation—a 'propaedeutic' as [Kant] termed it—for everything else. While, therefore, geography was obviously a 'precritical' or 'prescientific' state, its foundational role required that [Kant pay] close attention" (530).

The point Harvey makes here calls us to consider more closely geography as a metaphor that carries out a specific sort of intellectual work in Wright's novella: North/South, urban/rural, transatlanticism, colonialism, and exile are all issues that inform Wright's oeuvre to such an extent that they must be considered aspects of his poetics. Certainly, Wright felt that the locus of the city exerted a powerful force on his own fashioning of his characters, his plot lines, and the imagery of his texts. For example, in his introduction to *Black Metropolis*, from which I quote in the epigraph to this chapter, Wright points out that the slums of Chicago produced Bigger Thomas; we see clearly that an urban space likewise produced Fred Daniels. And in a striking rhetorical move, Wright likens the pathology of his fictional progeny to that of Adolf Hitler. He warns his reader:

Do not hold a light attitude toward the slums of Chicago's South Side. Remember that Hitler came out of such a slum. Remember that Chicago could be the Vienna of American Fascism! Out of these mucky slums can come ideas quickening life or hastening death, giving us peace or carrying us toward another war. (xx)

In other words, then, America's urban centers, with their complex plight of poverty, industrialism, marginalization, and perhaps even fascism, have the potential to produce a deadly schism. Wright continues:

Lodged in the innermost heart of America is a fatal division of being, a war of impulses. America knows that the split is in her, and that that split might cause her death but she is powerless to pull the dangling ends together. An uneasiness haunts her conscience, taints her moral preachments, lending an air of unreality to her actions, and rendering ineffectual the good deeds she feels compelled to do in the world. America is a nation of a riven consciousness. (xxi)

The movement Wright describes in the novella does not serve as a transcendence of this "fatal division of being," the "riven" condition in which America finds herself. Instead, this movement is radical submersion into the break, as Ralph Ellison might put it,[15] a descent into a heterotopic space, for which Michel Foucault provides a helpful definition. Heterotopias are dimensions apart, heterogeneous spaces that are "disturbing probably because they secretly undermine language, because they shatter or tangle common names, because they make it impossible to name this *and* that . . . Heterotopias . . . desiccate speech, stop words in their tracks, contest the very possibility of grammar at its source" (Foucault, *The Order of Things*, xviii). Kevin Hetherington draws upon Foucault's thought to define heterotopias as "spaces of alternate ordering" that "organize a bit of the social world in a way different to that which surrounds them. That alternate ordering marks them out as Other and allows them to be seen as an example of an alternative way of doing things" (*Badlands of Modernity* viii). Hetherington sees even so-called "normative" spaces—such as that of industrial factories—as heterotopias, but for him, Foucault's heterotopias are neutral ground, spaces neither perfect (such as that described in Thomas More's *Utopia*) nor imaginary, but fitfully located somewhere between.

The alternative mode of action Wright depicts in his novella's underground space comments directly upon the epistemology Kant set out as definitive of the modern world and its modes of consciousness. Kant's treatise on *Geography* (marred, like his *Observations on the Feeling of the Beautiful and the Sublime*, with an inordinate but not surprising dose of racism) considers modern time to indicate a "richness, fecundity, and life," while space (like that of the underground cave) "was treated as the dead, the fixed, the undialectical, the immobile" (Foucault, "Questions on Geography" 70). Wright is clear in his refusal of this distinction; he compresses time and space in the novella, and thus delivers a radical revisioning of the historicity of conscious black being, and, therefore, the basis upon which we claim to know this or that.

If we look more keenly at what I shall call Daniels' tableau, the poem he has constructed in the cave from objects that constitute the detritus of modern materialism, we may come closer to an understanding of the significance of Wright's strategy in this regard. Because language—the ultimate conveyor of Western knowledge—ultimately fails the underground man, his poetry largely comprises the material: its lines of verse are drawn from the jewels he steals, the paper money he uses to veil the walls of his cave, the various objects that serve as talismans. Daniels amasses a complex pastiche of elements collected from the aboveground. We might say, in reviewing the final composition he renders, that the lines separating these elements themselves become blurred, to the extent that meaning is difficult, if not impossible, to decipher. Foucault describes the sort of disorder that characterizes heterotopias as that in which "fragments of a large number of possible orders glitter separately in the dimension, without law or geometry" (*Order of Things* xvii). The sort of "enigmatic multiplicity" of which Foucault speaks reflects the revolutionary prescience of the underground space in Wright's novella, with its incongruous orders: technology (represented by the radio, which regularly serves aboveground as a conduit of misinformation and an instrument of control); capitalism (represented by the money, jewels, and precious metals that are used as pure ornamentation—without exchange value—in Daniels' cave); weaponry (primal in the case of the cleaver, and modern in the case of the gun); and time (represented by the watches—each set to a random hour—Daniels hangs on the wall, alluding to his subversion of the ordering of time and history). Collectively, these pieces, along with Daniels' inability to grasp fully the sense and ontology at work in black folk expression, destabilize the provisional wisdom Wright assigns (in "Blueprint") to black vernacular and folk forms. They eventually constitute the fragmented and heterogeneous poetry of the underground man's cave, itself deconstructive of the ordering of the cosmos which it, geographically, precedes. They also suggest an alternative epistemology and, following Kant's thought, they impinge upon universal knowledge.

These are the spaces in which otherness and alterity might flourish in support of a revised ontology and a subversive epistemology, yet Harvey warns us against taking too much comfort in this theory. Heterotopias may allow us to "think of the potential for coexistence in the multiple utopian schemes—feminist, anarchist, ecological, and socialist—that have come down to us through history" (537). However, Harvey complains that the radical promise of the heterotopia has been reduced to theoretical commonplace, that its thick potential becomes watery banality if "power/knowledge is or can be dispersed into [multiple and many] spaces of difference" (Harvey 538). The disruptive effect of geographical thought "makes space a favorite metaphor in the postmodernist attack—inspired, for example, by Foucault's *The Order of Things*—upon all forms of universality" (Harvey 539). But these are only metaphors, he claims. They stop short of postulating "questions of real geography and even the production of space" (541).

Harvey argues that we should resist overvaluing geographical metaphors and instead pay attention to the ways in which "places and localized ways of life are relationally constructed by a variety of intersecting socioecological processes occurring at quite different spatio-temporal scales." We must also, he insists, give due consideration to "historical-geographical processes of place and community construction" (542). Wright constructs metaphorical spaces in his novella that are actually reflective of the "localized ways of life" and "processes of place and community construction" that are so important to Harvey, and they are not simple metaphors. It seems to me that the imagination of critical, metaphorical spaces such as those appearing in the novella are indeed productive of not only spaces that allow for conceptual and revisionist thought, but that might also be seen as having the potential to induce radical social action and consciousness on the part of the reader.

Here I return to my earlier point on cosmopolitanism: the disruptive nature of Wright's metaphorical underground space may be seen to attempt the sort of cosmopolitanism Harvey values, if one sees cosmopolitanism as an outcome of the erasure or mitigation of spatio-temporal boundaries through self-reflective, rhizomatic errantry rather than as the well-rooted growth of transnational corporations and international political formations (such as the European Union).[16] Consider, for example, Daniels' erratic encounters with black folk culture during his time in the underground, a folk culture that seems alien to him, and which he observes with a certain ambivalence. Wright's paradigmatic representation of black folk culture comes, in this instance, in Daniels' distant hearing of the Spirituals, sung during a church service going on in a sub-basement next to one of the caves of Daniels' underground world. He is both attracted to and repulsed by the singers; their songs at once "enchanted" him (1438) and appeared "abysmally obscene" (1439). On first spying the choir, with its "white robes" and "tattered songbooks" in "black palms," Daniels' "first impulse [is] to laugh" (1439). His second visceral emotion is that of guilt.

Why guilt? Even in his heterotopic space beyond the Cosmos, Daniels feared that God would "strike him dead" for ridiculing the devoted song-offerings of the choir (1439), which sang of love and a home beyond the world in which they lived, even as slave singers had done in foregoing generations. But unlike the improvised renderings that are characteristic of the Spirituals, the singers of Wright's underground sing from well-worn songbooks, an unusual occurrence. While hymnals are bought and broadly distributed throughout modern African American churches, it is unusual for African American choirs (especially black Baptist and apostolic choirs that continue the spiritual tradition Wright describes) to sing Spirituals (rather than hymns) from songbooks (rather than from memory) while in the choir stand on Sunday mornings. The guilt incurred by Wright's fictional choir appears to be that of being fed hopeful lyrics whose apparently dogmatic and seemingly unreflective rendering in song brings pain to the protagonist, because it seems to him that the singers are unconscious of their intrinsic freedom, what Jean-Paul Sartre (in *Being and Nothingness*) refers to as the ontological origins or foundation of freedom. Daniels shares some species of the choir's guilt since he feels himself to be existentially and morally a part of the singers' world, and he is thus unable to tear himself away from the church scene:

> After a long time he grew numb and dropped to the dirt. Pain throbbed in his legs and a deeper pain, induced by the sight of those black people groveling and begging for something they could never get, churned in him. A vague conviction made him feel that those people should stand unrepentant and yield no quarter in singing and praying. Yet *he* had run away from the police, had pleaded with them to believe his innocence. He shook his head, bewildered. (1439, italics in original)

When Daniels hears singing coming from this same church later in the novella, he has already made the decision to emerge from his heterotopic space, to act in the aftermath of the false accusations that had disrupted not only his own life (sending him into the solace of the chaotic subterranean realm), but also the lives of others, such as the night watchman, who, after being falsely accused of a theft that Daniels himself had committed, takes his very life before the underground man, who watches the death scene as though he were a spectator witnessing a performance. The singing convinces Daniels that he must "tell" the church folks what he has learned, perhaps to absolve both himself and them of their common guilt, and when he opens the door to the church, the "deluge of song" that washes over him confirms in him the necessity of this action, his deep-seated need to emerge from the underground into what he considers to be the realm of false light and "truth," to convey to the black folk much needed knowledge, subversive insight, and even salvation. As he approaches the church, he hears the choir sing:

> The Lamb, the Lamb, the Lamb
> Tell me again your story
> The Lamb, the Lamb, the Lamb
> Flood my soul with your glory

The lyrics cast Daniels as a black Christ figure, come to take on sin and guilt, and to save the black folk by way of the baptismal stream of his narrative, his "story." He is an ironic savior who comes to the surface of the earth not from the realm above, but from a space below, where blackness is not detrimental and evil, but affirming and good. The song that is next taken up by the choir confirms this metaphor of Daniels as a black Christ:

> Oh, wondrous sight upon the cross
> Vision sweet and divine
> Oh, wondrous sight upon the cross
> Full of such love sublime

While Daniels is certainly positioned as the savior of the folk, the folk, in turn, are transformed through this lyrical performance from a collective of automaton-like singers to a cautionary, insightful group, gifted with the second-sight of what Wright refers to in "Blueprint" as "racial wisdom." (Du Bois, as we recall, would often refer to the gift of second sight among those living within the veil.) The lyrical commentary of the choir alludes to the "wondrous sight upon the cross," and a "love sublime." It is perhaps like the moral commentary of a Greek chorus and recalls Wright's analogy in his Introduction to *Black Metropolis*, wherein black migrants to northern cities are likened to "characters in a Greek play," "driven and pursued" down "the path of defeat." It warns Daniels of both bodily sacrifice and a love

vast in its dimensions, yet still comprehensible: the transitional stage of the
death of the body (the knowledge of the graveyard and the "laying down"
of the body, in the language of the Spirituals) and the subsequent rising up
of the spirit of consciousness in a sublime, transcendent, and even victorious
fashion. Even so, the death of the body is required before one can achieve
such transcendence; it is the sacrifice one must make should one wish to
live in the presence of God. As I have noted, Wright warns of an analogous
sacrifice of the artist in "Blueprint for Negro Writing": "By his ability to fuse
and make articulate the experiences of men, because his writing possesses
the potential cunning to steal into the inmost recesses of the human heart,
because he can create the myths and symbols that inspire a faith in life,
he may expect either to be consigned to oblivion, or to be recognized for
the valued agent he is." The question is essentially one of life *and* death;
the Negro writer, Wright argues, "is being called upon to do no less than
create values by which his race is to struggle, live and die" ("Blueprint"
1407). The choir's mortal warning, which seems to emanate from Wright's
own theory of the poetics of African American literature, falls mute on
the ears of Daniels, who, intent upon conveying his own salvific message
rather than lending credence to the import of the Spiritual, is turned away
by the men of the church. Quite apart from the Biblical injunction to
take in strangers and anoint their feet with oil, Daniels, dirty, seemingly
intoxicated, and quite unruly, is turned out of the church to wander once
again the streets that precipitated his initial descent. He is, as Wright puts
it, consigned to oblivion.

The encounter with the church men, in particular, provides Daniels
with a new, but naïve purpose in his wandering above ground: to go to
the police and make a statement. "What statement? He did not know. He
was the statement" (1462). In yet another allusion to Christ—that Daniels
himself "was the statement," that he was the "word" made flesh—he would
confess and assume, like Christ, guilt that was not his alone, but rather,
to his mind at least, everyone's: "I'm guilty! . . . All the people I saw was
guilty" (1464). It is the scene in the church that most forcefully occupies
Daniels' thoughts as he struggles to word his confession, and thus reveal
himself, his consciousness, to the same policemen who falsely accused him:
"His smile faded and he was possessed with memories of the underground;
he saw the cave next to the church and his lips moved to speak. But how
could he say it?" (1464). As he becomes convinced of the need to "force the
reality of himself upon them" (1465), he tries again to structure the narrative
of his confession, which somehow is rooted in the songs that emanated
from the church: "First, he ought to tell them about the singing in the

church, but what words could he use?" (1465). When the policemen finally
agree to take him to the cave and see what he has done, Daniels not only
feels relieved of his "burden," but experiences a transcendental "selflessness"
(1468). He wanted "to prance about in physical ecstasy, throw his arm about
the policemen in fellowship," and the song he sings as he is being driven
back to the manhole, "the song that had brought him to such a high pitch
of terror and pity," underscores this sensation of "selflessness" and "ecstasy"
as he intones lyrics expressing his joy that the spirit of Christ now resides
in his soul: "*Glad, glad, glad, oh, so glad / I got Jesus in my soul*" (1468).

When they finally arrive at the manhole, Daniels is convinced that
by showing them his underground space, along with his inversion of the
meaning of material objects—his inversion of the "order of things"—he
will provoke in them a feeling of sympathy and empathy that would be
transformative:

> He was eager to show them the cave now. If he could show
> them what he had seen, then they would feel what he had felt
> and soon everybody would be governed by the same impulse of
> pity. (1469)

For Daniels, the cave is a space of poetic meaning whose content,
the material objects he refashions and reorders, has been reduced to pieces,
fragments that are themselves metaphors of the modern condition, capable
even in their fractured state of producing meaning by way of what Daniels
refers to as "feeling." Such feeling, Daniels believes, would lead others to
be "governed by the same impulse of pity," a conclusion that, in Daniels'
mind, might advance in a number of hopeful directions. Not least of these
is compassion, which would indicate a "suffering with" another, signaling the
importance of strengthening the bonds of communal affinity and emotion
that would lead individuals to grant succor and care to other human beings.

Caring, then, as a fundamental humanistic act and construed as
a characteristic of Being-in-the-world by Heidegger, emerges as the
cornerstone of Daniels' project, conveyed by the tableau he composes in
his underground cave, a poetic tableau that requires a reader/viewer in order
that its import and the possibilities it intimates do not fall soundlessly
into oblivion. Diamonds, jewelry, money, a typewriter, a radio, a cleaver, a
gun: all are forms that Daniels has emptied of their prior meaning as he
assembles a collage of sorts, leaving only structures that function as symbols
and metaphors at play in a heterotopic realm of chaos and formlessness.

Time, for example, loses its force in the cave: the underground man is not sure of how long he sleeps, how long he has been underground, or even whether it is night or day. His memory is likewise thrown into chaos. He forgets his name and where he lives; he forgets where he was arrested (1463). His mind and feelings work together to "reconstruct events in reverse . . . his feelings ranged back over the long hours and he saw the cave, the sewer, the bloody room where it was said that a woman had been killed" (1463). It is perhaps the murdered woman who appears to Daniels in a dream. Rather than her murderer (he maintains his innocence in this regard, though he deems himself to be culturally and socially "guilty"), he symbolically dreams himself her savior, one who walks toward her on water just as Christ walked on the surface of the sea toward his disciples to save them during a storm. Daniels' dream reads as follows, introduced by Wright's characteristic ellipsis, itself another insistence upon fragments and reordering. The dream is narrated using a Joycean stream-of-consciousness technique to string together a number of fluid metaphorical images through which Wright fleshes out the symbols that are central to his conveyance of meaning:

> . . . His body was washed by cold water that gradually turned warm and he was buoyed upon a stream and swept out to sea where waves rolled gently and suddenly he found himself walking upon the water how strange and delightful to walk upon the water and he came upon a nude woman holding a nude baby in her arms and the woman was sinking into the water holding the baby above her head and screaming *help* and he ran over the water to the woman and he reached her just before she went down and he took the baby from her hands and stood watching the breaking bubbles where the woman sank and he called *lady* and still no answer yes dive down there and rescue that woman but he could not take this baby with him and he stooped and laid the baby tenderly upon the surface of the water expecting it to sink but it floated and he leaped into the water and held his breath and strained his eyes to see through the gloomy volume of water but there was no woman and he opened his mouth and called *lady* and the water bubbled and his chest ached and his arms were tired but he could not see the woman and he called again *lady lady* and his feet touched sand at the bottom of the sea and his chest felt as though it would burst and he bent his

knees and propelled himself upward and water rushed past him and his head bobbed out and he breathed deeply and looked around where was the baby the baby was gone and he rushed over the water looking for the baby calling *where is it* and the empty sky and sea threw back his voice *where is it* and he began to doubt that he could stand upon the water and then he was sinking and as he struggled the water rushed him downward spinning dizzily and he opened his mouth to call for help and water surged into his lungs and he choked . . . (1443–1444)

Daniels emerges from the dream at this point, having dreamt himself as both savior and apostle working desperately to save the nude Madonna and child: for it was the apostle Peter who began to sink into the sea when his fear and doubt overtook him as he tried to walk on the water toward Christ. Wright's use of stream-of-consciousness writing in this passage exemplifies the dessication of speech Foucault sees as characteristic of heterotopias, and heightens the sense of urgency conveyed in the manifest dream content as well as in its latent meanings: the underground man is portrayed as a moral and upstanding person who risked his own life to save that of two others, but it is an ethic he is hard-pressed to articulate. Walking on water in the midst of an underground heterotopia becomes an ironic and ambivalent metaphor of ethics: seemingly, the narrator implies, he would have acted to save another human being in real life, and would not have been able to commit an act of murder such as that of which he stood accused, although he himself had not acted to relieve the suffering he had witnessed while underground. It is as though his doubt and inaction render his morality ambiguous; ironically, they are two aspects of his character that had propelled him to an existence beneath the city.

The trauma of the underground space—its oscillations between morality and guilt, freedom and entrapment, and its movement between the past, the present, and the imaginary, eventuate in a failure of language and a retreat into emotion. As Wright puts it in the novella, "He could no longer think with his mind; he thought with his feelings and no words came." The ineffable here is connected to affect and emotion, an inability to create content to fill a language that might convey his feelings. The story itself is most obviously an allegory that encompasses metaphor, irony, and what might be described as strivings to express that which is inexpressible, ineffable, unspeakable. One essentially senses this striving in Wright's quotation of the Spirituals sung by the church choir that attracts the underground man and names him, as he names himself, their savior.

However, like Christ the Savior, Daniels is destined to die. The choir's ironic warning of Daniels' fate is foreshadowed in the numerous images of death that appear in the underground space: the dead baby (both in reality and in his reverie); the dead man at the undertaker's; the woman who drowns in his dream; and finally his own body, first as he lies "dead upon the table" in his dream (1456), and again once he is shot by the policemen. As the policemen plan his murder and conduct him back to the underground, Daniels gleefully lowers himself one final time into the manhole that "gaped round and black" (1469). After he is shot, Daniels' body floats lifelessly away, water blossoming around his head even as it had bloomed around the dead baby (and here Wright continues the Christ theme, given that the baby in the novella is an aspect of the Madonna and child trope). His own mouth "gaped soundless" in death, just as the lifeless infant's mouth had "gaped black in a soundless cry." Daniels and the Christ child alike pay the wages of guilt.[17] He, in a fate risked by the generalized "Negro writer" who figures centrally in "Blueprint for Negro Writing," is consigned to oblivion rather than agency.

Daniels' murder at the novella's conclusion indicates a literal "death of the author," such that the contents of yet another form, one whose meaning is generally occupied by the person of the author or creator, is obviated. Even so, the death of Daniels, and his purposeful emptying of forms and obviating of language, do not relieve the reader of the need and demand for interpretation of content. Herein lies the paradox of Daniels' cave. Daniels, an iconoclast, comes face to face with the inevitability of the icon. He is, as Giorgio Agamben might term him, a revolutionary who is forced to consider the futility of his revolt. Agamben writes:

> In order to leave the evanescent world of forms, [the revolutionary] has no other means than form itself, and the more he wants to erase it, the more he has to concentrate on it to render it permeable to the inexpressible content he wants to express. But in the attempt, he ends up with nothing in his hands but signs—signs that, although they have traversed the limbo of non-meaning, are no less extraneous to the meaning he was pursuing. (*The Man without Content* 10)

The signs Daniels refashions and reorders are extraneous to the meaning he pursued because even as he completes his wordless poetic masterpiece, he still feels compelled to move beyond it in order to accomplish its destiny. The only remaining gesture available to Daniels near the end of the novella (before his death) is that belonging to the double artist, who, not yet satisfied with the mere production of art, wishes to effect the communion of art and spectator. So long as no one else remarked the success of his masterpiece, Daniels remained overtaken by the desire for community and for the recognition of his thought and renewed sense of being.

～

I have underscored that Wright was unequivocal in his fiction as in his criticism about the importance of community and the need for an engaged art, and these demands eventually become the foundation of his poetics, his artistic principle. In his conception of a poetics, which we see clearly at work in *The Man Who Lived Underground*, he was not interested in what Nietzsche referred to (in a fanciful but disparaging manner in *The Gay Science*) as an art for artists only. Were this so, Daniels would not have been so concerned to share his newfound point of view, his worldview based upon a transformative aesthetics of materialism. In the 1957 essay, "The Literature of the Negro in the United States," Wright did not shift position from his earlier work of criticism, "Blueprint for Negro Writing." He continued to insist that the craft of writing should maintain a certain autonomy, but that it should also reach beyond itself to communicate with a community of writers and readers, even if one of the tasks he assigns the text is the responsibility of creating readers or implying readers. There is a way in which Wright strives to set before the implied or created reader the scenes and images that beset his protagonist, and this setting forth is most regularly accomplished through metaphors such as rift and descent, and symbols such as darkness and light.

We often, mistakenly, consider metaphor to be simple ornamentation, loosely called a figure of speech. However, metaphor, at its very foundations—as the somatic phrase "*figure* of speech" suggests—is ontological in nature. As metaphor is related to action or movement (physical, cognitive, or both), it depends fundamentally upon the primal verb of existence, the verb "to be," whether that verb is explicit or implied. Paul Ricoeur has argued that there is a harmony between the verb "to be" and the noun "reason": being is rational, while non-being is irrational; non-being is the chaos Fred Daniels negotiates in life as in death. Yet if as Martin Heidegger writes, true poetry "awakens the largest view" and "makes World appear in all things," we must look a little more closely at what the ontological and epistemological metaphors in Daniels' underground space do, what work they perform. That is to say that if Fred Daniels' chaotic poetry "makes World appear in all things," then it does, as Daniels insists, give birth to a true and radically new cosmos. It associates with imagistic knowledge a mystery of sensibility, an intuitive grasping of intent and import that is akin to perceiving in darkness, to listening in silence.

It is perhaps because Daniels insists upon such paradoxes of metaphor and symbol that he meets his end in tragedy. In spite of his amassing of objects to adorn his underground cave, the tragedy of Daniels' life is that he cannot overcome the split between art and spectatorship any more than he can heal what Wright describes as America's riven consciousness, a split similar to that endured by Bigger Thomas, who longs not simply to spectate upon life, but to participate in what he considers to be "real" life, and thus to *know* life. Bigger remains an enigma to himself, yet Daniels, gazing upon the art he has made, is placed in contact with an innermost truth that he is driven to share. To his mind, he has achieved perfect knowledge, which he senses will displace and supercede the false logic of the upper world. Nonetheless, Daniels' creation does not ensure the erasure of his sense and state of alienation; in fact, his act of creation seals his ultimate alienation through death. The creative-destructive force and tragedy of his art is that it eventually serves as a poetics of perversion that calls for a thoughtful, even morally outraged response from the reader. Wright's dynamic critique in *The Man Who Lived Underground* demands that the reader engage in a tensional imagination of truth, and makes of the tragedy that ensues from an unjust death a heuristic that construes a new sphere of meaning opened by metaphorical discourse. He makes of the death-laden split that inhabits America, and the West more generally, the foundation from which a new human existence and ethical human action become possible and necessary.

8

A Love Called Democracy

Ralph Ellison's *Invisible Man*

By Way of Conclusion

In the Prologue of Ralph Ellison's 1952 novel *Invisible Man*,[1] the narrator encounters an old slave who speaks to him of love. An "old singer of spirituals," the slave woman comes to him in a dream, a fissure "where time stands still" (7). Not unlike the eighteenth-century autobiographer Equiano, Harper's Aunt Chloe, the spiritual singers who invisibly populate Du Bois's *The Souls of Black Folk*, or who again play a central, epistemic role in Wright's *The Man Who Lived Underground*, Ellison's singer also has critical knowledge to impart. In the dream's depths she confesses to him that she "dearly loved" her master, the father of her children, although she "hated him too" (8). The invisible man, writing of his dream from the critical distance of the underground, admits that he also has "become acquainted with ambivalence." When he asks the singer why she moans, she replies:

'I moan this way 'cause he's dead,' she said.
'Then tell me, who is that laughing upstairs?'
'Them's my sons. They glad.'
'Yes, I can understand that too,' I said.
'I laughs too, but I moans too. He promised to set us free, but
    he could never bring hisself to do it. Still I loved him . . .'
'Loved him? You mean . . . ?'
'Oh yes, but I loved something else even more.'
'What more?'
'Freedom.'
'Freedom,' I said. 'Maybe freedom lies in hating.'

313

> 'Naw, son, it's in loving. I loved him and give him the poison
> and he withered away like a frost-bit apple.' (9)

This passage is instructive, for it introduces a theme that Ellison develops throughout the novel. Love, or at least its expression and representation in metaphorical language, is held to be ambiguous, always threatening to teeter over into its opposite, hate. For the woman, the white master she loves symbolizes the law and the oppressor, one who has used her both for her labor and for sexual gratification. Nevertheless, she saves him, at least temporarily. The narrator recounts that her sons would have cut their father to bits had it not been for their mother holding them in abeyance. Finally, the mother's love leads her to kill her master; her moral spirit demands his murder, and thus his death takes on a certain symbolic significance. Not allowing her black sons to kill their white father, she herself poisons the one who represents the nation-state's law. Instead of guaranteeing her and her sons the freedom stipulated by its own democratic ideals, the law legitimates and ensures their continued oppression and enslavement under the insufficient and negligent practice of democracy in America.

My reading of love in the invisible man's early dream serves as both a prolegomenon to the work of this chapter and an apt conclusion to the work I have undertaken in this book. Over the course of this study, I have attempted to underscore the ways in which many African American authors employ philosophical metaphors that, while often drawn from the vernacular tradition of African American expression, evince not only the author's sense of being and consciousness, but also the author's exhortation to contemplative and speculative thought that should lead to moral action on the part of the engaged reader. The field of metaphor and tropes of love in *Invisible Man* will be the focus of this final chapter, which examines how the conceptual metaphor of love in the novel functions in connection with its veiled, liminal spaces of consciousness, such as dreams and allegorical undergrounds, wherein Ellison's protagonist, in a fashion that is resonant with yet ultimately distinct from that of Wright's underground man, devises plans for moral, democratic action.

Throughout this study, I have discussed the conceptual metaphors by which the authors whose works I examine negotiate such ontological and epistemological spheres or boundaries of thought. In the writings of Olaudah Equiano, Frances E. W. Harper, and W. E. B. Du Bois, the transgression and inhabitation of the liminal spaces between these realms are ultimately regenerative: while inhabiting such interstitial sites allows for a certain opacity that shields the individual from racist overdetermination and oppressive aggressions, they also bring about new life, new identity, and a renewed quest for a sense of purpose. In Equiano's *Narrative*, the sphere of thought he promulgates takes shape through a discourse of spirit and ethics. In Harper's poetry, we find ourselves ushered into the realm of slave being and moral contemplation in ways that Equiano does not neglect, but that befit the context of Reconstruction. These metaphoric life-ways are closely related to those traced by Du Bois, who likewise charts and chronicles the onto-theologies of slave being and, importantly, archives its experiences and expressions. Du Bois, having performed a critical ontology of race in "The Conservation of Races" (showing race to be a specific sort of social mythology that could and should be used strategically by oppressed African Americans), guides his reader into the inner recesses of the veil as he explores the varied meanings of black being in *The Souls of Black Folk*. In Wright's novella, the testing of ontological boundaries ends in a tragedy that calls the reader to question yet again racialized epistemologies of being and non-being as these impact black existence. The experience of the liminal—the crossing of boundaries and the testing of limits—regularly serves as sites of being and becoming in the conceptual metaphors devised by these writers, sites of personal transformation and radical politics.

Ralph Ellison's novel likewise dwells in such a site. A masterwork of peculiar dimensions, *Invisible Man* was the only major work of fiction published by Ellison before his death in 1994. Although his reviews, opinion pieces, short stories, and essays appeared from the mid-1930s onward, *Invisible Man* remains the yardstick by which Ellison's literary talent and intellectual acumen continue to be judged by twenty-first-century critics, even those who consider the posthumous publication of *Juneteenth* (1999) and, more recently, *Three Days before the Shooting* (2011).[2] Each centimeter on the yardstick appears to count as a mile, and justly so. Ellison's debut novel immediately propelled him to the heights of literary success, garnering the coveted National Book Award in 1953, and helping him to win numerous fellowships and teaching posts. However, some responses to the novel, such as the white critic Irving Howe's belated critique in the 1963 essay "Black Boys and Native Sons,"[3] appear truculent, complaining with an almost perceptible pout that with the appearance of *Invisible Man*, social realism's spell over the African American novel, a magic that had been most assiduously practiced by Wright before his untimely death in 1960, was broken. Ellison's novel is remarkable not only because of the willfulness he showed in breaking away from his own Marxist leanings, along with those of his erstwhile mentor, Wright,[4] by composing a text that openly critiqued communism and its grand scheme regarding the "liberation" of blacks in America. He also defiantly concerned himself with artistic form and the craft of writing over and above social and political propaganda of the sort advocated by Howe. However, Ellison did not want to be misread on this point. "Now mind! I recognize no dichotomy between art and protest," he declared while being interviewed by the *Paris Review* three years after the publication of his novel ("The Art of Fiction" 169). He later clarified his stance in a 1966 *New York Times* interview with John Corry: "I am a novelist, not an activist . . . but I think that no one who reads what I write or who listens to my lectures can doubt that I am enlisted in the freedom movement" (*Conversations with Ralph Ellison* 101). Indeed, Ellison's propensity to commingle a number of novelistic devices—the use of complex and philosophical metaphors, the layering of narrative voices, the combination of the symphonic and the folkloric, and the use of a Prologue and an Epilogue to frame his work—make his novel one that may be approached from a number of critical and theoretical perspectives. They also render any singular or simplistic approach regarding his poetics and politics inadequate to a sentient assessment of the novel in all its complexity.

Acknowledging such limitations, my argument works toward an analogy between Ellison's conception of the liminal as an allegorical site of preparation for democratic action, which insists upon "love" as an Emersonian principle of democratic inclusion, and the unconscious as the seat of the linguistic function, where a figure of speech, such as the metaphor of love, takes shape. In this analogy, the skepticism in various trajectories of poststructuralist and postmodernist theories toward the primacy of absolute knowledge in Western epistemologies (articulated and conveyed via a system of language that functions in accordance with the symbolic order) will be useful. It aids me in tracing the contours of the discursive value of love as metaphor and this metaphor's imbrication with racial difference and national belonging (which Ellison articulates through the trope of invisibility) that carry out Ellison's critique of exclusionary nationalist practices. In particular, contemporary applications of Kristevan psychoanalysis, which extrapolates from the Freudian psychoanalytic theory with which Ellison was quite familiar, and focuses on the condition of the speaking subject as s/he enters the symbolic realm and interacts and makes meaning with an Other, offer a preliminary framework for reading the economies of language that have crafted, in a variety of contradictory ways, the historical production of race. Likewise, Paul Ricoeur's interpretations of Freudian thought in relation to aesthetics and philosophical thinking have aided me in seeing more clearly the interrelation of psychoanalytic theories of the self and the philosophy of being as these meet in the occasion of metaphor. Finally, the thought of

Audre Lorde and Hortense Spillers has encouraged me to attend to what I call a latent but insurgent black maternal feminism in *Invisible Man*, a discourse with which Ellison's name does not usually resonate.

Through an analysis that acknowledges the social symbolism, linguistic symbolism, and what Fred Moten has called the "ocularcentrism" at work in at least Lacan's version of psychoanalytic theory,[5] I read Ellison's metaphor of love as democracy as emerging from the multiple folds of his Americanist discourse. Following the intentionality of both Ellison's fiction and his criticism, the American nation-state emerges as a problematic metaphysical construct of the symbolic realm, subtended by the Law of the (white) Father. Via the specific organization of its metaphysics, the American nation-state early on established a set of meanings attached to the raced, gendered black body that impacted in tension-filled ways how this speaking subject broached questions of blackness and being in the realm of the symbolic. Ellison, as he demonstrates in a number of his critical essays, takes note of this sort of metaphysical discourse used in founding the nation-state in the eighteenth century and in outlining its criteria for membership.[6] These criteria fell in line with the ideals of Western civilization, and were given pointed force through a practice of political and scientific racism wherein various populations, separated into ostensible racial groups, were placed along a hierarchical chain of being that curtailed, to a great extent, their right to citizenship in the nation-state as well as their freedom to be "at home in the world," to borrow a favored phrase of Ellison's. The metaphysical discourse used to establish the nation-state—and this discourse is furthermore, as I have shown, quite metaphorical in nature—did not simply outline an epistemology of being-in-the-world that stipulated the non-being of black folk. It also established guidelines for what sort of speech may be "heard" by society, what sort of speech is recognizable. This has, in ways that will become clear over the course of this chapter, much to do with the metaphoric symbolization of the body that speaks of love, particularly if this body has been raced as black.

What Ellison gets at in depicting certain situations of physical love (that is, sexuality or sexual behavior that the invisible man often characterizes in terms of his love for the white women he is with) alongside his critical adaptation of Emerson's theory of a loving, democratic society, is a critique of an "empty narcissism" on the part of both his protagonist and his nation. The invisible man's quest for sexual love, which is not unrelated to his quest for a sense of self and being or consciousness, is fueled by his narcissism (his limited self-love), his unactualized being, and his lack of social and personal recognition. In short, the invisible man is invisible because he does not love morally and is not morally loved by the socius in return. He "plunges"—another verb that repeats in the text of *Invisible Man*—outside of the nation's democratic embrace, and thus into the realm of invisibility.

In this way, I see the novel's highly celebrated metaphor of invisibility as fully dependent, for its philosophical and psychoanalytic import, upon the metaphor of love. The movement Ellison effects between the invisible man's immature, naïve, and narcissistic expressions of love, which all take place within a Freudian context of sexual tension that is at work throughout the main body of the novel, is at odds with the greater love the invisible man insists upon (in the Prologue and Epilogue) from his underground cell. In being forced underground, the invisible man is forced out of his narcissism: he is compelled to depart from a state of self-love, which is really a non-loving, non-reciprocal state of non-being, and to enter a critically reflective space that provides for contemplation and enactment of a greater, moral love. In the chaotic space of the underground, a womb-like and ultimately maternal space that is the opposite of the symbolic, cosmological realm of the father, Ellison's protagonist benefits from its nurturing even as he envisions the rebirth of a world that makes newly possible the realization of a beloved community.[7]

Speaking for the Beloved

The philosophical and psychoanalytic questions of black being that found my inquiry into *Invisible Man* will first require contextualization. I provide that in this section by discussing the politics of speaking and black representation with which Ellison contended in mid-twentieth-century America, and preface it with a turn to the contextualization Ellison himself affords regarding his protagonist's act of writing.

The metaphor of love as democracy, or democracy as love, rings forcefully when we recall that Ellison drew its inspiration, as I have mentioned, from the work of the man for whom his father named him, Ralph Waldo Emerson. Ralph Waldo Ellison was convinced that "Emerson's essays fulfilled a need, precisely because Americans existed in a society and in a country which was not tightly structured and in which no one, at that time especially, could set a limit upon possibility, certainly not at the level of imagination" ("The Novel as a Function of American Democracy" 311). In "Politics" (1841), Emerson posited the utopian and optimistic notion that the nation-state could and should be re-envisioned as founded upon the "principle of right and love." Within this guiding ideal lies morality, a "reliance upon the moral sentiment," Emerson opined (125). Ellison, prodding the conscience of his protagonist in the mournful aftermath of Brotherhood member Tod Clifton's death and reprising Emerson's sentiment, puts the question to all of his readers: "And could politics ever be an expression of love?" (*Invisible Man* 341). The question the invisible man poses provides an apt contextualization of the very act of writing his memoir, and reveals the role of moral love in the novel's theme and overall import. Through the metaphor of love, Ellison proposes a political agenda with real implications for the actualization of American democracy, and he seeks to bring his agenda to agency through the act of writing itself.

The invisible man differs greatly from Wright's underground man in this regard, though Wright's novella clearly influenced the shape of Ellison's novel to an important extent. While the invisible man evolves a language of love, Fred Daniels abandons spoken language in his heterotopic underground space—or, perhaps it is better said that Wright purposely allows love's discourse to desert Daniels. In our reading of the two texts, we move from the fragments of poetry in Wright's novella to the open unity of prose in Ellison's novel. Ellison's protagonist, undoubtedly speaking with the voice of his creator in the Prologue and the Epilogue, describes the memoir as an act of love whereby he hopes to advance not only toward an understanding of the "principle" of moral democracy on which the country is founded, but also toward a plan of right action that would permit him to breathe life into that principle.

In his grotto, for instance, he pauses in deep contemplation of this principle while querying his grandfather's advice to "overcome 'em with yeses" (13): "Did he mean say 'yes' because he knew that the principle was greater than the men. . . . Did he mean to affirm the principle? . . . Or did he mean that we had to take the responsibility for all of it, for the men as well as the principle, because we were the heirs who must use the principle because no other fitted our needs?" (433). He works through these questions by connecting the space of writing and the concept of love to a space of moral action, or at least to a preparation for principled action that will achieve ideal democracy and work against nationalistic exclusions. The invisible man tells us in the Epilogue that he tortures himself "to put it all down" in writing because he has, in fact, learned things that came to him once he stepped away from normative and constraining discourses, such as those espoused by the Brotherhood's version of communism and by Ras's variety of black nationalism. His concluding thoughts near the end of the Epilogue reveal the very schisms from which the question has arisen:

So it is now I denounce and defend, or feel prepared to defend. . . . I denounce because though implicated and partially responsible, I have been hurt to the point of abysmal pain, hurt to the point of invisibility. And I defend because in spite of all I find that I love. In order to get some of it down I have to love. I sell you no phony forgiveness, I'm a desperate man—but too much of your life will be lost, its meaning lost, unless you approach it as much through love as through hate. So I approach it through division. So I denounce and I defend and I hate and I love. (437–38)

The protagonist's conclusion sheds meaningful light on the psychical fractures from which arise his revised "approach" to the meaning of his life. His mode of response to the painful experience of a racialized and fragmented existence emerges as a philosophy of moral love—a higher love toward which he strives, but which he has not yet achieved. Were we to heed the invisible man's example, which he describes as a "divided" strategic approach, defining his ultimate philosophy of moral love in light of Ellison's view of the novel as a function of American democracy would require that we approach it piecemeal through the idea of nation and the construct of race and, more specifically, through varied inscriptions and discourses of blackness. That which lies at the heart of discourses on the nation is regularly articulated, as I discuss in the foregoing chapters of this study, through metaphors of purity and blood, of community and belonging, of authenticity and legitimacy (including jurisprudence), and by extension, metaphors of desire. So much of what lies at the heart of nationalist discourses evolves out of figural language that we regularly use to describe families and our membership in them at the same time that it echoes tropological language used to talk about racial belonging and our longing to belong to a community, society, or nation.

In fact, as I discuss in chapter 4 of this study, the idea of the nation is theorized by W. E. B. Du Bois, Ernest Gellner, and Hans Kohn, among others, as a political entity that grew out of family units—biological unions that came together in work and cultural groups to form the basis of the city-state, a precursor of the nation-state. Thus the notions of blood that give life to our ideas of race likewise engender our concept of the modern nation-state. In chapter 3 of this study, I discuss *The Metaphysics of Morals* by Immanuel Kant, whom many scholars recognize as providing the modern definitions of both race and nation at a moment in Western history that has left an indelible mark on our considerations of the Enlightenment. Kant writes that the members of the nation can be "represented as analogous to descendants from a common ancestry (*congeniti*). . . . [I]n an intellectual sense or for the purposes of right, they can be thought of as the offspring of a common mother (the republic), constituting, as it were, a single family (*gens, natio*) whose members (the citizens) are all equal by birth." Thus, the essence of racial thinking (underscoring here the essentialism that is caught up with racialism) is situated in founding metaphors that overlay with discursive sediment the politics of the nation-state and underscore through tropes of mother and family the idea of the nation-state as a home to which we belong, a dwelling or habitation. The essence of racial thinking is imbricated with the question of national belonging, which we often metaphorically imagine in terms of home and community: mother, family, membership, as well as the republic, the citizenry, and its culture.

In light of such discourse as this, it is telling to consider once more Ellison's by now well-known theory of the aims and function of the American novel. Similarly, the relation of the ideas of nation-state and "home"—a concept-metaphor, really, in Ellison's thought—should lead us to meditate further upon his pert attention to conceptual metaphor as he composed his text. Ellison's theory of the novel linked love and being, as well as nation and home. Likening the novel to an existential habitation, Ellison argued that the novel could provide a portal to a realization of the democratic ideals upon which the country had been founded. For instance, when considering what he felt to be the "chief significance" of *Invisible Man* as a novel, Ellison concluded: "Its experimental attitude, and its attempt to return to the mood of personal moral responsibility for democracy which typified the best of our nineteenth-century fiction" in the tradition of Mark Twain ("Brave Words for a Startling Occasion" 102). Ellison argued that the twentieth-century American novel was in crisis precisely because of its inattention to the moral problems facing the nation. These had to do with what he describes as "the conflicts within the human heart which arose when the sacred principles of the Constitution and the Bill of Rights clashed with the practical exigencies of human greed and fear, hate and love" (104). Specifically, for Ellison, the Negro in American fiction could aid us not only in redeeming the lost values of the novel, but also in achieving the lofty democratic aims of our nation. For the Negro in American fiction, he argued, "symbolized both the man lowest down and the mysterious, underground aspect of human personality. In a sense the Negro was the gauge of the human condition as it waxed and waned in our democracy" (104). He concluded that in order to "see America with an awareness of its rich diversity and its almost magical fluidity and freedom I was forced to conceive of a novel unburdened by the narrow naturalism which has led . . . to the final and unrelieved despair which marks so much of our current fiction" (104–5). And thus his extrapolated conclusion, coming in the penultimate paragraph of his acceptance speech upon winning the 1953 National Book Award: "The way home we seek is that condition of man's being at home in the world, which is called love, and which we term democracy" (105–6).

Ellison's metaphor of love as democracy is foundational to his novelistic poetics, especially as exemplified in *Invisible Man*. It takes shape through what he saw as the re-determined foundation of the nation-state, as well as by way of a number of deft theoretical framings. Ellison relates this metaphor to representations of embodied blackness that serve to undergird the central critique of his novel: blackness and democratic inclusion provisionally appear to be diametrically opposed in *Invisible Man*, and each in turn runs counter to the exclusionary principles that give shape to the nation-state.

Ellison's thought on this point resonates with that of two writers who occupy my attention earlier in this study—Equiano and Du Bois. Each approaches the idea of blackness by way of an analysis that destabilizes the concepts of blackness and whiteness alike, especially as these concepts pertain to ideas of national identity. The intellectual process subtending this outcome takes on different guises in the work of each writer, but mainly occurs within a debate over the notion of nationhood and national belonging. Equiano, for instance, speaks of his blackness as a disembodied African identity to which he no longer has full access. Yet the negative attributes associated with embodied blackness by Europeans disallow him the Englishness he desires and ultimately approximates and critiques. On the other hand, Du Bois's 1897 critical ontology of blackness or, more specifically, of a racialized identity called blackness or the Negro, is more pointed, yet nuanced. In "The Conservation of Races," Du Bois considers blackness a political tool that—once it has been historicized and deconstructed—may be used to unite Americans of African descent in the face of white American aggression. However, Du Bois points out that this uniting force is quite unstable. He reads race as metaphor and ephemeron: blackness is, for him, a limited identity that may be cast off when two important events have taken place. First, the "Negro people as a race" must make a lasting "contribution" to "civilization and humanity, which no other race can make." Blackness as *racial identity* may then finally be cast aside once "the ideal of human brotherhood" will have become a "practical possibility" ("Conservation" 825). But Du Bois never argues that the idea of black *culture* must be relinquished fully. Rather, he demonstrates the capacity of black culture to exact critique (in the manner that Hortense Spillers recognizes and advocates in "The Idea of Black Culture"[8]) through his attention to the transcendent and visionary power of the Sorrow Songs, his portraits of southern black life in America, and his construction of a sometimes transcendent, sometimes immanent narrative persona in *The Souls of Black Folk*.

Ellison's interpretation of blackness differs somewhat from that of Equiano and Du Bois, yet resonates in perhaps unexpected ways. In "The Art of Fiction," the 1955 interview conducted by the *Paris Review*, Ellison pronounces his ideas on the topic, and seems to imply that while conceiving *Invisible Man*, he had no intention of subverting the usual social implications of blackness in Western thought in favor of a critique that blackness might bring forth:

> [T]here are certain themes, symbols and images which are based on folk material. For example, there is the old saying amongst Negroes: If you're black, stay back; if you're brown, stick around; if you're white, you're right. And there is the joke Negroes tell on themselves about being so black they can't be seen in the dark. In my book this sort of thing was merged with the meanings which blackness and light have long had in Western mythology: evil and goodness, ignorance and knowledge, through blackness to light; that is, from ignorance to enlightenment: invisibility to visibility. ("The Art of Fiction" 173)

It would seem on first surmise that Ellison, for whom "the word," that is, language, is of utmost importance, incorporates conventional, negative perspectives on blackness into his aesthetic without challenging their connotations. As Ellison continued to restate his position on the point, however, his concept of blackness showed greater nuance, in a manner of speaking. Moving from a perspective of blackness framed and conditioned by what Ellison himself refers to in 1955 as a white "Western mythology," in a 1966 interview he launches a different sort of "definition," sprawling in its breadth and complex in implication. Although Ellison expresses concern over an "increasing emphasis on Negroness, on blackness" in certain quarters of the Civil Rights and Black Arts movements, he expands his perspective on blackness by distinguishing biological notions of race from the culture a so-called race possesses and shares with the world:

> [Blackness] grows out of despair. [. . .] It attempts to define Negroes by their pigmentation, not their culture. What makes

you a Negro is having grown up under certain cultural conditions, having undergone an experience that shapes your culture. There is a body of folklore, a certain sense of American history. There is our psychology and the peculiar circumstances under which we have lived. There is our cuisine, though we don't admit it, and our forms of expression. I speak certain idioms; this is also part of the concord that makes me a Negro. (*Conversations with Ralph Ellison*, 101)

Ellison agrees with Du Bois when he propounds blackness by way of culture and consciousness rather than biology. But to opine (seriously) that blackness is disgorged by a social condition of "despair" is to raise any number of pertinent questions. Does he insist that African Americans despair over their station in life, which is determined, as it were, by virtue of the color of their skin and not by their culture alone? Might one then go on to say, as Ellison seems to here, that the despair that engenders blackness reflects a rather desperate attempt on the part of the larger "white" society to constrain "black" people, to put them "in their place" by way of a restrictive process of determination reserved for "black skin"? If blackness entails a specific sort of psychology and "a certain sense of American history," as Ellison puts it, are these intrinsically negative fields of inquiry because they themselves sprout from the negativity that blackness—if we follow what seems to be Ellison's logic in this regard—appears to be?

Surely Ellison's sense of Americanness has something to do with how he frames blackness here, as he intimates when he comments on the "certain sense of American history" he feels Negroes possess. Even as Ellison quite presciently distinguishes between a biologically essentialist view of race and one that sees race as an amalgamation of cultural values, he is still less than precise in conveying his sense of the relationship between biology and culture, a relationship (nature vs. nurture) that has long been under debate. Blackness as despair seems harsh and jagged, especially coming from an intellectual of Ellison's stature, who articulated such thoughts at the height of the Civil Rights movement and on the eve of the Black Power movement. We could point our finger at Ellison and echo Ernest Kaiser's later condemnation of him as an "establishment writer" and, what is more damning, an "Uncle Tom."[9] But such angling would overlook the fact that Ellison's ideas on blackness, as stated in a number of interviews reprinted in the important collection, *Conversations with Ralph Ellison* (1995), are not far from the proclamations of black cultural nationalists such as Kaiser, who denigrated his work during the late 1960s and 1970s, and for whom Ellison had little appreciation in return.

For example, Ellison's emphasis on black vernacular as "part of the concord that makes me a Negro" is but a stone's throw from the exhortations of a certain Professor McWorter, who, according to James A. Emanuel, defines blackness in terms of black speech. Such a definition is, Emanuel writes, central to a "prescribed training for literary competition" ("Blackness Can" 213). Similarly, Sarah Webster Fabio echoes Ellison in deeming black language "an idiom of integrated insight," a poetic creation and an amalgam of "idiosyncrasies—those individualized stylistic nuances (such as violation of structured syntax [and somewhat esoteric metaphorical contrivances]) which nevertheless hit 'home' and evoke truth" (qtd. in "Blackness Can" 211).

Black Aestheticians such as Fabio and Emanuel shared a grand appreciation of the Afro-French Négritude movement, with its staunch valuations of African-oriented cultural artifacts. Whatever affinities Ellison might have unconsciously had for Black Aesthetic-tinged evaluations of African American culture (for he consciously distanced himself from the movement), he critiqued the Négritudinists openly. Going beyond the perspective of Jean-Paul Sartre, who characterized Négritude as an "antiracist racism" in his 1948 essay "Orphée noir," Ellison condemns Négritude as an ideology that "represents the reverse of that racism with which prejudiced whites approach Negroes. As a theory of art it implies precisely that culture is transmitted through the genes. It is a blood theory" ("A Very Stern Discipline" 303).

In his exceptionalism, Ellison not only failed to give Négritude its due by not examining its premises and evolution more carefully; he also "rejected any notion of a link [with Africans] just as [he] later rejected [Melville] Herskovits' ideas" about African cultural survivals (*Conversations with Ralph Ellison* 67). Ellison's position on blackness, read through his ostensible disdain for certain of its theoretical manifestations, were likely precipitators of the assaults lanced against him by writer John O. Killens and historians John Henrik Clarke and Herbert Aptheker. Harold Cruse's *The Crisis of the Negro Intellectual* (1967) gives an account of the verbal fracas that took place during the 1965 conference, "The Negro Writer's Vision of America," organized by Killens and held at the New School for Social Research in February of that year. The participants might well have burned Ellison's image in effigy, so intense was the defamation of Ellison's intellectual and artistic character recounted by Cruse. According to him, Clarke portrayed Ellison as "'standing outside his people's struggle.'"

Aptheker, a white Marxist historian who had been named W. E. B. Du Bois's literary executor in 1946, concurred, adding with what seems to be unconscious irony that " '[it] is unfortunate that Mr. Ellison is not here'" to voice a defense of himself. " '[He] has made himself not particularly visible in the struggles of the Negro people'" (Cruse 501–508).

Most likely, Ellison made himself a target of such ad hominem attacks because of his own theory of the novel and his ideas of cultural and literary aesthetics, which carefully merged his apparently anti-black nationalist ideas on blackness with his developing concept of Americanness and democracy. He was, perhaps, most culpable in the eyes of Killens and the AFNA cohort for saving his loftiest literary praise for white American and European writers. (Ellison did not even respond to "most mail addressed to him by his fellow black writers," John Henrik Clarke chided.) He admired Eliot's *The Waste Land* (1922) as an example of a great work of American literature, whose stature derived, in part at least, from its use of cultural forms and traditions in the text. He was also deeply intrigued by Russian literature, and, as is well known, held the work of Fyodor Dostoyevsky in the highest esteem. The French writer André Malraux became a good friend of Ellison's, and his *La Condition humaine* (1933; translated into English as *Man's Fate* in 1934) provided Ellison with an example of a novel influenced by Marxist ideology (as were the works of any number of the AFNA group), yet free from the limitations of socialist dogma, which often produced, Ellison was known to complain, dull, ineloquent fiction.

While Ellison's novel remained popular with a number of white mainstream critics, the widespread condemnation that flowed from Black Aesthetic and AFNA circles largely proscribed his work in the halls of black literary criticism, and rendered his pronouncements on blackness somewhat circumspect. As late as 1988, critic Valerie Smith accused him of denying "his intellectual links with and debt to earlier black writers" ("The Meaning of Narration in *Invisible Man*" 26). However, Ellison does acknowledge inheritances from his black literary antecedents, albeit implicitly. His belief in the importance of black cultural forms—folklore, Spirituals, the blues, and jazz—emerges as a guiding force in the invisible man's memoir. Frederick Douglass's 1845 *Narrative* (and more obliquely, that of Equiano) undoubtedly provided Ellison fertile ground for troping on the multiple naming his protagonist endures. Ellison's narrator remarks directly upon the renaming Douglass withstands in order to attain a position of social power, and by the time of the Prologue and Epilogue, as he undertakes the writing of his memoir, it is clear that he has read and critically digested Douglass's *Narrative*: "Douglass came north to escape and find work in the shipyards;

a big fellow in a sailor's suit who, like me, had taken another name. What had his true name been? Whatever it was, it was as Douglass that he became himself, defined himself" (*Invisible Man* 288). Du Bois's critique of black leadership, articulated searingly in his essay, "Of Mr. Booker T. Washington and Others," resonates in the scene where the invisible man is first introduced to Jack's mistress, Emma. "Their leaders are made, not born," she says cynically of black people (*Invisible Man* 230). Du Bois had written in *The Souls of Black Folk* that while others "had become leaders by the silent suffrage of their fellows," Washington, the founder of Tuskegee Institute (Ellison's alma mater, though he never earned a degree) whose image is so clearly evoked in the second chapter of the novel, was hoisted into leadership on the shoulders of white "national opinion" (*Souls* 397–98). Du Bois is quite direct in his criticism: "Mr. Washington represents in Negro thought the old attitude of adjustment and submission; but adjustment at such a peculiar time as to make his programme unique. . . . Mr. Washington's programme naturally takes an economic cast, becoming a gospel of Work and Money to such an extent as apparently almost completely to overshadow the higher aims of life. . . . [it] practically accepts the alleged inferiority of the Negro races" (398). The invisible man, from the critical distance of the underground, recalls the sight of a statue of Washington, and likewise wonders about the true aims of the founder's seemingly liberatory ideology:

> Then in my mind's eye I see the bronze statue of the college Founder, the cold Father symbol, his hands outstretched in the breathtaking gesture of lifting a veil that flutters in hard, metallic folds above the face of a kneeling slave; and I am standing puzzled, unable to decide whether the veil is really being lifted, or lowered more firmly in place; whether I am witnessing a revelation or a more efficient blinding. (28)

Certainly this ambiguous image of uplift calls to mind the title of Washington's 1901 autobiography, *Up from Slavery*, even as the concept-metaphor of the veil signifies at once the blindness and insight modeled by Du Bois in *Souls*, where Washington's motives were likewise cast into question. A further example of the black literary heritage resonant in the novel is found in the work of James Weldon Johnson, whose *The Autobiography of an Ex-Colored Man* (1912/1927) Houston Baker sees as a "prototype" for Ellison's experimental text.[10] Johnson's nameless narrator encounters the greatness of black cultural forms, and carries with him a talisman (the ten-dollar gold piece made worthless by the hole his father had drilled through it) that is recast as various fetishes in Ellison's work. Throughout the novel, the invisible man is adamant about keeping with him a leather briefcase bearing a number of "important papers," Mary Rambo's broken bank (the "cast-iron figure of a very black, red-lipped and wide-mouthed Negro"), and Tod Clifton's dancing sambo doll.

In implicitly and at times explicitly engaging Douglass, Washington, Du Bois, and Johnson through his fiction, Ellison nods to black literary antecedents, all male, it must be said. (While not sexist, Ellison was at least superficially masculinist in his fiction, a point I take up in the next section.) Assuming a public mantle that continues a long tradition of contending with notions of "manhood" (a topic that demands a chapter of its own), Ellison, unlike Wright in this regard, exempted himself from what Herbert Aptheker called the "visible" circles of activist black authorship, becoming hyper-visible in the "mainstream" world of white letters while (from his own perspective at least) fully immersing himself in writing with an aesthetic purpose and a latent, if not overt, political focus. Jerry G. Watts deems this the "conundrum" of the anti-black nationalist black intellectual: inscribing blackness as invisibility in a way that counters the concrete, essential black subject imagined by the Black Aestheticians, while at the same time speaking of blackness in ways that do not conform to the contours of the prescriptive boundaries of discursive black self-determination put into place by such powerful black nationalist artistic and intellectual circles as the Harlem Writers Guild, constituted a transgressive gesture on Ellison's part. In other words, in the eyes of many black nationalist thinkers, Ellison was hardly the ideal porte-parole of everyday black people facing bleak social and political situations. To speak plainly, Ellison was, in some circles, considered a sell-out who had abandoned his people.

Yet this conclusion, framed and clouded as it is by essentialist issues of racial and cultural authenticity, must be dismantled carefully and with insight. Watts, of course, begins this work by recuperating Ellison's image as an intellectual who might not have been openly political, but was certainly influenced by political thought and saw art as unavoidably social and political in nature. Nonetheless, in Watts' estimation, Ellison was also an elitist "who [believed] that disengagement from politics best [served] his creative ambitions" (*Heroism and the Black Intellectual* 21). More recently, Nicole Waligora-Davis sees Ellison's "racial philosophy" as one that constituted "a rubric as much an expression of black nationalism as it is the formation of an ethical system for human interaction and accountability."[11] Ellison's route in political thought was necessarily different because he conceived of the responsibilities of the artist in terms that demanded critical distance and space for reflection. His considerations and critiques of American society were generally informed by his broad and deep understanding of the historical principles that founded the concept of ideal democracy in America, and that generally meet staunch resistance when they run afoul of the exclusionary and racist practices of the nation-state on both sides of matters, by both white American racist, terrorist, and so-called "nativist" groups such as the Ku Klux Klan, and by extreme black nationalists, such as the African Blood Brotherhood, an organization of the 1920s not unlike the group of black nationalists led by Ras the Exhorter/Destroyer in *Invisible Man*.

We may conclude that Ellison was an apolitical, disengaged literary aesthete only if we deny that the novel, as a literary genre and social tool, bears any sort of politically symbolic power. I agree with Ellison that as a form, the novel does possess this sort of power. Ellison often alluded to the symbolic origins, form, and function of the novel in his many essays on the subject of literature and democracy in *Shadow and Act* (1964) as well as in *Going to the Territory* (1986). Therefore, what has often been called Ellison's Euro-Americanism, further remarked in his appreciation of the Irishman James Joyce's dual manipulation of and innovations in literary form and linguistic content, could also be interpreted in relation to the sort of cosmopolitanism and internationalism that framed the political era in which Ellison understood the novel to first rise and take shape as a new genre of writing.

Internationalism, from the early days of its conception in eighteenth-century liberalism, has always had to do with the formative ideals of individual nation-states as they relate to one another. It may be seen as yet another dialectical process whereby nation-states recognize in each other the merits of their respective civilizations, which may, in turn, be said to possess a specific exchange value. Evolved and developed societies are considered as such by other nation-states only to the extent that evidence of their development is tangible or material. Advancements in technology and, no less, in the sciences and the arts come to be of paramount importance in the display of high "culture," the major principle underlying concepts of civilization. Literature was thus widely held to be indicative of "high culture," and non-literate, or oral, societies were relegated to the hinterlands of savagery. Such purported "savages" as Africans and Native Americans were, of course, forbidden the communion of nation-states and their emerging democracies due to the oral—and thus "low"—foundations of their cultures. They were, hence, without civilization and were cast outside the boundaries of the international community of nation-states.

As I discuss in chapter 3, philosophical texts by writers such as Kant and Jean-Jacques Rousseau, along with those of their Romantic-era successor Georg W. F. Hegel, laid the theoretical foundations upon which the modern nation-state would rise and flourish. And with the rise of the modern nation-state came a fundamental change in the concept of democracy. Coined in the fifth century by the Greek historian Herodotus, "democracy" combined two words meaning, separately, "the people" and "to rule." Thus the original meaning of democracy was, in the literal sense, "rule of the people," a concept that was not widely popular with all political observers. Plato's attitude toward the concept was "decidedly hostile," Muhammed Rejai writes, and Plato's student Aristotle "accepted it with severe qualifications" (3). The concept fared no better as early modern philosophers and theorists began to imagine the birth of the nation-state. Analyses such as that of Niccolò Machiavelli underscored the tension between concepts of the nation-state and democracy. Rejai points out that the centralization of power proposed by Machiavelli in his 1532 book *The Prince* "was manifestly detrimental to the development of democratic" thought (11). Political philosopher Chantal Mouffe concurs. The forms of consensus postulated by the modern nation-state and required for its longevity "are by necessity based on acts of exclusion," she writes (378). Mouffe and her collaborator, the political theorist Ernesto Laclau, remind us that the "original forms of democratic thought were linked to a positive and unified conception of human nature" (181), and this nature, as theorized by Europeans and the American "founders," was not inclusive of African identities. Africans were thus cast outside of the community of human being and, hence, the community of national citizenry. They were excluded from the very ideal of the beloved community Ellison sought to promulgate.

The notion of community in these arguments over national belonging can be seen clearly in the foundational work of a number of Enlightenment-era nationalist theorists, Thomas Jefferson prominent among them. Jefferson, one of the "classical" theorists of modern democracy identified by Rejai, reflects this notion in his widely remarked *Notes on the State of Virginia* (1804). There, as Jefferson contemplates the maturing of the American nation-state, he insists that once slavery in the United States is abolished, blacks should be "removed beyond the reach of mixture." The objection to the presence of blacks is physical and moral as well as political, the statesman argues, fearing that "the real distinction which nature has made . . . will divide us into parties and produce convulsions which will probably never end but in the extermination of one or the other race" (46). Such a disruption in the space of the socius was, to Jefferson's mind, conducive neither to the principles of national belonging nor to the ideals of democracy as they were theorized in his day.

The Civil Rights–era image of democracy Ellison renders against Jefferson's classical version of it (we might just as likely say that Ellison undertakes a pointed diachronic exposition of America's democratic shortcomings) must therefore also be read as a critique of the traditional liberal concept of democracy and its limited notions of "freedom." Because the classical theorists of democracy, such as Jefferson and Rousseau, held as main values liberties in the forms of "inalienable" and "self-evident" rights (Jefferson) and community or social welfare (Rousseau), classical democracy such as that which they practiced stressed such ideas as the "common will" and the "common good" (Rejai 24). The principle of liberty was understood as a "non-interference with the right of unlimited appropriation and with the mechanisms of the capitalist market economy," and it is this notion—pointedly economic and laissez-faire capitalist—that constituted the eighteenth century liberal idea of individual freedom. This traditional view "exerts itself to discredit every 'positive' conception of liberty as being potentially totalitarian," Laclau and Mouffe write. "It affirms that a liberal political order can exist only in the framework of a capitalist free market economy" (172). Thus, twentieth-century conservatives, who hearkened to a profoundly anti-egalitarian defense of the free-market economy and concomitant ideas of individual freedom, did so on a platform provided by the anti-egalitarian principles of eighteenth-century liberalism. They worked "to redefine the notion of democracy itself in such a way as to restrict its field of application and limit political participation to an even narrower area" (Mouffe and Laclau 173).

The conservative definition of democracy underscored by Mouffe and Laclau finally ends in the emergence of a state ideology that contradicts and even at times seeks to render impotent the contemporary demands of democratic principles that evolved during various phases of the Civil Rights movement, from the late nineteenth century to Ellison's own time. Yet Ellison appears not to have wavered in his faith in the possibility of a beloved community, a revisionist sort of "ideal" democracy, and never failed to call upon the American nation-state to actualize the humanist ideals that founded its democratic principles, even if these were at odds with free-market principles.

Thus, he embodied what the black feminist legal scholar Dorothy Roberts elsewhere calls a "fidelity to the Constitution."[12] The invisible man's rejection of certain threads of political ideology, signified in his membership in the Brotherhood and his ultimate understanding, by the time of the Prologue and Epilogue and the beginning of his hibernation underground, that ideal democracy had been hijacked and obscured—and that it needed, above all, to be rescued and resurrected—finds an analogy in Frederick Douglass's democratic philosophy. Douglass's shift during the nineteenth century from a Garrisonian rejection of the Constitution, to a realization that the Constitution was being misused and willfully misinterpreted by the ruling class signals for Roberts the profound degree of trust that African Americans and their intellectuals have traditionally placed in the founding documents of this country. Douglass, who once dramatically intoned that the Founding Fathers, in crafting the Constitution while neglecting to abolish racial bondage, had "attempted to unite Liberty in holy wedlock with the dead body of Slavery," later turned from this position to embrace the Constitution. For surely, he wrote, this document "could not well have been designed at the same time to maintain and perpetuate a system of rapine and murder like slavery."[13]

Central to my point here are the familial ("holy wedlock") and sexual ("system of rapine") metaphors Douglass crafts in order to exact his early and late critiques of the nation-state's biopolitics and practices of racial exclusion. Douglass clearly recognizes, in his early statement, not only the foundational nature with which family was considered in relation to the edification of the nation-state. (This is a point I examine and discuss in chapter 5 of this study.) He also sees the sexual contradictions at work in joining a false conception of liberty and liberalism with the moribund and sinful practice of human bondage. Douglass's critique of the sexual disparagement of black womanhood (which I see in his choice of the word "rapine," a word full of classical connotations of the vengeful sexual assault of the women of a community), alongside the effacement of black existence (in his use of "murder") render his analysis one that cannot be ignored. Further, it resonates with the use of familial and maternal metaphors in writings on the nation-state by figures such as Kant. Again, Kant's metaphorical rendering of the republic as the "common mother" of the citizenry, a figure who can provide a sense of cohesion, belonging, and "home" even to disparate, heterogeneous nations lacking consanguinity, places the mother at the center of the discourse on nation and democracy, as I see it. I will return to this point shortly.

Douglass's thought continues to resonate with that of contemporary intellectuals, who have no more released the Constitution from its responsibility toward democracy than did he and Ellison. As I discuss at greater length in chapter 2 of the present study, Wahneema Lubiano, in her introduction to the collection of critical essays entitled *The House that Race Built* (1997), an outgrowth of the Race Matters Conference convened by Lubiano and others at Princeton University in April of 1994, the very month when Ralph Ellison died, writes:

> The United States is not just the domicile of a historically specific form of racial oppression, but it sustains itself as a structure through that oppression. If race—and its strategic social and ideological deployment as racism—didn't exist, the United States' severe inequalities and betrayal of its formal commitments to social equality and social justice would be readily apparent to anyone existing on this ground. (vii)

Here the question of race interrupts the notion of national community. If race did not exist, Lubiano argues, then each person living within the nation-state's borders could easily apprehend the country's critical failure to ensure social justice and social equality for its citizens. However, because race and racism are alive and well in America, most Americans are blinded (by race itself) to these problems. While Lubiano supplies, in short order, a most insightful and incisive critique of the shortcomings of our democratic order ("The idea of race and the operation of racism," she writes, "are the best friends that the economic and political elite have in the United States"), she proposes no alternative to a democratic society founded upon Constitutional ideals. Instead, she forcefully appeals to the doctrines of equality and justice in her introduction, and part of the purpose of the collection is to "call into question and to account a liberal majority that trivializes racism by turning its attention to individual remedies, to attitude adjustment, to 'color-blind' legal adjudications" (vii).

In the same collection, Toni Morrison uses her introductory essay, "Home," to expound a similar point, while putting forward a different argument in favor of democratic inclusion:

> From the beginning I was looking for a sovereignty—an authority—that I believed was available to me only in fiction writing. . . . I believe . . . that my own writerly excursions and my use of a house/home antagonism are related to the topics addressed [at the Race Matters Conference held at Princeton University in 1994] because so much of what seems to lie about in discourses on race concerns legitimacy, authenticity, community, [and]

belonging. . . . The anxiety of belonging is entombed within the central metaphors in the discourse on globalism, transnationalism, nationalism, the break-up of federations, the rescheduling of alliances, and the fictions of sovereignty. Yet these figurations of nationhood and identity are frequently as raced themselves as the originating racial house that defined them. When they are not raced, they are . . . imaginary landscape, never inscape; Utopia, never home. (passim)

Morrison's house/home metaphor appears to pay implicit homage to analogous metaphorics Ellison unfolded in his acceptance speech upon receiving the National Book Award in 1953 for *Invisible Man*. Indeed, during the previous year, 1993, Morrison had been awarded the Nobel Prize for Literature an emblematic forty years after Ellison garnered the National Book Award, so it is not unreasonable that his words would have resonated with her thoughts in the month of his death. Ellison, retelling the tale of Menelaus in the Odyssey and thus allegorizing the quest for self-identity that lies at the heart of his novel, concludes his remarks on the political and cultural contributions he felt *Invisible Man* made by devising a metaphor that explicitly connected the home metaphor at work in his novel to both love and democracy. In fact, as I mention earlier, the syntax of his sentence draws a metaphorical equivalence between each of these terms: "The way home we seek is that condition of man's being at home in the world, which is called love, and which we term democracy" ("Brave Words" 105–6).

We might say that love, home, and democracy form a tripartite conceptual metaphor of the ideal human condition in Ellison's thinking on both the novel and the nation. In his critical writings as well as in his fiction, Ellison, like Morrison, seeks to refashion the American domicile into a site where politics might actually be something other than an expression of the will and desire of the white ruling classes, which often demand the exclusion and marginalization of "lower" classes based on racial determination and socioeconomic positioning. Rather, he hopes that the American house, a sphere dominated by the racist, gendered, and class-oriented ideology of the nation-state, might be transformed into a home shaped instead by the principles of moral democracy and capable of accommodating pluralism and hybridity, or what Ellison often refers to in terms of "possibilities." As Ellison addresses himself to this concept, he insists upon the responsibilities of citizenship, and in *Invisible Man* this democratic dilemma is, we might say using Ellison's own metaphor, "acted out upon the body of a Negro giant who, lying trussed up like Gulliver, forms the stage and the scene upon which and within which the action unfolds" ("Twentieth-Century Fiction" 28). In *Invisible Man*, Ellison renders the black body as a metaphorical liminal space upon which and within which the conflicts engendered by the struggle for true democracy are acted out. For him, the Negro represents, as he maintains in "Brave Words for a Startling Occasion," "the gauge of the human condition as it [waxes] and [wanes] in our democracy'" (104). In Ellison's concept of the American novel, the black body serves as a metaphorical barometer of the nation's democratic sensibilities. It clarifies the effects of America's racial house upon the black body that seeks a home, a habitation.

Ellison's project in *Invisible Man*, and the later projects of Lubiano, Morrison, and other participants in the Race Matters conference, work to point out the peculiar nature of racial construction in the United States, with particular attention to historical circumstances and the exigencies of nationalist thought that are in regular and at times tensive articulation with traditionally democratic notions such as liberty and equality. This work of unmasking, as it were, the specificities of American power structures that inhere in the nation-state generally approaches its object via a tripartite vocabulary of power, authority, and legitimacy. Ellison's own recognition of the eighteenth-century roots of the novel, which "rose," as Ian Watt[14] points out, at the very moment when a number of Western nations were coming to see themselves as nation-states, when ideologies of race were crystallizing and when modern capitalism began to exert its force, means that we as readers must arrive at an understanding of the impact of nationalist ideology, racial thinking, and political theory on Ellison's text and his response to these discourses. Because he saw the novel in general, and thus *Invisible Man* in particular, as having always been "tied up with the idea of nationhood," ("The Novel as a Function of American Democracy" 310), and because the tension that begat *Invisible Man* commences with Ellison's—and his narrator's—metaphorical formulations regarding the implications of blackness upon blackness (that persistent and progressive blackness brings about both social invisibility and hypervisibility), we must further contextualize *Invisible Man* as the outgrowth of Ellison's consideration of a particular historical moment in the West, when ideas of race and homelessness most forcefully collide with those of home and national belonging, when raced bodies take on a value coeval with the dictates of a new market economy, and where speech has a certain and dynamic role in the realm of political power.

All such roads lead to the metaphor of love, and ideally so if we follow Ellison in his critique of American democracy. Ellison gives us to know as well that love's discourse in the novel must come from and demonstrate its relation to the linguistics and stylistics of the community. Otherwise, it can hold no cultural or political authority. That the work of Lubiano and, especially, Morrison is emblematic of black feminist critical discourse on love and democracy, and that the maternal is conceptually and historically at the core of notions of "home" in the modern nation-state, form the occasion for my return to the maternal in this next section.

Love's Habitation: Blackness, The Uncanny Maternal, and American Democracy

The "body" of Ellison's novel is itself, like the black body of his metaphorics, situated in a caesura: set in the placeless place that is at once Harlem and America, yet neither one of these in reality. This textual body is love positioned in and emergent from the void, since Ellison names the occasion of the novel as the occasion of love, the event and necessary condition of his having to "put it all down" (437) even as he locates Harlem "nowhere,"[15] the site of both the common black man and this marginal man's lived condition of existential chaos. Harlem is thus not a utopia—the dreamed of place to come. It is, rather, an atopia, the no-place or abyss where black being is presumed to fall inexorably into nothingness. Because Ellison titles his novel with the very name most of us have come to bestow upon his protagonist, and because the novel serves as the fictional memoir of a self that exists symbolically in autobiographical narration, I want provisionally to consider the novel and its text as a body. It may be considered a living, symbolic, and exiled being cast out of doors as well as outside of home and love. It is cast instead into an atopic habitation that both skirts and limns the biopolitical realities of an exclusionary nation-state. One might say that it is a body birthed from a certain womb that served as both home and reprieve from a racist onslaught: the body of the black mother.

   I have noted how Ellison tropes upon Wright's underground man and the poetic revolution of his chthonic heterotopia. Wright's protagonist, as we have seen, constructs out of the fragments of his existence a poetry that threatens the ontology, the epistemology, and even the politics of the above ground. Thus his is a *stanzaic* space, the nucleus of dessicated poetic thought, a "dwelling" or "room" (following the etymology of the word "stanza") in which both his thought and his lyrical spirit simultaneously expand and contract. Wright's caesura—even in its emphasis upon song, which recalls the meaning of the word "caesura" when used as a verb, an elongation of utterance in a "singsong" style that evokes Daniels's impulse to sing as the police drive him back to the manhole—calls us once more to reconsider the scission Western philosophy has long upheld between poetry and philosophy. What is regularly overlooked by this insistence is that all poetic projects—even those articulated in the vernacular—are aimed toward not only beauty, but also thinking and knowledge.[16] With Daniels's annihilation we read not only of the silencing of the black body that seeks a habitation. Perhaps more importantly, we see Wright's broader critique of the hegemonic marginalization of black epistemology, an epistemology that, from the perspective of the black metaphorics I have examined throughout this study, nonetheless looks persistently for and towards a brighter world to come; a world that can serve openly as a dwelling—a home—rather than as a refuge.

In the Prologue, the invisible man's first descent into his memory, history, and imagination comes by way of song. Precipitated by the "lyric of sound" (6) intoned by Louis Armstrong, he quickly enough perceives the mournful strains of the slave mother's Spiritual. The bluesman Armstrong and the Spiritual-singing mother alike sing songs of existential angst and disappointment that mirror the state of the invisible man's unconscious. It is as though by descending from Armstrong's conscious world into the unconscious realm of the black mother, Ellison's character descends into a preternatural site rife with sacrament and mystery. The love of which she later speaks to him appears primordial and, in fact, antecedent to all other moral concerns. Love begets freedom, the woman tells him (9), and thus it bears some inherent relation to the principle on which the invisible man mediates at length in the Epilogue. It is, in fact, that which prompts his further reflection, his writing of his life's exploits in the pages of a fictitious memoir.

Ellison, as was often his wont, crafted his fiction with an eye toward the cultural practices that constitute the rituals of the Western world, and thus his descent into the underground, following the path taken not only by Wright, but also by such classical figures as Orpheus and Odysseus, comes by no accident. Few students of Ellison's fiction and essays will be surprised that he saw in ritual the source of literary inspiration and Western culture, more generally. Ellison was, as he notes in "The Art of Fiction" and elsewhere,[17] a great observer of the archetypal contradictions that were the ironic cultural artifacts of these rituals. His return to the space of the maternal—the movement toward the maternal is always a "return," since the maternal is antecedent to human life—obviates the simple trope that would make of Ellison's descent and prospective ascent a rescinding of the West's normative negation of black being. Ellison's return to the womb of the maternal is, rather, a complex return to the very embrace of human life that idealizes *agape* love, makes *eros* possible, and holds *thanatos*, or the death wish so often identified in Wright's fiction, at bay.[18] Again, Ellison seems to say, the descent into the womb, while seemingly a remanding to a daemonic place, is a prolegomenon, a propaedeutic to the world that love demands.

Audre Lorde has written of this maternal space as the "Black mother" who "exists more in women; yet she is a name for a humanity that men are not without." Men who deny the primordial feminine being Lorde names as central to the existence of all humanity "have taken a position against that piece of themselves, and it is a world position, a position throughout time" (*Sister Outsider* 101). Lorde's feminist worldview may seem far in intent and time from Ellison, but in fact, she was (writing in 1979 and specifically assuming a transhistorical stance) much more contemporary to his thought than it would seem were we to glance only briefly between them. This appears especially so if we take the additional step of pointing out the resonances between the feminist and womanist position Lorde upholds, and that of one of the most astute feminist and poststructuralist readers of Ellison, Hortense Spillers.

Where Lorde speaks of the "Black mother within" who provides a creative and epistemic power that men must, if they will, learn to recognize and prize, Spillers writes in "Mama's Baby, Papa's Maybe" (1987), that she as a black woman, like Lorde before her, has been named, but hers is a case of ritual misnaming. Dubbed "Sapphire," "Peaches," or "Earth Mother," did she not exist she "would have to be invented" (203). For Spillers, the "black woman," devised in a masculinist and sexist language that demands the bracketing qualification of quotation marks, is central to a conceptual metaphorics that is analogous to Du Bois's powerful concept-metaphor of the color line: "We could add to [Du Bois's] spatio-temporal configuration [of the color-line] another thematic of analogously terrible weight: if the 'black woman' can be seen as a particular figuration of the split subject that psychoanalysis posits, then this century marks the site of 'its' profoundest revelation" (203).

I will return to Spillers's fruitful analogy shortly, but will here underscore how her extrapolation of Lorde's humanistic metaphor of the "Black mother" eventuates in her argument that the

> African-American male has been touched, therefore, by the mother, handed by her in ways that he cannot escape, in ways that the white American male is allowed to temporize by a fatherly

reprieve. This human and historic development—the text that has been inscribed on the benighted heart of the continent—takes us to the center of an inexorable difference in the depths of American women's community: the African-American woman, the mother, the daughter, becomes historically the powerful and shadowy evocation of a cultural synthesis long evaporated—the law of the mother—only and precisely because legal enslavement removed the African-American male not so much from sight as from mimetic view as a partner in the prevailing social fiction of the father's name, the father's law. (Italics in original, 228)

Turning once more with these words in mind to the scene from the invisible man's dream that I quote at the outset of this chapter places before us a quite different notion of Ellison's psychoanalytic of race and descent (which signifies doubly here as both a genealogy and a movement into the depths of the psyche). Ellison seems to challenge white Western metaphysics of blackness with a differential symbolic of black feminism and maternality with which he is not generally credited. More often, he has been critiqued for eliding black women in his novel of black invisibility, much in the same way that Ellison himself critiques Ernest Hemingway for erasing blacks from his fictional portrayal of America in a fashion that is analogous, in Ellison's striking metaphor, to a denial of their very humanity,[19] a literary lynching. Or, he has been criticized for silencing them through, for instance, Jim Trueblood's blues ballad of father-daughter rape and incest, which has received such outstanding readings from Spillers and Baker. Yet is there not something more to these "marginal" figures of black women in *Invisible Man*, especially since most of them are depicted as maternal figures?[20]: the slave mother whom the invisible man encounters and queries at the outset of his dream; the young slave woman being auctioned at yet a deeper level of his reverie, "a beautiful girl the color of ivory pleading in a voice like [his] mother's as she stood before a group of slaveowners who bid for her naked body" (7); the evicted Mrs. Provo, a former slave mother whose scene of dispossession (he has seen, among her possessions strewn along a Harlem sidewalk, "an old breast pump with rubber bulb yellowed with age") evokes in the invisible man a mental vision of his mother "hanging wash on a windy day . . . her hands white and raw in the skirt-swirling wind" (206–7); and Mary Rambo, whose earnest nurturing of the protagonist and cloying rambunctiousness recall the stereotype of the mammy figure earlier redeemed and refigured by Harper in her Aunt Chloe poems.[21]

That each of these maternal figures appears in the oneiric, multiple folds of the invisible man's Prologue, analogous to the unconscious levels of the mind where, Ellison has contended, the Negro is repressed in the American psyche, should give us some indication of the ritual significance of these elided feminine black figures. I would argue that it is from their repressed yet mythological presence—narrative myth being one of the primary ways in which human beings seek to make sense of their existence by configuring a story of origin and roots, in short, a narrative of originary birth and home, and thus a narrative of originary maternality—that springs a metaphorics of black being.

The Repression of the Black Maternal

The idea of an originary yet repressed black maternal in Ellison's fiction is fairly analogous to his general theory of repression in the novel. Such a reading can be supported by a glance at the theme of repression Ellison develops over the course of his criticism. In "Twentieth-Century Fiction," for instance, he writes that while the "conception of the Negro as a symbol of man . . . was organic to nineteenth-century literature" (88), after "[Mark] Twain's compelling image of black and white fraternity [in *Huckleberry Finn*] the Negro generally disappears from fiction as a rounded human being" (89). The Negro was "thoroughly . . . pushed into the underground of the American conscience" to such an extent that even a writer of Hemingway's stature (in addition to the early Faulkner) "missed completely the structural, symbolic and moral necessity for that part of the plot in which the boys rescue Jim" (90). The "dual function" of such a "dissociation seems to be that of avoiding moral pain and thus to justify the South's racial code," Ellison concludes. For the Southerner, if not for American writers more broadly, Ellison argues, "the Negro becomes a symbol of his personal rebellion, his guilt and his repression of it" (98).

   This often rehearsed point of Ellison's poetics (and for Ellison, a moral American "conscience" was necessary to an American consciousness capable of realizing its ideals of democracy) reads compellingly in light of Spillers's theory, which calls us to see the black female as that "insurgent" "social subject" that "breaks in upon the imagination with a forcefulness that marks both a denial and an 'illegitimacy'" ("Mama's Baby" 228–29). Her insurgency goes against the law of the white father while re-instantiating the lost law of the black mother. Spillers, like Ellison, identifies a repression (a denial) that is both secondary and peculiarly "American" (228). Such a denial ironically enables the black American male (writer) to "[embody] the only American community of males handed the specific occasion to learn who the female is within itself" (228). When Ellison's American male, himself a writer and thinker still caught within the depths of his dreams, returns to the old slave singer to ask her, "what is this freedom that you love so well?" one of her sons seizes him "in a grip like cold stone" and roars, "next time you got questions like that, ask yourself!" (10). Playing on the vernacular phrase "ask your mama," the son's exhortation that the invisible man should instead ask himself rings with the tones of the oracular black female within. Upon hearing his question, the old slave woman of his unconscious had become confused, muttering a string of disjointed sentences that leaves the invisible man "dizzy" (9). She had first looked "surprised, then thoughtful, then baffled" as she uttered her response. She seemed as helplessly obscure as the oracle of Delphi had been deliberately ambiguous, and equally as enigmatic. It is the ritual riddle of maternal blackness that thus sets the invisible man into motion toward waking, toward consciousness: he suddenly comes out of the dream, "ascending hastily from this underworld of sound to hear Louis Armstrong innocently asking, 'What did I do / To be so black / And blue?'" (10).

The ambivalence that Ellison here ascribes to the mother's language and elsewhere to language writ large, questioning its standing as the unassailable repository of meaning, resonates in the slave mother's Delphic inscrutability even as it rings in Armstrong's bluesy "silence of sound" (10), the "invisible music of [his] isolation" (11). The mother's riddle of freedom, prefacing the jazzman's invisible sound of solitude, proves to be the insurgent ground that precipitates the invisible man's intellectual and ontological quest. Most readers attribute this impetus to the grandfather's dying words in chapter 1 of the novel. That may be so in the chronological time of the invisible man's life. Yet in the time of the novel, the memoir in which the invisible man reflects upon his life, the paternal is fully absent from this formative moment when the invisible man explains his self-reflexion. (Indeed, the patriarch—the white father—has been murdered by the mother in an act of moral outrage.) His experience assumes iterability and expression through the crafting of this body of text, and he determines to narrate his story only after his encounter with the primordial slave mother. The mythological symbolism of the slave mother as Delphic origin, the womb to which the invisible man returns and from which he must emerge, reborn anew, marks the underground as a site of the sanctuary of thought whose portal must be a two-way street.

But somehow, if I may be permitted a dialectical leap that promises to bridge the distance between the slave mother's riddle of freedom and the lesson of love she offers the invisible man, the rebirth that love appears to herald offers as well a philosophy of love, one that tries to get at the heart of the human quest for life. To love is somehow to live again, as Kristeva has put it in *Tales of Love*.[22] Love is a primordial state to which human beings can take recourse through memory and dream and upon which humans can take meaningful action. In *Invisible Man*, the true knowledge of love is discovered and revealed only in the space of the womb, as the invisible man queries love's Pythia in the labyrinth of the underground, that semiotic chora[23] that, as Kristeva would have it in *Revolution in Poetic Language* (1974), "precedes and underlies figuration" (2170) and is identified with the uncanny maternal body.

And yet love is also, in the psychoanalytic framing that was so instructive to Ellison's fiction, the coming together of *eros* and *agape*, of Freudian sexuality and loving democratic ideals. Kristeva writes of the "twisted commingling of sexuality and ideals that makes up the experience of love" (1). Love is a possibility that can transform the Manichean relation between I/other into a dynamic relation of "the I with the Other" (15). Here she does not speak of the emotion in individuals' love for one another or the affect of romantic or courtly love (her initial reference is to the transference and counter-transference of love between analysand and analyst in the clinical setting), but of love as an experience, and hence as the "act" of love, of love as "doing." Love's absence is a death, Kristeva tells us (15). The absence of love—of, perhaps, Du Boisian humanism, Wright's notion of "care," and Ellisonian democracy—is non-Being.

Ellison seems to say, in part, that one thing Wright's Bigger Thomas and Fred Daniels lack is love, love of a certain kind that the invisible man comes to possess and understand only in the critical distance of his grotto. It is a higher form of love, a democratic love, that the invisible man postulates in the realm of the underground through his interlocution with the maternal, and thus the love he exhorts is the loving act of moral responsibility: an ability to respond critically and morally to one's social context, an ability to enact and foster positive change. "Irresponsibility" is part of his "invisibility," the invisible man tells us: "any way you face it, it is a denial. . . . Responsibility rests upon recognition, and recognition is a form of agreement" (11), a relation.

In this intellectual framing that defines the function of his invisibility, and naming himself as one who suffers from "hysteria," the protagonist deems his invisibility a "sickness" that is "not unto death" (11), but rather that for which he has found a cure. (Interesting to note here that the word hysteria is drawn from the Greek for womb. Ellison would have been quite conscious of this point as he cast his protagonist into a state of hysteria that eventuates in a descent into a womb-like, underground space.) Invisibility, a conceptual metaphor that Ellison develops out of the Freudian theory of repression, is an insufficiency and a social illness whose antidote lies in Ellison's concept of love.

Freud claimed to have discovered repression, according to his biographer Peter Gay. He likened it to resistance, and in this way he drew an equivalence between the act of repression and that of deviance. Freud used the notion of deviance to characterize repression, and in fact, saw defensiveness—such as that which Ellison describes as the response of many whites when faced with the presence of black people—as the most significant expression of repression. In Freud's theory, repression is not an "original" defense mechanism, but arises when "a sharp cleavage has occurred between conscious and unconscious mental activity . . . the essence of repression lies simply in turning something away, and keeping it at a distance, from the conscious" (italics in original 569–70). The primal stage of repression, a first phase (570), consists in "the psychical (ideational) representative of the instinct being denied entrance into the conscious" (570). From this denial, a fixation emerges. "The second stage of repression, repression proper, affects mental derivatives of the repressed representative, or such trains of thought as, originating elsewhere, have come into associative connection with it. On account of this association, these ideas experience the same fate as what was primally repressed. Repression proper, therefore, is actually an after-pressure" (570). Secondary repression occurs with the "surplus" of repressed representations (experience, memory, image, language, etc.). One should not overemphasize the repulsion of the object/representative that is at the center of repression, Freud tells us. Equally important if not more so is the "attraction exercised by what was primally repressed upon everything with which it can establish a connection." These two forces necessarily "co-operate," he argues (570). That which is repressed "proliferates in the dark," he writes in tones that likely long reverberated with Ellison. Repression does not take place only once, but "demands a persistent expenditure of force." Its "mobility" is expressed in the "psychical characteristics of the state of sleep, which alone renders possible the formation of dreams. With the return to waking life the repressive cathexes which have been drawn in are once more sent out" (572).[24]

The act of repression Freud describes is directly related to the act of the metaphorical, as Jacques Lacan has underscored in his work. Lacan argues that metaphor "consists in the substitution in a signifier-signified relationship of the new signifier, S´, used as the signifier of the original signifier S, which now becomes a signified."[25] Metaphor is itself a new signified, overwriting another signified as if it were a palimpsest, yet destined to be sedimented under a future signified, it seems.

The implications of this point in relation to *Invisible Man* are telling. Such sedimentation does occur, but only at the level of secondary repression, a refusal, as Ellison argues through the prose of his Prologue, but also an admission of existential guilt: the invisible man is a victim of others' refusals to "see" him, yet he is also guilty because he has not taken responsibility for his own humanity; he assumes that his is a quest for being through others—that his being requires the determination of others—rather than seeing his being as self-determined and fully human. He suffers from a double repression, a double refusal that differs subtly from Du Bois's concept-metaphor of double consciousness. Rather than experiencing a Du Boisian sense of multiple being that results from the processes of racism and nationalism, the invisible man suffers from an Ellisonian construct of infra-humanity—he lacks what Charles Mills terms the Ellisonian *sum* (see chapter 2). He is thus guilty for not possessing the wherewithal to impose a humanistic and loving pattern on the social chaos that casts him as an outsider. That is, the organizing model of love, the "beloved community" or "a love called democracy," the concept-metaphor of democratic love first suggested by the insurgent and uncanny figure of the slave mother—who symbolizes home (*heimlich*) but is undoubtedly displaced and dispossessed (*unheimlich*)—constitutes what I see as Ellison's overcoming of the invisible. Invisibility, as conceptual metaphor, is an insufficiency and a social illness whose antidote lies in Ellison's concept of love.

I speak of such invisibility in relation to an "empty narcissism," after the fashion in which Kristeva describes this phenomenon. In the language of the unconscious, she tells us, one finds floating signifiers that are themselves metaphorical. This would be, following Freud's theory of secondary repression, word-presentations that have risen from the unconscious into the consciousness, only to be repressed into the unconscious by the pre-consciousness. These re-emerge as memory traces, those formed by experience as well as by myth, history, and ritual, and may be written on the body as wounds.

Invisibility is such a wound. For Kristeva, who re-reads and revises Freud's theory of love[26] as she surveys it in what she calls the "field of metaphor," narcissism is a "screen for emptiness"; it is a wound that "displays itself in feelings of solitude and emptiness—those temporary freezings of the death drive" (*Tales of Love* 21, 337, emphasis in original). The invisible man's provocative yearnings for sexual love are what Kristeva might refer to as a fragile "narcissistic elaboration" (43), a complex and empty act that, for him, can only be narrated from the invisibility of the underground as he recounts his "pre-invisible days" (37), the time before he understood his condition of invisibility. The sexual acts he narrates—each of those that occurs during his time of hyper-visibility—are charged with such conflicting, death-driven emotions as hate and fear. The love he expresses in that realm thus cannot be but compromised, in moral terms, by the "temporary freezings" of *thanatos*, the death drive.

In this light, the ultimate fulfillment of the invisible man's quest for being cannot come through a simple pursuit of sex (acts of *eros*) that he narrates in detail throughout the novel. Rather, it comes via his movement toward a moral, democratic love (*agape* love) whose value and possibility he comes to recognize only in the fissure of his underground existence, the realm of mother love. Again we see here how Ellison's metaphor of invisibility is wholly dependent, for its psychoanalytic and philosophical import, upon the metaphor of love.

Ellison quite skillfully demonstrates that the concept of moral love can take shape only through the choric example of black maternal love—itself seemingly repressed—that he encounters in the underground of both Harlem and his consciousness, the mother's law that is not only antecedent to the stasis and constraints of the white father's law in the realm of the symbolic (Spillers), but also to the conceptual metaphorics of invisibility Ellison deploys there. I am certainly ascribing to Ellison a feminist sensibility which he nowhere, to my knowledge, claims, but which is indeed in evidence in the workings of the text, and thus may be said to be rendered only unconsciously. A reading of the invisible man's encounters with many of the white women of the text bears out the argument that they not only differentially symbolize the white father's law and proscriptions (as Freud gives them in *Totem and Taboo* and elsewhere), but that his sexual "love" or desire for them can only be morally insufficient, even as the invisible man recognizes their humanity in relation to his own.

For instance, while above ground, the invisible man is ambivalent about love, and his claims to love truly some of the white women he encounters are thus placed in doubt even as we juxtapose them to the black maternal figures he describes and encounters in the underground. There is something illicit and immoral about his relations with the white women of the story, from his encounter with the stripper of the battle royal scene, to the lewd demands of Sybil. The reader finds not the *agape* ideals of moral love that would help found a beloved democratic community; rather one finds the pure *eros* of Freudian theory, a theory of sexuality rather than moral love. The protagonist desires to both "love and murder" the stripper (16); for the unnamed wife of a Brotherhood leader he feels a certain "poignancy," "the sensation of something precious perilously attained too late" (315); and he calls Sybil his "too-late-too-early love" (399). When we turn to Ellison for an explanation of these relationships, we find that he has little to say on the point. One of his few statements appears in "The Art of Fiction," where, when asked about the "love affairs—or almost love affairs" of his character, he responds laughingly:

> I'm glad you put it that way. The point is that when thrown into a situation which he thinks he wants, the hero is sometimes thrown at a loss; he doesn't know how to act. After he made this speech about the Place of the Woman in Our Society, for example, and was approached by one of the women in the audience, he thought she wanted to talk about the Brotherhood and found that she wanted to talk about brother-and-sisterhood. Look, didn't you find the book at all funny? I felt that such a man as this character would have been incapable of a love affair; it would have been inconsistent with his personality. (emphasis in original 180)

Ellison's comments certainly caution us against opening ourselves to believing the invisible man's professions of deep and abiding—moral—love for white women in the novel. This is especially so in light of his attention to Freud's writings on repression and sexuality. However, there are enough references to sexual love in the text to allow us to formulate our own conclusions.

The Irresponsible Dreamer: Reveries of Sexual Love

Let us look first to the Trueblood encounter, which Ellison laces with resonances that repeat in the invisible man's own experiences. After leaving Trueblood's farm and being vehemently accosted at the Golden Day, he drives Mr. Norton, the white philanthropist, back to the campus. The protagonist's behavior with the donor has, of course, landed him in a vat of hot water, and he is ordered by Dr. Bledsoe, the college president, to attend services in the chapel and to report directly to the administration building afterwards. The invisible man's description of the college choir at the chapel mirrors his first impressions of the student body. Upon arriving on campus, he recognizes immediately the military-style uniformity with which the students are trained: "shoes shined, minds laced up, eyes blind like those of robots" (28). Such an impression strikes him once more as he describes the student choir as a group of enunciating automatons who move "with faces frozen in solemn masks" and "mechanically" sing songs that effortlessly please white campus visitors. The songs are rendered in the spirit of an "ultimatum accepted and ritualized, an allegiance recited for the peace it imparted and for that perhaps loved. Loved as the defeated come to love the symbols of their conquerors" (86).

I want to underscore the way the narrator recounts not only his early formation as an ardent and quite willing participant in the automatization of his own thoughts and emotions—the vet from the Golden Day describes him as a "walking zombie," the "perfect personification of the Negative" (72)—but also the "love" of the defeated for the symbols of their conquerors. It takes no great critical powers to point out that the American white woman serves as an iconic symbol of the nation and its purported ideals of freedom. This is seen quite clearly in the nation's statuary: blind Justice holding a balance; Lady Liberty bearing the torch of Enlightenment; and Armed Liberty (the Statue of Freedom) gracing the dome of Washington DC's Capitol building are among the most visible examples. Equally obvious and more ironic is the nationalism Ellison ascribes to the stripper, whose iconography—an American flag—is inscribed on her very body, and whose body is laid bare for all to regard and "read," even the black boys to whom it is forbidden. Of further note in this regard is the white paint of Brockway's factory, used to blanch national monuments to a perfect alabaster. The irony of both scenarios should not be lost on the reader. The illusory whiteness of Brockway's "optic white" (165) paint comes only by way of a crucial but imperceptible number of drops of "black dope" (151–52), added and mixed to perfection. And the stripper is a white woman of questionable morals whose sexual value increases as it is denied to black males.

As he does so many times in the narrative, the invisible man slips into an interval in time whence he observes and interprets the scene: the stripper "seemed like a fair bird-girl girdled in veils calling to me from the angry surface of some gray and threatening sea. I was transported" (16). After being groped by the "town's big shots" (15), she tries to escape, an exit the narrator and the other boys trapped in the room also long to make. For a brief moment, the invisible man sees beyond her mask of paint and rouge;

he sees his own emotions mirrored in her eyes: "above her red, fixed-smiling lips I saw the terror and disgust in her eyes, almost like my own terror and that which I saw in some of the other boys" (17). As she finally escapes, the invisible man likewise believes he has been released, that he is free to leave. However, he and the other boys are herded into the ring and blindfolded. As the band of cloth is placed over his eyes, he silently goes over his speech: "In my mind, each word was as bright as flame" (17).

The day's mishaps—the occasion of the smoker in lieu of the high-toned social gathering he had anticipated; his being pressed into the battle royal when his only purpose had been to give his speech; and the mauling of the stripper by the town's leading white figures—all fail to make a lasting impression on the invisible man. Even as the battle royal takes place, and he and the other boys subsequently are made to scramble upon an electrified rug for what turns out to be worthless gold-colored tokens, the protagonist still thinks of his speech: "I felt myself bombarded with punches. I fought back with hopeless desperation. I wanted to deliver my speech more than anything else in the world, because I felt that only these men could truly judge my ability" (20). It is perhaps best said that the invisible man fails to grasp the implications of the unfortunate turn of events. He fails to allow the faint connection he makes with the stripper upon looking into her eyes to impress upon him the utter inappropriateness of the speech he is about to give; he fails to rebel against the will of a malicious collective force. Instead, conjuring his best Washingtonian air, he later intones as he stands bleeding before the still raucous crowd of men, " 'Cast down your buckets where you are'" (24).

The narrator's reward for his accommodationist reprisal of Washington's 1895 Atlanta Exposition speech is a "gleaming calfskin briefcase" (25), which contains a college scholarship (26). That night in his dream, his grandfather torments him, forcing him to open a seemingly endless succession of envelopes until he finally comes upon one that holds a message of ominous proportions: "To Whom It May Concern. [. . .] Keep This Nigger-Boy Running" (26).

This line is usually read as the motor that powers the picaresque nature of the narrative. While the Prologue is often considered a prolegomenon to the important work of the invisible man's memoir, the opening sequence of chapter 1 itself is taken to give the reader the most central understanding of the structure by which the text progresses. Yet it is clear that time intervals and dream states that appear throughout the text are pivotal nodal points that are instructive and regenerative in the Prologue. However, they are mainly ignored or misunderstood in the action of the novel as the invisible man moves to the next phase of his life. In this regard, he calls to mind yet again Wright's underground man, who ignores the warnings of the church choir and sets the stage for his own death and permanent descent. The invisible man's first glimpse of Harlem (which the insane vet from the Golden Day had described to him as a Mecca of sorts, and which appears to the protagonist as "not a city of realities, but of dreams"[27]), and his arrival at the meeting place of the Brotherhood, the "Chthonian" (an etymologically significant hellish place where he felt he had "been through it all before"[28]) all serve to propel the protagonist somewhat mindlessly across the action of the novel. Often such intervals of time and space are mitigated by the actual or dreamed presence of a white woman. Trueblood's story, the invisible man's seduction by Red, and the Harlem riot scene, each contain the presence of a white woman. That the narrator fails to benefit from the dream states, fails to learn from his mistakes time and again in the main body of the narrative, demands the attention of the reader regarding any profession of emotion the protagonist utters regarding the women with whom he becomes sexually involved.

Ellison's overlapping conceptions of time, space, and rhythm, an imbrication that is most evidently manifested in the novel's Prologue, are cogent in the Trueblood incident. As Houston Baker points out, "The multiple narrative frames and voices in Ellison's Trueblood episode include the novel *Invisible Man*, the protagonist's fictive autobiographical account, Norton's story recalled as part of the fictive autobiography, Trueblood's story as framed by the fictive autobiography, the sharecropper's own autobiographical recall, and the dream narrative with in that autobiographical recall" (*Blues* 176). I am most interested in the lowest frequency of Ellison's narrative range in this section of the novel, and that is the allegorical dream that Trueblood points to as the impetus behind his violation of his child. It is this scene that seals for many the absence of any sort of feminist perspective that could be at work in the text.

In a sequence of events that culminate in what seems to be a strange *non sequitur*, Trueblood describes how he came to his dream state. His daughter, Matty Lou, slept between him and his wife out of necessity in order that they might keep warm. Jim Trueblood's version of the story, the only version to which we are privy, contends that Matty Lou called out in her sleep, and threw her arm around her father's neck, turning and squirming against him (44). Trueblood turned his back and tried to move away, but Matty Lou continued to draw near. "Then I musta dropped into the dream," he said abruptly, recalling for us the way the invisible man more smoothly slipped into the breaks of Louis Armstrong's music and "look[ed] around" in the novel's Prologue as he descended into the depths of his reefer-induced reverie (7). Trueblood compares his daughter's call of "Daddy" (mumbled, Trueblood supposes, while dreaming of her own beau) to the soft moans made by a woman he used to date, Margaret. Jim and Margaret used to lie in bed together and listen to the music that emanated from the riverboats as they drifted by (43–44). Both the woman and girl, as well as the riverboats' music, in some strange way precipitate his descent into the dream.

Although the dream is important, as Baker points out, for its depiction of the black male as bearer of the phallus[29] (and therefore as possessor of some socio-sexual power), it is also significant as another instance of premonitory warning against a facile belief in sexual love that the invisible man refuses to recognize. It foreshadows both his experience at the Liberty Paint factory hospital and his involvement with the unnamed seductress of the Brotherhood, whom I shall call "Red." The nameless woman in red symbolizes for the young orator beauty and femininity, purity and fertility (309). Yet she is clearly immoral: she uses him for her sexual pleasure, and the invisible man becomes lost in her in a way that reminds us of Jim Trueblood's dream, where Trueblood momentarily becomes lost in the body of a white woman, who, like a succubus, enters the room through the door of a grandfather clock. Trying to break free of her—she had wrapped her arms about his neck in a motion mimicking that of Trueblood's sleeping daughter—Trueblood "throws her on the bed and tries to break her holt" (45). "That woman just seem to sink outta sight, that there bed was so soft. It's sinkin down so far I think it's going to smother both of us. Then swoosh! all of a sudden a flock of little white geese flies out of the bed like they say you see when you go to dig for buried money" (45).

Echoing Trueblood's dream, in the seduction scene with Red, the invisible man sees himself in a mirror

standing between her eager form and a huge white bed, myself caught in a guilty stance [. . .] and behind the bed another mirror which now like a surge of the sea tossed our images back and forth, back and forth, furiously multiplying the time and the place and the circumstance. [. . .] [O]ne free hand went up as though to smooth her hair, and in one swift motion the red robe swept aside like a veil, and I went breathless at the petite and generously curved nude, framed delicate and firm in the glass. It was like a dream interval [. . .]. I was heading for the door, torn between anger and a fierce excitement, hearing the phone click down as I started past and feeling her swirl against me and I was lost, for the conflict between the ideological and the biological, duty and desire, had become too subtly confused. I went to her thinking, Let them break down the door, whosoever will, let them come. (314–15)

In Trueblood's dream, it is Mr. Broadnax, the woman's husband, who enters the scene and looks upon them disinterestedly, saying " 'They just nigguhs, leave 'em do it'" (45), no doubt a reflection of the implications of Trueblood's act speaking to him in the judgmental voice of the white Father as Trueblood rapes his own daughter. He gives in to his weakness and his desire, and his cowardice is exposed when he describes his daughter to Norton and the invisible man as part child, part woman, part angel, part whore: "sometimes a man can look at a little ole pigtail gal and see himself a whore—you'all know that?" (46). In his dream, the grandfather clock, which represents a cessation of time, accords the only means of escape from the room where Trueblood, like the invisible man with Red, is being seduced by a white woman. After disentangling himself from her, Trueblood finally gets the door open and steps inside the clock:

I goes up a dark tunnel, up near where the machinery is making all that noise and heat. It's like the power plant they got up to the school. It's burnin' hot as iffen the house was caught on fire, and I starts to runnin', tryin' to get out. I runs and runs till I should be tired but ain't tired but feelin' more rested as I runs, and runnin' so good it's like flyin' and I'm flyin' and sailin' and floatin' right over the town. Only I'm still in the *tunnel*. Then way up ahead I sees a bright light like a jack-o-lantern over a graveyard. It gits brighter and brighter and I know I got to catch up with it or else. Then all at once I was right up with it and it burst like a great big electric light in my eyes and scalded me all over. Only it wasn't a scald, but like I was drownin' in a lake where the water was hot on the top and had cold numbin' currents down under it. Then all at once I'm through it and I'm relieved to be out and in the cold daylight agin. (45–46, emphasis in original)

Trueblood describes his escape from the white woman as the sensation of moving through a tunnel that, nonetheless, imparts the feeling that he is flying. He moves toward a huge electric light emanating from the eye of the jack-o-lantern, which bursts and scalds him, drowning him in cold currents (the reflection of his orgasmic incest with Matty Lou). His experience resembles the invisible man's surfacing from Lucius Brockway's basement, into the factory hospital, and, later, his emergence from the subway into the arms of Mary Rambo. After the explosion in "the basement" "three levels underground" (recalling again the three levels of descent in the novel's Prologue), the invisible man feels as if he is sinking "in the center of the lake of heavy water" (175). He awakens to a "bright third eye that glowed from the center of [a man's] forehead" (176). The "cold numbin' currents" of Trueblood's dream are translated into "cold-edged heat" that pounds the invisible man's body "between crushing electrical pressures" (177) as the medical staff administers an experimental "shock treatment" that will produce the "effects of a prefrontal lobotomy without the negative effects of the knife" (180). The procedure results in an excisionless castration intended to cure a case that, according to a white doctor, "has been developing some three hundred years" (180).

The scene in the hospital responds to Trueblood's indecision over how to extricate himself from his intercourse with Matty Lou: "There I was tryin' to git away with all my might, and yet having to move *without* movin'. I flew in but I had to walk out. [. . .] There was only one way I can figger that I could git out: that was with a knife. But I didn't have no knife, and if you'all ever seen them geld them young boar pigs in the fall, you know I knowed that was too much to pay to keep from sinnin'" (emphasis in original 46).

Trueblood emerges from his nightmare with a sense of self-determination: "I ain't nobody but myself" (51). He finds a sympathetic audience in Norton, whose feelings for his own daughter border on the incestuous. Norton describes her to the protagonist as "a being more rare, more beautiful, purer, more perfect and more delicate than the wildest dream of a poet. [. . .] Her beauty was a well-spring of purest water-of-life, and to look upon her was to drink and drink and drink again. [. . .] I found it difficult to believe her my own" (33). When Norton confronts Trueblood after first hearing of his transgression, he is amazed that Trueblood has acted upon his desire for his daughter, the desire Norton never dared fulfill. Trueblood had "looked upon chaos" and was not "destroyed": "'You did and are unharmed!' he shouted, his blue eyes blazing into the black face with something like envy and indignation" (40).

The invisible man also escapes unscathed from his encounter with Red. Similar to Mr. Broadnax, who looks upon Trueblood's coupling with the white woman of Trueblood's dream and walks away unconcerned, Red's husband returns home after she has conquered the invisible man, who lies stated in her bed:

I didn't know whether I was awake or dreaming. [. . .] It was strange. My mind revolved. I was chased out of a chinkapin woods by a bull. I ran up the hill; the whole hill heaved. I heard the sound and looked up to see the man looking straight at me where he stood in the dim light of the hall, looking in with neither interest nor surprise. His face expressionless, his eyes staring. (315)

The hill Trueblood climbs to get to Mr. Broadnax's house (44) reappears in this dream sequence. After Red's husband reminds her, "Wake me early, I have a lot to do," she wishes him good night and drifts back into sleep. The invisible man studies her, touches her, ponders their night together and, becoming anxious, wonders how he can best extricate himself from the situation without becoming the main attraction of a "lynching bee" (*Shadow and Act* 37). Wondering how he, too, can escape the knife (a ritual that regularly accompanied a lynching), he experiences a range of emotions:

I leaned over her, feeling her breath breezing warm and pure against my face. I wanted to linger there, experiencing the sensation of something precious perilously attained too late and now to be lost forever—a poignancy. But it was as though she'd never been awake and if she should awaken now, she'd scream, shriek. [. . .] Why had I gotten myself into such a situation? (315)

The invisible man expects that at any moment he will become a sacrificial goat, a victim of white society's totemic retribution: "My heart pounded as I closed the door and went down the hall, expecting the man, men, crowds—to halt me. Then I was taking the stairs" (315–16).

The lynching motif arises twice more before the dénouement of the novel. The first comes during the riot scene when the invisible man sees a feminine figure dangling by her neck from a lamppost in Harlem. The second comes in the final dream sequence, in which the invisible man is finally castrated by a gang of his tormentors: Bledsoe, Norton, Jack, and Ras all play a part in the illusory castration of our hero. The riot in Harlem erupts after Brother Hambro has informed the invisible man that the people of the Harlem district must be sacrificed for the greater good of the Brotherhood (380–81). After the invisible man has whipped the community into a frenzy over the injustice of Tod Clifton's death, the Brotherhood leadership decides to withdraw from the uptown district, leaving the crowds vulnerable to the charisma and influence of Ras the Exhorter/Destroyer. Ras's exhortation to violence comes at the expense of the people: as the Brotherhood had planned and anticipated, the police retaliate full force, effecting a massive devastation of black life and property. Once the invisible man realizes he has been duped, but before he learns of the riot brewing in Harlem, he decides to infiltrate the inner circle of the Brotherhood with the help of a white woman, and he eventually settles on Sybil.

Just as Aeneas consults the sybil, or priestess, before his descent into the underworld, the invisible man attempts to elicit information from Sybil, the wife of a Brotherhood big shot, before his eventual retreat underground. Ironically, however, the protagonist's Sibyl has no information to give him. She is the diametrical opposite of Virgil's creation, for she can neither offer him any helpful advice, nor can she escort him about the underworld to assist him in his search for himself.

The scene with Sybil turns from one in which the invisible man had planned to seduce her into one where she attempts to run a pathetic seduction game on him. "Who's taking revenge on whom?" he asks himself (393), going on to describe what was happening with Sybil in terms of a different paradigm. Instead of loving the symbol of the conqueror, that is, the black man loving the white woman as a sexualized representation of American nationality and white male power, Sybil becomes a sybaritic sign of the "conquerors conquered" (393). The invisible man interprets her hedonism as a reflection of the myth of the black phallus—the black man as simply a less powerful figure of power to worship alongside the white man. When Sybil whispers in the invisible man's ear her wish for their evening's pleasure, he is shocked to find out that she wants him to create a rape scene in which he, a "beautiful" black man, takes on the role of a big black "brute." "With all the warnings against it, some are bound to want to try it out for themselves," he quips (393). He is even less offended by Sybil than by Red, who had confided to him that he frightened her a bit because of the "primitive" tone of his voice (312). However, he chooses not to have intercourse with Sybil while allowing her to believe that they had been intimate. A pitiful figure without, it would appear, any redeeming graces, Sybil nonetheless draws the invisible man to her. He believes himself to be attached to her emotionally, lovingly, and in fact mourns the times that will not allow for their relationship (399). Later, while negotiating the streets of Harlem after the riots that follow Clifton's death, he sees a number of naked white feminine bodies swinging from the steel arms of streetlamps, and thinks immediately of Sybil, afraid that she might have been trapped and lynched (420).

The bodies are actually mannequins; they are unreal, yet they sway in the wind and give the illusion of life, of white life sacrificed to black violence. The narrator grieves over the possibility of Sybil's death, of her sacrifice, and wonders if he is somehow responsible, if he had gone too far in initiating a sexual relationship with her for the express purpose of gaining inside information regarding the plans the Brotherhood has for the Harlem district (397). What is the significance of Ellison's use of the white female body in this instance? And why lynching, as if to signify upon the lynching of black males with the lynching of white females?

Sacrificing Sexual Desire

I would like to elaborate two ideas here in response to Ellison's evocation of Freud's *Totem and Taboo* (1912–1913) in chapter 9 of the narrative, and these are the image of the white woman as repository of white male and black male desire, and the issue of retribution and violence in response to the prohibition set about the body of the white female. It is no accident that Freud's text is found lying open on young Mr. Emerson's desk (137). As with other elements of the novel, the presence of *Totem and Taboo* is meant to provide another source of meaning for the reader. Ellison, as I mention above, was quite familiar with Freud's work. Biographer Mark Busby observes that Ellison became acquainted with Freudian theory while a student at Tuskegee, "and again as an aide to psychologist Harry Stack shortly after his arrival in New York" (Busby 70). I will discuss Freud's ideas of "taboo" along with René Girard's critique of taboo and social retaliation in *Violence and the Sacred* (1977). These two analyses will shed light on Ellison's construction of lynching in the closing sequences of the novel, and it is my hope that this analysis will bring the conversation neatly back round to one in which Ellison's theory of moral democracy as love will come clear, for it resonates with the images of the black maternal with which he opens the text.

I read Freud here as myth and narrative, and I think in this way his theory can be quite useful to our discussion. Freud defined taboo as something sacred, yet uncanny and forbidden (*Totem and Taboo* 26). He writes, "taboo expresses itself essentially in prohibitions and restrictions" (26), and asserts that man's early "systems of punishment are also connected with taboo" (29). Thus, taboo becomes the law (34). Girard critiques Freud on a number of points, specifically on substitution in sacrifice, and the role of desire in Freud's Oedipus theory.

Relative to the first point, in *Totem and Taboo*, Freud tells the story of a father who is jealous and violent. He decrees that his sons are not to touch sexually any woman of the clan. Driven by sexual desire and rage, the sons come together and slaughter their father and eat him; they thereby take on the father's essence, incorporating him. Guilt subsequently sets in, and the sons mourn their father—he becomes the sanctified father. They render into law the father's prohibition against the women, insisting on exogamy and the incest taboo. Women then become tokens of exchange between tribes, and, borrowing a term from the work of both Claude Lévi-Strauss and Gayle Rubin, a "traffic in women" ensues.

Girard, who is anti-modern, disputes Freud. He feels that *Totem and Taboo* is very close to Freud's idea of the Oedipus complex, and to set this paradigm on its head Girard renders the positions of victim and victimizer, object and subject, interchangeable. That is, the (white) woman, as object of desire, assumes a mutable position from which she emerges as actor instead of merely as the sexual object that is acted upon. Furthermore, where in Freudian theory the (white) woman as object of desire stands apart from any scene of action, in Girard's model, desire is mediated by the (white) father, with whom the subject, in our case the black man, identifies.

As I discuss above, it has often been observed by both Ellison and his critics that *Invisible Man* is replete with reflections of myth and ritual, and not only those emerging from the heritage of African American folklore. In this respect, the myth of black male sexual prowess, and the ritual of lynching that accompanies this myth, align themselves with Girard's revision of Freudian sexual taboos. In addition to mitigating Freud's more rigid stance on the position of the (white) woman solely as the object of desire, Girard elaborates a theory of retribution and vengeance in response to transgression of social norms and regulations. His theory of violence and sacrifice, which does not specifically discuss the ritual of lynching but to which I will relate this act, posits violent acts of sacrifice as measures that work to "restore harmony to the community, to reinforce the social fabric" (*Violence and the Sacred* 8). The victim of sacrifice serves as a substitute, and the sacrifice itself may be described as an "active mediation" between the sacrificed and a higher power (6). Expanding on this idea and adapting Girard's own thought, I will define lynching for our purposes as a racist, "deliberate act of collective substitution performed at the expense of the [black] victim and [provisionally] absorbing all the internal tensions, feuds, and rivalries pent-up within the [white] community" (7). (I write "provisionally" since history has taught us that no one violent act of substitution such as lynching ever seemed to satiate the white "community.") By definition, the victim of sacrifice is generally an outsider, a marginalized individual or collective existing on the fringes of society and often feared by the hegemonic group (12).

Such a description is operative in both the scene where the invisible man believes he has seen Sybil swinging from a lamppost by a rope around her neck, and in his own dream where he is castrated—another form of lynching—by his motley crew of tormentors. Sybil fulfills Girard's prescription of the mutability of woman as the object of desire. She alternately plays the role of aggressor and victim in the novel. The narrator chooses Sybil as his oracle not only due to the fact that she is the wife of a high-ranking Brotherhood member, but also because in spite of her pathetic demeanor, she regularly and persistently pursues him. She "was one of those who assumed that my lectures on the woman question were based upon a more intimate knowledge than the merely political and had indicated several times a willingness to know me better. I had always pretended not to understand [. . .]" (390). Once the invisible man chooses her and finds she has no information that will benefit him, he is nonetheless forced to go ahead with the seduction scene he has set because she assumes the role of seducer perforce:

'Come on, beautiful,' she said, 'pour.'

I poured her another and another; in fact, I poured us both quite a few. [. . .] Then she looked at me, her eyes bright behind narrowed lids and raised up and struck me where it hurt.

'Come on, beat me, daddy–you–you big black bruiser. What's taking you so long?' (394)

The invisible man restrains himself from striking her back, and as she loses control with each glass she imbibes, she reverts to helplessness and passes out. It is then, oddly enough, that her humanity comes to appeal to the narrator: "She lay anonymous beneath my eyes until I saw her face, shaped by her emotion which I could not fulfill, and I thought, Poor Sybil, she picked a boy for man's job and nothing was as it was supposed to be. Even the black bruiser fell down on the job" (395).

The myth of the black macho dispelled (the invisible man appears in this scene to have been unable to perform sexually—he "fell down on the job"), the invisible man puts Sybil in a cab and heads uptown, where he encounters the riot in full rage. Having been grazed by a policeman's bullet and after participating in the arson of a rundown tenement house, the invisible man once more feels himself to be running "as in a dream":

Ahead of me the body hung, white, naked, and horribly feminine from a lamppost. I felt myself spin around with horror and it was as though I had turned some nightmarish somersault. I whirled, still moving by reflex, back-tracking and stopping and now there was another and another, seven—all hanging before a gutted storefront. [. . .] I steadied long enough to notice the unnatural stiffness of those hanging above me. They were mannequins—'Dummies!' I said aloud. Hairless, bald and sterilely feminine. [. . .] But are they real, I thought; are they? What if one, even one is real—is . . . Sybil? I hugged my briefcase backing away, and ran. . . . (419–20)

The symbolic lynching of a white woman enacts a complete reversal of the lynching of a black man. In the text there is a simultaneous critique of blackness and emasculation of black manhood, as well as a commentary upon the state of American democracy. The white woman as national icon, as pure, fertile, sexual yet forbidden—all images Ellison evokes and toys with in the narrative—culminate in the tragicomical figure of Sybil and her lynching in effigy. Not only is the white woman desexualized and sterilized in this gesture (and hence her force as a tool of the white man in the battle for black male sexuality is nullified); a portion of the illusion of American democracy as unassailable has been put to death (the white woman as a symbol of the nation and of the conquerors is liquidated). The invisible man, however, is left powerless—he can do nothing to ensure that none of the mannequins is in fact Sybil; he cannot discern reality. In running from the scene of Sybil's symbolic lynching—an action that repeats his running from Ras and his henchmen, his running from a gang of white men looking for trouble after the riot, and, as the invisible man states, his running "within myself" (403)—he falls blindly into the manhole. Later in his subterranean dream, his own castration is the mode by which Jack and the others purport to free him of his illusions, and thereby, as Girard observes, restore a false sense of order and stability to white society.

Yet the most significant dream that appears in the entirety of the novel is that of the slave mother, for it is to her principle of love—not yet perfected—that the invisible man returns when he writes of his preparatory, divided strategy of denouncing and defending, saying yes and saying no, loving and hating (437–38). This is especially clear since the morally loving import of that dream stays with him as he writes his memoir, while in the memoir itself, he admits that he cannot, finally, identify (with) the real

Sybil. The uncanny slave mother instructs him on a new taboo—pure hate, against which she forms a law. The insurgent mother's law against hatred is a law against narcissism (insufficient love) and the death drive, which Kristeva names as "[hatred's] psychological equivalent" (43). Hatred and the death drive result from a sense of the abject allowed to "run wild": "Narcissism and its lining, emptiness, are in short our most intimate, brittle, and archaic elaborations of the death drive. The most advanced, courageous, and threatened sentries of primal repression" (43–44).

Ellison understood well the need to confront and deconstruct the concept of repression when it was psychologically experienced by and socially applied to the figure of the Negro. As he makes clear in the essay, "Harlem is Nowhere," the city in which he sets his novel is "the scene of the folk-Negro's death agony," "the symbol of the Negro's perpetual alienation in the land of his birth" (*Shadow and Act* 296). Yet by developing "insight into the relation between his problems and his environment" (302), the African American could realize the possibility of what Ellison calls in this essay "transcendence" (296). *Invisible Man* seems to offer a corrective to certain aspects of Freud's psychology of love, which would better be called a psychology of sexuality. Ellison's text begins with a critique of which he is fully aware. As he puts it, the end is in the beginning, and thus the mother's law of love, which the protagonist engages after the exploits of his youth, in fact informs his reflections on the morality (and lack thereof) of his life. Through the framing perspective of the mother's law, Ellison as novelist undertakes a variety of representations (symbolic, imaginary, and real) that call the reader, who perhaps, in this context, functions as the analysand, to attempt to reconcile his or her own divided reality with that faced by the protagonist.

Black Being's Moral of Love

After a fashion, the reader's engagement with the text (and not Ellison's act of writing alone) is an act of love, a display of moral responsibility. By the time of his writing, which is chronicled in the Prologue and Epilogue, the narrator's self-consciousness is effected through memory, the consciousness of a past that he has examined, set down, and disseminated through novelistic discourse. Though he loves as well as hates, love is the criterion for emerging from his "hibernation," as he learns from the slave mother in the Prologue. As he seeks new life and rebirth—he anticipates his coming out, his re-emergence from the womb of the earth, and his quitting the realm of chaos for the space of the cosmos—he does so not only for himself, but for all of humanity. What takes place as this new vision of democratic love encounters the limits and static resistance of the symbolic realm Ellison does not show us. But the transition is certain not to be smooth. Black being, in this sense among others, is radical.

Notes

Introduction

1. "The Conservation of Races," 817.

2. Various disciplines have different but strikingly related perspectives on the question. Critical and human geographers often discuss identity as constructed in relation to national and other geo-political formations. Philosophers investigate identity in terms of equivalence, sameness, and similarity of varying types and degrees. And sociologists inquire into the psychodynamic and sociological forms of identity, theorizing it with relation to the symbolic interactionism that emerges from the pragmatic theories of William James and George Herbert Mead. Of course, in literary theory, our current perspectives on identity have been strongly influenced by structuralist and poststructuralist theory. Saussurean linguistics, Freudian and Lacanian psychoanalysis, and Foucauldian ideas of discursive formation have held sway over the field for the past three decades, with studies of the hybridity and creolization of identity coming about in the seminal works of Édouard Glissant, Homi Bhabha, and Paul Gilroy. Black feminist theory, womanism, and feminist theory have also addressed and critiqued the question. On this score, see work by Patricia Hill Collins, Audre Lorde, and Naomi Zack (a philosopher of race and mixed race identity), among others.

3. Two years before he left the United States in 1946 to begin life as an expatriate in Paris, Richard Wright took an interest in Heidegger's philosophy of being, not in a simplistic effort to glean ideas from Heidegger's thought, but in order to assess Heidegger's perspective on Western being (a point that Heidegger specifies in *On the Way to Language*, 1959) against Wright's own philosophical conception of black being. Once his move to France was complete, he was introduced by Gertrude Stein to many of the prominent members of French intellectual society. Through his interactions with them, his concept of black being continued to evolve, an evolution that I discuss at length in chapter 7.

4. See Fanon's well-known essay, "L'Expérience vécue du Noir" in *Peau noire, masques blancs* (Paris: Éditions du Seuil, 1952): 90–114. Fanon writes: "Si les études de Sartre sur l'existence d'autrui demeurent exactes (dans la mesure, nous le rappelons, où L'Etre et le Néant décrit une conscience aliénée), leur application à une conscience nègre se révèle fausse. C'est que le Blanc n'est pas seulement l'Autre, mais le maître, réel ou

imaginaire d'ailleurs." (112). ["If the studies of Sartre on the existence of others remain correct (insofar as, we recall, *Being and Nothingness* describes an alienated conscience), their application to a Negro consciousness appears false. It is that the white man is not only the Other, but the Master, real or, moreover, imaginary." My translation.]

5. In Paris, Wright would, of course, become a friend and interlocutor of the existentialist philosopher Jean-Paul Sartre. Long established in Paris by the time Wright arrived, the philosopher Jean Beaufret—who knew Sartre personally—taught at the École Normale Supérieure from 1946–1962, and was a member of a social circle that included Maurice Merleau-Ponty, Louis Althusser, and Jacques Lacan. Though he would come to oppose Sartre's perspective on existentialism, he was deeply invested in identifying a synthesis between Sartrean existentialism and Marxism, a quest that led him to the writings of Heidegger. (Beaufret credits Sartre with guiding him to Heidegger.) Beaufret was, thus, in great measure, responsible for introducing Heidegger's work to French philosophers and intellectuals. Believing Heidegger to be innocent—by Heidegger's own account, which did not escape dispute—of charges of Nazism, Beaufret committed himself to the study and dissemination of Heidegger's thought. By this time, Wright had already discovered Heidegger for himself, having asked Dorothy Norman, the prominent photographer, editor, author, and activist, "to instruct him on existentialism and the writings of Kierkegaard, Nietzsche and Heidegger, whom she had read. She invited Paul Tillich and Hannah Arendt over so that they could discuss the topic with him" (Michel Fabre, *Unfinished Quest* 299). Importantly, Wright did not look to Heidegger for inspiration on ways to theorize black being, but appraised Heidegger as he analyzed the works of various thinkers who were contemplating the deep and complex problems of modern being. See the "Translator's Introduction" to Jean Beaufret, *Dialogue with Heidegger: Greek Philosophy*, trans. Mark Sinclair (Bloomington, IN: Indiana University Press, 2006): vii–xiii; and *Generation Existential: Heidegger's Philosophy in France, 1927–1961* (Ithaca: Cornell University Press, 2005): 157–206.

6. See "Letter on Humanism," in Heidegger, *Basic Writings* (Ed. David Farrell Krell. New York: HarperPerennial, 2008), 247.

7. See Derrida, "White Mythology: Metaphor in the Text of Philosophy," in *Margins of Philosophy*. Trans. Alan Bass (Chicago: University of Chicago Press, 1982), 207–273; and Heidegger, "Lecture Six," in *The Principle of Reason* (Bloomington, IN: Indiana University Press, 1991), 48.

Chapter 1

1. Please see Gates' 1988 study *The Signifying Monkey: A Theory of Afro-American Literary Criticism* (New York: Oxford University Press).

2. Of particular interest are Plato's *Republic* and the *Poetics* and the *Rhetoric*, by Aristotle.

3. *Metaphor and Continental Philosophy: From Kant to Derrida*, (New York: Routledge, 2007), 3.

4. *Heidegger and Derrida on Philosophy and Metaphor: Imperfect Thought* (Amherst, NY: Humanity Books, 2000), 24.

5. Aristotle, *The Rhetoric and The Poetics of Aristotle* (New York: Modern Library, 1984), 173.

6. Quobna Ottobah Cugoano, *Thoughts and Sentiments on the Evil and Wicked Traffic of Slavery and Commerce of the Human Species.* Ed. Vincent Carretta (New York: Penguin, 1999).

7. Please see *Black Culture and Black Consciousness: Afro-American Folk Thought from Slavery to Freedom,* by Lawrence W. Levine (New York: Oxford University Press, 1977), and *Slave Culture: Nationalist Theory and The Foundations of Black America,* by Sterling Stuckey (New York: Oxford University Press, 1987) for pertinent discussions of African American oral traditions and the politics associated with them.

8. Please see Albert Murray, *Stomping the Blues* (Cambridge, MA: Da Capo Press, 1976) for a full and engaging discussion of this form and its history.

9. Murray, *Stomping the Blues,* 88. See also Angela Davis, *Blues Legacies and Black Feminism: Gertrude 'Ma' Rainey, Bessie Smith, and Billie Holiday* (New York: Vintage, 1990). Davis explains that the "formal blues played a minimal role in Billie Holiday's repertoire." Even so, "her music, deeply rooted in the blues tradition, recalled and transformed the cultural product of former slaves and used it to powerfully contest and transform prevailing popular song culture" (161).

10. For an extensive discussion of this point, see Henry Louis Gates, Jr., *The Signifying Monkey,* chapter 4, "The Trope of the Talking Book," 127–169.

11. Sojourner Truth, *The Book of Life* (London: Black Classics, 1999): 74.

12. Ellison writes of the importance the Harlem Renaissance writers, James Weldon Johnson among them, held for him in "Hidden Name and Complex Fate," published in *Shadow and Act* (1964) and reprinted in *The Collected Essays* of *Ralph Ellison,* ed. John F. Callahan (New York: Modern Library, 2003): 202. For critical commentary drawing comparisons between the two works, see Houston A. Baker, Jr., "A Forgotten Prototype: *The Autobiography of an Ex-Colored Man* and *Invisible Man,*" in *Singers of Daybreak: Studies in Black American Literature* (Washington, DC: Howard University Press, 1974): 17–32; Lawrence Jackson, *Ralph Ellison: Emergence of Genius* (New York: John Wiley & Sons, 2002): 411; and Henry Louis Gates, Jr., Introduction to *The Autobiography of an Ex-Coloured Man* (New York: Vintage, 1989): xvi.

13. In his review, "Between Laughter and Tears" (*New Masses,* October 1937), Wright condemned Hurston's novel on the very grounds James Weldon Johnson (in his Preface to the *Book of American Negro Poetry*) used to declare dialect poetry moribund and passé: it could convey only two limited emotions: humor and pathos. Wright's dismissal of Hurston's novel as a book that had no "basic idea or theme that lends itself to significant interpretation" (22) was searing. He roared on: "Miss Hurston *voluntarily* continues in her novel a tradition which was *forced* upon the Negro in theatre, that is, the minstrel technique that makes 'white folks' laugh. Her characters eat and laugh and cry and work and kill; they swing like a pendulum in

that safe and narrow orbit in which America likes to see the Negro live: between laughter and tears" (emphasis in original, 25). Hurston, stung by Wright's reproval, returned the favor in April 1938 when she pointed out what were, to her mind, the myriad failings in Wright's short story collection, *Uncle Tom's Children*, published earlier that year. Hurston wrote in her review, which appeared in the April 2, 1938 issue of *The Saturday Review of Literature*, that Wright's fiction was so overburdened with hatred that he had neglected to take note of what she called "the broader and more fundamental phases of Negro life" (Hurston 32). The lines between the two writers could not have been more clearly drawn: each was the other's antithesis of his or her own ideal. For Hurston, Wright, despite his humble beginnings as a Mississippi sharecropper's son, could in no way measure up to the "characteristic" Negro, whose expression was creative and full of life in spite of the obstacles and oppressions that African Americans faced. And for Wright, Hurston was far from the radical visionary artist whose works reflected Wright's dictates in "Blueprint for Negro Writing." See Zora Neale Hurston, "Stories of Conflict," *The Saturday Review of Literature* 17 (April 2, 1938): 32; and Richard Wright, "Between Laughter and Tears," *New Masses*, 5 (October 1937): 22, 25.

14. One exception to this claim may be found in Lorenzo Dow Turner's 1949 study *Africanisms in the Gullah Dialect*. Turner was one of Hurston's linguistics professors during her matriculation at Howard University in the 1920s, and was a pioneer in his field. His book is cited by Margaret Wade-Lewis (in her 2007 intellectual biography *Lorenzo Dow Turner: Father of Gullah Studies*) as the first and still most important study of African linguistic and cultural retentions among the Gullah people. Even so, it is not widely cited among scholars of African American literature and culture, likely because, as the introduction to the 2002 edition of Turner's work puts it, "the Sea Islands" where Gullah is spoken "do not represent wider African American culture (even in the rural South), and much of what Turner found there was not found elsewhere." As her English professor, Turner was a strong influence on Hurston; she speaks of him in *Dust Tracks on a Road* (1942) as the man whose commanding and sensitive voice made her feel that she "must be an English teacher." Apparently, he did not make her feel as though she must be a linguist or, more precisely, a sociolinguist and anthropologist. This urge would come later, once she had left Howard for Columbia to study under the preeminent Franz Boas.

15. In his Preface to his own translation of Homer's *Iliad*, Pope writes that "Invention . . . in different degrees distinguishes all great Genius's," [sic] and that "in *Homer* and in him only, it burns every where clearly, and every where irresistibly. . . . That which *Aristotle* calls the *Soul of poetry*, was first breath'd into it by *Homer*. . . . *Aristotle* had reason to say, He was the only Poet who had found out *living words*; there are in him more daring figures and metaphors than in any good author whatever [sic]." *The Iliad of Homer. Translated by Alexander Pope.* Ed. Steven Shankman (London: Penguin, 1996). 3–9, *passim*. Homer's epic hexameter poem the *Iliad* relied upon Greek mythology and folk traditions, and though it was "composed" about the eighth or ninth century before the common era, it was not written down until much later. It and the *Odyssey* alike belong to the Western oral

tradition, mixing legend and history, fiction and fact. In their oral states, both may arguably be related to folk literature. According to J. A. Cuddon, folk literature is the provenance of "primitive and illiterate people" (*The Penguin Dictionary of Literary Terms and Literary Theory* 346). Cuddon argues that folk literature is a vague term that may include folksongs, drama, and legend, and that it only becomes true literature "when people gather it together and write it down" (346). Examples of folk literature are found, according to Cuddon, in the work of the philologists and folklorists Jacob and Wilhelm Grimm, whose collection of folktales, *Grimms' Fairy Tales* (1812–1822), emerged as a leading text of nineteenth-century German Romanticism. It may be worthwhile to investigate any existing links between a text of folklore, such as that published by the Grimms, who influenced the development of German romanticism, and the publication of African American folklore by Zora Neale Hurston and others, who influenced the development of the Harlem Renaissance. Just as German Romanticism was deeply intertwined with a German sense of national identity, so the Harlem Renaissance was characterized by a literary aesthetic indelibly marked with notions of blackness and social belonging. It is this note that Du Bois and Johnson—in their own analyses of black cultural expression—strike so forcefully in their works.

16. Hurston enrolled in Columbia University's Barnard College in 1925, and began to study anthropology under Franz Boas that year. She had studied linguistics under the prominent African American linguist Lorenzo Dow Turner at Howard University, where she earned an associate's degree in 1920. In 1926, according to Cheryl Wall, she began to undertake field work "for Boas in Harlem, measuring the skulls of passersby to disprove theories of racial inferiority." After meeting with the patron Charlotte Mason, Hurston began to collect folklore and information on various types of African American cultural artifacts in 1927. That year, Boas also arranged for her to receive a research fellowship that would fund her study and collection of African American folklore. Hurston's work took her to Florida as well as the Bahamas, and she published her findings in such prominent periodicals as the *Journal of American Folklore* during the 1930s. During this time, she wrote plays and transcribed source material that included folktales, work songs, sermons, proverbs, children's rhymes, and blues lyrics. She organized folk concerts, one of which, *The Great Day*, played on Broadway at the John Golden Theatre in 1932. Her first novel, *Jonah's Gourd Vine*, was begun and completed in 1933; it would be published the following year. This intense flurry of intellectual, artistic, and academic activity all preceded the composition of Hurston's signal essay on African American vernacular expression, "Characteristics of Negro Expression," which was published in 1934. For Wall's quote, please see "Chronology," *Hurston: Folklore, Memoirs, and Other Writings* (New York: Library of America, 1995), 964.

17. See the *Poetics* 1457b.

18. Aristotle describes simile in this fashion in the table of contents that prefaces the *Rhetoric*. See the description of Chapter Four in Book III.

19. Lévi-Strauss is well-known for his opposition to racism, yet a number of scholars have pointed out that his analyses did not deal adequately with questions of

racial inequality and injustice. See, for instance, Kamala Visweswaran, "The Interventions of Culture: Claude Lévi-Strauss, Race, and the Critique of Historical Time," in *Race and Racism in Continental Philosophy*, eds. Robert Bernasconi and Sybol Cook (Bloomington: Indiana University Press, 2003): 227–248.

20. *Course* 71; *Signifying Monkey* 47.

21. Space will not allow for an analysis of the more troubling aspects of Hurston's discourse in this essay: the issues of class it presents, its posture on race and essentialized being, and so on. For a fuller treatment of the text, see Karla F. C. Holloway, *The Character of the Word: The Texts of Zora Neale Hurston* (New York: Greenwood Press, 1987). Most commentaries on "Characteristics" avoid this aspect of the writing, possibly due to what Ann duCille has described as the iconization of Hurston, what she terms "Hurstonism." She calls it "the conspicuous consumption of Zora Neale Hurston as the initiator of the African American women's literary tradition," and thus it functions as a lionization and mythologizing of Hurston that would logically render any pointedly critical examination of perceived weaknesses in Hurston's arguments and positions difficult if not blasphemous in black feminist thought. Please see duCille's essay, "The Mark of Zora: Reading between the Lines of Legend and Legacy," in *The Scholar and Feminist Online* 3.2 (Winter 2005), n. p.

22. The interested reader should reference the special issue on metaphor, *Critical Inquiry* 5.1 (Autumn 1978): 1–201. This issue contains wide-ranging yet in-depth treatments of metaphor and its theories.

23. "That Same Pain, That Same Pleasure," in *The Collected Essays of Ralph Ellison*, 67.

24. See "Spirituals and Neo-Spirituals" in *Zora Neale Hurston: Folklore, Memoirs, and Other Writings*, ed. Cheryl Wall (New York: The Library of America, 1995), 870.

25. *Norton Anthology of Theory and Criticism*, 1st ed. New York: Norton, 2001. 1256–57.

26. Lacan did so in the essay, "From Interpretation to the Transference," in *The Four Fundamental Concepts of Psychoanalysis: The Seminar of Jacques Lacan, Book XI* (New York: Norton, 1981), 249. He writes, "It was thought to be very clever to do this with metaphor, arguing from the following—to that which carries the weight, in the unconscious, of an articulation of the last signifier to embody the metaphor with the new meaning created by its use, should correspond some kind of pinning out, from one to the other, of two signifiers in the unconscious. Such a formula is quite definitely unsatisfactory. First, because one ought to know that there can be no relations between the signifier and itself, the peculiarity of the signifier being the fact that it is unable to signify itself, without producing some error in logic." Lacan did not deem Laplanche's interpretation to be wholly useless, however, since it identified in his schema certain characteristics of elementary signifiers. A useful discussion of Laplanche's interpretation and Lacan's thought in response to it is found in Anika Lemaire's *Jacques Lacan*, preface by Jacques Lacan, trans. David Macey (London: Routledge & Kegan Paul, 1977), especially the section

titled "Critical Study of 'The Unconscious: A Psychoanalytic Study' by J. Laplanche and S. Leclaire. Clarifications as to Lacan's Thought," p. 113–131.

27. On this point, please see Ricoeur, *The Rule of Metaphor*, pages 145–8. Even as Ricoeur rebuts Jakobson's opposition of metaphor and metonymy, the classical comparatist Michael Silk argues not against Ricoeur's opposition to what Silk calls Jakobson's "dyarchy of metaphor and metonymy" (121), but against what he sees as Ricoeur's refusal to acknowledge the various forms metaphor can take, specifically those forms of poetic metonymy that actually function as metaphors. Ricoeur does acknowledge that metonymy can, in certain instances, serve as metaphor. He also, as I have discussed, argues against a parallelism between poetic metaphors and philosophical metaphors. Without taking up this aspect of Ricoeur's argument, Silk chides Ricoeur for allowing his analysis of metaphor to become "remote from poetic actuality" (143). The "experience of poetry," Silk asserts, may not be "sufficient" to a theory of metaphor, but it is "plainly necessary for any adequate theory" (144). "Poetic usages" are not the "scaffolding" of philosophical theory, he insists: "they are their bricks" (146). This point, of course, runs counter to Ricoeur, who argues that though it may offer an event in thinking, metaphor is ever only anterior to the type of speculative thought in which philosophy engages. See Michael Silk, "Metaphor and Metonymy: Aristotle, Jakobson, Ricoeur, and Others," in *Metaphor, Allegory, and the Classical Tradition: Ancient Thought and Modern Revisions* (Oxford: Oxford University Press, 2003): 115–147.

28. The implications of this may be traced not only in Ricoeur's work, but also in that of Jacques Derrida in *Of Grammatology* (1967), trans. Gayatri Chakravorty Spivak, corrected edition (Baltimore: The Johns Hopkins University Press, 1997); and in *The Margins of Philosophy* (1972), trans. Alan Bass (Chicago: University of Chicago Press, 1982).

29. First published in 1987; reprinted 1993 in *A Postmodern Reader*. Ed. Natoli and Hutcheon (New York: State University of New York Press), 273–286. Citations here refer to the Natoli and Hutcheon edition.

30. Derrida's pronouncement comes in *Of Grammatology* and should be considered in its context. It reads as follows: ". . . [I]f reading must not be content with doubling the text, it cannot legitimately transgress the text toward something other than it, toward a referent (a reality that is metaphysical, historical, psychobiographical, etc.) or toward a signified outside the text whose content could take place, would have taken place outside of language, that is to say, in the sense that we give here to that word, outside of writing in general. That is why the methodological considerations that we risk applying here to an example are closely dependent on general propositions that we have elaborated above; as regards the absence of the referent or the transcendental signified. There is nothing outside of the text [there is no outside-text; *il n'y a pas de hors-texte*]. And that is neither because Jean-Jacques's life, or the existence of Mamma or Thérèse themselves, is not of prime interest to us, nor because we have access to their so-called "real" existence only in the text and we have neither any means of altering this, nor any right to neglect this limitation.

All reasons of this type would already be sufficient, to be sure, but there are more radical reasons. What we have tried to show by following the guiding line of the 'dangerous supplement,' is that in what one calls the real life of these existences 'of flesh and bone,' beyond and behind what one believes can be circumscribed as Rousseau's text, there has never been anything but writing; there have never been anything but supplements, substitutive significations which could only come forth in a chain of differential references, the "real" supervening, and being added only while taking on meaning from a trace and from an invocation of the supplement, etc. And thus to infinity, for we have read, in the text, that the absolute present, Nature, that which words like "real mother" name, have always already escaped, have never existed; that what opens meaning and language is writing as the disappearance of natural presence." (158–159)

31. I bracket the "negation" of Gates's intentionality in this sentence to underscore the inevitable risk Gates and other theorists, including I myself, run when examining African American literature through the lens of a white Western metaphysics that has, from at least the early modern period onward, denied the very possibility of a metaphysics of black being, even if that lens is a critical one. If the African American philosopher Lewis Gordon is correct in arguing that possibility itself is the philosophical precondition and propadeutic of human freedom, denial of the sheer possibility of a metaphysics of black being not only relegates black being to enslavement; it also remands it to the realm of oblivion, or non-being. Thus the African American theorist seeking to promulgate black being must carefully devise ways, as Hortense Spillers and Ronald Judy have both pointed out, of having our metaphysics and eating it too.

32. The reader may refer to the well-known passage in Thomas Jefferson's *Notes on the State of Virginia* (1784), where he speaks of "the black" as unknowable, and thus as ill-suited for full incorporation into the American body politic, because of the thick "veil of blackness" that deflects whites' attempt to divine the emotions and thoughts—the humanity—of the black "other." Jefferson's perspective was not simply influential and representative of the raciology of his time, which was marked by the rise of racial pseudosciences in an era of humanistic "enlightenment"; it was also quite Platonic in its formulation, given that Plato's dictum in the *Republic* regarding those who were best suited as the guardians of his ideal society were those whose bodily form aptly reflected their inner goodness. Thus physical beauty was indicative of intellectual, moral, and ethical "goodness." In Plato's words, "a good soul will, by its excellence, render the body as perfect as it can be" (*Republic* Bk III 403c). Some commentators on Plato's work may see this as simply one aspect of his program of education for elite young men. Yet when read as a text whose influence on Jefferson was formative, the dicta of both men resonate one with the other in clear tones. Of course, Plato did not conflate beauty of the body with the goodness of one's soul, and argued, through the figure of Socrates, that a beautiful body could never on its own form a good soul. However, he does imply that goodness of soul, that is, of character and consciousness, will undoubtedly be reflected in the physical human form. Given that Plato and Jefferson alike were, in their respective texts, contemplating the attributes of the ideal republic and the place of the citizen

within it (and notwithstanding that this critical aspect of Socrates's dialogue at this point in the text shortly follows a discussion of legitimate love—as opposed to vulgar conduct—between male lovers), one can easily draw these two thinkers into discourse one with the other, even across the millennia of time that separate them.

33. *Rhetoric* 1355 b 25.

34. In *The Philosophy of Rhetoric*, first published in 1936 and reissued in 1965, I.A. Richards seeks to resuscitate the waning discipline Ricoeur describes: "These lectures are an attempt to revive an old subject. I need spend no time, I think, in describing the present state of Rhetoric. Today it is the dreariest and least profitable part of the waste that the unfortunate travel through in Freshman English! So low has Rhetoric sunk that we would do better just to dismiss it to Limbo than to trouble ourselves with it—unless we can find reason for believing that it can become a study that will minister successfully to important needs. As to the needs, there is little room for doubt about them. Rhetoric, I shall urge, should be a study of misunderstanding and its remedies" (3).

35. "The Art of Fiction." *Shadow and Act* (New York: Random House, 1964), 169.

Chapter 2

1. Space will not allow for discussion of a good number of thinkers who likewise take up the implications of literature's imbrication with philosophy even as they devote critical space to the role of language and writing in the expression of black being. Significant among these thinkers is Nahum D. Chandler, author of the forthcoming book *The Problem of Pure Being: Annotations on W. E. B. Du Bois and the Discourses of the Negro*. This study has benefited in myriad ways from Professor Chandler's generosity of spirit and acute intellectual work.

2. *Moorings and Metaphors*, 78.

3. The illimitable character of black being is, as I discuss fully in the chapter on "The Conservation of Races," both deferred and anticipated by Du Bois in this 1897 essay, which is perhaps his most controversial piece of writing. The concept is treated at length by Nahum Chandler in his unpublished manuscript, "The Question of the Illimitable in the Thought of W. E. B. Du Bois" (n.d.).

4. Georg W. F. Hegel, *The Philosophy of History*. Rev ed. Trans. J. Sibree. (London: The Colonial Press, 1900): 8.

5. G. W. F. Hegel's *Philosophy of History* was published in 1831, rather than in 1813, as given in this quote. In his preface to the second edition of his father's work, Charles Hegel writes that the first lectures on which the book is based were not delivered until the "winter of 1822–23" as a graduate course (xi). The first edition of the *Philosophy* came after Hegel's death in 1831, drawn from his lecture notes for the course as given from 1830 to 1831. The revised, 1900 edition hearkens back to the earlier set of notes, from 1822–23 and 1824–34. See Georg Wilhelm Friedrich Hegel, *The Philosophy of History*, trans. J. Sibree, rev. ed. (London: The Colonial Press, 1900).

6. See pgs 92–93 of *Figures in Black.*

7. Du Bois, "The Conservation of Races." *Writings.* Ed. Nathan Huggins. (New York: Library of America, 1986): 825.

8. Tommie Shelby, *We Who Are Dark: The Philosophical Foundations of Racial Solidarity.* Cambridge, MA: Harvard University Press, 2005; Stuart Hall, "Subjects in History: Making Diasporic Identities" in *The House that Race Built* (New York: Vintage), 1998: 295.

9. "Subjects in History," 298.

10. Hortense Spillers, "Mama's Baby, Papa's Maybe: An American Grammar Book," in *Black, White, and in Color: Essays on American Literature and Culture* (Chicago: University of Chicago Press, 2003): 204–205. Officially titled *The Negro Family: The Case for National Action,* The Moynihan Report, as it is widely known, appeared in 1965. Steven Steinberg names the report as a pivotal point in liberal America's disengagement from race-based policies of social equality. See his essay "The Liberal Retreat from Race during the Post-Civil Rights Era" in *The House that Race Built,* 13–47.

11. See N. Katherine Hayles, *How We Became Posthuman: Virtual Bodies in Cybernetics, Literature, and Informatics* (Chicago: University of Chicago Press, 1999), 3. In Hayles's view of the posthuman, "consciousness, regarded as the seat of human identity in the Western tradition long before Descartes thought he was a mind thinking, [is considered] as an epiphenomenon, as an evolutionary upstart trying to claim that it is the whole show when in actuality it is only a minor sideshow" (2–3).

12. Barnor Hesse, "Self-Fulfilling Prophecy: The Postracial Horizon" in *The South Atlantic Quarterly* 110.1 (Winter 2011): 155–178. While Hesse's argument is quite valid, there is, of course, more to the story. Taking pre-1492 Spain into consideration, with its purity of blood trials and its ultimate "expulsion," in 1492, of the Moors and the Jews, religious "difference" between Europeans as well as whites and nonwhites must be seen as a precursor to modern ideas of racial difference. Likewise, the concept of social otherness was quite alive in pre-modern ideas on ethnicity, as well as in early modern quasi-medical (or proto-medical) discourses on the body and its humors. See, for instance, Mary Floyd-Wilson's *English Ethnicity and Race in Early Modern Drama* (2003) for a discussion of a number of points regarding race and bodily humors. David Levering Lewis's recent book, *God's Crucible: Islam and the Making of Europe, 570–1215* (2008), explores an even earlier time period and its struggles over race and difference. See also María deGuzmán's *Spain's Long Shadow: The Black Legend, Off-Whiteness, and Anglo-American Empire* (Minneapolis: University of Minnesota Press, 2005), which touches upon Spain's purity of blood trials and treats fully Spain's lingering shadow of "blackness."

13. See, for instance, Wright's introduction to *Black Metropolis,* by St. Clair Drake and Horace Cayton (1945), where Wright cites James not as the source of his own social philosophy, but as affirmation of thoughts he developed independently.

14. I am borrowing by allusion from the title of Robert Gooding-Williams's 2009 study, *In the Shadow of Du Bois: Afro-Modern Political Thought in America* (Harvard University Press). Though he credits *Souls* as being the most influential Afro-Modern contribution to black political philosophy, Gooding-Williams sees

Du Bois's thought as inherently limited in ways that demand its surpassing, even as its example is instructive. To this end, he uses Du Bois's work as a segue back to the earlier political thought of Frederick Douglass, whose aims and methods Gooding-Williams sees as more promising for twenty-first-century African American political thought. My own perspective, of course, diverges from that of Gooding-Williams.

15. See Mark C. Taylor, *Journeys to Selfhood: Hegel and Kierkegaard* (New York: Fordham University Press, 2000), p. 134; Gulnara Bakieva, *Social Memory and Contemporaneity*, ed. Maura Donohue (Washington, DC: The Council for Research in Values and Philosophy, 2007), v; David Kettler and Volker Meja, *Karl Mannheim and the Crisis of Liberalism: The Secret of these New Times* (New Brunswick, NJ: Transaction Publishers, 1995), p. 17; Julius Stone, *Province and Function of Law: Law as Logic, Justice, and Social Control* (Sydney, Australia: Assoc. General Publication, Pty Ltd, 1946; Rpt. 1973), p. 479; Jacques Derrida, *Specters of Marx*, trans. Peggy Kamuf (New York: Routledge, 1994), p. xviii.

16. Spillers, "The Idea of Black Culture," *CR: The New Centennial Review* 6.3 (Winter 2006): 7.

17. As Glissant's translator Betsy Wing explains, Glissant's sense of wandering, given in the French as *errance* (or errantry), is not mindless roaming, "but includes a sense of sacred motivation" (*Poetics of Relation* [Ann Arbor: University of Michigan Press, 1997] 211ff1).

18. First published in *boundary 2* 21.3 (Fall 1994): 65–116.

19. Du Bois's final book, *The Autobiography of W. E. B. Du Bois*, was published posthumously in 1968, the year after Cruse's *Crisis* appeared. Du Bois counted *Souls* and *Darkwater: Voices from within the Veil* (1920) among his autobiographical writings; however, *Dusk of Dawn: An Essay toward an Autobiography of a Race Concept* would remain his fullest autobiographical work to appear before *The Autobiography*. While James Baldwin's *Notes of a Native Son* (1955), *Nobody Knows My Name* (1961), and *The Fire Next Time* (1962) are each autobiographical to greater or lesser extents, and each speak to the vocation and responsibility of the black writer, Baldwin does not figure in Spillers's account here.

20. I use this term as it was developed in writings by Linda Hutcheon: *The Politics of Postmodernism* (New York: Routledge, 1989) and *A Poetics of Postmodernism* (New York: Routledge, 1988).

21. See Judy's "Writing Culture as Nonrecuperable Negativity" in *(Dis)forming the American Canon*, p. 92–98.

22. Naomi Zack's work on mixed race identity has been critiqued by Michele Elam as celebrating racial hybridity, seeing it as racelessness. Elam's 2011 book, *The Souls of Mixed Folk: Race, Politics, and Aesthetics in the New Millennium* (Stanford: Stanford University Press), works to counter simplistic, congratulatory perspectives on mixed race identity as the treasured result of the Civil Rights gains of America. Naomi Zack, *Race and Mixed Race* (Philadelphia: Temple University Press, 1993) and the edited volume *American Mixed Race: The Culture of Microdiversity* (Lanham, MD: Rowman and Littlefield, 1995).

Chapter 3

1. Page numbers refer to Hawkes, *Metaphor*. London: Methuen, 1972.

2. In the Norton Critical Edition of the *Narrative*, Werner Sollors includes a helpful selection of contemporary and early nineteenth-century reviews of Equiano's work. Pertinent to my point here are assessments that appeared in the *Monthly Review* (1789), the *General Magazine and Impartial Review* (1789), and a review of the *Interesting Narrative* by Mary Wollstonecraft (1789). Sollors also includes later reviews by the Abbé Grégoire (1808) and Lydia Maria Child (1833). Please see *The Interesting Narrative of the Life of Olaudah Equiano, or Gustavus Vassa, the African, Written by Himself.* Ed. Werner Sollors. New York: Norton, 2001. 295–302.

3. David Punter, *Metaphor*. New York: Routledge, 2007. 71.

4. A quick sampling of titles supports this point. The inclusion of the phrase "interesting narrative" was popular throughout the eighteenth and nineteenth centuries on both sides of the Atlantic. It and another phrase that draws so much attention when appended to memoirs and autobiographies by former slaves, "written by himself," was also used with some frequency by whites who were in no way part of the tradition of slave literature, but who wished to underscore the fact of their authorship. Such titles number in the hundreds, and are hardly dominated by writers of African descent. I will list only a few and will limit this list to titles that appear close to the publication date of Equiano's *Narrative* and that were published, like Equiano's work, in London: *The Interesting Narrative of the Life and Adventures of David Doubtful* by Henry Brooke (London: n.p., 1798); *An Interesting Narrative of the Travels of James Bruce, Esq. into Abyssinia, to Discover the Source of the Nile* by James Bruce (London: Printed for H. D. Symons, 1800); *An Interesting Narrative of the Voyage, Shipwreck, and Extraordinary Adventures of Mr. Drake Morris* by Drake Morris (London: John Abraham, 1797); *An Authentic and Interesting Narrative of the Late Expedition to Botany Bay, as Performed by Commodore Phillips, . . . and Safe Arrival on the Coast of New Holland: With Particular Descriptions of Jackson's Bay & Lord Howe's Island, . . . Written by an Officer just Returned* (London: printed by W. Bailey, 1789); and *The Authentic Memoirs and Sufferings of Dr. William Stahl, a German Physician. Containing His Travels, Observations, and Interesting Narrative during Four Years Imprisonment at Goa, . . . Written by Himself*, by Wilhelm Stahl (London: printed for J. Barker, 1792).

5. Linda Nochlin, *The Body in Pieces: The Fragment as a Metaphor of Modernity*. New York: Thames and Hudson, 1995. Vincent Carretta's biography of Equiano, entitled *Equiano, the African: Biography of a Self-Made Man* (Athens: University of Georgia Press, 2005), contains a full discussion of portraits used by Equiano's eighteenth-century African contemporaries.

6. Jean-Jacques Rousseau, from *The Geneva Manuscript*. In *The Nationalism Reader*, ed. Omar Dahbour and Micheline R. Ishay (New Jersey: Humanities Press, 1995), 22–26.

7. Immanuel Kant, *The Metaphysics of Morals*. In *The Nationalism Reader*, 38–47.

8. David Hume, "Of National Characters." In *David Hume: The Philosophical Works*. Vol. 3. Ed. Thomas Hill Green and Thomas Hodge Grose (Scientia Verlag Aalen, 1964), 248.

9. Peter Gay, *The Enlightenment: An Interpretation*, vol. 2 (New York: Knopf, 1966–69), 410; John Locke, *Two Treatises of Government*, 2nd ed. Ed. Peter Laslett (Cambridge: Cambridge University Press, 1970); and Baron de Montesquieu, *De l'esprit des lois*, (Paris: Garnier, 1945). Locke's text was originally published between 1684 and 1689; Montesquieu's appeared in 1748.

10. *Observations on the Feeling of the Beautiful and Sublime*, 110–11.

11. Père Labat was the author of nineteen volumes of travelogues that documented the years he spent as a missionary in the West Indies. He published *Voyage du père Labat aux îles de l'Amérique* in 1724.

12. Please see "Author's Note," *The Interesting Narrative of the Life of Olaudah Equiano*. Ed. Rebecka Rutledge Fisher (New York: Barnes and Noble, 2005), xix–xxviii. Page references to Equiano's *Narrative* are drawn from this edition.

13. Richard Steele, ["Brunetta and Phillis"]. *The Spectator* Vol 1 No 80 (June 1, 1711). Ed. G. Gregory Smith (London: J.M Dent, 1897), 302–305. Image taken from *Paintings from Books: Art and Literature in Britain, 1760–1900*, by Richard D. Altick. The painting, titled simply "Brunetta and Phillis" (1803) and completed by Thomas Stothard, was inspired by Steele's vignette. Stothard avoids Steele's explicit dressing of the slave in an undergarment of the same fabric as Brunetta's gown, an even more daring insult than the portrayal he gives here. This image from Steele's vignette, and the attendant dialectic of the black body in European apparel, was quite popular, as it was rendered again as a painting in 1853 by a Mr. A. Solomon. Solomon's rendering was first displayed at the Royal Academy in 1853, and again at the Paris Exposition Universelle of 1855, in the Palais des Beaux-Arts.

14. There were a number of translations of Homer's *Iliad* in the early eighteenth century. Prominent among them was a translation undertaken by Anne Dacier in 1711; Houdard de la Motte published what was considered to be a distorted version of the *Iliad* in 1714, to which Dacier replied with disdain. Pierre Marivaux, well known for his novel *La vie de Marianne* (1731–1741), but also respected as a playwright and an essayist whose work is compared to that of Addison and Steele, also responded derisively to this translation in a tract entitled "L'Homère travesti, ou l'Iliade en vers burlesques" (1717). Pope devoted six years' work to his 1720 translation of the *Iliad* when he was but twenty-five years old; his translation, though unfaithful to the Greek in the literal sense, was widely respected in his day because it was deemed foremost among the translations that permitted one to read the *Iliad* as a poem rather than as a cultural artifact. In her 1985 evaluation of Pope's translation (the second edition of which was published in 2002), Felicity Rosslyn maintains that Pope's translation "remains the best available," even considering what she calls its "defects." Please see *Pope's Iliad: A Selection with Commentary*. 2nd Edition. Ed. Felicity Rosslyn. London: Bristol Classical Press, 2002: xii.

15. Under the Spanish Asiento, Spain contracted with non-Spaniards to manage the slave trade between Spain, Africa, and the Spanish American Empire. The

contractors were originally Genoese. From 1595 to 1640, they were Portuguese; from 1702 to 1713, French, and from the Treaties of Utrecht in 1713 to 1750, British.

16. Alexander Pope, "Windsor Forest" in *Poetry and Prose of Alexander Pope*. Ed. Aubrey Williams (Boston: Houghton Mifflin, 1969), 76.

17. *Spectator* 69, 1711.

18. "The Royal Exchange." In *The Oxford Anthology of English Literature*, vol. 1 (New York: Oxford University Press, 1973), 2027–29. Addison employs metaphors that reflect his interest in the interwoven nature of humankind, facilitated by the burgeoning capitalistic system that was growing during his era. He uses metaphor as well as synecdoche in conveying his thoughts.

19. Paul Ricoeur, *Time and Narrative*. Vol 2. Trans. Kathleen McLaughlin and David Pellauer (Chicago: University of Chicago Press, 1985): 6.

20. See Toni Morrison, "Home," in *The House that Race Built* (New York: Pantheon, 1997), 3–12.

21. Terry Eagleton, *Literary Theory: An Introduction*. 2nd edition. Minneapolis: The University of Minnesota Press, 1996: 15.

22. "On the Mimetic Faculty." *One-Way Street and Other Writings*. London: Verso, 1985: 160–163.

23. *Narrative of the Most Remarkable Particulars in the Life of James Albert Ukawsaw Gronniosaw* (1772). In *Slave Narratives* (New York: Library of America), 11–12.

24. *Interesting Narrative*, 64. Equiano was obviously mistaken. He felt that he was free because of his baptism at St. Margaret's Church in 1759. Although the baptism of blacks, a growing community in seventeenth and eighteenth-century England, was not an irregularity, such a sacrament still caused a stir of disapprobation among those who supported slavery. James Walvin writes, "From the early arrival of Africans in England, their religion (or apparent lack of one) was a sensitive issue. The 1601 Elizabethan Proclamation, ordering the expulsion of early black settlers in England, was linked to their heathenism." The debate continued throughout the seventeenth century: "a number of seventeenth-century legal cases had suggested that the 'heathenism' of imported blacks confirmed their bondage" (*An African's Life* [London: Continuum], 43). Christianity and slavery were held to be mutually exclusive; for a time, blacks who had been baptized felt that under English law, they were essentially freed through the ritual. However, pro-slavery forces actively worked against any such claims, and English courts, not willing to endanger the stability of the plantation society upon which the colonial system was built, were careful not to allow challenges to slavery on English soil to go unchecked. They understood that to condemn slavery in the metropole would clearly spell imminent doom for slavery in the colonies. A ruling in 1729 by the Attorney and Solicitor General (stating that "baptism doth not bestow freedom [on a slave], nor make any alteration in his temporal condition in these kingdoms") appeared to settle the matter, and it was confirmed once more by Yorke (Lord Hardwicke) in 1749. However, as Equiano's remarks indicate, the mythic connection between baptism and freedom persisted. See Walvin's *An African Life*, 43. Also see Anthony J. Barker, *The African*

Link (London: Frank Cass, 1978), 67–68; and Peter Fryer, *Staying Power: The History of Black People in Britain* (Atlantic Highlands, NJ: Humanities Press, 1984), 23–24.

25. As Pascal concludes the sale of Equiano to Captain James Doran, he makes clear his conviction that Equiano, being his slave, possessed nothing, not even the coat he wore to ward off the December winter on the day of his sale. Pascal took Equiano's only coat from him.

26. For more on the African cultural elements that remain legible in Equiano's text, see April Langley, *The Black Aesthetic Unbound: Theorizing the Dilemma of Eighteenth-Century African American Literature* (Columbus: Ohio State University Press, 2008).

27. The word "Bible" is derived from the Greek "biblia," meaning small books. The Christian community, of course, prefers "The Book" to "The Books," and did so in Equiano's time after the death of Elizabeth I in 1603 and the ascension of James I, who commissioned the King James Version, completed in 1611.

28. Equiano does not actually quote from the 126th Psalm, as he states he does, but instead adapts verses from Ephesians 1: 12–13, which reads: "That we should be to the praise of his glory, who first trusted in Christ. In whom ye also trusted, after that ye heard the word of truth, the gospel of your salvation: in whom also after that ye believed, ye were sealed with that holy Spirit of promise." The 126th Psalm, a short chapter of 6 verses, bears no semantic resemblance to the verses from Ephesians, but shares an emphasis upon placing one's trust in the Lord.

29. The account of Peter's liberation to which Equiano refers comes in Acts 12:1–9: Peter "wist not that it was true which was done by the angel; but thought he saw a vision." The translators of the King James Version link this passage from Acts to Psalms 126, to which Equiano likewise alludes here, though he does not cite it directly.

30. This metaphor is, of course, taken up and repeated in the work of Wright and Ellison, where it is secularized and rationalized by way of Freudian thought.

31. Matthew 25:41 reads: "Then shall he say also unto them on the left hand, Depart from me, ye cursed, into everlasting fire, prepared for the devil and his angels."

32. Quite symbolic here would be the telling of Equiano's life in three evolutions, using the number three to symbolize perfection of existence, as in the Biblical perfection of "God in three persons." This, however, is not a narrative strategy Equiano chooses to employ.

33. Luke 4:16–20 tells of the beginnings of Christ's ministry, when he went into the synagogue on the Sabbath and stood up to read from the Book of Isaiah [given in the New Testament as "Esaias"]: "And there was delivered unto him the book of the prophet Esaias. And when he had opened the book, he found the place where it was written, 'The Spirit of the Lord is upon me, because he hath anointed me to preach the gospel to the poor; he hath sent me to heal the brokenhearted, to preach deliverance to the captives, and recovering sight to the blind, to set at liberty them that are bruised, to preach the acceptable year of the Lord.' And he closed the book, and he gave it again to them minister, and sat down. And the eyes of all

them that were in the synagogue were fastened on him. And he began to say unto them, 'This day is scripture fulfilled in your ears.'" This passage is taken from the King James Version; italics reproduced here are given in the original.
  34. Micah 6:8.

Chapter 4

1. See James Weldon Johnson's Preface to the first edition of *The Book of American Negro Poetry*, rev. ed. (1922; repr., San Diego: Harcourt Brace, 1931), 26. See also J. Saunders Redding, *To Make a Poet Black* (Chapel Hill: Univ. of North Carolina Press, 1939), 40–43.

2. Frances Ellen Watkins Harper, *A Brighter Coming Day: A Frances Ellen Watkins Harper Reader*, ed. Frances Smith Foster (New York: Feminist Press, 1990); Frances Smith Foster, *Written by Herself: Literary Production by African American Women, 1746–1892* (Bloomington: Indiana Univ. Press, 1993); Hazel V. Carby, *Reconstructing Womanhood: The Emergence of the Afro-American Woman Novelist* (New York: Oxford Univ. Press, 1987); Melba Joyce Boyd, *Discarded Legacy: Politics and Poetics in the Life of Frances E. W. Harper, 1825–1911* (Detroit: Wayne State Univ. Press, 1994).

3. Smith Foster, introduction to Harper, *Brighter Coming Day*, 19–20.

4. See Michel de Certeau, *The Writing of History*. Trans. Tom Conley. New York: Columbia University Press, 1988.

5. Patricia Liggins Hill, " 'Let Me Make Songs for the People': A Study of Frances Watkins Harper's Poetry." *Black American Literature Forum* 15.2 (Summer 1981): 60–65; " 'We Are Rising as a People': Frances Harper's Radical Views on Class and Racial Equality in *Sketches of Southern Life*." *American Transcendental Quarterly* 19.2 (June 2005): 133–53.

6. Frances Smith Foster lends interesting texture to our understanding of this period. She writes: "Harper knew that nineteenth century popular audiences preferred poems with rhymes and rhythms that were easy to memorize and to recite. The aesthetics of popular poetry also required familiar verse forms such as the sonnet and the ballad, simple and didactic metaphors, and readily comprehensible word order" (*A Brighter Coming Day* 28). Poets of Harper's day who practiced these aesthetics included the so-called "Fireside poets": Longfellow, Lowell, and Whittier figured among their numbers. Since Harper wanted to succeed with the same audience that read these poets, Smith Foster argues, she employed the popular aesthetics of her day in order to best reach this audience.

7. The rhythm of the poem may also be traced to a source earlier than that of Howe. Howe's "The Battle Hymn of the Republic" is a hymn based not only on the popular song "John Brown's Body," but also the African American camp song, "Say Brothers, Can You Meet Me?," a song that actually predates "John Brown's Body." Thus Harper may be seen to signify multiply here. She was friends with John Brown and, according to William Still's *The Underground Railroad*, corresponded

with Brown's wife as Brown and his comrades awaited execution. Further, Still points out, Harper spent two weeks with Mrs. Brown "at the house of the writer [Still] while she was awaiting the execution of her husband, and sympathized with her most deeply" (Still 762).

8. It was again during the Reconstruction period that Harper published what I see as her most striking work of poetry, *Moses: A Story of the Nile* (1869). A book-length narrative poem divided into nine chapters, this work is a sharp departure from Harper's earlier compositions. In it, she neglects the form of rhyming quatrains that had characterized so much of her poetry in favor of a free verse form. Moses, a Christian archetype who appears in a number of Harper's works, aided her in formulating a symbolic system in her poetry, whereby the plight of African Americans was allegorized through the plight of the Hebrews. Harper's poetics shine forcefully in this work. It is, perhaps, the pinnacle of her compositions. Its analysis remains a project to undertake at another time.

9. Harper referenced Stowe's work through at least two additional poems that appeared shortly after the publication of *Uncle Tom's Cabin*: "Eva's Farewell," and "To Harriet Beecher Stowe" were directly inspired by Stowe's novel.

10. See Graham's introduction to *The Complete Poems of Frances E. W. Harper*. Ed. Maryemma Graham. New York: Oxford University Press, 1988. xxxiii–lvii.

11. The late Martinican poet and philosopher Édouard Glissant proposes and develops this term in *Poetics of Relation* (Trans. Betsy Wing, Ann Arbor: The University of Michigan Press, 1997), 5–37.

12. Giorgio Agamben, *Remnants of Auschwitz: The Witness and the Archive*, trans. Daniel Heller-Roazen (New York: Zone Books, 2002), 33, 12. Readers familiar with Agamben's text will note the influence of his thought upon this chapter.

13. Toni Morrison, "The Site of Memory," in *Inventing the Truth: The Art and Craft of Memoir*, ed. William Zinsser, rev. and exp. ed. (New York: Houghton Mifflin, 1995), 94.

14. Morrison, "Site of Memory," 92, 95, 97.

15. Martin Heidegger's use of this term in "The Origin of the Work of Art" defines it as a narrative clearing that functions doubly; it is both an opening in the midst of a textual locus (from which an imaginative, possible world is set forth), and an illumination of the events of the past. This essay, first delivered in 1935 as a lecture titled *Der Ursprung des Kunstwerkes*, is translated and reprinted in *Poetry, Language, Thought*, trans. Albert Hofstadter (New York: Perennial Classics, 2001), 15–86.

16. Heidegger, "Origin," 44.

17. Heidegger, "Origin," 51–52.

18. I find it useful here to underscore Michel Foucault's definition of episteme as a way of referring to the ideologies that shape the perception of knowledge and the act of knowing in any particular period of history.

19. My use of the term "semiotic" follows the work of Julia Kristeva. Drawing on the word's Greek etymology, Kristeva defines it as a distinctive mark or trace that exists prior to the symbolic, the relational space governed by rules of syntax,

categorization, and structure. The semiotic, through its inclusion in the genotext (the energies Kristeva sees as bringing a text into being, including the vitality of the language user's body), leaves its imprint on the phenotext (Kristeva's term for the physical literary work that, in its correspondence to the symbolic, conforms to the rules of language and categorization). See *Revolution in Poetic Language* (New York: Columbia Univ. Press, 1984), 25.

20. Frances Ellen Watkins Harper, *Sketches of Southern Life*, repr. in *Complete Poems of Frances E. W. Harper*, ed. Maryemma Graham (New York: Oxford Univ. Press, 1988), 117, 118; hereafter cited parenthetically as *SL*.

21. It is only in this final poem that we learn Chloe's last name, the use of which a number of nineteenth-century writers, including William Wells Brown in his *Narrative* (1847), emphasize as a significant mark of social recognition and respect. When Wells Brown takes on the name of his Quaker benefactor in chapter 14 of his autobiography, he purposefully quotes this "good Quaker friend," who tells him, "Since thee has got out of slavery, thee has become a man, and men always have two names." See *The Narrative of William Wells Brown*, in *Slave Narratives*, ed. William L. Andrews and Henry Louis Gates Jr. (New York: Library of America, 2000), 420.

22. Luke 2:25–30; esp. 2:25, 2:28–30 (King James Version).

23. We see this concern at work in the short story "The Two Offers," a tale of morals Harper published in 1859. The poem "Vashti" (1857), which revises the Biblical story found in the book of Esther, is equally concerned with contemplation coupled with moral action. For other instances, see the poem "An Appeal to the American People" (1871), which calls upon the American people to demonstrate their democratic, moral sensibilities; "An Appeal to My Country Women" (1894), a patriotic poem written in the same meter and accent pattern as "The Star-Spangled Banner" (1814); and "Woman's Political Future," a speech given in 1893 at the World's Columbian Exposition. Christianity, temperance, family, and human rights are all themes that Harper forcefully explores in this essay, which is one of her finest.

24. Grant's tenure was marked by scandal and lavish living. Yet he supported freedmen's rights and won passage of the KKK Act of 1871, one of a number of "Force bills" passed between 1870 and 1875 to protect rights granted to African Americans by the Fourteenth and Fifteenth Amendments. W. E. B. Du Bois discusses these acts in *Black Reconstruction in America, 1860–1880* (New York: Atheneum, 1935), 682–84.

25. See Harper's essay "Christianity," published in *Poems on Miscellaneous Subjects* (Philadelphia: Merrihew and Thompson, 1857), 40–44. I discuss this essay fully in chapter 8 of this study.

26. Many writers construe Harper as a woman from the North. Though she was, in fact, freeborn, she was born in the state of Maryland, one of the fiercest states of the Confederacy and the home state of Frederick Douglass. Harper was indeed a southerner; even her experiences in the northern state of Ohio could not take her far from slavery's reach. Harper's poetic memorialization of Margaret Garner, whose infanticide in the face of slave catchers has been commemorated and celebrated in works ranging from Harper's own poetry to Toni Morrison's Pulitzer

Prize-winning 1988 novel, *Beloved*, was set on the outskirts of Cincinnati, Ohio, a mere river's span away from the slave-holding state of Kentucky.

27. This community of free African Americans was established after the American Revolution. A strong community based largely in religious activism and attentive to the benefits of education, this free community was one to which Frederick Douglass's wife, Anna Murray, belonged. Complex labor relations existed in Baltimore through the Civil War, and it was not uncommon for enslaved and free blacks to work side by side. Further, the free population increased as the slave population decreased; that is, the free black population in Baltimore tended to rise with the manumission of slaves once their period of indentured servitude came to an end. This shift only exacerbated race relations of the time; it was likely the impetus behind Maryland's statute of 1853. See Delano Greenidge-Copprue, "Baltimore, Maryland, Slavery in." *Encyclopedia of African American History, 1619–1895: From the Colonial Period to the Age of Frederick Douglass*. Ed. Paul Finkelman. See also Frederick Douglass, *The Narrative of the Life of Frederick Douglass, An American Slave*. Ed. David W. Blight. New York: Bedford/St. Martin's, 2003. Douglass writes: "I had resided but a short time in Baltimore before I observed a marked difference, in the treatment of slaves, from that which I had witnessed in the country. A city slave is almost a freeman, compared with a slave on the plantation. He is much better fed and clothed, and enjoys privileges altogether unknown to the slave on the plantation. There is a vestige of decency, a sense of shame, that does much to curb and check those outbreaks of atrocious cruelty so commonly enacted upon the plantation. He is a desperate slaveholder, who will shock the humanity of his nonslaveholding neighbors with the cries of his lacerated slave. Few are willing to incur the odium attaching to the reputation of being a cruel master; and above all things, they would not be known as not giving a slave enough to eat. Every city slaveholder is anxious to have it known of him, that he feeds his slaves well; and it is due to them to say, that most of them do give their slaves enough to eat. There are, however, some painful exceptions to this rule" (64–65).

28. See Orlando Patterson, *Slavery and Social Death: A Comparative Study* (Cambridge: Harvard Univ. Press, 1982).

29. Agamben argues that there is an "intimacy" to the relation of subject and consciousness in testimony (*Remnants*, 146). The intimacy of the two is inseparable. We might speak of the relation of Harper to Chloe in these terms.

30. See chapter 2, pages 76–83, for a discussion of this concept.

31. Martin Heidegger, "The Thinker as Poet," in *Poetry, Language, Thought*, 10.

32. Heidegger, "Origin," 35, 43.

33. Agamben, *Remnants*, 147–48.

34. Agamben, *Remnants*, 146.

Chapter 5

1. For instance, Robert Bernasconi, in his 2009 essay " 'Our Duty to Conserve': W. E. B. Du Bois's Philosophy of History in Context," argues that Du Bois's

essay is less a contribution to the debate over the validity of the concept of race, and more of an intervention in the debate over the impact of racial mixing on African American political solidarity. He provides a useful rebuttal of the charge of essentialism leveled against Du Bois by Anthony Appiah, and while our work shares a similar perspective on Du Bois's philosophy of history, my study uses that historicist foundation to erect an argument that draws the metaphorics of "Conservation" into relation with those of *Souls*. Bernasconi's essay, which is a testament to the continued interest in "Conservation" among humanists, appears in *SAQ: South Atlantic Quarterly* 108.3 (Summer 2009): 519–540.

2. Moses defines classical black nationalism as an "ideology whose goal was the creation of an autonomous black nation-state, with definite geographical boundaries—usually in Africa" (1). He rightly argues that " 'The Conservation of Races' reveals how concepts of black independence and racial destiny were present in [Du Bois's] thinking from the beginning of his career" (228). In an incomplete memorandum to Paul Hagemans, the consul general of Belgium who was stationed in Philadelphia during the years Du Bois spent there undertaking sociological research that would be published as *The Philadelphia Negro* in 1899, Du Bois inquired whether it might be possible for the government of Belgium to work with the American Negro Academy in determining whether the Congo Free State might be an appropriate locale for the establishment of a colony of "skilled, intelligent [American Negro] colonists which the Congo Free State needs" (48). Although Du Bois would early on contemplate the possibilities that lay in repatriating Americans of African descent to Africa, he does not propose such in "The Conservation of Races" either directly or indirectly. Thus the essay itself does not aptly serve as the example of classical black nationalist thought that Moses intends to demonstrate. Herbert Aptheker dates Du Bois's memorandum to Hagemans as 1897, but does not specify whether the note was ever sent to or received by the consul general. The memorandum does make clear, however, that some months after the ANA's founding, Du Bois did indeed consider such expatriation to be a viable solution for some, if not in fact all, of America's Negro population. He advocated the selection of a "small but steady stream . . . of emigrants who could go to Africa, knowing the conditions, equipped for meeting them and desiring to work to the credits of the Congo Free State." "On Migration to Africa." 1897. *Against Racism: Unpublished Essays, Papers, Addresses, 1887–1961*. Ed. Herbert Aptheker. Amherst: The University of Massachusetts Press, 1985. 43–49.

3. In her book, *Silence in the Land of Logos* (Princeton: Princeton University Press, 2000), Silvia Mantiglio writes that *muthos* denotes "an oratorical performance that takes place in public. *Muthos* is speech in action, that is, speech viewed from the standpoint of the speaker who is seeking to act upon his audience through a lengthy display of his authority" (65). In his introduction to *Logos and Muthos: Philosophical Essays in Greek Literature* (Albany: SUNY Press, 2009), William Wians writes that *muthos* may be defined as "literary, usually poetic, texts" (1), some of which may be mythical in nature, that relate demonstrable or even undemonstrable philosophical truths. In my usage of the term, I intend it to denote both speech

and writing of a conceptual, denotative sort, as is the case in "The Conservation of Races." Here, I use this term to underscore Du Bois's reliance upon the modes of epic narrative as he presents a complex argument deconstructing the validity of race as a biological concept.

4. See Gates's introductory essay in *"Race," Writing, and Difference* (Chicago: University of Chicago Press, 1986), 1–20. Entitled "Writing 'Race' and the Difference it Makes," it reads, in part: "Race, as a meaningful criterion within the biological sciences, has long been recognized to be a fiction. When we speak of 'the white race' or 'the black race,' 'the Jewish race' or 'the Aryan race,' we speak in biological misnomers and, more generally, in metaphors" (4).

5. Blumenbach submitted his doctoral thesis, *De generis humani varietate nativa*, to the medical faculty at the University of Göttingen in Germany in 1775, "as the minutemen of Lexington and Concord began the American Revolution. He then republished the text for general distribution in 1776, as a fateful meeting in Philadelphia proclaimed our independence. The coincidence of three great documents in 1776—Jefferson's *Declaration of Independence* (on the politics of liberty), Adam Smith's *Wealth of Nations* (on the economics of individualism), and Blumenbach's treatise on racial classification (on the science of human diversity)—records the social ferment of these decades, and sets the wider context that makes Blumenbach's taxonomy, and his decision to call the European race Caucasian, so important for our history and current concerns" (Gould, 1996, p. 402).

6. Anthony Appiah, "The Uncompleted Argument: Du Bois and the Illusion of Race." In *"Race," Writing, and Difference.* Ed. Henry Louis Gates, Jr. Chicago: University of Chicago Press, 1986, 21–37.

7. David Levering Lewis, *W. E. B. Du Bois: Biography of a Race* (New York: Henry Holt, 1993); Wilson J. Moses, *Afrotopia: The Roots of African American Popular History* (New York: Cambridge UP, 1998); Anthony Appiah, *In My Father's House: Africa in the Philosophy of Culture* (New York: Oxford UP, 1992).

8. In fact, this study presumes the articulations of the text itself to be sufficient evidence against the willful misreadings of the sort indelibly marked in the thought of Anthony Appiah, which I have discussed fully elsewhere. Please see Rebecka R. Rutledge, "Metaphoric Black Bodies in the Hinterlands of Race; Or, Towards Deciphering the Du Boisian Concept of Race and Nation in 'The Conservation of Races.'" In *Race and Ethnicity: Across Time, Space, and Discipline.* Ed. Rodney D. Coates. Boston: Brill, 2004. 331–349.

9. Hans Gadamer, *Truth and Method* (New York: Continuum, 1975); Mikhail Bakhtin, *The Dialogic Imagination: Four Essays* (Austin: University of Texas Press, 1981).

10. On this point, I express my gratitude to Dr. Donald H. Matthews, without whose dogged pursuance of the connection between Du Bois and Dilthey I would not have seen fully the importance of a specific concept of "understanding" in the former's work.

11. "Speaking in Tongues: Dialogics, Dialectics, and the Black Woman Writer's Literary Tradition." In Napier (Ed.) *African American Literary Theory: A Reader* (New York: NYU Press): 350.

12. "Strivings of the Negro People" (1897), which I have already mentioned, will be discussed in the following chapter, as it is virtually indistinguishable from the later form in which it appears in Chapter One of *The Souls of Black Folk* as "Of Our Spiritual Strivings."

13. Parenthetical page references for "Woman's Political Future" are drawn from *The Norton Anthology of African American Literature*, 1st ed. (New York: Norton, 1997), 436–439.

14. Andrew Carnegie, "Value of the World's Fair to the American People," *Engineering Magazine* 6.4 (1894), 417–422.

15. "The Reason Why the Colored American is not in the Columbian Exposition," Chicago, 1893 (rprt. Urbana: University of Illinois Press, 1999).

16. *Philosophy of History*, 1831, 2nd ed. (London: Colonial Press, 1900).

17. One remarkable omission in Hegel's overview of Africa's place in world history is the question of color. Earlier philosophers writing during the time of the Enlightenment, such as Immanuel Kant and Thomas Jefferson, regularly hearkened to the color of the African's skin in their conclusion that Africans were not world historical beings and, thus, could not aspire to national belonging, to the sort of national "becoming" to which Hegel refers in the passage I cite above. Enlightenment philosophers such as Jefferson, writing in his *Notes on the State of Virginia* (1804), was willing to abandon the economic crutch of slavery, but strongly doubted that blacks would ever "fit in" in America's landscape due to their "veil of blackness," the essential difference that would forever render them outsiders. An extended discussion of this question may be found in chapter 3 of this study.

18. Kristeva discusses this point in "Throes of Love: The Field of Metaphor," *Tales of Love*, trans. Leon S. Roudiez (New York: Columbia University Press, 1987): 267–279.

Chapter 6

1. See W. E. B. Du Bois, Review of *The Souls of Black Folk*. *The Independent* vol. 57, Nov. 17, 1904.

2. Hebrew nationalism holds a special place in the history of nationalist thought. Hans Kohn writes in *Nationalism: Its Meaning and Its History* (1965) that the concept of modern nationalism originated in three essential tenets espoused by the Hebrews: "the idea of the chosen people; the emphasis on a common stock of memory of the past and hopes for the future; and finally national messianism" (11). John Bracey, August Meier, and Elliott Rudwick, editors of *Black Nationalism in America* (1970), point out that black religious nationalism, a close relative of cultural nationalism, not only entails the establishment and administration of churches by blacks, for blacks; it may also claim that Jesus and God are Black, and extend itself into messianism with the assertion that African Americans are the chosen people (xxvii).

3. Du Bois does credit Native Americans with developing folklore in story, but reserves the creation of American song for African Americans. His reasoning behind this is less than clear. Perhaps due to the language barrier, or the perceived insular nature of American Indian culture, the contributions of Native Americans to American song culture were less apparent to him, even though Native Americans attended historically black colleges such as Hampton Institute.

4. I am thinking here of the relation between the slaves' embodiment—their blackness—and the sort of Western phenomenology (which descends from Plato's notions of "the good" and moral understanding) wherein blackness is theorized as absence, ahistorical, comedic, ugly, unknowing, and unknowable. See Plato's *Republic*, Kant's *Observations on the Feeling of the Beautiful and the Sublime*, and Hegel's *The Philosophy of History*.

5. See Alexander Weheliye, *Phonographies: Grooves in Sonic Afro-Modernity* (Durham: Duke University Press, 2005); and Donald H. Matthews: *Honoring the Ancestors: An African Cultural Interpretation of Black Religion and Literature* (Oxford: Oxford University Press, 1998).

6. A sampling of work by these authors includes Erskine Peters' *Lyrics of the Afro-American Spiritual: A Documentary Collection* (Westwood, CT: Greenwood Press, 1993) and "The Poetics of the Afro-American Spiritual" in *Black American Literature Forum* (23.3 Autumn 1989): 559–578; Jon Michael Spencer's *Protest and Praise: Sacred Music of Black Religion* (Minneapolis: Fortress Press, 1990); and Sterling Brown's "Negro Folk Expression: Spirituals, Seculars, Ballads and Work Songs" in *Phylon* (14.1, 1st Qtr, 1953): 45–61. Alain Locke has written interestingly but somewhat conservatively on "The Negro Spirituals" in his seminal 1925 anthology *The New Negro*. In his 1928 pamphlet, *A Decade of Negro Self-Expression* (John F. Slater Fund Occasional Papers, No. 26), Locke described *The Souls of Black Folk* as a "classic of intimate spiritual interpretation of the Negro."

7. W. K. McNeil. Introduction to *Slave Songs of the United States*, p. 9.

8. Du Bois's underscoring of mourning here recalls for me Fred Moten's work on mourning (in *In the Break: The Aesthetics of the Black Radical Tradition*), and its relation to the primal scream, such as that which is rendered by Frederick Douglass's Aunt Hester and described in his *Narrative*. The distinction between sound and language at work there seems to have been effaced here, though the sounds that the slaves made find their interpretation in a world system beyond the one in which they lived. It seems quite logical to construct an empiricism of an imagined world when the phenomenological world that surrounds one is—day after day—alienating and horrific.

9. Canto II, lines 673–676.

10. Frederick Douglass, *The Heroic Slave*. In *Autographs for Freedom*. Ed. Julia Griffiths. Boston: John P. Jewett and Co, 1853. 174–239. <http://docsouth.unc.edu/neh/douglass1853/douglass1853.html>

11. Wright seems to have had a penchant for ironically naming institutions he founded after conservative and even racist white organizations. In addition to the *States Rights Sentinel*, whose name would undoubtedly evoke images of southern segregation-

ists, he founded in Philadelphia, upon retiring from the presidency of Georgia State Industrial College, the Citizens and Southern Bank, which was named after a bank in Georgia where his daughter had been disparaged. *The Booker T. Washington Papers*, 115.

12. In another version of the poem, of which there are a number, Whittier wrote, "Massa, tell 'em we're rising."

13. Wright's support of Washington's policies went only so far, however. He fell out of favor with Georgia State Industrial College trustees when he decided to include Classics among the curricular offerings there. He and Washington nonetheless maintained good relations.

14. See Genesis, ch 10.

15. For an extended discussion of Du Bois's views on sociology at the turn of the century, please see Rebecka Rutledge Fisher, "Cultural Artifacts and the Narrative of History: W. E. B. Du Bois and the Exhibiting of Culture at the 1900 Paris Exposition Universelle" (*Modern Fiction Studies* 51.4 [2005]). See also *W. E. B. Du Bois on Sociology and the Black Community*. Ed. Dan S. Green and Edwin D. Driver. Chicago: University of Chicago Press, 1978.

16. Such is most visible in the final stanza of "The Brute," where Moody writes:

Then, perhaps, at the last day,
They will whistle him [the Brute] away,
Lay a hand upon his muzzle in the face of God, and say:
"Honor, Lord, the Thing we tamed!
Let him not be scourged or blamed.
Even through his wrath and fierceness was thy fierce wroth world
    reclaimed!
Honor Thou thy servant's servant; let thy justice now be shown."
Then the Lord will heed their saying, and the Brute come to his
    own,
'Twixt the Lion and the Eagle, by the arm-post of the throne.

17. The most focused commentary by Du Bois on the Exposition appears in "The American Negro at Paris" (*The American Monthly Review of Reviews*. Nov. 1900: 575–77). A more concise reflection on the Paris Exhibit is found in *The Autobiography of W. E. B. Du Bois* (np: International Publishers, 1968), p. 220–221.

18. Du Bois writes in *Darkwater* that he was in attendance at the Crystal Palace for "one of the earliest renditions of *Hiawatha's Wedding Feast*" (194), but writes mistakenly in *The Autobiography* that he attended the first rendition of *Hiawatha's Wedding Feast* at the Crystal Palace during his time in London with the Coleridge-Taylors (219). *Hiawatha's Wedding Feast* was completed and delivered to the publisher Novello in the spring of 1898 and was first performed at the Royal College of Music on November 11 of that year. The complete Hiawatha trilogy, including *Hiawatha's Wedding Feast*, actually premiered at the Royal Albert Hall on March 22, 1900, a few months before Du Bois arrived in Europe. Du Bois likely attended a performance of either the entire suite or a portion of it during the summer of

1900. The Crystal Palace performance drew high critical praise as well as a strong appreciative reaction from the audience. See Avril Coleridge-Taylor, *The Heritage of Samuel Coleridge-Taylor* (London: Dennis Dobson, 1979), p. 40; Geoffrey Self, *The Hiawatha Man: The Life and Work of Samuel Coleridge-Taylor* (Hants, England: Scolar Press, 1995), 70–72; "Mr. S. Coleridge-Taylor's 'Hiawatha.'" *The Musical Times and Singing Class Circular* 41.686 (April 1, 1900): 246–247.

19. Arthur Sherburne Hardy, *Passe Rose* (London, Sampson Low, Marston, Searle, & Rivington), 1889.

20. William Sharp authored a biography of Robert Browning, first published in 1890, the year following Browning's death. He writes there: "Though there are plausible grounds for the assumption, I can find nothing to substantiate the common assertion that, immediately or remotely, his people were Jews. As to Browning's physiognomy and personal traits, this much may be granted: if those who knew him were told he was a Jew they would not be much surprised. In his exuberant vitality, in his sensuous love of music and the other arts, in his superficial expansiveness and actual reticence, he would have been typical enough of the potent and artistic race for whom he has so often of late been claimed. What however is more to the point is that neither to curious acquaintances nor to intimate friends, neither to Jews nor Gentiles, did he ever admit more than that he was a good Protestant, and sprung of a Puritan stock" (*Life of Robert Browning* [London: Walter Scott, 1897], pp. 15–16). Sharp would have been slow to believe that, as Du Bois asserted often, Browning was partly of African origin.

21. See Mrs. William A. Sharp, "Bibliographic Note." *Poems and Dramas by Fiona Macleod (William Sharp)* (New York: Duffield and Co., 1911): 454.

22. Please see "The Religion of the American Negro" in *New World: A Quarterly Review of Religion, Ethics, and Theology* 9.36 (December 1900): 614–625.

23. Du Bois's letters to his wife Nina, which he would have written during this period and which might have chronicled some of his leisure activities that summer, have not survived, according to David Levering Lewis (*Biography of a Race*, 247). And, as I have mentioned, his writings on his time in Paris and London are few outside of his brief mentions of the Paris Exhibit, the London Conference, and his outing with the Coleridge-Taylors.

24. Du Bois would also focus upon African American religion as the central theme of the 1903 Atlanta University Conference.

25. As I discuss in chapter 5, such anarchy was obvious not only in the assassination of William McKinley at the 1901 Pan-American exposition in Buffalo, NY, for example, but also in the rampant lynching that tainted America's social atmosphere in the 1890s and the early twentieth century.

26. Please see *The Negro Problem* (Amherst, NY: Humanity Books, 2003).

27. See *Black Reconstruction in America* (New York: Athenum, 1992).

28. See John 1: 20–21. Du Bois will reference John the Baptist again in chapter 13 of *Souls*, "Of the Coming of John."

29. Mark 9:4

30. Quoted in Margaret Homans, *Royal Representations: Queen Victoria and British Culture* (Chicago: University of Chicago Press, 1998), p. 184. Homans points

out that *Idylls of the King* was written as an encomium to the recently deceased and beloved husband of Queen Victoria, Prince Albert, and reports that the Queen found great solace in the verse of Tennyson, her poet laureate. She was likewise a great admirer, as her husband had been before his passing, of the poem "In Memoriam, A.H.H.," which had been penned in 1850. This poem is quoted—quite often—by Du Bois throughout his oeuvre.

31. For an excellent discussion of such sedimentation in Du Bois's, please see Nahum Dimitri Chandler, "The Economy of Desedimentation: W. E. B. Du Bois and the Discourses of the Negro" *Callaloo* 19.1 (Winter 1996): 78–93.

32. See Matthew 3: 13–17.

33. The libretto originally reads : Treulich gefürht, ziehet dahin" ("Faithfully led, move along").

Chapter 7

1. See, for instance, Joyce Ann Joyce, *Richard Wright's Art of Tragedy* (Iowa City: University of Iowa Press, 1986); Abdul R. JanMohamed, *The Death-Bound Subject: Richard Wright's Archaeology of Death* (Durham: Duke University Press, 2005); and Eugene E. Miller, *Voice of a Native Son: The Poetics of Richard Wright* (Jackson: University Press of Mississippi, 1990). Joyce sees an "ideological relationship" (13) between the naturalism and existentialism that generally serve as interpretive lenses for much of Wright's fiction, and tragedy, which she feels "extends the limits of existentialism" (14). Seeing Wright, and rightly, I think, as preeminently concerned with the human and human expression, Joyce argues that Wright's art of tragedy "not only finds meaning in human existence but also celebrates it" (14). Yet Joyce concerns herself with the Western traditions of tragedy in ways that diverge sharply from my intent; while she purports to read Wright primarily through Aristotelian notions of tragedy, feeling that this is the most advantageous approach to Wright's work, I examine the philosophical underpinnings of phenomenology (that is, ways and categories of perceiving and knowing as aspects of consciousness or being) that undergird Wright's art of metaphor. JanMohamed's study addresses the "ways in which 'subjectivities' are bound and hence formed by the threat of death" (4) and, indeed, as he draws upon the notion of "social death" promulgated by Orlando Patterson (in *Slavery and Social Death* [Cambridge: Harvard University Press, 1982]), he somewhat problematically uses the terms *"slave* and *black* interchangeably to refer to the black man or woman living in the South between 1900 and the 1950s as well as to Wright's characters" (5). Wright was, as many critics have noted, preoccupied with the depiction of death, yet JanMohamed argues that many of Wright's critics, including Paul Gilroy, "overlook the agency of death in Wright's work" (11). For JanMohamed, the " 'willing acceptance of death' functions as the most viable form of liberation in the fiction of Wright" (22).

I see the trope of death to be at the center of the novella's concerns, yet, surprisingly, neither of these critics focuses to any extent on *The Man Who Lived Underground.* Joyce, though her book is titled *Richard Wright's Art of Tragedy*, does not focus on Wright's oeuvre at large, but solely upon *Native Son*. No mention is made of *Underground*, nor is any but passing mention made of Wright's other works of long fiction. JanMohamed, who moves with chronological acuity through Wright's major works (from *Uncle Tom's Children* (1938) to *The Long Dream* (1958)), gives no critical attention whatsoever to the novella, though it would seem quite germane to the thrust of his book (he explains this omission briefly in a footnote, p. 303ff15). Miller's *Voice of a Native Son* remains focused on Wright's poetics (gleaned through an examination of Wright's published and unpublished manuscripts) throughout its pages. Drawing upon Wright's own words, Miller underscores the ways in which Wright sought to push art " 'beyond mere contemplation. In short its expression must become an objective act, having immediacy as its aim' " (xviii). This sort of understanding of Wright's poetics is central to reading *The Man Who Lived Underground*, and accords with my analysis of the novella, since I view Wright as moving the reader toward a sense of moral outrage at the murder of his protagonist, an outrage that would ideally extend beyond the act of reading and compel the reader toward constructive social action. However, Miller views guilt as the unifying "symbol" of *Underground*, a reading I cannot support firstly because guilt itself cannot be a *symbol*, though it may be a major theme that is symbolized in various ways. Further, I see the novella proposing a number of critical and conceptual metaphors (existentialist guilt among them) that emerge from the symbolic opposition of chaos and cosmos, as I argue here. Though his method is quite different from mine, Houston Baker's reading of the novella in *Blues, Ideology, and Afro-American Literature* (Chicago: University of Chicago Press, 1984), which insists upon a "tropology" of the "black (w)hole," and thus a metaphorics of consciousness, echoes my intention here.

2. Indeed, in the past decade, *The Man Who Lived Underground* seems to have fallen out of critical favor: as I completed this study, my review of current bibliographies on Wright revealed very few analyses of the novella published during the first decade of this century. This is a serious oversight in Wright scholarship, one I attempt to ameliorate through this contribution. Certainly in light of Wright's centennial, which was celebrated in 2008, additional studies of this text will emerge.

3. See, for instance, Robert Bone's early study, *Richard Wright* (Minneapolis: University of Minneapolis Press, 1969), which is exemplary in this regard. Bone argues that *Underground* is one of three enduring texts by Wright (the others are *Native Son* [1940] and *Black Boy* [1945]) that will lead the reader to a discovery of "the central thrust of Wright's imagination" (14). Yet Bone's perspective on the pessimism in Wright's work is clear. As he concludes, "Wright's subterranean world is a symbol of the Negro's social marginality. Thrust from the upperworld by the racial exclusiveness of whites, he is forced to lead an underground existence. Wright was groping for a spatial metaphor that would render the Negro's ambiguous relationship to Western culture. In *Native Son*, seeking to express the same reality, he hit upon the metaphor of No Man's Land. It conjures up a bleak and sterile landscape in which a hapless soldier crouches, in constant danger of annihilation by enemy or friend" (26). In Bone's reading, the Negro, and by extension the reader, is left without sanctuary or reprieve.

4. My use of the term "ek-static" draws upon readings in both Heidegger and Jean-Paul Sartre. Sartre adapts Heidegger's concept of "ek-static temporality"

to refer to the quality (rather than the quantity) of "lived" time. The emphasis here would be upon the situational and existential conditions faced by the slave. Also of concern would be the care for others exhibited in the Spirituals, as well as action described and prescribed in their lyrics.

5. Wright's idea that the blues were an urban form of the Spirituals—expressed in an introduction to *Southern Exposure* (a three-album recording of folk songs by Josh White)—certainly accords with the perspective on this point that most musicologists who study the subject embrace. It is striking that though Wright calls the blues the "spirituals of the city" (qtd. in Fabre, *Unfinished Quest* 238), he does not draw upon the blues in the urban setting of *Underground*.

6. I am using "sublimation" in the psychoanalytic sense of this term, such that cathexes that might be seen as the motility behind black folk expression such as Spirituals and "dialect poetry" would be redirected towards other more "socially acceptable" avenues of affect and utterance. Du Bois might characterize such cathexes as emanating from an instinct to live and thrive, requiring no such redirection; Wright might seem them as coming from the death drive, demanding their own transcendence. Though he does not give pointed attention to *The Man Who Lived Underground*, Abdul JanMohamed explores at length the poetics of what he calls the "death-bound-subject" which, he argues, is central to the "teleological structure of [Wright's] work." See JanMohamed, *The Death-Bound-Subject*, 2. These points merit further discussion, especially given Wright's deep investment in psychiatry and Freudian psychoanalysis, but I do not have space to pursue them here.

7. See Johnson's Preface to the *Book of American Negro Poetry* (1922); I discuss this preface and Johnson's perspective below.

8. "Moral" is used here to underscore the morality that was expounded as a central aspect of the concept of freedom in eighteenth and nineteenth century continental philosophy.

9. I discuss "Criteria of Negro Art" more fully in my essay, "The Anatomy of a Symbol: Reading W. E. B. Du Bois's *Dark Princess: A Romance*," in *CR: The New Centennial Review*. Special issue, "W. E. B. Du Bois and the Question of Another World." Vol 6 no 3 (Winter 2006). There as here, I investigate Du Bois's poetics and theory of literature as stated in "Criteria," and evaluate his ability to achieve his own criteria in *Dark Princess*.

10. Inspired by the New Critics I. A. Richards, author of many books, including *Principles of Literary Criticism* (1924), and T. S. Eliot, renowned poet and critic who lectured on metaphysical poetry, Leavis maintained that cultural analysis and critique should grow out of close readings of cultural artifacts emanating from the folk. He would write in *Culture and Environment: The Training of Critical Awareness* (1933):

> What we have lost is the organic community with the living culture it embodied. Folk song, folk dances, Cotswald cottages, and handicraft products are signs and expressions of something more; an art of life, a way of living, ordered and patterned, involving social arts, codes of intercourse, and a responsive adjustment growing out of immemorial experience, to the natural environment and the rhythm of the year. (1–2)

11. Of course, a number of scholars have argued that the conclusion of the Harlem Renaissance was marked by the 1929 crash of the stock market and the subsequent drying up of philanthropic support for the literary arts in Harlem and elsewhere. Yet just as many scholars regularly include *Their Eyes Were Watching God* on undergraduate and graduate syllabi for courses on the Harlem Renaissance. Any study of this period would be incomplete without consideration of this second novel by Hurston, which most critics consider her finest work of long fiction. I have not included Hurston's "Characteristics of Negro Expression" (1934) in my discussion here because for all of Hurston's indispensable analyses of Negro speech and cultural aesthetics—such as the aesthetics of private domestic spaces among the folk, dancing, bodily styling, and so forth—she does not discuss *literature*, as such. This is a striking and, one must assume, purposeful omission on Hurston's part. A treatment of "Characteristics" appears in chapter 2.

12. This is my reading of Wright's positionality, but as my colleague John Charles reminds me, Wright's strategy as I describe it here resonates well with William James's version of pragmatism. Wright was a devoted reader of James, and quoted him in his introduction to *Black Metropolis* as philosophical support for his own feelings and experience.

13. Two excerpts from the final section of the novella—the section that appears in *Eight Men* (1961) and that was also published in *Cross Section*—appeared in 1942 in the magazine *Accents* (Spring 1942 pp. 170–176), according to Michel Fabre (*Unfinished Quest* 242). *The Man Who Lived Underground* went through a number of versions, and began as a 150-page manuscript that Wright gradually trimmed down to suit the interests of publishers. The third section of the novella was published as a short story in *Cross Section* by Seaver (who had tried to help Wright publish the full text), and is the version most widely read today. It is to this version that my reading refers, and it has become customary for scholars to refer to this short version as a novella. I continue that convention here. For readings that reference earlier versions, see Fabre (239–243) and Miller (95–124).

14. See, for instance, *Difference and Repetition* (New York: Columbia University Press, 1994), in which Deleuze upholds what he sees as Nietzsche's rejection of the dialectical opposition between chaos and cosmos, embracing instead a "chaosmos" (299).

15. Here I am thinking of the Prologue to Ellison's *Invisible Man*, where the protagonist, after having been slipped "a reefer," which he sat enjoying in his underground hole, slips "into the breaks" of the "swift and imperceptible flowing of time" he hears "vaguely" in Louis Armstrong's music. Armstrong's music "demanded action," the narrator tells us, "the kind of which I was incapable, and yet had I lingered there beneath the surface I might have attempted to act" (8; 12). Ellison comments directly on Wright's underground story and speaks to the subversive potential provided by such heterotopic, chaotic spaces. The spaces are formative for both main characters: Daniels' unorthodox artistic production and the invisible man's memoir alike prepare each "to emerge," as Ellison puts it.

16. The eighteenth-century *philosophes* foresaw the idea of the European Union in their vision of a European internationalism, which was fostered by the rise of the

nation-state as feudal and religious institutions began to decline. Jean-Jacques Rousseau went so far as to envision a world federation (see his "Judgment on Saint-Pierre's Project for Perpetual Peace" in *The Nationalism Reader* [1995]). The philosophy of Immanuel Kant is especially instructive in this regard, as he theorizes the foundations for a new international commerce that was peaking along with the transatlantic slave trade. In *The Metaphysics of Morals* (1797), Kant developed a perspective that placed newly emerging national entities into relation with a burgeoning international community. On the question of the commerce that would necessarily arise among them, Kant proposed the term "cosmopolitan" as an apt descriptor: "Thus all nations are originally members of a community of the land. . . . It is a community of reciprocal action (*commercium*). . . . Each may *offer* to have commerce with the rest, and they all have a right to make such overtures without being treated by foreigners as enemies. This right, in so far as it affords the prospect that all nations may unite for the purpose of creating certain universal laws to regulate the intercourse they may have with one another, may be termed *cosmopolitan (ins cosmopoliticum)*" (44).

17. Romans 6:23 reads, "The wages of sin is death; but the gift of God *is* eternal life through Jesus Christ our Lord." Writing to the faithful in an effort to exhort their rejection of sin and embrace of the salvation of Christ, Paul works to convince them that even as they were baptized in the name of Christ, they were baptized into Christ's death as much as into his salvation. In the narratives of the New Testament, the sacrificial figure of Christ is essential to salvation, making guilt, sin, and death the nucleus of innocence, purity, and rebirth. In drawing upon this striking metaphor, Wright conveys to his reader the absolute necessity of the artist, whose sermon of enlightenment might bring about his own death, but through whose death the people might be lifted up. All of this Wright does by hearkening to the folk wisdom familiar to his African American readers, even though his aim is the surpassing of such religious dogma.

Chapter 8

1. Parenthetical page references are drawn from *Invisible Man* (New York: Quality Paperback Book Club [Book-of-the-Month Club], 1994); hereafter referenced by page number parenthetically as *Invisible Man*.

2. *Juneteenth* gains only scant notice from Ellison's two major biographers, Lawrence Jackson and Arnold Rampersad. Jackson's *Ralph Ellison: Emergence of Genius* (2002) mentions the novel only in its preface (ix), and, in fact, Jackson's treatment of Ellison's life stops with the publication of *Invisible Man*. Arnold Rampersad's *Ralph Ellison: A Biography* (New York: Random House, 2007) chronicles Ellison's life from his childhood to the very day of his death, briefly mentioning not the publication of *Juneteenth* the novel, but "Juneteenth" the story, which appeared in 1965 (422). John S. Wright aptly sums up the feeling of many critics, including the present author, toward *Juneteenth* when he refers to its publication as the "vexed matter of Ellison's unfinished novel . . . published . . . at Fanny Ellison's request and

with John Callahan's editorial existence" (*Shadowing Ralph Ellison* [Jackson: University of Mississippi Press, 2006], 8). *Juneteenth* attests at various moments to Ellison's continued brilliance as a writer, but does not cohere as a novel. It is, rather, a set of fragments drawn from Ellison's later work, and should by most critical accounts be approached in this manner. *Three Days before the Shooting* (New York: Random House, 2011) seeks to provide avid readers and scholars of Ellison's fiction with a more complete portrait of his narrative vision, method, and form by gathering a good portion of the fragments of Ellison's unfinished novel, though it does not pretend to present a completed work.

3. Irving Howe, "Black Boys and Native Sons," *Dissent* 10 (Autumn, 1963).

4. Though Wright is credited with introducing Ellison to communism in the mid 1930s, Wright's most forthright statement on his ultimate rejection of communism is found in the essay "I Tried to be a Communist," which appeared in the August–September 1944 issue of the *Atlantic Monthly*.

5. Please see Fred Moten, *In the Break: The Aesthetics of the Black Radical Tradition* (Minnesota: University of Minnesota Press, 2003). Referring to Lacanian psychoanalysis, he writes: "I'm after a way of rethinking the relation between the mirror stage and the *fascinum/baraka* of the gaze, to think the gaze as something other than necessarily maleficent, but not by way of a simple reversal or inclusion within the agencies of looking; rather within another formulation of the sensual, within a holoesthetic nonexclusionarity that improvises the gaze by way of sound, the horn, that accompanies the blessing, that has effects that Lacan cannot anticipate in part because of his ocularcentrism, because of the way his attention to language is always through an implicit and powerful visualization of the sign [. . .]" (183). For Moten, the prologue of *Invisible Man* "would set the specifically musical conditions for a possible redetermination of the ocular-ethical metaphysics of race and the materiality of the structure and æffects of that metaphysics" (68). While Moten focuses upon the sonic aspects of Ellison's writing that he rightly feels are capable of redirecting the metaphysics of race, my focus is upon the metaphorical discourse that Ellison crafts in response to Western metaphysics, a discourse that he draws from African American vernacular speech and thought, and that he brings to bear upon the metaphysics of Western bio-politics in an analogous redeterminative gesture.

6. See, for example, "Society, Morality, and the Novel" (1957), and "The Novel as a Function of American Democracy" (1967).

7. Of course, this phrase resonates with Dr. Martin Luther King, Jr's use of it in his many speeches and writings. Many scholars attribute its early usage to W. E. B. Du Bois's Harvard philosophy professor, Josiah Royce. As it was espoused by King through his readings in the Christian realist philosophy of Richard Niebuhr, among others, the beloved community was conceived as the "subsequent transformation of the social landscape [through] love (*agape*) and directed by the Creator with integration as its final goal" (Richard W. Wills, *Martin Luther King, Jr. and the Image of God* [Oxford: Oxford University Press, 2009]: 158).

8. *CR: The New Centennial Review* 6.3 (Winter 2006): 7–28. This essay is discussed at length in chapter 2 of the present volume.

9. See "A Critical Look at Ellison's Fiction and at Social and Literary Criticism by and about the Author." *Black World* 20.2 (December 1970): 53–59, 81–97.

10. See Baker's "A Forgotten Prototype: *The Autobiography of an Ex-Colored Man* and *Invisible Man*," in *Singers of Daybreak: Studies in Black American Literature* (Washington, DC: Howard University Press, 1974), 17–32.

11. Nicole Waligora-Davis, "Riotous Discontent: Ralph Ellison's 'Birth of a Nation,'" in *MFS: Modern Fiction Studies* 50.2 (Summer 2004), 386.

12. Dorothy E. Roberts, "The Meaning of Blacks' Fidelity to the Constitution" in *Constitutional Stupidities, Constitutional Tragedies,* ed. William N. Eskridge and Sanford Levinson (New York: New York University Press, 1998): 227.

13. Douglass's early anti-constitutional stance is conveyed in his article, "The Constitution and Slavery" in *The North Star* 2.12 (March 16, 1849): 2. He explains his disunionist perspective with vigor and conviction: "All attempts to explain [the Constitution] in the light of heaven must fail. It is human, and must be explained in the light of those maxims and principles which human beings have laid down as guides to the understanding of all written instruments, covenants, contracts and agreements, emanating from human beings, and to which human beings are parties, both on the first and second part. It is in such a light that we propose to examine the Constitution; and in this light we hold it to be a most cunningly-devised and wicked compact, demanding the most constant and earnest efforts of the friends of righteous freedom for its complete overthrow. It was 'conceived in sin, and shapen in iniquity.' But this will be called mere declamation, and assertion—mere 'heat without light'—sound and fury signify nothing.—Have it so. Let us then argue the question with all the coolness and clearness of which an unlearned fugitive slave, smarting under the wrongs inflicted by this unholy Union, is capable. We cannot talk 'lawyer like' about law—about its emanating from the bosom of God!—about government, and of its seat in the great heart of the Almighty!—nor can we, in connection with such an ugly matter-of-fact looking thing as the United States Constitution, bring ourselves to split hairs about the alleged rule of interpretation, which declares that an 'act of the Legislature may be set aside when it contravenes natural justice.' We have to do with facts, rather than theory. The Constitution is not an abstraction. It is a living, breathing fact, exerting a mighty power over the nation of which it is the bond of Union. . . . Slaveholders took a large share in making it. It was made in view of the existence of slavery, and in a manner well calculated to aid and strengthen that heaven-daring crime."

By the time of *My Bondage and My Freedom* (1855; New York: Library of America, 1994), Douglass would moderate this stance. To his mind, as he had written in 1849, such an about face was not self-contradiction, but an intellectual course dictated by his steadfast principle of honesty and truth. In "The Constitution and Slavery," Douglass had written that the "only truly consistent man is he who will, for the sake of being right today, contradict what he said wrong yesterday." To this end, it seems, he opined in 1855: "My new circumstances compelled me to re-think the whole subject, and to study, with some care, not only the just and proper rules of legal interpretation, but the origin, design, nature, rights, powers, and duties of civil government, and also the relations which human beings sustain to it. By such a course of thought and reading, I was conducted to the conclusion that the constitution [sic] of the United States . . . could not well have been designed at the same time to maintain and perpetuate a system of rapine and murder like slavery; especially as not one word can be found in the constitution to authorize such a belief. Then, again, if the declared purposes of an instrument are to govern the meaning of all its parts and details, as they clearly should, the constitution of our country is our warrant for the abolition of slavery in every state in the American union" (392–393).

14. Ian Watt, *The Rise of the Novel: Studies in Defoe, Richardson, and Fielding* (Berkeley: University of California Press, 1957).

15. Here I borrow from the title of Ellison's well-known 1948 essay, "Harlem is Nowhere," published in *Shadow and Act* (1964): 294–302.

16. Studies that recognize this point include, for instance, Helen Vendler's *Poets Thinking: Pope, Whitman, Dickinson, Yeats* (2006); Giorgio Agamben's *Stanzas: Word and Phantasm in Western Culture* (1977, trans. 1993); and the aforementioned work by Fred Moten, *In the Break: The Aesthetics of the Black Radical Tradition* (2003) as well as that of Paul Ricoeur in *The Rule of Metaphor: The Creation of Meaning in Language* (1975; trans. 1977). Ricoeur, of course, upholds a separation between poetic metaphors and philosophical metaphors, although he allows that significant conceptual metaphors that appear in creative works can create and introduce new meanings in society.

17. Ellison discusses the importance of ritual to American culture and society in many of the essays included in *Shadow and Act* (1964), as well a number of those appearing in *Going to the Territory* (1984).

18. Abdul JanMohammed has put forward a particularly compelling reading of Wright's poetics in this regard in *The Death-Bound-Subject: Richard Wright's Archaeology of Death* (Durham: Duke University Press, 2005).

19. "Twentieth-Century Fiction and the Black Mask of Humanity." *Shadow and Act*, 35.

20. As Claudia Tate has pointed out in "Notes on the Invisible Woman in Ralph Ellison's *Invisible Man*" (*Ralph Ellison's Invisible Man: A Casebook*, ed. John F. Callahan [Oxford: Oxford University Press, 2004]: 253–66), the novel's Mary Rambo is an underdeveloped character when compared with her fuller portrayal in the short story "Out of the Hospital and Under the Bar," published in *Soon, One Morning: New Writing by American Negros, 1940–1962* (New York: Knopf, 1963). "Out of the Hospital" was excised from the final version of *Invisible Man*.

21. Even Matty Lou, the daughter Trueblood rapes in his sleep, and Trueblood's wife, Kate, are presented as maternal figures. Each woman—impregnated alike by Trueblood—is far along in her pregnancy when the invisible man and Mr. Norton encounter them.

22. *Tales of Love*. Trans. Leon S. Roudiez. New York: Columbia University Press, 1987.

23. While Derrida (in *Positions* [Chicago: University of Chicago Press, 1981]: 75, 106n39) has critiqued the concept of the *chora* for what he sees as its ontological essence, Kristeva's description of the *chora* seems to have anticipated such a critique. Disallowing the *chora* any consistent stasis, she adapts it from Plato's *Timaeus* "to denote an essentially mobile and extremely provisional articulation constituted by movements and their ephemeral states" (2170). For her, the concept of *chora* can be deployed as one that "precedes" the "evidence, verisimilitude, spatiality, and temporality" so necessary to the ontological, and so should be differentiated from "a *disposition* that already depends on representation, lends itself to phenomenological, spatial intuition, and gives rise to a geometry" (2170). The *chora* as Kristeva describes it, may lend itself to a concept of mapping or a topology of the psyche and of discourse, "if necessary." Yet it is neither a sign nor a signifier, but a propadeutic to the very possibility of signification, metaphorization, and specularity. "Neither model nor copy, the *chora* precedes and underlies figuration and thus specularization, and is analogous only to vocal or kinetic rhythm" (2170). "Revolution in Poetic Language" in *The Norton Anthology of Theory and Criticism* (New York: Norton, 2001): 2169–2179.

24. These two essays, along with an excerpt of the 1923 piece *The Ego and the Id,* are reprinted in *The Freud Reader* (ed. Peter Gay, New York: Norton, 1989). Each of these pieces is pertinent to Ellison's conception of the invisible and the motility of the repressed. Freud's essay on repression was published in the same year as his essay "The Unconscious," which specified that the repressed is a mobile part of the unconscious. It is in this essay, with which Ellison also seems familiar, that Freud describes the topography and dynamics of repression.

25. Quoted in Anika Lemaire, *Jacques Lacan* (New York: Routledge, 1977): 97. See the chapter entitled "The Constituting Metaphor of the Unconscious," in which Lemaire takes exception with a number of Laplanche and Leclaire's interpretations of Lacan's theory where metaphor is concerned. Lemaire's correction was sanctioned by Lacan, who wrote the preface to her study. A number of Lacan's ideas on repression, metaphoricity, and love are found his *The Four Fundamental Concepts of Psychoanalysis: The Seminar of Jacques Lacan Book XI* (New York: Norton, 1988), where Lacan also responds to Laplanche and Leclaire's misreading of his formula of metaphor (248–53), though he points out that the importance of their work in this regard is the underscoring of metaphor as an effect of secondary repression, rather than primary repression.

26. Freud wrote three papers focusing on the role of love in psychoanalysis, specifically in the clinical context and (drawing upon the comments Freud makes in the essay "Observations on Transference-Love") from the perspective of the analyst rather than the analysand. He published these papers in 1918 under the title *Contributions to the Psychology of Love* (New York: Penguin, 2007) in Series IV of his papers on neuroses. Freud sees himself as taking from the realm of poetry and fiction the authority to describe, define, and analyze "the necessary conditions for loving" (387). Freud felt that creative writers were not fully qualified to define love, for while they take great pains to depict love's unfolding in "the hidden impulses in the minds of other people" and exemplify "the courage to let [their] own uncon-

scious speak," they nevertheless "are under the necessity to produce intellectual and aesthetic pleasure, as well as certain emotional effects." Thus, they are quite unable, he argues, "to reproduce the stuff of reality unchanged, but must isolate portions of it, removing disturbing associations, tone down the whole and fill in what is missing. These are the privileges of what is known as 'poetic license'" (387). Since writers "can show only slight interest in the origin and development of the mental states which they portray in their completed form," it is left to science to take up the slack, Freud argues. "These observations will, it may be hoped, serve to justify us in extending a strictly scientific treatment to the field of human love. Science is, after all, the most complete renunciation of the pleasure principle of which our mental activity is capable" (387–88). Of course, Freud seems a bit hasty here in vaunting the methodology of "science" over that of humanism, but the idea that he insists upon a science of love without first defining the object of his study (love itself) must be duly noted. And his comments are limited to the "abnormal" love expressed by neurotics, a point not unrelated to Ellison's depictions of love in *Invisible Man*. Interestingly in Freud's text as in Ellison's, the focus is upon "masculine love" and its preconditions, and he generally analyzes love in terms of sexuality rather than emotional or moral commitment.

27. *Invisible Man*, 122.

28. Ibid., 228.

29. See *Blues, Ideology, and Afro-American Literature: A Vernacular Theory* (Chicago: University of Chicago Press, 1984), 172–199.

Bibliography

Agamben, Giorgio. *The Coming Community*. Minneapolis: University of Minnesota Press, 1993.

———. *Idea of Prose*. Albany: State University of New York Press, 1995.

———. *Means without End: Notes on Politics*. Minneapolis: University of Minnesota Press, 2000.

———. *Remnants of Auschwitz: The Witness and the Archive*. New York: Zone Books, 2000.

———. *Stanzas: Word and Phantasm in Western Culture*. Minneapolis: University of Minnesota Press, 1993.

Alaya, Flavia. *William Sharp—"Fiona Macleod," 1855–1905*. Cambridge, MA: Harvard University Press, 1970.

Aristotle. *The Rhetoric and Poetics of Aristotle*. New York: The Modern Library, 1984.

Badiou, Alain. *Briefings on Existence: A Short Treatise on Transitory Ontology*. Albany: State University of New York Press, 2006.

Baker, Houston. *Blues, Ideology, and Afro-American Literature: A Vernacular Theory*. Chicago: University of Chicago Press, 1984.

———. *The Journey Back: Issues in Black Literature and Criticism*. Chicago: University of Chicago Press, 1980.

Barthes, Roland. *A Lover's Discourse: Fragments*. New York: Hill and Wang, 1978.

———. *Camera Lucida: Reflections on Photography*. New York: Hill and Wang, 1982.

———. *Image-Music-Text*. Trans. Stephen Heath. Glasgow: Collins, 1977.

———. "From Work to Text." *Debating Texts: Readings in 20th Century Literary Theory and Method*. Ed. Rick Rylance. Toronto: University of Toronto Press, 1987. 117–122.

Benveniste, Emile. "The Nature of the Linguistic Sign." *Debating Texts: Readings in 20th Century Literary Theory and Method*. Ed. Rick Rylance. Toronto: University of Toronto Press, 1987. 77–81.

Bernasconi, Robert. Introduction. *Race and Racism in Continental Philosophy*. Bloomington: Indiana University Press, 2003. 1–7.

Bhabha, Homi K. *The Location of Culture*. London: Routledge, 1994.

Bigger, Charles P. *Between Chora and the Good: Metaphor's Metaphysical Neighborhood*. New York: Fordham University Press, 2005.

Browning, Elizabeth Barrett. *The Seraphim, and Other Poems*. London, Saunders and Otley, 1838.

Busby, Mark. *Ralph Ellison*. Boston: Twayne Publishers, 1991.

Butler, Judith. *The Psychic Life of Power: Theories in Subjection*. Stanford: Stanford University Press, 1997.

Carretta, Vincent. *Equiano, The African: Biography of a Self-Made Man*. Athens, GA: University of Georgia Press, 2005.

Cazeaux, Clive. *Metaphor and Continental Philosophy: From Kant to Derrida*. London: Routledge, 2007.

Chandler, Nahum Dimitri. *X—The Problem of the Negro as a Problem for Thought*. New York: Fordham University Press, 2014.

Coleridge-Taylor, Jessie. *A Memory Sketch: Or, Personal Reminiscences of My Husband, Genius and Musician, S. Coleridge-Taylor, 1875–1912*. Ed. J. H. Smither Jackson. London: J. Crowther Ltd., 1943.

Costanzo, Angelo. *Surprizing Narrative: Olaudah Equiano and the Beginnings of Black Autobiography*. New York: Greenwood Press, 1987.

Cruse, Harold. *The Crisis of the Negro Intellectual: A Historical Analysis of the Failure of Black Leadership*. New York: New York Review Books, 2005.

Cugoano, Ottobah. *Thoughts and Sentiments on the Evil of Slavery and Other Writings*. Ed. Vincent Carretta. New York: Penguin Books, 1999.

Cunard, Nancy, ed. *Negro: An Anthology*. London: Published by Nancy Cunard at Wishart & Co, 1934.

Dahbour, Omar, and Micheline Ishay, eds. *The Nationalism Reader*. Atlantic Highlands, NJ: Humanities Press, 1995.

Davis, Charles T. and Henry Louis Gates, Jr., eds. *The Slave's Narrative*. Oxford: Oxford University Press, 1985.

De Man, Paul. *Allegories of Reading: Figural Language in Rousseau, Nietzsche, Rilke, and Proust*. New Haven: Yale University Press, 1979.

DeGuzmán, María. *Spain's Long Shadow: The Black Legend, Off-Whiteness, and Anglo-American Empire*. Minneapolis: University of Minnesota Press, 2005.

Derrida, Jacques. *Margins of Philosophy*. Chicago: University of Chicago Press, 1982.

———. *Monolingualism of the Other, Or, the Prosthesis of Origin*. Stanford: Stanford University Press, 1998.

———. *Specters of Marx: The State of Debt, the Work of Mourning and the New International*. Trans. Peggy Kamuf. New York: Routledge, 2006.

———. "Structure, Sign, and Play in the Discourse of the Human Sciences." *Debating Texts: Readings in 20ᵗʰ Century Literary Theory and Method*. Ed. Rick Rylance. Toronto: University of Toronto Press, 1987. 123–136.

Douglass, Frederick. *Autobiographies*. New York: Library of America: 1994.

Drake, St. Clair, and Horace Cayton. *Black Metropolis: A Study of Negro Life in a Northern City*. New York: Harcourt, Brace and Company, 1945.

Du Bois, W. E. B. *The Autobiography of W. E. B. Du Bois*. Ed. Herbert Aptheker. N.p.: International Publishers, 1968.

————. *Against Racism: Unpublished Essays, Papers, Addresses, 1887–1961*. Ed. Herbert Aptheker. Amherst: University of Massachusetts Press, 1985.

————. *Black Reconstruction in America: 1860–1880*. New York: Athenum, 1992.

————. *The Brownies' Book*. New York: Du Bois and Dill, 1920.

————. "The Conservation of Races." 1897. *Writings*. Ed. Nathan Irvin Huggins. New York: Library of America, 1986. 815–26.

————. "Criteria of Negro Art." *Writings*. New York: Library of America, 1986. 993–1002.

————. *Dusk of Dawn: An Essay toward an Autobiography of a Race Concept*. 1940. *Writings*. 549–802.

————. "Fifty Years After." *The Souls of Black Folk*. Jubilee Edition. New York: Blue Heron Press, 1953.

————. *The Souls of Black Folk*. *Writings*. 357–547.

————. "Strivings of the Negro People." *Atlantic Monthly* 80 (1897): 194–98.

————. *Writings*. Ed. Nathan Irvin Huggins. New York: Library of America, 1986.

————. *W. E. B. Du Bois: A Reader*. Ed. David Levering Lewis. New York: Henry Holt, 1995.

Dunbar, Paul Laurence. *The Collected Poetry of Paul Laurence Dunbar*. Ed. Joanne M. Braxton. Charlottesville: University Press of Virginia, 1993.

Eagleton, Terry. *Literary Theory: An Introduction*. Minneapolis, MN: University of Minnesota Press, 1996.

Early, Gerald. "Decoding Ralph Ellison." *Dissent*. 44.3 (Summer 1997).

————. Introduction. *Speech and Power: The African-American Essay and Its Cultural Content from Polemics to Pulpit*. Ed. Gerald Early. 2 Vols. Hopewell, NJ: Ecco Press, 1992.

————, ed. *Lure and Loathing*. New York: Penguin, 1994.

Edwards, Paul. "Introduction to *The Life of Olaudah Equiano*." *The Interesting Narrative of the Life of Olaudah Equiano, or Gustabus Vassa, the African. Written by Himself*. Ed. Werner Sollors. New York: Norton, 2001.

Edwards, Paul, and David Dabydeen, eds. *Black Writers in Britain: 1760–1890*. Edinburgh: Edinburgh University Press, 1991.

Eliot, T. S. *The Waste Land. Selected Poems*. San Diego: Harvest Books, 1964. 51–74.

Ellison, Ralph. *The Collected Essays of Ralph Ellison*. Ed. John F. Callahan. New York: Modern Library, 2003.

————. *Conversations with Ralph Ellison*. Eds. Maryemma Graham and Amritjit Singh. Jackson: University Press of Mississippi, 1995.

————. *Going to the Territory*. New York: Random House, 1986.

————. *Invisible Man*. New York: Quality Paperback Books [Book-of-the Month-Club], 1994.

————. *Shadow and Act*. New York: Vintage International, 1995.

Equiano, Olaudah. *The Interesting Narrative of the Life of Olaudah Equiano, or Gustavus Vassa, the African: An Authoritative Text*. Ed. Werner Sollors. New York: Norton, 2001.

Equiano, Olaudah. *The Interesting Narrative of the Life of Olaudah Equiano*. Ed. Rebecka Rutledge Fisher. New York: Barnes and Noble, 2005.

Fabre, Michel. "From Tabloid to Myth: 'The Man Who Lived Underground.'" *The World of Richard Wright*. Jackson: University Press of Mississippi, 1985. 93–107.

——. *Richard Wright: Books & Writers*. Jackson: University Press of Mississippi, 1990.

——. *The Unfinished Quest of Richard Wright*. Trans. Isabel Barzun. 2nd Edition. Urbana: University of Illinois Press, 1993.

Fackler, Herbert V. "William Sharp's "House of Usna" (1900): A One-Act Psychic Drama." *The South Central Bulletin* 30.4, Studies by Members of SCMLA (1970): 187–9.

Fanon, Frantz. *Peau Noire, Masques Blancs*. Paris: Éditions du Seuil, 1952.

Fiedler, Leslie A. *Love and Death in the American Novel*. New York: Dell, 1966.

Felman, Shoshana. *Literature and Psychoanalysis: The Question of Reading, Otherwise*. Baltimore: Johns Hopkins University Press, 1982.

Fisher, Rebecka Rutledge. "The Anatomy of a Symbol: Reading W. E. B. Du Bois's *Dark Princess: A Romance*." *CR: The New Centennial Review* 6.3 (Winter 2006): 91–128.

——. "Cultural Artifacts and the Narrative of History: W. E. B. Du Bois and the Exhibiting of Culture at the 1900 Paris Exposition Universelle." *Modern Fiction Studies* 51.4 (Winter 2005): 743–774.

——. Introduction. *The Interesting Narrative of the Life of Olaudah Equiano*. Ed. Rebecka Rutledge Fisher. New York: Barnes and Noble, 2005.

——. "Metaphoric Black Bodies in the Hinterlands of Race; Or, Towards Deciphering the Du Boisian Concept of Race and Nation in "The Conservation of Races.'" *Race and Ethnicity: Across Time, Space and Discipline*. Ed. Rodney Coates. Leiden, Netherlands: Brill, 2004. 331–349.

——. "Remnants of Memory: Testimony and Being in Frances E. W. Harper's *Sketches of Southern Life*." *ESQ: A Journal of the American Renaissance* 54.1–4 (2008): 55–74.

Foster, Frances Smith, ed. *A Brighter Coming Day: A Frances Ellen Watkins Harper Reader*. New York: The Feminist Press, 1990.

Foucault, Michel. *The Foucault Reader*. Ed. Paul Rabinow. New York: Pantheon Books, 1984.

——. *The Order of Things: An Archaeology of the Human Sciences*. New York: Vintage Books, 1994.

——. "Questions on Geography." *Power/Knowledge: Selected Interviews and Other Writings,1972–1977*. Ed. Colin Gordon. New York: Pantheon, 1980. 63–77.

Freud, Sigmund. *The Freud Reader*. Ed. Peter Gay. New York: W. W. Norton, 1989.

——. "The Uncanny." 1919. *The Norton Anthology of Theory and Criticism*. New York: Norton, 2001: 929–952.

Frye, Northrop. *Fables of Identity: Studies in Poetic Mythology*. New York: Harcourt, Brace & World, 1963.

——. *The Great Code: The Bible and Literature*. Toronto: University of Toronto Press, 2006.

———. *Myth and Metaphor: Selected Essays, 1974–1988.* Ed. Robert D. Denham. Charlottesville: University Press of Virginia, 1990.

Fryer, Peter. *Staying Power: The History of Black People in Britain.* Pluto Press, 1984.

Gates, Henry Louis, Jr. *Figures in Black: Words, Signs, and the "Racial" Self.* New York: Oxford University Press, 1987.

———, ed. *"Race," Writing, and Difference.* Chicago: University of Chicago Press, 1986.

———. *The Signifying Monkey: A Theory of Afro-American Literary Criticism.* New York: Oxford University Press, 1988.

Gayle, Addison. *The Black Aesthetic.* Garden City, NY: Doubleday, 1971.

Gilroy, Paul. *Against Race: Imagining Political Culture Beyond the Color Line.* Cambridge, MA: Belknap Press of Harvard University Press, 2000.

———. *The Black Atlantic: Modernity and Double Consciousness.* Cambridge, MA: Harvard University Press, 1993.

———. *Small Acts: Thoughts on the Politics of Black Cultures.* London: Serpent's Tail, 1993.

Girard, René. *Violence and the Sacred.* Baltimore: Johns Hopkins University Press, 1977.

Glissant, Édouard. *Poetics of Relation.* Trans. Betsy Wing. Ann Arbor: University of Michigan Press, 1997.

Gordon, Lewis R. *Existentia Africana: Understanding Africana Existential Thought.* New York: Routledge, 2000.

Harper, Frances Ellen Watkins. "Christianity." *Poems on Miscellaneous Subjects.* Philadelphia: Merrihew and Thompson, 1857. 40–44.

———. *Complete Poems of Frances E. W. Harper.* Ed. Maryemma Graham. New York: Oxford University Press, 1988.

———. *Sketches of Southern Life.* 1870. Philadelphia: Merrihew & Sons, 1887.

Harvey, David. *The Condition of Postmodernity: An Enquiry into the Origins of Cultural Change.* Cambridge, MA: Blackwell, 1990.

———. "Cosmopolitanism and the Banality of Geographical Evils." *Public Culture* 12:2 (Spring 2000): 529–64.

Hawkes, Terence. *Metaphor.* London: Methuen, 1972.

Hegel, Georg Wilhelm Friedrich. *The Philosophy of History.* Trans. John Sibree. New York: The Colonial Press, 1902.

———. *Philosophy of Mind.* Trans. William Wallace. Oxford: Clarendon, 1971.

———. *Reason in History: A General Introduction to the Philosophy of History.* Trans. Robert S. Hartman. New York: Bobbs-Merrill, 1953.

Heidegger, Martin. *Basic Writings: From Being and Time (1927) to the Task of Thinking (1964).* Ed. David Farrell Krell. New York: Harper Perennial Modern Thought, 2008.

———. *Being and Time.* Trans. John Macquarrie and Edward Robinson. New York: HarperPerennial/Modern Thought, 2008.

———. *On the Way to Language.* New York: Harper & Row, 1971.

———. "The Origin of the Work of Art." *Poetry, Language, Thought.* Trans. Albert Hofstadter. New York: Perennial Classics, 15–86.

Hesse, Barnor. "Self-Fulfilling Prophecy: The Postracial Horizon." *SAQ: The South Atlantic Quarterly* 110.0 (Winter 2011): 155–178.

Hetherington, Kevin. *The Badlands of Modernity: Heterotopia and Social Ordering.* London: Routledge, 1997.

Holloway, Karla F. C. *Moorings & Metaphors: Figures of Culture and Gender in Black Women's Literature.* New Brunswick, NJ: Rutgers University Press, 1992.

Homans, Margaret. *Royal Representations: Queen Victoria and British Culture, 1837–1876.* Chicago: University of Chicago Press, 1998.

Hurston, Zora Neale. "Characteristics of Negro Expression." *The Norton Anthology of African American Literature.* 1st Edition. Eds. Henry Louis Gates, Jr., and Nellie McKay. New York: Norton, 1997. 1019–1032.

———. *Dust Tracks on a Road.* New York: HarperPerennial, 1996.

———. *Folklore, Memoirs, and Other Writings.* Ed. Cheryl A. Wall. New York: Library of America, 1995.

———. *Jonah's Gourd Vine: A Novel.* Eds. Rita Dove and Henry Louis Gates Jr. New York: HarperPerennial, 2008.

———. *Their Eyes Were Watching God.* Urbana: University of Illinois Press, 1978.

Hutcheon, Linda, and Joseph P. Natoli, eds. *A Postmodern Reader.* Albany: State University of New York Press, 1993.

Jackson, Lawrence P. *Ralph Ellison: Emergence of Genius.* New York: Wiley, 2002.

James, William. *Pragmatism, and Other Essays.* New York: Washington Square Press, 1963.

———. *Selected Papers on Philosophy.* London: J. M. Dent, 1917.

JanMohamed, Abdul R. *The Death-Bound Subject: Richard Wright's Archaeology of Death.* Durham: Duke University Press, 2005.

Johnson, Charles R. *Being & Race: Black Writing since 1970.* Bloomington: Indiana University Press, 1988.

Johnson, James Weldon. *The Autobiography of an Ex-Coloured Man.* New York: Vintage Books, 1989.

———. "The Creation." *God's Trombones.* New York: Viking Press, 1927. Documenting the American South. 2004. University Library, University of North Carolina at Chapel Hill. 4 August 2013. <http://docsouth.unc.edu/southlit/johnson/johnson.html#p17>

———. Preface. *Book of American Negro Poetry.* New York: Harcourt, Brace and Co., 1922.

Joyce, Joyce Ann. *Richard Wright's Art of Tragedy.* Iowa City: University of Iowa Press, 1986.

Judy, Ronald A. T. *(Dis)forming the American Canon: African-Arabic Slave Narratives and the Vernacular.* Minneapolis: University of Minnesota Press, 1993.

Kant, Immanuel. *Critique of Judgment.* Indianapolis, IN: Hackett Pub. Co, 1987.

———. *Immanuel Kant's Physical Geography.* Trans. Ronald L. Bolin. [Translator's thesis. Indiana University, 1968.]

———. "The Metaphysics of Morals." Excerpt. In *The Nationalism Reader.* Eds. Omar Dahbour and Micheline R. Ishay. Amherst, NY: Humanity Books, 1995. 38–48.

———. *Observations on the Feeling of the Beautiful and Sublime*. Trans. John Goldthwait. Berkeley: University of California Press, 1960.

Kettler, David and Volker Meja. *Karl Mannheim and the Crisis of Liberalism: The Secret of these New Times*. New Brunswick, NJ: Transaction Publishers, 1995.

Kinnamon, Keneth. *Richard Wright: An Annotated Bibliography of Criticism and Commentary, 1983–2003*. Jefferson, NC: McFarland & Co, 2006.

Kristeva, Julia. *Revolution in Poetic Language*. New York: Columbia University Press, 1984.

———. *Tales of Love*. New York: Columbia University Press, 1987.

Lacan, Jacques. *Feminine Sexuality: Jacques Lacan and the École Freudienne*. Eds. Juliet Mitchell and Jacqueline Rose. New York: W.W. Norton, 1985, c1982

———. *The Seminar of Jacques Lacan: Book XI: The Four Fundamental Concepts of Psychoanalysis*. Ed. Jacques Alain Miller. Trans. Alan Sheridan. New York: Norton, 1998.

Lakoff, George and Mark Johnson. *Metaphors We Live By*. Chicago: University of Chicago Press, 1980.

Leavis, F. R., and Denys Thompson. *Culture and Environment: The Training of Critical Awareness*. London: Chatto and Windus, 1933.

Leitch, Vincent B. *The Norton Anthology of Theory and Criticism*. New York: Norton, 2001.

Lemaire, Anika. *Jacques Lacan*. London: Routledge & Kegan Paul, 1977.

Lewis, David L. *God's Crucible: Islam and the Making of Europe, 570 to 1215*. New York: Norton, 2008.

———. *W. E. B. Du Bois: A Reader*. Ed. David Levering Lewis. New York: Henry Holt, 1995.

———. *W. E. B. Du Bois: Biography of a Race, 1868–1919*. New York: Henry Holt, 1993.

———. *W. E. B. Du Bois: The Fight for Equality and the American Century, 1919–1963*. New York: Henry Holt, 2000.

Lévi-Strauss, Claude. *The Savage Mind*. Chicago: University of Chicago Press, 1966.

Locke, Alain. *The New Negro: Voices of the Harlem Renaissance*. New York: Simon and Schuster, 1992.

Lorde, Audre. *Sister Outsider: Essays and Speeches*. Berkeley, CA: Crossing Press, 1984.

Lubiano, Wahneema H. *The House that Race Built: Original Essays by Toni Morrison, Angela Y. Davis, Cornel West, and Others on Black Americans and Politics in America Today*. New York: Vintage Books, 1997.

Majors, Monroe A. *Noted Negro Women, Their Triumphs and Activities*. Chicago: Donohue & Henneberry, 1893.

Malraux, André. *La Condition humaine*. Paris: Gallimard, 1946.

Marrant, John. *A Narrative of the Lord's Wonderful Dealings with John Marrant, a Black*. New York: Garland Pub, 1978.

Miles, Kevin Thomas. " 'One Far Off Divine Event': 'Race' and a Future History in Du Bois." *Race and Racism in Continental Philosophy*. Bloomington: Indiana University Press, 2003. 19–31.

Miller, Eugene. *Voice of a Native Son: The Poetics of Richard Wright.* Jackson: University Press of Mississippi, 1990.

Mills, Charles W. *Blackness Visible: Essays on Philosophy and Race.* Ithaca, NY: Cornell University Press, 1998.

Mitchell, W. J. T. *Iconology: Image, Text, Ideology.* Chicago: U of Chicago P, 1986.

Morel, Lucas E., and Alfred L. Brophy, eds. *Ralph Ellison and the Raft of Hope: A Political Companion to Invisible Man.* Lexington: University Press of Kentucky, 2004.

Morrison, Toni. *Playing in the Dark: Whiteness and the Literary Imagination.* Cambridge, MA: Harvard University Press, 1992.

Moses, Wilson Jeremiah, ed. *Classical Black Nationalism: From the American Revolution to Marcus Garvey.* New York: New York University Press, 1996.

Moten, Fred. "The Case of Blackness." *Criticism: A Quarterly for Literature and the Arts* 50 (2008): 177–218. Web.

———. *In the Break: The Aesthetics of the Black Radical Tradition.* Minneapolis, MN: University of Minnesota Press, 2003.

Myrdal, Gunner. *An American Dilemma: The Negro Problem and Modern Democracy.* New York: Harper and Brothers, 1944.

Napier, Winston, ed. *African American Literary Theory: A Reader.* New York: New York University Press, 2000.

Nochlin, Linda. *The Body in Pieces: The Fragment as a Metaphor of Modernity.* London: Thames and Hudson, 1994.

Outlaw, Lucius T. *On Race and Philosophy.* New York: Routledge, 1996.

Plato. *The Republic.* New York: Penguin, 2003.

Punter, David. *Metaphor* London: Routledge, 2007.

Rabaka, Reiland. *W. E. B. Du Bois and the Problems of the Twenty-First Century: An Essay on Africana Critical Theory.* Lanham: Lexington Books, 2007.

Rampersad, Arnold. *Ralph Ellison: A Biography.* New York: Alfred A. Knopf, 2007.

Rejai, M. *Democracy: The Contemporary Theories.* New York: Atherton Press, 1967.

Ricoeur, Paul. *The Conflict of Interpretations: Essays in Hermeneutics.* Evanston, IL: Northwestern University Press, 1974.

———. *Du Texte à l'action.* Paris: Éditions du Seuil, 1998.

———. *Figuring the Sacred: Religion, Narrative, and Imagination.* Ed. Mark I. Wallace. Minneapolis: Fortress Press, 1995.

———. *Freud and Philosophy: An Essay on Interpretation.* New Haven: Yale University Press, 1970.

———. *From Text to Action.* Evanston, IL: Northwestern University Press, 2007.

———. *Interpretation Theory: Discourse and the Surplus of Meaning.* Fort Worth: Texas Christian University Press, 1976.

———. *On Translation.* London: Routledge, 2006.

———. *Oneself as Another.* Chicago: University of Chicago Press, 1992.

———. *The Rule of Metaphor: Multi-Disciplinary Studies of the Creation of Meaning in Language.* Toronto: University of Toronto Press, 1977.

———. *Time and Narrative*. Vol 1. Chicago: University of Chicago Press, 1988.

Robinson, Cedric J. *Black Marxism: The Making of the Black Radical Tradition*. Chapel Hill: University of North Carolina Press, 2000.

Rydell, Robert. *The Reason Why the Colored American is not in the World's Columbian Exposition*. Urbana: University of Illinois Press, 1999.

Sartre, Jean-Paul. *Being and Nothingness: An Essay on Phenomenological Ontology*. New York: Philosophical Library, 1956.

———. *L'Existentialisme est un humanisme*. Paris: Éditions Nagel, 1970.

Saussure, Ferdinand de. *Course in General Linguistics*. 1915. New York, Philosophical Library, 1959.

Sayers, W. C. B. *Samuel Coleridge-Taylor, Musician; His Life and Letters*. Ed. J. H. Smither Jackson. Chicago: Afro-Am Press, 1969.

Self, Geoffrey. *The Hiawatha Man: The Life and Work of Samuel Coleridge-Taylor*. Brookfield, VT: Ashgate Pub, 1995.

Sharp, Elizabeth A. *William Sharp (Fiona Macleod): A Memoir*. London: W. Heineman, 1910.

Sharp, William. *The House of Usna, A Drama*. Portland, ME: Thomas B. Mosher, 1903.

———. *Life of Robert Browning*. Ed. John Parker Anderson. London: W. Scott, 1890.

———. *Poems. Selected and Arranged by Mrs. William Sharp*. Ed. Elizabeth A. (Elizabeth Amelia) Sharp. London: W. Heinemann, 1921.

Shelby, Tommie. *We Who Are Dark: The Philosophical Foundations of Black Solidarity*. Cambridge, MA: Harvard University Press, 2005.

Spillers, Hortense J. *Black, White, and in Color: Essays on American Literature and Culture*. Chicago: University of Chicago Press, 2003.

———. "The Crisis of the Negro Intellectual: A Post-Date." *Boundary 2: An International Journal of Literature and Culture* 21.3 (1994): 65–116.

———. "The Idea of Black Culture." *CR: The New Centennial Review* 6.3 (2006): 7–28.

Stellardi, Giuseppe. *Heidegger and Derrida on Philosophy and Metaphor: Imperfect Thought*. Amherst, NY: Humanity Books, 2000.

Stepto, Robert B. *From Behind the Veil: A Study of Afro-American Narrative*. Urbana: University of Illinois Press, 1979.

Sterling, Dorothy, ed. *We are Your Sisters: Black Women in the Nineteenth Century*. New York: W. W. Norton, 1997, 1984.

Still, William. *The Underground Railroad*. New York: Ayer, 1992.

Sundquist, Eric J., ed. *Cultural Contexts for Ralph Ellison's Invisible Man*. Boston: Bedford Books of St. Martin's Press, 1995.

Synge, J. M. *The Playboy of the Western World and Other Plays*. New York: Signet Classic, 1997.

Taylor, Mark C. *Journeys to Selfhood: Hegel & Kierkegaard*. New York: Fordham University Press, 2000.

Toomer, Jean. *Cane*. New York: Modern Library, 1994.

Tortolano, William. *Samuel Coleridge-Taylor: Anglo-Black Composer, 1875–1912*. Lanham, MD: Scarecrow Press, 2002.

Truth, Sojourner. *The Book of Life*. London: Black Classics, 1999.

Waligora-Davis, Nicole. *Sanctuary: African Americans and Empire*. New York: Oxford University Press, 2011.

Washington, Booker T. *Up from Slavery: An Autobiography*. New York: Modern Library, 1999.

Watts, Jerry Gafio. *Heroism and the Black Intellectual: Ralph Ellison, Politics, and Afro-American Intellectual Life*. Chapel Hill: University of North Carolina Press, 1994.

West, Cornel. *Race Matters*. Boston: Beacon Press, 1993.

Wheatley, Phillis. *The Collected Works of Phillis Wheatley*. New York: Oxford University Press, 1988.

Williams, Heather. *Self-Taught: African American Education in Slavery and Freedom*. Chapel Hill: University of North Carolina Press, 2005.

Wright, John S. *Shadowing Ralph Ellison*. Jackson: University Press of Mississippi, 2006.

Wright, Richard. *Black Boy (American Hunger): A Record of Childhood and Youth*. New York: Harper Perennial Modern Classics, 2006.

———. "Blueprint for Negro Writing." *The Norton Anthology of African American Literature*. 2nd Edition. Ed. Henry Louis Gates Jr. and Nellie Y. McKay. New York: Norton, 2004. 1403–1410.

———. Introduction. *Black Metropolis: A Study of Negro Life in a Northern City*. New York: Harcourt, Brace and Co., 1945.

———. "The Literature of the Negro in the United States." *Black Power: Three Books from Exile: Black Power; The Color Curtain; and White Man, Listen*. New York: Harper Perennial, 2008. 731–773.

———. *The Man Who Lived Underground*. *The Norton Anthology of African American Literature*. 2nd Edition. Eds. Henry Louis Gates, Jr. and Nellie McKay. New York: Norton, 2004. 1436–1470.

———. *Native Son*. New York: Harper Perennial Modern Classics, 2005.

———. *The Outsider*. New York: Perennial, 2003.

Index